# Land Banking

JOHNS HOPKINS STUDIES IN URBAN AFFAIRS
Center for Metropolitan Planning and Research
The Johns Hopkins University

David Harvey, *Social Justice and the City*

Ann L. Strong, *Private Property and the Public Interest: The Brandywine Experience*

Alan D. Anderson, *The Origin and Resolution of an Urban Crisis: Baltimore, 1890–1930*

James M. Rubenstein, *The French New Towns*

Malcolm Getz, *The Economics of the Urban Fire Department*

Ann L. Strong, *Land Banking: European Reality, American Prospect*

Jon C. Teaford, *City and Suburb: The Political Fragmentation of Metropolitan America, 1850–1970*

# Land Banking

## European Reality, American Prospect

Ann L. Strong

The Johns Hopkins University Press
*Baltimore and London*

Manufactured in the United States of America

The Johns Hopkins University Press, Baltimore, Maryland 21218
The Johns Hopkins Press Ltd., London

Library of Congress Catalog Card Number 78–11804
ISBN 0–8018–2169–X

Library of Congress Cataloging in Publication data
will be found on the last printed page of this book.

What one proposes now is that a bad land policy, which confused stable occupation and security of tenure with the irrelevant concept of individual ownership, should be obliterated. In its stead, one proposes a sound land policy which shall vest ownership in the community, and guarantee tenure, for definitely assigned periods, to those who work the land thriftily and pay their communal taxes. This policy can be put into effect piecemeal, by permitting cities to buy up land necessary for their development and to hold it permanently: an indispensable aid in four-dimensional planning.

LEWIS MUMFORD,
*The Culture of Cities*

# Contents

## Maps

## Tables

**Figures**

# Acknowledgments

I owe my husband, Michael L. Strong, the largest measure of thanks for his support and encouragement. His willingness to take a leave of absence from his law firm, despite the professional hardship this entailed, in order to accompany me on my five-month trip to Sweden, the Netherlands, and France meant much to me.

The support of the National Endowment for the Humanities, through the award of a Senior Fellowship, made the trip and the ensuing research work during my sabbatical year financially possible.

In the three European countries many people were generous with their time and responsive to my inquiries. A few made exceptional commitments to the study.

In Sweden, Thomas Atmer, Head of Research and Long Term Planning, Stockholm City Planning Commission, and his wife, Ann Katrin, welcomed us and educated me about Swedish planning. They found us a place to live, took us to see new and old development in the Stockholm region, introduced me to leading planners, and in general contributed substantially to the pleasure of our stay. Per Holm, Professor of Regional Planning at the Technical High School, provided funds to pay for a Swedish research assistant and offered valuable insights into the rationale of Swedish land policy. Christina Engfeldt, the research assistant, was a great asset, finding Swedish texts, translating appropriate sections, contacting people, and assisting with interviews. Carl F. Ahlberg, Director of the Stockholm Regional Planning Commission, contributed an office and, more important, almost daily thoughtful advice and opinions. To the extent that I have understood and described accurately the principles underlying the Stockholm region's land bank programs, the above people are those to whom I am most grateful.

xii    ACKNOWLEDGMENTS

In the Netherlands, Jacobus P. Thysse, former Director of the Institute of Social Studies in The Hague, volunteered to work on this study jointly with me. Unfortunately for me, a United Nations mission took him to southeast Asia and made this collaboration impossible. However, Professor Thysse made numerous suggestions and arranged contacts for me prior to his departure. J.W.N. Droog, Head, International Relations Bureau, and J.A.C. de Jonge, Senior Adviser at the Ministry of Housing and Physical Planning, were unfailingly gracious and went to considerable trouble to arrange interviews for me in Amsterdam, Rotterdam, Utrecht, The Hague, and Tilburg.

In France, Max Falque, formerly an environmental planner with the Société du Canal de Provence and now a principal partner of SOMI (Société Méditerranéenne d'Ingénierie), was of immeasurable help. He and his wife, Ursula, housed us until we found an apartment and welcomed us at their home often thereafter. He determined whom it was useful for me to interview and frequently joined me for the interviews. He explained much to me about the land use problems and the political crosscurrents of the Marseilles region. Both while I was in France and subsequently he helped me obtain the reports needed to document this chapter of the study. Lastly, he solicited comments on the draft of the French chapter and offered his own useful critique.

One person has spent about as many hours as I producing this book. Laura Kessler, of the University of Pennsylvania, has typed the successive drafts, prepared the bibliographies, and checked the footnotes, all with great care and accuracy. Some references are less complete than one would wish because, on occasion, people provided me with staff memos, drafts, and other materials lacking full attribution. These sources have been used where appropriate and are referenced as fully as possible.

Scott Middleton, while a student in the landscape architecture and regional planning program at the University of Pennsylvania, prepared most of the maps, graphs, and figures. Satish Jindel, while a student in the urban design program at the University of Pennsylvania, prepared most of the maps and graphs for the Swedish chapter and some of the illustrations for the Dutch chapter.

I thank all of the above and hope that they feel that this book, made possible by their contributions, advances the prospects for better land management, both in the United States and elsewhere.

# Land Banking

# Introduction

The initial impetus for this book on land banking in Europe and its potential for use in the United States grew out of my research, during the late 1960s, for *Planned Urban Environments*.[1] My aim in that book was to examine a diverse range of European urban planning programs, the national contexts of these programs, their principal objectives, and the means used to implement them. Land banking was one of the many implementation techniques that were in widespread use. In looking at the array of methods of plan implementation, I was struck by the apparent relative efficiency and equity of land banking and began to wonder whether it might possibly gain acceptance in the United States. As I said in *Planned Urban Environments*:

Public landownership has been a crucial element of almost all successful European planning. Tapiola is a major exception, although public acquisition of land prior to development is common in Finland. Stockholm's satellite centers, the British and Israeli new towns, the polder new towns in the Netherlands, Rotterdam's port development and urban expansion, and the Languedoc-Roussillon resort towns and coastal development share the common element of public land acquisition in advance of development. In most of these instances, as well as in much of the European planning of which they are illustrative, the land is leased rather than sold for development. If the desired use of the land changes over time, the public can secure the altered use—as well as increments in land values—through negotiation of new lease terms.

In the United States, there is an antipathy to public landownership and a conviction that the increment in land value accruing from increased development potential should go to the successful speculator rather than to the public at large to offset public development costs. We have been ready to compensate the landowner damaged by public planning decisions, but, unlike the Europeans, we have refused to charge the landowner benefited by such decisions.

Given the increasing attribution of incidences of development value to public decisions and investments, the irrationality of our current posture is ever more costly to us as a nation, and to us as individual taxpayers.[2]

With the advent of a sabbatical year in 1973/74 and the receipt of a senior fellowship from the National Endowment for the Humanities, I was able to devote a sustained period of time to an inquiry into land banking in Western Europe. I was particularly anxious to compare the operation of land banking in countries whose value systems are strongly supportive of public land ownership and public retention of development value with its operation elsewhere in a less hospitable climate, in order to determine whether its attributes remained substantial enough in the latter situation to recommend land banking as a preferred tool for plan implementation in the United States. My conclusion is that land banking does have considerable potential for use here.

Land banking is defined rather broadly as public, or publicly authorized, acquisition of land to be held for future use to implement public land use policies. The general nature of the future use of the land may or may not be known at the time of the acquisition. The term is not used here to describe advance acquisition of sites for specific uses such as schools or community facilities.

A number of attributes have been ascribed to land banking. Among them are:

(a) Land can be acquired well ahead of need as it comes on the market;
(b) Land can be acquired before development value attaches to it;
(c) Land can be assembled into tracts large enough for major developments;
(d) Public investment in land and improvements can be averaged over a long term and over the entire land bank program, so that specific site costs do not dictate site use;
(e) Gains in land value from public development decisions will accrue to the public at large;
(f) All landowners are treated equitably, whether or not their land is purchased for a land bank;
(g) Speculation is curbed;
(h) Land can be committed to the building of infrastructure and then to development in an orderly, efficient manner; and
(i) If land is leased rather than sold, the public will continue to profit from its increasing value.

Realization of the greatest benefits from land banking requires popular support for public retention of gains in land value resulting from public planning decisions. It also depends upon adequate initial financing for large-scale acquisitions. Some of the benefits of a land bank program can be realized even where these conditions do not prevail. Where the underlying value structure of the society calls for landowners to receive some share of the development value of their land, land still can be acquired, but at a higher price than in a society that accepts rural land value as fair compensation. If funding is not adequate for the land bank to acquire most of the land that will be developed, a limited scale land bank can acquire sites for the most intensive development.

### The Choice of Countries

Given a desire to contrast land banking under ideal conditions with land banking subject to limitations attributable to public values and to scale of financing, I began the process of determining which group of countries would provide the most appropriate range of experience. The first step was to inquire about the level and nature of activity in the countries of Western Europe known to engage in land banking. These countries were: Austria, Belgium, Denmark, Finland, France, Great Britain, Israel,[3] the Netherlands, Norway, Spain, Sweden, and Switzerland.

Response to the initial inquiries and a survey of the available literature pointed to three countries—Sweden, the Netherlands, and France—as outstanding choices for detailed study. Different factors led to the elimination of the other countries.

Lack of information made it impossible to determine the extent of land bank programs in Austria, Spain, and Switzerland. Because of Spain's three decades of extremely conservative government, exploration of the conceptual basis for municipal land purchase there would be interesting. Switzerland, because of its federal structure, may well have developed variations among intercantonal and cantonal-federal relationships that would have relevance to the United States. Both countries may well warrant future investigation.

Neither Great Britain nor Israel has an on-going land bank program. Great Britain's land acquisitions for the most part have been limited to the new towns, and the bulk of the acquisition is over. In Israel, 92 percent of the land has been in public hands since the formation of the country. While much urban fringe land is private, there has been no program to acquire any of it for a land bank, and the new towns have been built on the public land.

Finland, Norway, and Sweden all engage in land banking, and all three programs operate within similar legal structures and value systems concerning land use. However, lesser growth pressures and more limited financial resources have resulted in much lower levels of activity in Finland and Norway than in Sweden. Positive reasons for selecting Sweden were that some excellent work already had been done on aspects of the Swedish system and that a number of planners in Stockholm expressed enthusiasm for the proposed research and offered their assistance. Denmark does not have programs comparable to those in the other Scandinavian countries.

Belgium and the Netherlands both have a historic commitment to land banking and active current programs. Among those with some knowledge of programs in both countries, however, there was agreement that the Dutch experience was more diverse and the documentation more extensive.

France's position is unique among those countries about which information is available. It came to land banking late and from a perspective toward land ownership quite close to that of the United States. Although funding has not been sufficient, France has initiated programs with more variations—among goals, groups authorized to act, and means of financing —than those of any other country. For these reasons it provides an excellent contrast with Sweden and the Netherlands and is the most useful illustration of what might be possible in the United States.

Canada could have been a candidate for inclusion in this study. It often is cited for its land bank undertakings, and there is fairly extensive documentation both of specific programs and of the array of efforts. A number of these reports are cited in the bibliography for those interested in learning in some detail about the Canadian programs. Because so much material is already available, and because the Canadian experience is limited in extent and variety, only these references and a brief summary of Canadian activities are included here.[4]

The context of land ownership and attitudes toward land within which the various Canadian land bank efforts have occurred is very different from that which exists in the United States. First, the federal government of Canada owns 90 percent of the land[5] as compared with 33 percent federal ownership in the United States. Second, it is widely accepted that, in a conceptual sense, the British Crown holds a residual interest in all land. There is no Canadian equivalent in either statutes or case law of the "taking" language of the Fifth and Fourteenth amendments to the United States Constitution (saying that no property shall be taken without just compensation). Zoning ordinances are not subject to challenge, therefore, on the ground that their provisions constitute such a taking. In this setting, zoning of land in conformity with its natural capabilities or limitations— agricultural zoning, steep slope zoning, and flood plain zoning, for example —is widely used and enjoys public backing.

As in Israel, it is true that the private land in Canada tends to be in and near urban areas. For instance, in 1966, the federal government owned only 5 percent of the land in metropolitan Montreal, 6 percent in Vancouver, 3 percent in Winnipeg, and 1 percent in Toronto.[6] The Canadian urban fringe is subject to intense speculation, and the market is controlled by a handful of investors. This creates a situation that many Canadians believe calls for public acquisition. The other area in which there is considerable support for land banking is farmland preservation. The principal agricultural land bank program, that of the Saskatchewan Land Bank Commission, was inaugurated in 1972, to advance objectives over and above those that zoning could secure. These objectives were to help young farmers obtain land and to assure that land was used in accordance with its capability. The commission buys land, often from farmers who wish to retire; it determines whether cultivation should continue or whether the land should be leased for grazing or committed to some other use; and it seeks young farmers to enter into lifetime leases, with an option to purchase, of the land suited to cultivation. Between 1972 and 1974, the commission purchased 0.6 percent of the farmland of Saskatchewan.[7]

None of the other provinces matches this level of activity in land banking, either for agricultural or urban fringe land, although they have participated in a limited manner to acquire land under two sections of the National Housing Act. Under the Section 40 program, the federal government pays 75 percent and the provincial government 25 percent of land costs. Between 1948 and 1974, a total of 31,861 acres had been approved for land bank purchase under this program,[8] which is a very low level of activity. The Section 42 program of the National Housing Act is a loan program for acquisition of land for housing. Provinces, municipalities, and housing authorities may receive 90 percent federal loans; the loan term is up to fifty years for sites to be leased, twenty-five years for sites to be sold. During the early 1970s, approximately thirty loans per year were granted under this program, with the loan commitment ranging from six to $15 million.

Saskatoon and Edmonton, two of the municipalities frequently cited for their land bank activity, owe their present stocks of land to foresight during the 1930s. Both acquired substantial amounts of tax-delinquent land at that time and held on to it as a reserve for future development. Today 80 to 90 percent of their development is on municipally owned land. A Canadian study reported, with reference to Saskatoon,

the municipal government has been able to provide land for private development at reasonable prices while at the same time planning the development pattern in a comprehensive sense and retaining, again on a planned basis, sufficient land at the proper sites for public uses such as schools, libraries, parks and the like. Starting with the original depression "windfall," Saskatoon has continued to acquire land, sufficiently ahead of development to keep prices down, to the point where it has been able to accommodate current urban expansion and still build up an inventory of some 5,000 acres which should meet development needs for the next 20 years.[9]

As this brief account suggests, public ownership of land does not clash with Canadian concepts of property, and Canada is not a stranger to land banking. Currently, there is considerable debate in Canada about the need for a much more vigorous program of public land acquisition in the fast-growing urban areas in order to gain more control over the price of housing and the pattern of development.

### The Structure of the Book

The closely related issues that this book explores are how land banking has functioned under two quite divergent value systems—those of Sweden and the Netherlands and that of France—and whether land banking may be compatible in the near future with the American value system. My thesis is that land banking functions optimally in societies like those of Sweden and the Netherlands in which there is a long history of belief that all land is impressed with a public trust and that private rights to use of land are subordinate to the public interest. However, I also believe that land banking can be a valuable means of carrying out land use policies in societies occupying some intermediate position between that of Sweden and the Netherlands and laissez-faire capitalism. France's recent reliance on and successes with land banking are the primary evidence in support of this position.

Since the United States for almost two centuries venerated unfettered free enterprise in land, one must ask whether it is reasonable to anticipate that, despite a several decade trend toward greater public control, land banking soon will be both acceptable and useful here. For a number of reasons I am moderately optimistic.

First, current attitudes toward public control of land use in the United States parallel quite closely those in France, and land banking there is increasing in scale and applications. Both countries today accept public controls that limit to some extent the land use choices open to the landowner, yet neither is prepared to limit possible return from land to its rural value. Both countries have begun to test means of recapturing for the public some of the gains resulting from land development.

Second, there has been a substantial increase in the discussion of land banking in the United States.[10] The inclusion in the American Law Institute's Model Land Development Code[11] of a section on land banking is one of the more encouraging recent developments. There have been several proposals for state legislation. Among them is the proposal of the Pennsylvania Office of State Planning and Development, which recommends that the Pennsylvania Legislature establish thirteen metropolitan area development corporations and empower them to create land banks.[12] All of this suggests that the concept is becoming more familiar and less threatening.

Third, there is an increasing recognition in the United States that our natural resources—prime farmland, mineral deposits, wetlands—are finite and that difficult land use choices must be made between resource protection and development. A commitment to public intervention through land banking is more likely in a setting of resource scarcity.

If land banking does become palatable here, it will be one measure of the extent and rapidity of the shift in our views of the proper role of government in dealing with land. To understand our immediate heritage, and why it is so different from that in most Western European countries, this book opens with an exploration of the sources of Western attitudes toward land, the imprint of the American Revolution, the major post-Revolutionary land ownership decisions, and the nature of recent trends.

The following three chapters describe land banking in the Stockholm region, in the Netherlands, and in France. The questions that I have sought to answer with respect to land banking in these countries were: What objectives has the country sought to advance by the use of land banking? How has the system of land banking been influenced by the country's concepts of land ownership and of the public interest? What is the context of planning and land use controls within which land banking operates? How has the system evolved, and what are its current constraints and prospects?

While the answers to these questions are likely to be of interest to people in different countries who are concerned with implementation of land use policies, my particular focus here is on the shortcomings of the American land use control system and on an exploration of the potential of some form of land banking for bringing about improvements in our system.[13] Therefore, the final chapter contrasts the Swedish and Dutch programs with the French, compares their achievements, and explores what forms of land banking might win support in the United States in the near future.

NOTES

1. Ann Louise Strong, *Planned Urban Environments: Sweden, Finland, Israel, the Netherlands, France* (Baltimore: The Johns Hopkins Press, 1971).

2. Ibid., pp. xxxi, xxxii.

3. Israel, of course, is not located, in Western Europe, but its planning orientation is grounded there.

4. Maurizio Favretto, a former student in the Department of City and Regional Planning at the University of Pennsylvania, located much of the information cited here.

5. A. J. Greiner, "Land Policy in Canada," mimeographed (Ottawa: Ministry of State for Urban Affairs, 1974).

6. Department of Public Works, *Central Real Property Inventory*, March 1972.

7. The Saskatchewan Land Bank Commission, *Third Annual Report, 1974*.

8. Central Mortgage and Housing Corporation, *Annual Report, 1974* (Ottawa: Queen's Printer, 1974).

9. Canada, Task Force on Housing and Urban Development, *Report 40* (Ottawa: Queen's Printer, 1969).

10. See, for instance, Harvey L. Flechner, *Land Banking in the Control of Urban Development* (New York: Praeger Publishers, 1974); Carol Van Alstyne, ed., *Land Bank Handbook: Advance Acquisition of Sites for Low and Moderate Income Housing* (Greensboro, N.C.: Piedmont Triad Council of Governments, 1972); Kermit C. Parsons et al., *Public Land Acquisition for New Communities and the Control of Urban Growth*, Center for Urban Development Research (Ithaca, N.Y.: Cornell University, 1973).

11. The American Law Institute, *A Model Land Development Code* (Philadelphia: The American Law Institute, 1976).

12. Office of State Planning and Development, "Urban Growth Strategy," Statewide Land Policy Report (Harrisburg: Office of State Planning and Development, 1977).

13. See Ann L. Strong, *Private Property and the Public Interest: The Brandywine Experience* (Baltimore: The Johns Hopkins University Press, 1975), for a discussion of American attitudes toward land and a case study of an experiment with planning for use of public acquisition of development rights.

# 1

# Concepts of Land Ownership

Private land ownership ranks high in the constellation of American values. Thomas Jefferson's sentiment that "it is not too soon to provide by every possible means that as few as possible shall be without a little portion of land"[1] still finds widespread endorsement. Landowning is held to foster many favored attributes; chief among them are responsibility toward the land and toward society, independence, and self-sufficiency. Many feel that public land ownership is antithetical to democracy. Yet, at some time in our history 79 percent of the land of the United States has been owned by the federal government; today federal holdings total 761 million acres, or over one-third of the nation's land (see map 1.1). Another 8 percent is owned in trust for the Indians or held by the states (see map 1.2). Is there an anomaly between the private ownership values professed by many and the reality of the 58 percent private–42 percent public split in the distribution of ownership?

From the founding of our nation until the close of the nineteenth century, almost all new territory acquired became part of the public domain. The federal government endeavored to sell this land—and, later, to give it away—as rapidly as possible after acquiring it. Individuals, corporations, and states all were beneficiaries of policies that removed over one billion acres from the public domain. By the close of the nineteenth century, attitudes had begun to change. Much of the public domain existing at that time was residual or mismanaged acreage with little market value. People began to appreciate the need to manage resources for watershed protection, timber production, and scenic preservation. The pressure to sell abated. Today there is much public domain land that remains undeveloped

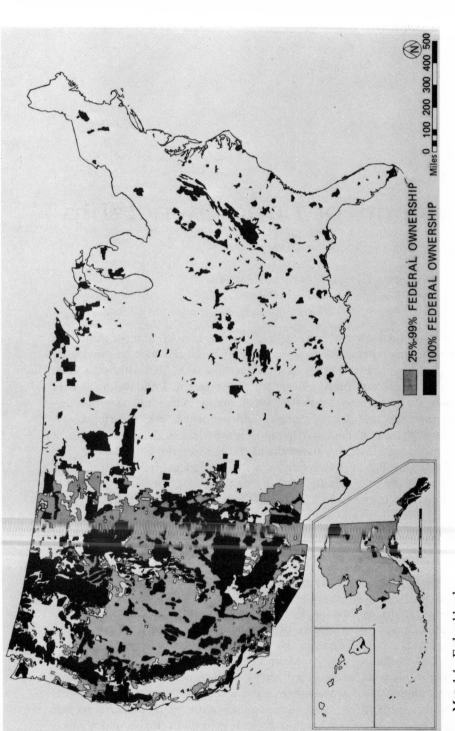

MAP 1.1. Federal lands

SOURCE: Adapted from U.S., Department of the Interior, Geological Survey, *Federal Lands: Principal Lands Administered or Held in Trust by Federal Agencies, January 1, 1968* (map) (Washington, D.C.: Government Printing Office, 1968)

25%-99% FEDERAL OWNERSHIP

100% FEDERAL OWNERSHIP

Miles

0 100 200 300 400 500

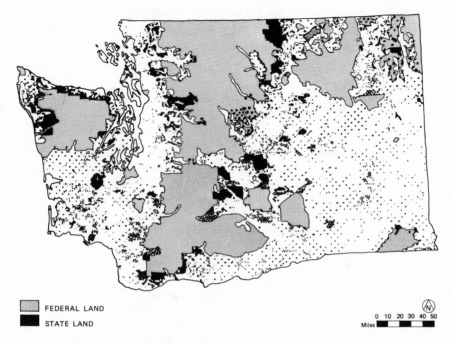

FEDERAL LAND

STATE LAND

0 10 20 30 40 50
Miles

MAP 1.2. Washington's public lands

SOURCE: Adapted from State of Washington, Department of Natural Resources, *Washington's Major Public Lands* (Olympia, 1973)

for any use, subject to no development pressures. Other land has substantial market value but is retained in public ownership because of a legislative recognition that the public interest may be better served by public management. Leases of timber, grazing, and mineral rights to public lands have been accepted as a means of permitting regulated private use of public resources. The states, on a lesser scale, mirror the federal ownership and management practices within which resource management is the dominant theme.

There is no sense of public outrage over the current scale and forms of government ownership of land. The recent expansion of park and open space holdings has been widespread. However, is there any sentiment for expansion of the reach of public ownership to embrace land banking? This would require an aggressive public program to acquire key sites for active future use. Government in the United States has, in this century, ceased to act as a land huckster and instead has become a land manager. Are we now ready for it to be an active intercessionist in the land market, seeking by its ownership to determine the location of intensive use of land and to redirect the gains from this use? This is the question to be explored. This chapter opens the inquiry by asking what attitudes toward public and private land ownership have been, how these attitudes were shaped, and what they are today.

### The Western Heritage

Control of land always has meant power, and the search for a conceptual base to justify claims to land has been an essential part of the power struggle. Rulers, ecclesiastics, rich men, poor men—all have bent theories of land ownership to support their political ends.

The fundamental question addressed in structuring a concept of land ownership is whether the governing law is held to be natural or man-made. In the Western tradition, natural law is equated with the law of God. If one accepts that, at the creation, law was natural, from that point there are two divergent conceptual paths. Either God, having designed ownership principles for a state of nature, intended these principles to remain binding on man, or He empowered man to make a new set of laws upon establishment of a society. If land is held to be governed by natural law, God remains the owner of the land and some component of society occupies the role of trustee for God. Different cultures adhering to the natural law concept have vested the role of trustee in the church, government, or people as a whole. If the law governing land is held to be man-made, the premise is that God gave title to the land to some sector of society and, with the title, the authority to structure laws of property ownership.

If we in the United States endorse the Jeffersonian view that, ideally, our society should offer each person the opportunity to own land, we are supporting a version of the concept of law as man-made that is both relatively new and antithetical to Christian and Jewish theology. It is a concept that flowered with John Locke and that gained a strong foothold in most of the countries that settled North America. While the views existing in England and France, and, to a lesser extent, in Sweden and the Netherlands during the early years of European colonization most strongly influenced American attitudes toward land ownership, one must look further back than John Locke to find the origins of these views.

### Greece, Rome, and the Early Christians[2]

One can trace to Plato one principle for the distribution of property that was employed in many early New England towns. The ideal society of Plato's *Republic* was one in which the rulers, or Guardians, owned nothing and lived a monklike existence, with no money, no family, and only the simplest of food. The other members of the society owned all forms of property but had no voice in shaping laws or policy. Recognizing that this ideal society was incompatible with men as they are, Plato proposed an alternate society in which the citizens would hold political power and also own property. The number of citizens and the number of shares of land would remain constant within the society, governed by laws of inheritance. If any citizen managed to acquire more than four times his original share of land, the excess would become state property. The parallel design for some colonial New England towns was that there should be a fixed maximum population and that no one citizen should hold more than eight times as much land as any other.

Aristotle agreed that some rough sort of parity among citizens was necessary to preserve a community. He justified slavery as being the natural condition of some men, and for slaves the rules of parity had no applicability. Unlike Plato, Aristotle did not express a clear conviction about the nature of land ownership in an ideal society. He did describe one possible pattern:[3] half of the land would be privately owned in equal shares by citizens and worked by the owners' slaves, while the other half would be owned in common by all citizens and worked by publicly owned slaves for the benefit of all. This concept of the division of ownership between common and private land found acceptance in societies from the Roman to the American colonies.

Neither Plato nor Aristotle discussed land ownership in the context of natural versus man-made law. The Bible, however, explicitly supports the natural law view. Leviticus 25:23–24 says: "And the land shall not be sold in perpetuity. For the land is mine; for ye are strangers and sojourners with me. And in all the land of your possession ye shall grant a redemption for your land." This injunction that land only be leased was interpreted as imposing a maximum term of forty-nine years. Every fiftieth year was denominated a jubilee year, in which no crops were to be planted and in which all debts could be redeemed. These teachings of the Bible are observed today in Israel for the more than 90 percent of the nation's land held by the state. The role of trustee for God has been vested in the national government.

Early Christian theology did not dispute the Biblical teaching that all property belongs to God. However, faced with the fact that men wanted to own property, not just the right to use it, the theologians devised a set of premises to justify private ownership. In the Garden of Eden—the ideal state—there was no private property; however, the fall from paradise so corrupted man that society no longer could function without a system of ownership. Thomas Carlyle described the early Christian rationalization:

The world was made for the common benefit of mankind, that all should receive from it what they require. . . . Human nature being what it is, greedy, avaricious, and vicious, it is impossible for men to live normally under the condition of common ownership. For mankind in general, some organization of ownership became necessary, and this was provided by the state and its laws, which have decided the conditions and limitations of ownership.

A further refinement of this argument is that after the fall some men were less corrupt than others, and the difference in merit justified rewarding them unequally through an unequal distribution of property.

The Romans tended to agree with the view that men had all been equal in a state of nature and had used and benefited from property without owning it. Seneca explained individual ownership of land in Rome by saying that, now that man's nature had become selfish and greedy, it no longer was possible to satisfy wants from common holdings. Roman law, however, did provide that people owning tillable land should hold in common ownership some forest and pasture land. Rights to the timber crop and to the pasturage were allocated in proportion to the tillable acreage held. This provision for common ownership of pastures and woods was replicated in many colonial New England town charters.

## The Feudal Era

During feudal times, heads of church and state and their logicians contributed to the embellishment of the doctrines of natural law and man-made law. During the Middle Ages, the church was the largest landowner in Europe and was committed to keeping what it had and getting more. Its theologians faced the double task of moral justification of the church's actions and defense of church property against government. St. Thomas Aquinas gave lip service to the ideal state with no individual ownership of property but urged that rulers as a practical matter recognize the concept of private land ownership. He, too, rested his argument on the theory of the fall from paradise and bolstered it with the pragmatic observation that property ownership encourages men to work harder. Aquinas agreed with the early Christians that some men are superior to others and that property is a fit reward for superiority. Since the church had great merit, this constituted a warrant for massive land ownership.

In the thirteenth century, Aegidius developed different conceptual glosses to defend church property against civil powers and to justify the aggrandizement of church holdings. He relied on natural law and argued that men, before forming governments, had recognized God's ownership and had entered into a compact to observe the natural law. Under this compact the church, and specifically the pope, held property as a custodian for God. One practical result of this, he argued, was that church property was not subject to French civil law or taxes. The church also could justify a form of escheat. Since by the compact the church was the trustee, it was entitled to allocate rights to land to sovereigns, and they, in turn, could grant some or all of these rights to men. Whenever any man holding property rights was excommunicated, these rights would revert to the church, since men outside the grace of God could not be parties to contracts allocating rights to use of God's land.

Those who were sovereigns rather than popes didn't fancy the theologians' arguments. For them, the divine right of kings meant that God had given *them* property to allocate and regulate as they saw fit. From the Roman Conquest on into the sixteenth century this was by feudal tenures, in which there were hierarchies of rights and obligations descending, roughly, from kings to lords to peasants.

A description of the major changes in the English feudal system from the time of the Saxons down through the sixteenth century gives a sense of the slow evolution of the distribution of power over land under feudalism in Europe.

Prior to the Norman Conquest in 1066, the Saxons held land in two ways: "folcland," or land granted by the king to be held in common, and "bocland," or land granted to an individual by a written document. Bocland could be inherited, and the holder of it might owe duties to the king. Both folcland and bocland grants could be allodial, meaning that full title went from the king to the grantees. It is important to distinguish between the interests in land defined during the feudal period by the terms allodial and fee, because today's definition has changed materially. A grant of land subject to no obligations to the king or other grantor was termed allodial. The opposite form of grant, which required the rendering of services, goods, or money, was termed a fee. Fief and feud were terms synonymous with fee; all described a limited, or less than free, estate in land. Today the term allodial is not in common use, and fee is the term that has come to be applied to what formerly were called allodial holdings.

The coming of William the Conqueror signaled the cessation of allodial grants. All property was granted in tenancy, with the king holding and retaining the fundamental title. Tenancies granted by the king were called *in capite* tenancies. Subtenancies granted by mesne (middle) lords were called "tenancies as of a manor." The manor referred to consisted of a lord, the lord's court, and others—bailiffs, freeholders, and villeins. Tenancies as of a manor governed most rights to land in the colonies.

There were two types of tenure, free and unfree, and these were applicable to either *in capite* tenancies or tenancies as of a manor. Types of free tenure included: knight service, the most common form of tenure for tenants holding from the king; serjeanty, which was an obligation to perform ceremonial duties, usually for the king; frankalmoin, or free alms, which was an ecclesiastic tenure with an obligation to perform religious services; and socage, which was an obligation to pay rent or to provide agricultural services. Socage—often called free and common socage—was the conventional form of tenure in the colonies. Unfree, or villein, tenure required the tenant to perform services on the king's or lord's land.

In this early period tenants might be subject to some of the following nine types of obligations or incidents: fealty, homage, wardship, marriage, relief, primer seisin, aids, fines for alienation, and escheats. The exact requirements of each obligation could vary with the type of tenancy but their general nature was as follows

1. Fealty: an oath of fidelity taken by all tenants
2. Homage: a personal allegiance to the king owed by *in capite* tenants
3. Wardship: a guardianship of minor heirs that, under some tenures, entitled the guardian to profits from the land of the heirs
4. Marriage: a guardianship of minor heirs that entitled the guardian to contract for the marriage of the heir
5. Relief: a payment of one year's rent by the tenant to the landlord on entering into the tenancy
6. Primer seisin: a payment of one year's profits from the land due to the king on succession of an heir to a knight's fee
7. Aids: a payment of one-twentieth of the annual income from the land, earmarked for the lord's expenses in knighting his son or providing a dowry for his eldest daughter
8. Fines for alienation: payment due the grantor of the fee upon the tenant's sale of his interest in the land
9. Escheat: the reversion to the landlord of the interest in land upon either the tenant's commission of a felony or death without lineal descendants

The thirteenth century saw several significant changes in feudal tenure. It became customary for a lord to make available to his tenants common land—"allmend"—for their use as pasture or for cutting timber. The Magna Carta, in 1215, guaranteed that no one would be deprived of his rights to land without a judgment rendered by his equals, and it limited what could be demanded under some of the feudal incidents. The Statute of Mortmain, passed in 1279, barred further grants of land to the church. At that time, the church held half of the land of England and paid no money to the king in the form of incidents of tenure. The Statute of Quia Emptores, in 1290, made two major changes: It allowed the sale of interests in land without payment of a fine to the lord, and it barred further subinfeudation, or creation of new tenancies, by those holding tenancies as of a manor. Since the statute did not apply to the king, grantees of *in capite* tenancies could continue to create subtenancies but could not sell their interests without obtaining a license from and paying a fine to the king. Centuries later, the king created tenancies *in capite* for the settlement of Pennsylvania and South Carolina, which meant that these tenants alone out of all colonial settlers could subinfeudate. William Penn, one such *in capite* tenant, in fact did make socage grants. The result of the Statute of Quia Emptores was that gradually the hierarchy of feudal ownership dissolved and, over several hundred years, most people came to hold socage tenancies granted directly by the sovereign. This is the prevailing nature of ownership in England today.

### Post-Reformation Ferment

Contemporaneous with the colonization of America, a number of new theories of land ownership were sweeping Europe. There was ferment against both church and feudal power over land and an emerging capitalist class was demanding greater property rights.

In England, plagues and migration to the cities had left the lords short of help and had altered the balance of power between them and their tenants. The tenants had become strong enough to obtain passage by Parliament of a law that abolished almost all of the incidents of tenure. What remained after adoption of the Statute of Tenures of 1660 were the obligations of the tenant to pay rent and relief.

The Reformation brought considerable expropriation of Catholic church lands in Protestant countries and the redistribution of these lands to a new class of land holders. Yet Luther and other voices of Protestantism had found no theory of property to warrant their acts. From the premise that land should be used efficiently, they argued, rather weakly, that capitalist landowners would achieve higher productivity than indolent priests. They failed to consider what ownership or regulatory roles should accrue to the state after expropriation.

The Calvinists, in the seventeenth century, did offer a theory, one that guided the Dutch and Swedes in their colonial settlements. God, at the creation, gave property in common to all men, not to a pope or a king. The American Indians were cited as a people who had continued to hold land in common, as a trust. However, most men, by social contract, had created governments and allocated to them certain rights to regulate use of property and certain obligations to defend the property interests of individuals. Governments had misconstrued the powers granted them, appropriating too much control and discriminating in favor of the aristocracy. It was now time to redress the balance.

John Locke moved boldly beyond this explanation of the origins of property to proclaim that property ownership by individuals, not in common, was a right of man. He justified differences in the size of land holdings by arguing that men take what they need and make it theirs by

their labor. Some need more than others. Throughout Europe, protagonists
of land reform for peasants and the growing middle class argued Locke's
liberal theories of property in efforts to weaken the grip of government and
big estate holders. Locke became the idealogue of the Glorious Revolution
of 1688 in England and, later, of the French and American revolutions. His
ideas did not triumph in England, but they did win adoption in France and
the United States. Life, liberty, and property, the triad of rights that Locke
argued that government should guarantee, were incorporated into the
wording of the French Declaration of the Rights of Man of 1789 and into
the bills of rights of Virginia and Massachusetts.

The Declaration of the Rights of Man stated: "The aim of every political association is the preservation of the natural and imprescriptable rights
of man. These rights are liberty, property, security and resistance to op-
pression." The drafters debated whether to rely on the social contract
theory to defend property rights but decided in favor of natural law. They
believed that there should be some limit on the accumulation of property
and concluded that it was the proper role of government to even out
disproportionate holdings. Although the French embraced Locke to support diffusion of property ownership to peasants and the lower middle
class, not everyone became a landowner, and voting, by the Constitution
of 1795, was restricted to landowners.

Jefferson averred that his three gods were Locke, Bacon, and Newton
and that there was little to learn from Aristotle.[4] About Jefferson's concept of law as it influenced him in drafting the Declaration of Independence, Filmer Northrop states that

the most significant person in Jefferson's trinity is Locke. It was Locke who
gave the natural law philosophy of Jefferson and our founding fathers its
particular modern content. In his classic treatise *Of Civil Government,* Locke
affirms that the sole justification of the existence of government is the preservation of the property of the individual, . . . In other words, the content of the
natural law of the Declaration of Independence is Newtonian and Lockian
rather than Aristotelian, Thomastic and Roman Catholic.[5]

The Massachusetts Bill of Rights, written by John Adams, another
adherent of Locke, stipulated that "all men . . . have certain natural,
essential and unalienable rights; among which . . . that of acquiring, pos-
sessing, and protecting property."

The First Continental Congress, in 1774, stated that "by the immutable
laws of nature" the colonists were entitled to "rights of life, liberty, and
property." By the time of passage of the United States Constitution, the
concept of a right to ownership of land was subject to debate. The Fed-
eralists, unwilling to offer such an assurance to all, succeeded in having the
wording of the Fifth Amendment reflect their preference: property rights

are to be protected but there is no policy statement that all men have a right to acquire property. Equality of opportunity, not equality of ownership, was the ideal reflected in the Constitution.

There was also concern in the United States about disparities in ownership. Jefferson, on visiting France in 1795, observed enormous inequalities in land holding, as well as in the accumulation of other forms of wealth, and recommended that "another means of silently lessening the inequality of property is to exempt all from taxation below a certain point, and to tax the higher portions of property in geometrical progression as they rise."[6]

Thus, in both post-Revolutionary France and the United States the ideas of Locke had won out, but modified so that property ownership could be available to all depending on ability. The issue of excess concentration of property was acknowledged and debated, but not resolved.

## Land Ownership during the Colonial Period

The European settlers arrived in America with different theories of land ownership. These theories had been shaped by many forces, including the power of the sovereign, the degree of religious freedom allowed, and the advance of the middle class in the countries from which the settlers came. Attitudes toward land ownership colored their views of Indian rights and shaped settlement patterns.

One aspect of the English view was that land held by non-Christians was vacant land, available upon discovery for taking in the name of the crown. "A Christian nation could move in at any time and occupy space needed by its own people. . . . Such occupancy was essential to the process of bringing heathens into the saving knowledge of the new religion, which was born out of the then teeming Reformation."[7] As Justice Marshall said, in commenting on the English foundation of American law:

That from time immemorial . . . all the Indian tribes . . . held their respective lands and territories, each in common, the individuals of each tribe or nation holding the lands and territories of such tribe, in common with each other, and there being among them no separate property in the soil. . . .

So early as the year 1496, her monarch granted a commission to the Cabots, to discover countries then unknown to Christian people, and to take possession of them in the name of the king of England. . . . The right of discovery given by this commission, is confined to countries "then unknown to all Christian people," and of these countries, Cabot was empowered to take possession, notwithstanding the occupancy of the natives, who were heathens. . . .

The United States, then have unequivocally acceded to that great and broad rule by which its civilized inhabitants now hold this country. They hold, and assert in themselves, the title by which it was acquired. They maintain, as all others have maintained, that discovery gave an exclusive right to extinguish the Indian title of occupancy.[8]

Only where the practical considerations of peace and safety dictated did the English compensate the Indians. The Puritans and Quakers were exceptions to this prevailing practice, feeling a moral obligation to pay. Their perspective had been shaped by their religious persecution in England and by their exclusion from government.

The Dutch and the Swedes respected the Indians' title and believed that the land must be acquired by purchase or gift before title could pass to them. In part, this attitude was shaped by Calvinism. The Dutch, as well, had a long history of survival depending on cooperation and were better able to understand the Indians' concept of land rights.

The Spaniards claimed title in the name of the pope. They did not explain the source of the pope's claim to ownership and did not pay for what they took. The French tended to pay compensation and, not infrequently, acquired title by intermarriage with the Indians.

The Indians' misfortune was that they had a concept of ownership so totally different from that of any of the Europeans that they did not seek what, by European terms, would be adequate compensation. Since they believed in sharing the land in common,[9] they generally failed to realize that, on accepting payment, all of their rights to use of the land would be extinguished.

### Grants from the King of England

The English settlers arrived under three types of grants of authority from the crown: royal colonies, proprietorships, and corporate colonies. Under each type of grant, the king was sovereign and held title to all land. All of the grants, except those to William Penn and Lord Baltimore and those in South Carolina, were tenancies as of a manor, held in free and common socage.

In the royal colonies, the king appointed the governor and upper house of the colonial legislature. Freemen could vote for representatives in the lower house, although in some colonies the franchise also depended on one's religion. In New Hampshire, for instance, Catholics and Quakers were not entitled to vote. By the time of the Revolution, there were seven royal colonies: New Hampshire, New York, New Jersey, Virginia, North Carolina, South Carolina, and Georgia. The land in New York was seized from the Dutch under a grant from Charles II to James, Duke of York. It became a royal colony when the duke became James II. Georgia was settled under a form of tenure as of a manor called tenure of the bishop of Durham. The Spaniards in Florida had treated the neighboring French so viciously that the English anticipated difficulty in getting settlers to go to Georgia. Therefore, they wanted to provide the least restrictive tenure in order to lure people to provide a buffer between the Spaniards and the other English colonies. The royal charters specified obligations owed the king; Virginia and New York, for instance, owed one-third of all gold and silver and one-fifteenth of all copper discovered. The charters often covered thousands of square miles and were subject to revocation if the king became dissatisfied with the return received.

Three colonies—Pennsylvania, Delaware, and Maryland—were settled as proprietary colonies. William Penn and Lord Baltimore were granted charters to overlapping sites, and the division of territory was not settled until the Mason-Dixon Line was fixed, between 1763 and 1768. The area that is now Delaware had been bought by the Swedes from the Indians in 1638, taken over in 1655 by the Dutch, who allowed those Swedes who wished to keep their land to remain, and then taken by the English and made part of the grant by the king to Penn in 1681. Penn received an *in capite* tenure and so, not being barred by the Statute of Quia Emptores, was able to subinfeudate. One example of Penn's subinfeudation was his 1731 grant of thirty acres at West Grove, Pennsylvania, to a rose grower, subject to an annual payment or quitrent of one red rose. Even today, the Star Rose Company makes its annual payment to the heirs of William Penn. A major benefit to the charterer of the right to subinfeudate was that if a tenant died intestate the property escheated to the grantor of the tenure, not to the crown.

The corporate colonies were Massachusetts, Rhode Island, and Connecticut. The charters from the king to the corporations gave them considerable leeway in the control of land use and the establishment of colonial government. The corporations sometimes made grants to individuals but customarily granted land to groups of settlers called town proprietors. Because of great confusion over boundaries, the settlers did not always establish towns within their charterer's jurisdiction. The Pilgrims, for instance, received a grant of land from the Virginia Company, but, since Plymouth was outside the Virginia Company's territory, they were, in effect, squatters.

### Land Distribution in the English Colonies

Distribution of land varied from colony to colony, influenced by the class background of the colonists, the natural environment, the rate of immigration, and the form of the colonial charter. Some holders of charters sold land in fee, some sold it subject to payment of an annual quitrent, and some offered a choice. As competition for settlers mounted, the quitrents tended to become more of a token payment. Lord Baltimore frequently leased land, and this custom still is prevalent in Maryland. Other charterers also made a practice of leasing, often for twenty-one-year terms. Only William Penn granted land subject to the stipulation that, for every five acres cleared, one acre should remain in forest.

The pattern of land grant or sale throughout New England was fairly standard. A group of between twenty and sixty men subscribed money to obtain a grant to "plant" a town. The grant was made by the colonial legislature, if it was a royal colony, or by the company holding the charter. Grants of land from royal colonies were free except for survey costs and payments to Indians, if any were made. However, they were subject to two conditions: the settlers had to be numerous enough to support a church, and the town had to be established and populated within two or three years of the grant. If these conditions were not met, the grant lapsed and the land could be granted anew to another group of would-be settlers.[10]

The grants were made based on the theory that there was an ideal size, population, and distribution of land for a town. It was assumed that the initial fixed area would not change in the future and that once the town had grown to its planned population it would remain stable, with any excess people moving away to establish towns elsewhere. Customarily, no one held more than eight times as much land as anyone else.

The towns were six to eight square miles in area. The land might previously have been surveyed or the prospective settlers might obtain a license to survey it. Once the boundaries were established the settlers designated land for one of four types of use: the town proper, including streets, a commons, and home lots; adjacent arable land; pasture; and woodland. The commons was fenced and provided a place to graze cows and to erect the church. Home lots, which provided enough space for the house, barns, chicken run, and garden, were granted to individual settlers. These lots varied considerably in size from town to town and, often, within a town, but generally were not less than one-half acre in area. The acreage variations within a town were to accommodate families of different size, composition, and/or wealth: "as seventeenth-century Englishmen and Puritans the settlers recognized hierarchy to be the natural and desirable order of society, men of means or status were given larger allocations or subsequent land bonuses."[11] Bachelors, families with female children, and widows might be discriminated against in the allocation. Arable land sometimes was held in common, and sometimes divided into strips and allocated in the same proportion as the home lots. One allocation system, for instance, granted eighteen acres of arable land per male child or ten acres per female.

The pasture and woodland customarily were held in common by the town.

From the earliest days, the king allowed towns and colonies to tax land. It also was customary in New England for the towns to retain the power to approve any sale of land, so that incompatible people could be kept out and also so that the town could prevent concentration of land ownership in the hands of a few people. Connecticut went even farther, in 1666, when it enacted a law specifying that no one could sell land without first offering it for sale to the town.

The New England settlers were, for the most part, imbued with the ideas of Locke and were religious dissenters as well, while the Southern settlers came from traditional, aristocratic English society. In their view, the elite had the right and obligation to govern and by their merit were entitled to dominate land ownership.

In the South, settlement reflected this class origin and tended to be dispersed on large, feudal-type plantations, with ownership restricted to a small portion of the population. Purchasers bought land by headrights; a specified number of acres was required for each person to be settled on the land. One hundred acres was the average size per headright in the early years but, as land values rose and settlement increased, the average dropped to 50 acres. The headright cost included the cost of passage from England and the charterer's charge for the land. Large purchases of headrights were made by wealthy individuals who imported poor settlers and installed them on the land under conditions of indentured servitude. There was an enormous range in the total size of headright grants; the Virginia Company, before it was dissolved in 1625, had granted headrights ranging in size from 12 to 800,000 acres. Just as did the grants of towns in New England, the grants of headrights stipulated that the land had to be planted and a house built within a specified number of years or the grant could be revoked. Where the grants were large, this requirement applied to only a small portion of the land.

Under the headright system, when the indentured worker paid off his debt, he was entitled to receive half of the land covered by the headright affecting him. Although the plantation owner retained the other half, under this system he eventually stood to lose up to one-half of his total land holdings and many of his workers. Slavery was a more lucrative alternative for landowners, so the use of headrights declined starting in 1715, disappearing around the end of the eighteenth century.

Georgia was different, both from the other Southern colonies and from New England. It was founded "for the relief of poor subjects who, through misfortune and want of employment, were reduced to great necessity." Between 1732 and 1741, fifteen hundred poor settlers were induced to go to Georgia, where they formed a buffer between the rapacious Spaniards and the gentry of the Carolinas. They were granted holdings of up to 500 acres each and were excused from payment of a quitrent for the first ten years of their tenancy. While liberal in its conditions of tenure, only Georgia of all of the colonies limited inheritance to the children born to the male owner—a fee tail.

A few cities, including New York, Washington, and Savannah, offered some of the land that they had acquired for city development for sale and some for lease with the intention that the cities' leased holdings would rise in value as a result of private improvement of the land that had been sold. New York, for instance, acquired vast acreage under the Dongan Charter of 1686. The city platted the land and sold lots in a checkerboard pattern. The remaining lots, which it leased, rose steadily in value, and the city was able to renegotiate the lease terms so as to increase its yield. For a considerable period, lease income was so substantial that the city did not need to levy real estate taxes. This happy state of affairs terminated in 1845, when the city sold the land to cover the unexpectedly high cost of its Croton Aqueduct.[12]

The ownership patterns in the colonies prior to the Revolution showed considerable diversity, but there were two common elements: all grants of land were held in tenancy from the king,[13] and the grants required payments in money or in kind. Some holders of colonial charters made fee grants to towns, some to individuals, and some to both. Towns that received grants of land managed the land in a variety of ways: some land was sold, some was sold subject to the town's right of preemption, some was leased, and some was held by the town for common use. Both the New England towns, with their holding of common pasture and woods, and cities with a checkerboard pattern of private-public holdings were acting on the assumption that the public good would best be served by retention of substantial areas in public ownership.

## The Creation and Disposition of the Public Domain

The principal initial impact of the Revolution on land ownership patterns was that the new states laid claim to immense and often ill-defined holdings. The federal government initially was landless. Both the disparity of holdings among the states and the lack of federal land soon were recognized as problems. Some states worried about the potential advantage of other states with large holdings. Many saw federal land ownership as one means of funding the treasury of the new government.

The states came into possession of their lands in several ways. The land of loyalists was seized by the states and sold. In the South, this broke up some of the feudal plantations, which were sold in smaller tracts for family farms. Many successors to the original holders of royal grants also had their lands seized and sold. By laying claim to these grants, seven of the thirteen original states obtained land both within and far beyond their boundaries, since the grants had extended to the west of the Alleghenies, with some even purporting to stretch to the Pacific. Already in 1779, several states, principally those lacking extensive holdings, were agitating for transfer of the lands outside states' boundaries to the federal government. The two main objectives—that the land should be held for the mutual benefit of all of the states by the United States and that it should be held subject to later divestiture—were stated in a resolution of the state of Delaware:

That this State consider themselves justly entitled to a right, in common with the members of the Union, to that extensive tract of country which lies westward of the frontiers of the United States, the property of which was not vested in, or granted to, individuals at the commencement of the present war:—that the same hath been, or may be, gained from the King of Great Britain, or the native Indians, by the blood and treasure of all, and ought therefore to be a common estate, to be granted out on terms beneficial to the United States.

Initially a majority of those states with external lands favored retaining these lands but, after considerable and heated argument, the states one by one ceded the holdings. By 1802, the transfers to the United States were complete. This land was the nucleus of the public domain.

The nature of private land ownership initially continued as it had been under the British. Land was held in tenure by the owners, with the states substituted for the king as sovereign. Later, a number of state legislatures abolished tenure and made all holdings allodial.[14] In some states tenure still exists technically, as a residue of colonial law; it is, however, of no significance in determining ownership rights and duties. A decision in 1853 affirmed that the sovereign was the initial owner of all land. The Massachusetts Supreme Court, in sustaining state regulation of tidal land, held: "All property . . . is derived directly or indirectly from the government, and held subject to those general regulations which are necessary to the common good and general welfare."[15]

One persistent influence of the British tenure system is the abjuration even today by the federal government of the exercise of the power to tax land. The colonial settlers had resented deeply the payment of a quitrent to the king, and the founders of the nation decided that real property taxation by a new, remote federal system might breed antagonism to the central government. Therefore, use of the real property tax was left to the states and local governments. Today's land use patterns might have been very different had there been a nationwide real property assessment, collection, and distribution system.

TABLE 1.1. Acquisitions for the Public Domain

| Acquisition | Year | Size (in million acres) | Percentage of Total U.S. Area | Comments |
|---|---|---|---|---|
| Cessions by the original states | 1781–1802 | 237 | 10 | |
| Louisiana Purchase | 1803 | 560 | 24 | purchased from France |
| Florida | 1819 | 46 | 2 | ceded by Spain |
| Oregon Territory | 1846 | 183 | 8 | overlapped part of Louisiana Purchase land; acquired on settlement of British claim |
| Mexican Purchase | 1848 | 339 | 15 | covered California and parts of the Southwest |
| Texas public domain | 1850 | 79 | 3 | purchased from the state of Texas, which was annexed in 1845; land was outside the state's boundaries |
| Gadsden Purchase | 1853 | 19 | 1 | further purchase from Mexico |
| Alaska | 1867 | 375 | 16 | purchased from Russia |
| Total public domain | | 1,838 | 79 | |
| Total area of United States | | 2,312 | 100 | |

SOURCE: Marion Clawson and R. Burnell Held, *The Federal Lands: Their Use and Management* (Baltimore: The Johns Hopkins Press, 1957).

### Acquisitions for the Public Domain

After the creation of the United States, all new acquisition of land was carried out by the federal government. The lands, with the exception of Texas and Hawaii, became part of the national public domain. All told, between 1803 and 1867, 1.8 billion acres, or 79 percent of the present total area of the United States, passed into the public domain. For the land that was bought, the average cost was four cents per acre.[16] The principal acquisitions are shown in table 1.1.

It was decided very early that governmental functions in the public domain should be divided between newly created states and the central government. However, new states should not come into being until there were enough people and enough development in an area for it to support the functions of a state government. Just as cessions of land by seven of the original states had been spurred by a concern over inequality of power among the then existing states, so was the formation of new states affected by the desire of the existing states that the new states not surpass them in wealth or population. A comparison today between Nevada and California suggests how futile was the attempt to design boundaries with relation to equality of potential.

### Disposition of the Public Domain

If it was considered not only desirable but even urgent for the new nation to expand its land holdings, the prevailing view, at least for the first 100 years of the public domain, was that it was equally desirable and urgent that the land be committed to private ownership. Thomas Jefferson and Andrew Jackson represented the majority opinion, which emphasized rapid settlement and creation of a society of landowners. John Quincy Adams would have preferred stressing public return and more orderly settlement: "My own system, . . . which was to make the national domain the inexhaustible fund for progressive improvement, has failed."[17] As Marion Clawson observed:

National policy in the early days of our country revolved around land to a degree not readily appreciated now. Lawmakers and officials were critically concerned over territorial acquisitions. They recognized that the use made of this land would markedly influence the nature of the country. . . . The concept of public land as the basis for an agrarian democracy was rather widely held. After all, one of the major motives bringing people to the new country was to acquire land—to escape the landed estates and the systems of land inheritance in the old country which had made landownership so difficult for the masses. . . . There was a great popular hunger for land in those days, and an immense supply of the new public domain and of land belonging to the states, as well as of land acquired earlier in large private grants.[18]

The government's disposal policy was shaped by several factors, whose relative weights varied over time. These factors were: the desire to get land settled and into productivity as rapidly as possible, the need for revenue for the federal treasury,[19] the need for dispersed settlement of the West to provide a place for immigrants and to increase safety from the Indians, the commitment to reward soldiers with land, and the aim of promoting self-sufficiency in the newly formed states.

How best to get the land into private hands was not self-evident; there was no comparable experience in Europe on which to draw, and there were many conflicting opinions. Whether to sell land or give it away and whether to market it to large entrepreneurs acting as middlemen or directly to settlers were continuing issues. Among those favoring sale there was disagreement as to price, size of tracts, terms of sale, and places of sale. A wide range of methods was tried, but a fair generalization is that throughout the period of early settlement those who had most got most, while later the individual frontiersman had a better chance.

At the same time that the federal government was selling or giving the public domain to private owners, it also was granting land to the states, often for earmarked public purposes.

Over 1.1 billion acres, or 62 percent, of the public domain was disposed of by the federal government. Most—63 percent—was sold or given to individuals, while 29 percent was granted to the states and eight percent to railroad companies. By the close of the nineteenth century, almost no public domain remained in the eastern half of the country. (See table 1.2.)

*1780–1840.* Three features of the system for managing the public domain between 1780 and 1840 merit particular mention: creation of a uniform method of land surveying, grants of specified surveyed sections to the states as a source of school revenues, and periodic downward adjustment of the minimum acreage required for purchase.

The Act of 10 October 1780 was the first law to specify how land ceded to the United States by the states should be disposed of and how new states should be formed. It soon was followed by the Northwest ordinances of 1785 and 1787, which established the framework of United States land policy. The ordinances mandated a system of surveying the new lands, establishing square townships of thirty-six square miles, and subdividing each township into thirty-six sections of 640 acres each, all with boundaries running due north-south and east-west. Once surveyed, the land might be granted to the states, granted to private individuals, or sold.

Specified sections of land were given to the states, subject to use for designated objectives. Initially, section 16 in each township was given to the states provided that the revenue from the land be earmarked for financing state schools. Sections 8, 11, 26, and 29 in each township were reserved for later disposal. Under the Northwest Ordinance of 1787, the educational stipulation was expanded to provide for the granting of two townships per state to provide income for university purposes. The allocation of income from public land to support government functions had a European precedent. In Switzerland, villages commonly retained 10 to 20 percent of their land in public ownership. This land, which was that least suited to cultivation, often was rented for grazing or timber harvesting, with the income used to support the village school or church.[20]

Since the United States had promised free land to men who had fought in the Revolution—from 100 acres for a common soldier to 500 acres for a colonel—and to deserters from the British army, some tracts were drawn by lot from the public domain to meet these promises. Other land was allocated to satisfy private scrip claims. These claims had arisen where, as a result of poor surveying or duplicate grants, there were overlapping

TABLE 1.2. Disposition of the Public Domain

| Disposition | Acres (in millions) | Percentage |
|---|---|---|
| Grants to the states | | |
| For schools | 78 | |
| For other institutions; including | | |
| universities, hospitals, and asylums | 22 | |
| For swamp reclamation | 65 | |
| For canals and rivers | 6 | |
| For wagon roads | 3 | |
| For railroads | 37 | |
| Other | 117 | |
| Subtotal | 328 | 29 |
| Grants to individuals | | |
| Homesteads | 288 | |
| Military bounties | 61 | |
| Private land claims | 34 | |
| Subtotal | 383 | 33 |
| Grants to the railroads | | |
| Subtotal | 94 | 8 |
| Sales | | |
| Timber and desert land | 36 | |
| Miscellaneous, primarily preemption | 303 | |
| Subtotal | 339 | 30 |
| Total | 1,144 | 100 |

SOURCE: U.S., Dept. of the Interior, *Public Land Statistics, 1975* (Washington, D.C.: Government Printing Office, 1976), p. 6.

ownerships of the same tract or where a tract description was inadequate to locate the land.

The remaining public domain was available for sale. Sale was by auction for a minimum price of one dollar per acre plus surveying costs, payable within one year. All land was granted in fee, and all deeds were required to be recorded. Initially, the government tried to market land in township-sized tracts to private entrepreneurs who would further subdivide and sell it. However, most of the early land companies didn't prosper, and this idea foundered. In any event, many settlers were eager to buy parcels directly from the government for their own use. By 1796, about one-half of the land was being sold in quarter township parcels and the rest in 640-acre sections. By 1800, the minimum tract that could be offered for sale was reduced to 320 acres; the minimum price was $2 per acre, payable over five years. After 1820, the minimum area dropped to 80 acres and the minimum price to $1.25 per acre.

Until 1820, land could be bought on credit. Under this system, sales mounted steadily, from one-half million to three million acres yearly, but forfeitures and unpaid debts also mounted. The problems of dunning debtors and of foreclosure were overwhelming, given the scale of the operation, and so the credit system was abandoned. Cash sales between 1820 and 1841 yielded eleven percent of all federal revenues.

*1841–1900.* The years 1841–1900 saw a tremendous surge in immigration and settlement and in conversion of land from public domain to private ownership. First preemptive rights, then free grants to individuals and massive free grants to the railroads marked disposal policies to the private sector. The period also brought major expansion in the cession of lands to the states.

Two significant changes were incorporated into the law in 1841. Acquisition by preemption was authorized. A head of a household—a man of twenty-one or older or a widow—could settle on up to 160 acres of land not previously sold or granted, improve it, and later buy it at the minimum government price—then $1.25 per acre—without competition from other would-be purchasers. Those who favored granting preemptive rights urged that it was better to favor hard-working settlers over the speculators who otherwise would be likely to buy the land. Those who opposed the idea said that the government was giving up potential revenue to aid squatters. In fact, the law recognized realities. Squatting was rife; in Iowa alone there were between twenty thousand and thirty thousand squatters as of 1838. Auctions of land brought but a few cents per acre over the minimum price anyway.[21] The preemption law, modified from time to time, remained in effect until 1891, when it was repealed.

The other new provision declared that each new state was assured of the cession of 0.5 million acres to use as it saw fit. An alternative, the turning over of all the public domain land within the borders of a new state to the state when it came into being, had been debated but never achieved sufficient backing to be adopted. The states received more lands under laws passed between 1848 and 1850. The eight Western states admitted to the union between 1840 and 1890 received section 36 as well as section 16 in each township as a source of income for schools. Where parts of these sections already had been settled, the states often were allowed to choose other land in lieu of it. The Swamp Acts gave 64 million acres to several states with the intention that they could drain the land and earn revenue from its sale. More modest land grants were made to the states from time to time to provide income for many sorts of institutions, including colleges, hospitals, jails, and asylums. Some states were allowed to sell this land and segregate the income from the sale to create a fund for the benefit of the specified institution. More often, the states were prohibited from selling the land and were restricted to leasing it, indicating that Congress believed that retaining the fee in the hands of the state would prove to be more in the public interest over time.

Between 1850 and 1900, 91 million acres were given to railroad companies. In addition to this federal grant, another 49 million acres were given to the railroad companies by the states. The federal and state governments had several motives for these grants. Probably foremost was the desire to open up the country and make the West more accessible to settlers. Immigrants were flooding in: 20 percent of Europe's 1850 population emigrated between then and 1900. There were not enough jobs for these newcomers in the existing cities; particularly after the Civil War, unemployment in east coast cities was widespread. Therefore, rural and new town settlement in the West, served by a railroad network, was touted as the way to handle this influx. Another hope, which proved illusory, was that railroad construction would drive up land prices so that federal and state governments would profit from land sales.

The concept of the grants was similar to that of New York City's Dongan Charter. The railroads were given a right of way and a giant checkerboard of alternating sections extending somewhere between six and forty miles deep on either side of the right-of-way. Sales of this land were supposed to provide compensation for the costs of building the railroad. To assure construction, the railroad companies were barred from selling granted land until the railroad had been completed near those tracts that they wished to sell. The government had hoped to profit from rising land values in the alternate sections that it had retained along the railroad rights-of-way. However, it did not even recover the value of the land given to the railroads. Speculators had foreseen which routes would be awarded to the railroads and already had bought many of the choice sites. Between them, the speculators and the railroads held the best land and made the profits from subdividing it. Clawson observes:

The government doubled the sale price of its lands, if sold at public sale, on the grounds that its lands were more valuable because of the railroads, and that in this way the government lost no revenue while giving help to railroad construction. This was a crude form of capturing part of unearned increment, as a means of financing public investment. The railroads also agreed to carry government freight at half price—a provision which cost them, in the end, a great deal, especially during World War I—it was repealed before World War II. The whole idea of land grants to finance railroads had much to commend it, as well as some serious objections; in practice, there were extensive frauds, both in the financing and construction of the rail lines, and in the handling of the land grants. Where grant sections promised to be low in value, because arid or steep, the railroad would hire an individual to assert a homestead or other claim, so that it could get valuable in lieu lands.[22]

Much of the land granted to the railroads was offered by them for sale to unsuspecting European immigrants as sites in new towns. Land was huckstered in Europe as situated in towns that were to offer "a new way of life for Europe's downtrodden masses. We will seek to gather into localities communities of emigrants, taking some from every class and sending them out in a body to establish a town or village of their own."[23] Although most of these new towns were little more than stops along a rail line, they drained off investment that otherwise might have gone into the public lands.

The next landmark year for federal legislation affecting the public domain was 1862. As in 1841, both the states and individual settlers were beneficiaries. The states were given scrip convertible to public domain land valued at $1.25 per acre. Each state received allotments of scrip in units of thirty thousand acres, with one unit granted for each United States senator and representative. If the state had public domain land, it could offer the scrip for sale in exchange for specific tracts that had been withdrawn from the public domain. States having no public domain land within their borders could sell their scrip tied to tracts of public domain elsewhere. The income to the states from the sale of this scrip was restricted by the Morrill Act of 1862 to the use of state agricultural colleges, "where the leading object shall be . . . to teach such branches of learning as are related to agriculture and the mechanic arts" in order to promote "the liberal and practical education of the industrial classes." The offers by the states to sell their scrip met with only limited success. The scrip price averaged only $0.70–0.90 per acre until 1865, and approximately $0.50 per acre thereafter, or on an average about half the value placed by the government on the public domain land.

The Homestead Act of 1862 contributed to the weakening of the scrip market. For many years Congress had debated the desirability of giving away land to settlers. Prior to the Civil War, Southern plantation owners had fought against grants of free land, because they foresaw that it would foster small family farms and limit the spread of slavery, thus weakening their position. It was argued by some that free land was not constitutional and by some that it was unfair to the people, including speculators, who had bought land. Those favoring the legislation urged that land sales were slow and that it was important to get more land on the tax rolls. They pointed out that, despite a contrary intent, the public domain had not proven a money maker. The United States had spent $322 million to acquire land and had received only $201 million from sales. While much land remained, the choice areas were gone. Others favoring free grants revived the public trust theory and argued that the United States government, as trustee of the lands, had no right to sell them. The Free Soil Democrats, speaking in 1852, put it this way:

that all men have a natural right to a portion of the soil; and that as the use of the soil is indispensable to life, the right of all men to the soil is as sacred as their right to life itself. That the public lands of the United States belong to the people and should not be sold to individuals nor granted to corporations, but should be held as a sacred trust for the benefit of the people and should be granted in limited quantities, free of cost, to landless settlers.[24]

Finally, in 1862, a majority of Congress was persuaded and the Homestead Act was enacted, authorizing the granting of title to 160 acres free after five years' occupancy, provided that the land had been farmed and improvements made, including the construction of a house. People who had established land rights under the preemption law were allowed to commute their rights to those offered by the homestead law. Although 285 million acres were claimed by one and one-third million homesteaders, the availability of free land by no means ended speculation or cash sales.[25] This was in part because the tracts available under homesteading were small and the sites chosen by the government tended to be poorer grade land at some distance from the railroads.

Over the next several decades the law was amended to provide for larger homesteads west of the one hundredth meridian where the lands were arid, to shorten the period of homesteading required before ownership could vest, and to set different provisions for lands to be irrigated.

One remaining event in this period warrants mention. Starting in 1883, ranchers in fourteen states went out and fenced in pieces of the public domain. There was no claim of ownership or of right. Two companies in Colorado each fenced in one million acres.[26] These were barons in the tradition of the seventeenth-century feudal lords who used their power to enclose common land and keep the poor farmers out. It was a short-lived phenomenon of the West, with the fences down by 1890.

Not until the close of the century, with the establishment of forest reserves in 1891[27] and federal grazing permits in 1900, was there the beginning of a recognition that the public interest might be served by holding and conserving portions of the public domain. Paul Wallace Gates describes this time of transition:

Here was the first fundamental break with the underlying philosophy of our land system—the desire to dispose of the lands and hasten their settlement. The conservationists had now convinced the country that a part of our natural resources must be retained in public ownership and preserved for the future. Unfortunately conservation, when first adopted, was embedded in an outworn laissez-faire land system of a previous age, just as the free homestead plan had been superimposed upon a land system designed to produce revenue. In both cases the old and the new clashed with disastrous results.[28]

### The Pendulum Reverses

The colonial period was marked by public control of town settlement, by a tenancy form of land holding, and, in the North, by an unprecedented diffusion of ownership rights. The ownership patterns reflected both the English law as it had then evolved and the settlers' demand for greater autonomy.

The period from the Revolution to the close of the nineteenth century was marked by the abolition of tenancy in land and by the expansion of private control of land use. A commitment to individual and corporate freedom and initiative in the use of land was a cornerstone of public policy. This policy dictated that public domain land should be transferred to private hands as rapidly as possible.

The twentieth century has been notable for a reversal of the direction of public policy. An increasing recognition of the finiteness of our land resources and of the interconnections between land uses has led to increasing support for public land ownership or public control of land use. One can pair as opposites the land management themes of the late nineteenth and late twentieth centuries: expansion versus growth control, dispersion versus concentration, and exploitation versus conservation. With a growing understanding that, while vast, the land, water, and mineral resources of the country are not limitless, that some of these resources have been squandered, and that others soon will be exhausted, a conservation ethic has taken root and is spreading. Aldo Leopold wrote in 1949: "We abuse land because we regard it as a commodity belonging to us. When we see land as a community to which we belong, we may begin to use it with love and respect."[29] At that time his words, had they been widely read, would have struck most people as idealistic and ill-matched with the American way of life. Today, several decades later, many find that they state a principle fundamental to our survival.

## The Public Trust

In recent years a long-dormant concept of land ownership has gained new currency. Whether one uses the term public trust, sovereignty, or quasisovereignty, the meaning understood is much the same: government has a right and an obligation, rooted in its underlying title to land, to protect natural resources.

The best-known decision of the United States Supreme Court articulating this theory dates back to 1907. The state of Georgia sought to enjoin a copper company that operated in Tennessee from transmitting air pollutants across the border to Georgia, where they were damaging forests, orchards, and crops. The defendants argued that Georgia had no standing to bring the suit because it did not own the affected lands. In *Georgia* v. *Tennessee Copper Co.*,[30] the court held for Georgia, with Justice Holmes writing the opinion:

This is a suit by a State for an injury to it in its capacity of quasi-sovereign. In that capacity the State has an interest independent of and behind the titles of its citizens, in all the earth and air within its domain. It has the last word as to whether its mountains shall be stripped of their forests and its inhabitants shall breathe pure air. It might have to pay individuals before it could utter that word, but with it remains the final power.[31]

The following year the court, again in the words of Justice Holmes, reiterated this position:

It is recognized that the State as quasi-sovereign and representative of the interests of the public has a standing in court to protect the atmosphere, the water, and the forests within its territory, irrespective of the assent or dissent of the private owners of land most immediately concerned.[32]

This language is inconsistent with the nineteenth-century view of private ownership as absolute; it is, however, a revival of a concept in common currency until the spread of the beliefs of John Locke. This restatement of the traditional Western view that the state has fundamental ownership rights distinct from and underlying those of individual landowners has been cited frequently in cases concerned with jurisdiction over water. It did not receive further attention from or construction by the United States Supreme Court with reference to land until 1945. Then, in *Georgia* v. *Pennsylvania Railroad Co.*,[33] Justice Douglas cited it in support of a finding of a state quasisovereign interest in the fixing of rates by railroads crossing the lands of Georgia. Subsequent to this case, there have been a number of decisions affirming state actions undertaken to discharge quasi-sovereign responsibilities.[34] Several of these cases have held that the state's concern is broader than that of any individual property owner.

The most far-reaching of the recent opinions is a 1972 decision of the Wisconsin Supreme Court. The court upheld a state law requiring the regulation of use of all land within 1,000 feet of lakes and 300 feet of rivers, basing its affirmation of the law on the public trust obligation of the state:

The state of Wisconsin under the trust doctrine has a duty to eradicate the present pollution and to prevent further pollution in its navigable waters. . . . Lands adjacent to or near navigable waters . . . are subject to the state public trust powers. . . . The shoreland zoning ordinance preserves nature, the environment, and natural resources as they were created and to which people have a present right.[35]

A recent amendment to the Pennsylvania Constitution also articulates a state public trust role, "Pennsylvania's public natural resources are the common property of all the people, including generations yet to come. As trustee of these resources, the Commonwealth shall conserve and maintain them for the benefit of all the people."[36] This language and a footnote to the Wisconsin judges' opinion echo the Indian and Eskimo belief in ownership shared by members of one's society, only a few of whom are alive currently.

This belief also is common among African tribes, including those of central Africa, Ghana, and Kenya.[37] The Ashanti of Ghana say: "Land belongs to a vast family of whom many are dead, a few are living and a countless host are still unborn."[38] The Bantu of Kenya share this concept:

the individual had inheritable rights as a user of his arable lands. . . . This does not imply individual ownership of fields, nor individual rights to misuses of land. Ownership, insofar as there was such a concept, was usually vested in the ancestor spirits . . . who symbolized his community past, present and future. . . . Sale was normally unthinkable, if not forbidden.[39]

Contrary to the Indian, Eskimo, the African assumption of a common trusteeship for management of resources, both Wisconsin and Pennsylvania attribute the role of trustee to the state. Exercise of a trusteeship role to protect resources interferes with the free action of the market. *Georgia v. Tennessee Copper Co.* recognized that the state might have to pay compensation for this interference. The nature and extent of the obligation of government to compensate landowners for its actions have received extensive and inconsistent interpretation, but principally under a different rubric than that of public trust.

### The Unresolved Issue of Equity

The "taking" clause of the United States Constitution—"nor shall private property be taken for public use, without just compensation"[40]—is the primary recourse of those challenging government action affecting private use of land. There are two lines of attack under this clause: (1) the government action is an unconstitutional taking because there is to be no public use of the land, and (2) the government action is within the proper sphere of government activities but is invalid because uncompensated. The challenge to government authorization to take property goes to the scope of public power; this is an area in which past decisions offer a basis for predicting future outcomes. The demand for compensation reaches the question just raised in the discussion of sovereignty: when does equity dictate that government pay for losses caused by its restrictive actions? The answer here is far from certain, with much depending on a given court's weighting of the relative significance of protection of private interests and achievement of public benefits. One can say, in general, that government regulations may cause substantial declines in land values without giving rise to the requirement of compensation.

*Taking.* A taking occurs when the impact of government action is "so complete as to deprive the owner of all or most of his interest in the subject matter."[41] Acquisition of title or occupancy of the property is not necessary for there to be a taking. For instance, frequent flights at low altitude constitute a taking of an easement over the land beneath.[42]

Government may take property only for a public use. What legislatures and courts deem a public use is subject to change; the definition has been broadening steadily in the areas of protection of resources and management of development. Two important decisions that illustrate judicial support for innovative legislative definitions in those areas are *Berman* v. *Parker*[43] and *Kamrowski* v. *State of Wisconsin.*[44] *Berman* v. *Parker* upheld the constitutionality of the District of Columbia Redevelopment Act of 1945. The law authorized the designation of an area as blighted (even though some structures within the area were sound), the condemnation of all property within the designated area, and the resale of the property to private developers for redevelopment. Justice Douglas, writing for a unanimous supreme court, sustained the legislative finding that there was a valid public use:

We do not sit to determine whether a particular housing project is or is not desirable. The concept of the public welfare is broad and inclusive. See *Day-Brite Lighting, Inc. v. Missouri*, 342 U.S. 421, 424. The values it represents are spiritual as well as physical, aesthetic as well as monetary. It is within the power of the legislature to determine that the community should be beautiful as well as healthy, spacious as well as clean, well-balanced as well as carefully patrolled. In the present case, the Congress and its authorized agencies have made determinations that take into account a wide variety of values. It is not for us to reappraise them. If those who govern the District of Columbia decide that the Nation's Capital should be beautiful as well as sanitary, there is nothing in the Fifth Amendment that stands in the way.[45]

The *Kamrowski* case sustained legislation[46] authorizing condemnation of scenic easements by the state of Wisconsin. The purpose of the easements was to protect the view of the Mississippi River from Great River Road, the adjacent highway. The court agreed with the legislative finding that the view constituted a public use and that physical access to the site was not necessary:

The enjoyment of the scenic beauty by the public which passes along the highway seems to us to be a direct use by the public of the rights in land which have been taken in the form of a scenic easement, and not a mere incidental benefit from the owner's private use of the land.[47]

*Compensation and Equity.* Continuing enlargement of the definition of public use is readily discernible; interpretation of the compensation requirement of the Constitution, on the other hand, has followed an uneven course. The issue can be stated simply: to what extent may government regulation, undertaken for a public purpose,[48] deprive an owner of property value? The leading case, judging by frequency of citation, is still *Pennsylvania Coal Co.* v. *Mahon,* in which Chief Justice Holmes said:

The general rule at least is that while property may be regulated to a certain extent, if regulation goes too far, it will be recognized as a taking. . . . We are in danger of forgetting that a strong public desire to improve the public condition is not enough to warrant achieving the desire by a shorter cut than the constitutional way of paying for the change.[49]

In other words, if the reduction in value is too great, the regulation is invalid. To achieve the desired control, government is left with the option of acquiring the property and paying just compensation.

The language of Holmes states a principle founded on a commitment to equity but provides no guidance for interpretation of the principle. Over the years a number of tests[50] have been used to relate the principle to the facts of a case; none of these has gained a clear ascendancy, nor have they been applied with consistency. Therefore, one cannot predict with assurance whether compensation must be paid for a given government action affecting land use.

The most widely used test is an economic one, that of loss in market value due to government regulation. For courts using this test there is general agreement if the regulation has one of two extreme effects. If the regulation acts only to deprive a landowner of the most economically beneficial use of the land, no compensation is payable.[51] On the other hand, if the regulation renders the land economically worthless, it is invalid.[52] Between these poles different courts apply different standards and apply the standards differently from one set of facts to another. One standard often used is that the amount of the loss that regulation can impose without being held invalid may be substantial—for instance, a drop in value from $800 thousand to $60 thousand.[53] Another commonly used standard is that the owner must be able to obtain a reasonable return from the land as regulated; under this standard a zoning ordinance was sustained that prohibited the sale of farmland in parcels smaller than eighteen acres.[54]

A radical departure from the loss in market value test is a test that judges reasonable return from land with reference to the land's natural capabilities rather than its economic potential.[55]

All of the tests address the question of what is fair to the landowner whose property value is affected negatively by public action. Comparatively little attention has been given to the related question of fairness when a landowner's property escalates in value as a result of public actions. There has been little legislative action aimed at recovering any portion of publicly induced gain. The current system is not evenhanded, since it holds the public sector accountable—to varying extents—for losses in value of private land but does not credit it for gains. The landowner receives protection through the taking clause but, in return for this, foregoes no share of a possible bonanza due to public action.

A highly significant recent decision by New York's highest court, since affirmed by the United States Supreme Court, may well alter the measure of just compensation. The court of appeals, which sustained a regulation designating Grand Central Terminal as a landmark, said:

society as an organized entity, especially through its government, rather than as a mere conglomerate of individuals, has created much of the value of the terminal property. . . . It is the privately created and privately managed ingredient which is the property on which the reasonable return is to be based. All else is society's contribution by the sweat of its brow and the expenditure of its funds. To that extent society is also entitled to its due.[56]

Therefore, the court concluded, the owner, the Penn Central Transportation Company, could be entitled to compensation only with relation to property value created by private efforts.

We may be moving from a system that rewards speculation and protects landowners from losses based on public actions toward a system that defines public purpose more broadly and judges it equitable for society to retain the values resulting from its investment. If so, it is reasonable to predict that Americans will see land banking as an appropriate and prudent activity of government. This has been an attitude common to many countries of Western Europe throughout this century.

NOTES

1. Ford, *Writings of Thomas Jefferson*, 7: 33–36.
2. See Schlatter, *Private Property*, and Coulanges, *Origin of Property in Land*, for discussions of theories of property ownership.
3. Aristotle, *The Politics of Aristotle* (Oxford: Clarendon Press, 1946), bk. 7.
4. Jefferson, *Living Thoughts*, pp. 61, 62.
5. Northrop, *Legal and Ethical Experience*, pp. 37, 170.
6. Ford, *Writings of Thomas Jefferson*, 7: 33–36.
7. Harris, *Land Tenure System*, p. 63.
8. *Johnson* v. *McIntosh*, 8 Wheat 543, 5 L.Ed. 681 (1823).
9. A belief shared by the Eskimos:

for the Eskimos land is not treated as being property of any kind, so that any man may hunt wherever he pleases, for the idea of restricting the pursuit of food is repugnant to all Eskimos. Moreover, although game and most articles of personal use are objects of property notions, the Eskimos are strongly hostile to the idea of anybody accumulating too much property for himself and thereby limiting the amount of property that can be effectively used in the community. In one part of Alaska, prolonged possession of more goods than a man could himself use was regarded as a capital crime, and the goods were subject to communal confiscation. (Lloyd, *Idea of Law*, p. 237)

10. Warner, *Urban Wilderness.*
11. Ibid., p. 10.
12. Conversation with John Reps, October 1975.
13. Only in Pennsylvania and South Carolina could the charterers subinfeudate and create their own tenancies.
14. New York, for instance, acted at its 1846 Constitutional Convention.
15. *Commonwealth* v. *Alger*, 7 Cush. 53, Sup. Ct. Mass. (1853).
16. Hibbard, *Public Land Policies.*
17. Quoted in Delafons, *Land-Use Controls*, p. 17.
18. Clawson and Held, *Federal Lands*, p. 22.
19. Hibbard, *Public Land Policies*, p. 1, comments: "Under the Confederation the States could not, and would not raise the apportioned shares of government revenue. Thus to the leaders, charged with the stern duty of raising the money with which to pay necessary national expenses, were the nation to continue to exist, it was little wonder that the land belonging to the nation would be viewed as the most promising asset."
20. Coulanges, *Origin of Property in Land.*
21. Hibbard, *Public Land Policies.*
22. Clawson, *Land Use Planning*, p. 40.
23. As quoted in Eichler, *Community Builders*, p. 13.
24. As quoted in Hibbard, *Public Land Policies*, p. 357.
25. Ibid.
26. Ibid.
27. *Light* v. *United States*, 220 U.S. 523, 537, 31 S.Ct. 485, 55 L.Ed. 570 (1911), upheld the right of Congress to create a forest reserve. The court said:

All the public lands of the nation are held in trust for the people of the whole country [*United States* v. *Trinidad Coal Co.*, 137 U.S. 160]. And it is not for the courts to say how that trust shall be administered. That is for Congress to determine. The courts cannot compel it to set aside the lands for settlement; or to suffer them to be used for agricultural or grazing purposes, nor interfere when, in the exercise of its discretion, Congress establishes a forest reserve for what it decides to be national and public purposes.

28. Gates, "Homestead Law," p. 601.
29. Leopold, *Sand County Almanac*, p. x.
30. 206 U.S. 230 (1907). See also *Missouri* v. *Illinois and the Sanitary District of Chicago*, 180 U.S. 208 (1900), for recognition of the quasisovereign role of states. The term 'quasisovereignty' is used with reference to the states to distinguish their position from that of the sovereign, the United States.
31. 206 U.S. 230, at 237.
32. *Hudson County Water Co.* v. *McCarter*, 209 U.S. 349 (1908).
33. 324 U.S. 447 (1945).
34. *United States* v. *McElween*, 189 F.S. 14 (1960); *United States* v. *Rains*, 189 F.S. 134 (1960); *State of South Dakota* v. *The National Bank of South Dakota*, 219 F.S. 847 (1963); *Hackensack Meadowlands Commission* v. *Municipal Authority*, 8 ERC 1433 (1975).
35. *Just* v. *Marinette County*, 56 Wis.2d 7, 201 N.W.2d 761 (1972).

36. Art. 1, sect. 27. As interpreted in *Commonwealth* v. *National Gettysburg Battlefield Tower*, 6 ERC 1949 (1973), public natural resources include land in private ownership.

37. Arnold, "Common Heritage of Mankind," p. 156.

38. Annot., "Interests in Land," p. 852.

39. Munro, "Land Law in Kenya," p. 1075.

40. This clause from the Fifth Amendment is applicable to the states under the due process clause of the Fourteenth Amendment (*Chicago, Burlington, and Quincy Railroad Co.* v. *Chicago*, 166 U.S. 225 [1897]).

41. *United States* v. *General Motors*, 323 U.S. 373 (1945), at 377–78.

42. *Griggs* v. *Allegheny County*, 369 U.S. 84 (1962).

43. 348 U.S. 26 (1954).

44. 31 Wis.2d 256, 142 N.W.2d 793 (1966).

45. 348 U.S. 26, 33.

46. W.S.A. 15.60.

47. 142 N.W.2d 793, 797.

48. More and more land management objectives have been held to be within the regulatory scope of government. Among these objectives are preservation of flood plains and wetlands (*Turnpike Realty Co.* v. *Town of Dedham*, 284 N.E.2d 891, Sup. Ct. Mass. [1972]), esthetic enhancement (for instance, exclusion of junkyards, *Oregon City* v. *Hartke*, 400 P.2d 255, Sup. Ct. Ore. [1955]), protection of historic sites (one historic district ordinance regulated such details as the style, size, and number of panes of glass in windows, *City of Santa Fe* v. *Gamble-Skogmo, Inc.*, 73 N.M. 410, 389 P.2d 13 [1964]), and timing of development (*Golden* v. *Planning Board of the Town of Ramapo*, 30 N.Y.2d 359, 285 N.E.2d 291 [1973]).

49. 260 U.S. 393 (1922).

50. Loss in market value, residual market value, creating a public benefit versus avoiding a public harm, environmental value, and publicly versus privately created value.

51. *Goldblatt* v. *Town of Hempstead, New York*, 369 U.S. 590 (1962).

52. *Baltimore City* v. *Borinsky*, 239 Md. 611, 212 A.2d 508 (1965).

53. *Hadacheck* v. *Sebastian*, 239 U.S. 394 (1915).

54. *Gisler* v. *Madera County*, 38 Cal. App. 3d 305 (1974).

55. *Just* v. *Marinette County*, 56 Wis.2d 7, 201 N.W.2d 761 (1972).

56. *Penn Central Transportation Co.* v. *City of New York*, 42 N.Y.2d 324 (1977); 438 U.S. 104, 98 S.Ct. 2646, 57 L.Ed.2d 631 (1978).

## REFERENCES

Annot., "Interests in Land in the Customary Law of Ghana," 74 *Yale L.J.* 848, 852, no. 20 (1965).

Arnold, Rudolph Preston. "The Common Heritage of Mankind As a Legal Concept." *International Lawyer* 9, no. 1 (January 1975): 153–58.

Carstensen, Vernon, ed. *The Public Lands.* Madison: University of Wisconsin Press, 1963.

Clawson, Marion. *An Historical Overview of Land Use Planning in the United States.* Washington, D.C.: Resources for the Future, 1972 (?).

Clawson, Marion, and Held, R. Burnell. *The Federal Lands: Their Use and Management.* Baltimore: The Johns Hopkins University Press, 1957.

Coulanges, Numa Denis Fustel de. *The Origin of Property in Land.* New York: C. Scribner's Sons, 1904.

Delafons, John. *Land-Use Controls in the United States.* 2nd ed. Cambridge, Mass.: The M.I.T. Press, 1969.

Eichler, Edward. *The Community Builders.* Berkeley and Los Angeles: University of California Press, 1967.

Ford, Paul L., ed. *The Writings of Thomas Jefferson.* 7 vols. New York: G. P. Putnam's Sons, 1904–5.

Gates, Paul Wallace. "The Homestead Law in an Incongruous Land System." *American Historical Review* 41 (July 1936).

Harris, Marshall. *Origin of the Land Tenure System in the United States.* Ames: Iowa State College Press, 1953.

Hibbard, Benjamin H. *A History of the Public Land Policies.* Madison: University of Wisconsin Press, 1965.

Hurst, James Willard. *Law and the Conditions of Freedom in the Nineteenth Century United States.* Madison: University of Wisconsin Press, 1967.

Jefferson, Thomas. *The Living Thoughts of Thomas Jefferson.* Presented by John Dewey. New York: Longmans, Green and Co., 1940.

Leopold, Aldo. *A Sand County Almanac.* New York: Oxford University Press, 1966.

Letwin, William L. *Municipal Land Banks: Land-Reserve Policy for Urban Development.* Lexington, Mass.: Urban Land Research Analysts Corp., 1969.

Lloyd, Dennis. *The Idea of Law.* London: Penguin, 1964.

Munro, A. "Land Law in Kenya." 1966 Wis. L. Rev. 1071, 1075.

Northrop, F.S.C. *The Complexity of Legal and Ethical Experience.* Boston: Little, Brown, 1959.

Schlatter, Richard. *Private Property.* New Brunswick, N.J.: Rutgers University Press, 1961.

U.S. Department of the Interior. *Public Land Statistics,* 1975. Washington, D.C.: Government Printing Office, 1976.

Warner, Sam Bass. *The Urban Wilderness.* New York: Harper and Row, 1972.

# 2
# Land Banks in
# the Stockholm Region

## Swedish Objectives
## and Stockholm's Achievements

The publicly owned land in Stockholm County undoubtedly constitutes the largest land bank of any metropolitan area in Western Europe.
Twenty-seven percent of the county's 1,606,000 acres is in public ownership (see map 2.1). The national government, Stockholm County, the city
of Stockholm, and most of the twenty-two other municipalities in the
county each own some of this land. The city of Stockholm alone has acquired 138,000 acres since 1904, at a price of approximately $110 million.
Its holdings outside of the city are twice as large as the area of the city itself.
Most development in the region occurs on land held by the public for
several decades and bought at or near farm value.

Land banking is only one way of implementing Sweden's urban development objectives. While it has been the principal tool for medium and
large Swedish cities, its use cannot be separated from the context of land
use law and practice. Rapid urban growth and altered life styles have led
to recent, sweeping changes in Swedish land use law that have begun to
affect land bank practices. It is a bit soon to predict what will happen, but it
seems likely that the panoply of tax, acquisition, and regulatory laws
enacted in the late 1960s will hold land prices down and so make it
unnecessary for municipalities to buy land years ahead of development, as
many have in the past.

43

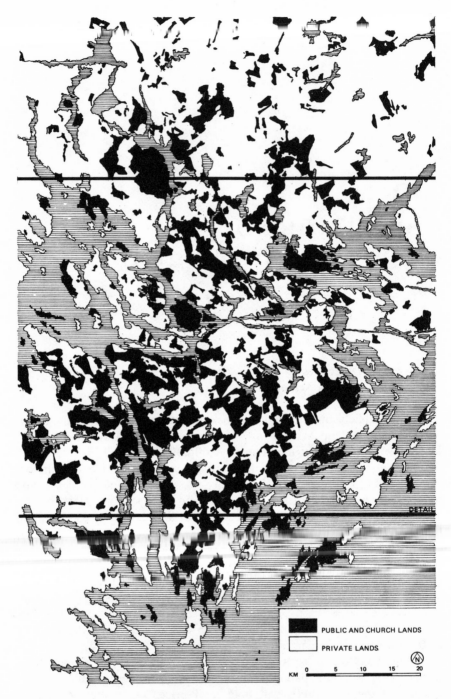

**MAP 2.1.** Public and church lands in Stockholm County

SOURCE: Adapted from Stockholm County Office, *Markägoförhållanden* [Land ownership situation] (map) (Stockholm, 1970)

Approximately 70 percent of the land in Swedish urban areas is in public ownership, and about 70 percent of residential development occurs on land either sold or leased by the municipalities. Thus, the municipalities are the dominant force in the urban land market. There is considerable variation among them as to when they began land banking, how long in advance of development they buy land, and whether land bank sites are sold or leased for development. Therefore, one cannot say that the Stockholm region—or, for that matter, any other urban area—is typical of Swedish land bank practices. However, there are a number of reasons for choosing the Stockholm region (today synonymous with Stockholm County) for detailed study.

Stockholm was one of the first Swedish municipalities to begin buying land for a land bank, and it continued to be one of the most active until 1967. Because Stockholm has been and continues to be a fast-growing urban area, it has faced problems of local government organization— central city annexations, city-suburban rivalry, and empowerment of regional organizations—that are so prevalent in the large metropolitan areas of the United States. The underlying urban problems of rapid growth, including the assimilation of rural in-migrants and foreign workers and the decline of the central city, also have parallels in the United States. The responses of the Stockholm region to these problems have differed from ours. Ascertaining whether these responses, particularly the creation of land banks, have been successful is difficult enough. Inquiring whether they have been more successful than actions in the United States implies the existence of a common goal. This I doubt. Many may disagree with me, suggesting that I overidealize Sweden's commitment and/or am too harsh in my judgment of American values. However, since it will color the evaluation to follow, it is essential to state my point of view.

Sweden's goal has remained constant since the initiation of land banking: the creation of a high-quality urban environment for all people. It is a goal that the United States Congress has enunciated more than once but about which there is considerable ambivalence and hypocrisy in this country. I would say that the Stockholm region has been more successful than any urban region in the United States in meeting this goal. Except for a few recent aberrations, the quality of the urban environment ranges from fair to good and truly is accessible to all. We, on the other hand, provide a superb environment for a few, a fair environment for many, and a devastating one for many more.

My personal scorecard for the Stockholm region, and particularly for the city of Stockholm, has many more pluses than minuses. Yet, because most of the minuses are of recent origin, I am concerned for the future.

On the plus side, its enormous land holdings have been the principal factor enabling Stockholm to develop in an efficient, orderly manner, assuring that public services will be available when each new area is opened to residents. Plans have indeed been implemented, and the new developments have provided high minimum standards of housing space and quality and ready access to open space, public transportation, and commercial and community facilities. Various national subsidy programs as well as municipal policies have assured that people of all incomes can live in the newly developed areas. Cooperative agreements between Stockholm and neighboring municipalities in which it owns land have enabled the city, with its greater financial resources, to build there as well. Stockholm's objective throughout the century has indeed been to create a good urban environment for all who come to the region. There is no doubt that ownership of so much land has been a powerful tool, affording choice and control.

It is commonly assumed in Stockholm that early acquisition also reduced the price of development. Whether this is, in fact, true has been impossible to determine, because the city administrators either have not kept records in such a manner that this can be calculated or are unwilling to have the calculation be made. Among the questions that one would like to be able to answer are:

1. How have the purchases of Stockholm and, later, of other municipalities affected prices in the Stockholm area land market?
2. How have Sweden's increasingly stringent land use controls affected the Stockholm area land market?
3. Have the enormous public investments in land paid off in lower development costs and capital appreciation?
4. Can Stockholm obtain an adequate return from development of its extraterritorial holdings?

There are many political factors that underlie an investigation of fiscal wisdom. Some of them will be described subsequently.

On the negative side, the city's most recent developments, including the regional center at Skärholmen and the satellites Tensta and Rinkeby, have drawn heavy fire. Commerce at Skärholmen has not flourished as predicted. At Tensta and Rinkeby the cold, massive monotony of the apartment buildings and the lack of neighborhood facilities have made it difficult to attract residents who have alternate choices. Had the city not had such absolute control of the development process, starting with ownership of land, the planners and other officials might have solicited and responded to public opinion. Their early sensitivity to human needs seems to have been lost in recent years in an absorption with quantification of individual components and with technological possibilities.

Another emerging problem is the difference in objectives between the city and the outlying municipalities. As the suburbs have become larger and more powerful, this divergence has become more open and explicit. The failure of the new county government to assume the city's prior land banking role, other than for public facilities, reflects the desire of the suburban municipalities to retain control over who moves in. Most of these municipalities now are active in land banking but also are competing with one another for the "best" development—usually that most lucrative to the municipality. Stockholm's long-time devotion to creating what its officials think to be the best living environment for all who come to the region is being supplanted in some municipalities of the region by a more parochial attitude that could foster social and economic segregation of a type very familiar to Americans.

Despite these reservations about what is current in the Stockholm region, there is no doubt that over the years the Swedes have enacted land use legislation and embarked on land investment programs that are consistent with placing the common good above protection of opportunities for personal gain. Our real priorities have been very different. Only if they change can we expect to benefit from Sweden's experiences.

Even given my strong personal reservations about the likelihood that we in the United States are ready to winnow out the best in the Swedish system and graft it onto our land use controls, I hope that an acquaintance with what has evolved in Sweden will prove useful in the not too distant future.

Before concentrating on the current situation in the Stockholm region, set in the context of national laws and programs, some historical perspective is essential. Stockholm's experience can be divided into three periods: (1) the turn of the century through 1939, the first great era of land banking for the city; (2) 1940 through 1967, when the focus remained on the city's activities, which rose to an all time peak in 1967; and (3) 1968–1973, a time of greatly altered laws and distribution of political power.

### The Early Years[1]

Too many people and too rapid growth have never been problems for Sweden. In fact, it was the vast emigration at the end of the nineteenth century that led to the land bank programs of the early twentieth century. By holding down land costs and making cheaper housing available to working people, Swedish cities sought to compete with the lure of the United States. It was an early version of urban homesteading, called the "Own-Home Movement," developed to stem the flow to American farm homesteads.

Between 1850 and 1900, one million Swedes emigrated. This was about one third of the total population. Net emigration peaked in the 1880s, when an average of thirty-eight thousand people left each year, while only five thousand immigrated.

Stockholm at this time was a city with a population of some one hundred thousand. The richer people lived in Norrmalm, the northern portion of the city, while the working class tended to live in Södermalm, the southern section. This historic economic segregation is of significance because it is a pattern that has been perpetuated. The first area bought by the city and leased for housing development for low- and middle-income people was the Enskede estate just to the south of the existing city. Even today, although the economic and social distinctions have blurred, the northern part of Stockholm and its suburbs is considered somewhat more desirable than those areas to the south.

The Stockholm City Council almost unanimously supported the initiation, in 1904, of a city land bank. Concern about emigration and a desire to make homeowning possible were the immediate reasons for action. For Sweden, with a long tradition of public landownership, starting a land bank was an unusual but not revolutionary undertaking.[2] From the Middle Ages until the nineteenth century, land was owned by the crown. As King Gustavus Vasa said in 1542, "Lands which are not under cultivation belong to God, Us, and the Swedish Crown, and to nobody else."[3] In some instances, town sites were given by the crown to the citizens of the town collectively, but not until 1810 were Swedish men given the right as individuals to acquire and possess land. Over the next several decades land exploitation became rampant. More and more people became convinced that, in urbanizing areas where speculation was rife, the cities must intervene to buy land and make it available for development at a reasonable price.

In Stockholm, the impetus came from Knut A. Wallenberg, a member of an aristocratic family who was one of the city's leading bankers and a member of the city council. Many of the other proponents also were wealthy and conservative businessmen. Yngve Larsson, long-time Liberal leader in the city council and staunch advocate of land banking, gave much credit to the city engineer for launching the program with the initial purchase at Enskede. He was "really the man who visualized purchase of the Enskede estate as the site for a new garden city with port facilities. He wanted this to be for low and middle class families."[4] (See fig. 2.1.)

From this start in 1904, Stockholm moved ahead steadily and ambitiously. As large estates in the outskirts came on the market, the city purchased them and added the land to its growing reserve. By 1939 and the advent of World War II, Stockholm had bought 33,074 acres, at a cost of 41,005,000 kronor. Much of the purchased land had been annexed to the city. Some of it had been developed, while the remainder was leased

FIGURE 2.1. 1930s apartment development, Enskede, Sweden (photo by Michael L. Strong)

for farming. From 1908 on, all public land developed for housing was leased to the developer. After 1938, all sites were leased. While the city hoped, eventually, to benefit from increases in the value of leased land, in the interim the rent systems favored the lessees. Since rents were not increased for terms of from twenty-six to sixty years, the city did not realize added income as site values rose. Rents also were not adjusted for changes in the value of the kronor.

### Acquisition

Even given widespread political support for the concept of municipal land purchase, the Stockholm City Council's initial venture was extraordinarily bold. In 1904 alone the city bought 4,940 acres. This figure is more remarkable when compared with the 4,199 acres that were then the total built-up area of Stockholm. The newly acquired land was in five parcels at Enskede and Bromma, both outside the city limits. The city paid $270 per acre for the Enskede land and $98 per acre at Bromma.[5]

The 1,590-acre site of Farsta, now one of the better known of Stockholm's satellite centers, was acquired in 1912, but not developed until the 1950s. Land for Vällingby, the first and probably best known of Stockholm's satellite centers, was bought in the late 1920s and early 1930s.

From 1904 until World War II, the pattern of land acquisition was much the same. As large estates in the Stockholm region came on the market, the city sought to buy them if they appeared to have potential for future development. Usually there were between one and five purchases annually, although in some years no land was bought. A few small parcels were acquired but the average size was over six hundred acres.

Acquisitions tapered off during the 1920s, when the Conservatives became somewhat stronger in the city council. They were concerned that the city was making too great a financial commitment to raising living standards in outlying areas. Also, it was evident that it would be many years before many of the tracts being purchased would be needed for development. Since, until 1946, a two-thirds vote of the city council was necessary to approve either the purchase or sale of land, not as many prospective purchases received city council approval as during earlier and later periods.[6]

In 1908, administration of the land bank program was placed in the hands of the newly created Agricultural Holding Committee of City Council. Previously, land transactions had been the responsibility of the city council Finance Commission, but it was decided that different skills were needed for the acquisition, planning, and development of outlying lands. In 1919, another reorganization grouped the city's land and housing policies together in a newly formed Real Estate Commission.

Each of these administrative arms of the city council continued the policy of acquiring land as it became available. By 1939, the city had acquired 43,810 acres, including a few parcels bought prior to 1904, when the land bank program was instituted. Acquisitions from 1904 to 1939 totaled 33,074 acres.

The price paid per hectare rose from 2,318 kronor in 1904–1909 to 3,136 kronor in 1910–1919, 3,407 kronor in 1920–1929, and 3,129 kronor in 1930–1939. During this entire period Stockholm financed the acquisitions without national government financial aid. In the early years, there was a revolving fund in the city budget, clearly distinguishable from other budget items. (See table 2.1.)

One new law affected the rate of turnover of land, influencing Stockholm's opportunities to buy as well as the land market in general. In 1928, a sliding-scale capital gains tax was adopted, under which 100 percent of the gain was taxable if land was sold within seven years of its purchase, 75 percent of the gain in the eighth year of holding, 50 percent in the ninth year, and 25 percent in the tenth year. None of the capital gain was taxable on sales made after holding the land for over ten years.[7]

TABLE 2.1. Stockholm City Land Acquisition, 1904–1939

| Year | Number of Purchases | Area | | Cost (in Thousands) | |
|------|---------------------|----------|-------|-------------------|---------|
| | | Hectares | Acres | Swedish Kronor | Dollars |
| 1904 | 5 | 1,962 | 4,846 | 3,599 | 955 |
| 1905 | 4 | 829 | 2,048 | 2,925 | 776 |
| 1906 | | | | | |
| 1907 | 1 | 297 | 734 | 275 | 73 |
| 1908 | 4 | 291 | 719 | 1,796 | 476 |
| 1909 | 1 | 393 | 971 | 150 | 40 |
| 1910 | | | | | |
| 1911 | | | | | |
| 1912 | 1 | 645 | 1,593 | 1,000 | 263 |
| 1913 | 2 | 196 | 484 | 263 | 69 |
| 1914 | 2 | 919 | 2,270 | 460 | 121 |
| 1915 | | | | | |
| 1916 | 1 | 5 | 12 | 40 | 11 |
| 1917 | 1 | 360 | 889 | 3,600 | 1,150 |
| 1918 | 1 | 111 | 274 | 55 | 18 |
| 1919 | 2 | 105 | 259 | 1,924 | 486 |
| 1920 | | | | | |
| 1921 | | | | | |
| 1922 | 3 | 942 | 2,327 | 3,396 | 887 |
| 1923 | | | | | |
| 1924 | | | | | |
| 1925 | | | | | |
| 1926 | 1 | 12 | 30 | 5 | 1 |
| 1927 | 1 | 508 | 1,255 | 1,580 | 424 |
| 1928 | | | | | |
| 1929 | | | | | |
| 1930 | 3 | 632 | 1,561 | 1,015 | 272 |
| 1931 | 4 | 2,023 | 4,997 | 4,180 | 1,040 |
| 1932 | 1 | 2 | 5 | 100 | 18 |
| 1933 | | | | | |
| 1934 | | | | | |
| 1935 | 2 | 450 | 1,112 | 2,045 | 515 |
| 1936 | 1 | 1,416 | 3,498 | 350 | 90 |
| 1937 | 5 | 301 | 743 | 4,221 | 1,074 |
| 1938 | 3 | 201 | 496 | 3,076 | 773 |
| 1939 | 3 | 790 | 1,951 | 4,950 | 1,187 |
| Total | 52 | 13,390 | 33,074 | 41,005 | 10,719 |

SOURCE: Shirley S. Passow, "Municipal Land Reserves in Sweden: Key to Planning Success" (Master's thesis, Columbia University, 1969). Thomas Atmer, Head of Division of the Stockholm Town Planning Department, provided annual conversion rates from kronor to dollars, as well as a cost of living index for Sweden during this period.

NOTE: Taking 1914 as 100, the cost of living index had reached 169 in 1939. See appendix for index and conversions, 1914–1974.

## Annexation

Most of the land purchased for the land bank was outside of the Stockholm city limits. The city's customary practice was to annex this land as it became ripe for development. Enskede, along with other large tracts, was annexed in 1913 and Bromma in 1916. Vällingby, because it was not developed until then, was not annexed until 1949.

## Disposition

When the Stockholm land bank program began, in 1904, Swedish law permitted the sale, but not the lease, of such land. In 1907, Parliament passed a law[8] enabling the state and municipalities to lease public land once it was planned and platted for development. Peter Heimbürger suggests that there was some conflict in the aims underlying this law. "Set against the desire for social reasons, to prevent housing costs—including those affected by rising land values—from becoming too high, there was a desire to enable the community to benefit from those very same rises in land values."[9] Thus, prospective homeowners did not need to make a capital investment in land and could obtain leases at low rates. At the same time, the municipalities hoped that, over the years, the land would rise in value and could eventually be sold at a considerable public profit. However, the economics of these early purchases and leases do not seem to have been well thought through, as will become evident from a description of Stockholm's program.

Following enactment of the 1907 law, the Stockholm City Council, in 1908, articulated the program it intended to follow:

1. While the national legislation permitted lease terms of 26 to 100 years, Stockholm would use a 60-year term for all residential properties. Sites for apartments and for commercial and industrial uses would be sold in order to obtain a recapture of some of the city's investment. Land owned by the city but not yet ripe for development would be leased for farm or forest use at a nominal rental.

2. The principal cost of the land would not be amortized. Lease charges would cover the cost to the city of interest payments on its borrowings for land acquisition and the cost of making the land ready for development, no more, no less. The annual rent charged would be 5 percent of these costs, allocated to a given site.

3. To prevent lessees from profiting from the municipality's subsidy, the amount that could be charged in a sublease was restricted.

The 1907 law did not provide for renegotiation of rates during whatever lease term a municipality chose, nor for adjustment to reflect changes in the value of the kronor. As a result, the rents paid in 1968 on a lease entered into in 1908 were absurdly low.

Initially, lessees had some problem mortgaging their leases. Because the law provided that, at the end of the lease term, the municipality had the choice of retaking possession of the land or renegotiating a new lease, lenders viewed the lease as less secure an interest than they sought. Partly as a consequence of this attitude in the lending community, Stockholm created a leasehold bank. Since all of the city's leases at this time were for single-family housing development, the bank loaned almost solely for this purpose.

The city made another contribution toward early development of single-family housing. At Enskede and other similar areas the prospective home-owner was likely to do much of the construction labor himself. The city provided housing plans and, on occasion, materials.

Stockholm's program for disposing of development sites continued in much the same manner from 1908 until the 1930s, when there were some shifts in policy. During the 1920s and until the mid-1930s, some five hundred to six hundred parcels of land were leased annually for single-family houses. Apartment construction was limited largely to central Stockholm on land either previously in private ownership or sold by the city to the highest bidder.[10] Rather suddenly the city altered its policy of fostering central city apartments ringed by single-family housing and committed itself to apartment construction in nuclei outside the central areas. A target was set of fifteen hundred apartments per year in addition to the single-family houses.[11]

Starting in 1934, much of this land for apartments was leased, rather than sold, as had been the practice since 1904. Then, in 1938, the minutes of the real estate board of the city note the decision "not to advertise any municipal ground for sale for the time being."[12] This decision included land intended for industrial and commercial use, as well as for apartments and single-family houses. Industrial land usually was leased for a seventy-five-year term, with a permitted rent increase of up to 30 percent at the midpoint of the lease term. Commercial lease terms tended to be twenty-six years, the minimum allowed by law.[13]

### The Peaking of Stockholm's Activity

Even though Sweden was neutral, the war years saw little land acquisition activity by Stockholm. Investment in land then picked up substantially from 1945 to 1951. After that, partly due to a very tight money market and partly due to a conservative shift in the political composition of the city council, land banking entered doldrums that lasted until 1958. Then the Social Democrats swept back into control, and with them came a revival in the land bank program. In 1961, the biggest land buying campaign in Stockholm's history began. This peaked in 1967 and fell off

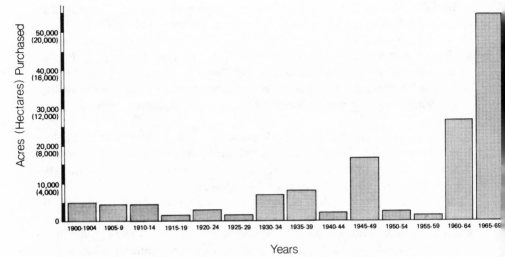

FIGURE 2.2. Stockholm city land acquisition, 1900–1969

SOURCE: Adapted from Shirley S. Passow, "Municipal Land Reserves in Sweden: Key to Planning Success" (Master's thesis, Columbia University, 1969)

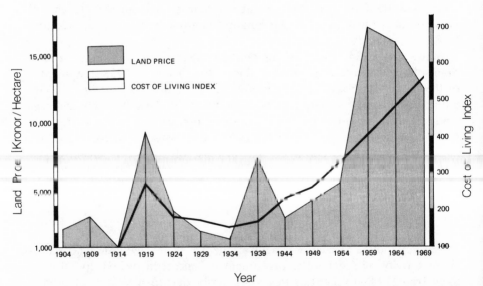

NOTE: LAND PRICES ARE FIVE-YEAR AVERAGES, WITH THE YEARS ENDING IN FOUR AND NINE AS MIDPOINTS. HOWEVER, THE 1904 PRICE INCLUDES ONLY 1904-1906, AND THE 1969 PRICE INCLUDES ONLY 1967.

FIGURE 2.3. Stockholm land prices: Swedish cost of living

NOTE: Land prices are five-year averages, with the years ending in four and nine as midpoints. However, the 1904 price includes only 1904–6, and the 1969 price includes only 1967.

TABLE 2.2. Stockholm City Land Acquisition, 1940–1967

| Year | Number of Purchases | Area | | Cost (in Thousands) | |
|---|---|---|---|---|---|
| | | Hectares | Acres | Swedish Kronor | Dollars |
| 1940 | 1 | 407 | 1,005 | 495 | 118 |
| 1941 | | | | | |
| 1942 | | | | | |
| 1943 | 1 | 90 | 222 | 140 | 33 |
| 1944 | 3 | 210 | 519 | 340 | 81 |
| 1945 | 4 | 1,510 | 3,730 | 3,040 | 724 |
| 1946 | 4 | 369 | 911 | 3,483 | 889 |
| 1947 | 2 | 110 | 272 | 4,345 | 1,207 |
| 1948 | 7 | 3,721 | 9,191 | 6,763 | 1,879 |
| 1949 | 3 | 956 | 2,361 | 3,028 | 750 |
| 1950 | 3 | 403 | 995 | 8,647 | 1,669 |
| 1951 | 4 | 543 | 1,341 | 1,487 | 287 |
| 1952 | | | | | |
| 1953 | 2 | 41 | 101 | 185 | 36 |
| 1954 | 2 | 10 | 25 | 29 | 6 |
| 1955 | 4 | 46 | 114 | 320 | 62 |
| 1956 | 1 | 1 | 2 | 18 | 3 |
| 1957 | 1 | 1 | 2 | 320 | 62 |
| 1958 | 3 | 672 | 1,660 | 2,552 | 493 |
| 1959 | 1 | 2 | 5 | 190 | 37 |
| 1960 | 1 | 1 | 2 | 375 | 73 |
| 1961 | 3 | 1,476 | 3,646 | 32,918 | 6,367 |
| 1962 | 3 | 952 | 2,351 | 3,757 | 728 |
| 1963 | 9 | 2,936 | 7,252 | 29,980 | 5,765 |
| 1964 | 13 | 4,863 | 12,012 | 36,640 | 7,101 |
| 1965 | 21 | 6,593 | 16,285 | 73,550 | 14,226 |
| 1966 | 16 | 5,513 | 13,617 | 190,525 | 36,852 |
| 1967 | 64 | 8,481 | 20,948 | 105,631 | 20,432 |
| Total | 176 | 39,907 | 98,569 | 508,758 | 99,880 |

SOURCE: Shirley S. Passow, "Municipal Land Reserves in Sweden: Key to Planning Success" (Master's thesis, Columbia University, 1969). Thomas Atmer, Head of Division of the Stockholm Town Planning Department, provided annual conversion rates from kronor to dollars, as well as a cost of living index for Sweden during this period.

NOTE: Between 1940 and 1967, the Swedish cost of living index rose from 190 to 540 (1914 = 100).

rapidly thereafter, influenced by several major factors, including new capital gains tax legislation, new land use controls, and the shifting of power and wealth from the city out to the suburbs. Although a number of the suburban municipalities were engaged in land banking during this period, the focus of the story continues to be on the city of Stockholm. (See figs. 2.2 and 2.3 and table 2.2.)

By 1967, Stockholm had bought 138 thousand acres for a price of some $110 million.[14] The total area of the city then was 456 thousand acres, so

municipal acquisitions were triple the city's size. The price paid per hectare rose from 2,934 kronor in the 1940s to 7,998 kronor in the 1950s
and to 15,362 kronor from 1960 through 1967. Until the late 1950s the
price paid for land closely paralleled the cost of living index. Acquisitions
continued to be of large tracts. Average parcel size was 560 acres during
this period; by decade, it was an average of 729 acres per parcel for
1940–1949, 203 acres for 1950–1959, and 585 acres for 1960–1967.
In 1966, of the publicly owned land, 26 percent was located in the city
and 74 percent in outlying areas. Seventy-four percent of the land within
the city limits was owned by the city.[15]

### The 1940s and 1950s

Stockholm emerged from the period of wartime retrenchment in construction with a tremendous pent-up demand for housing. Construction
had continued during the war, but at a slower pace. At the same time, the
Stockholm region had continued its rapid growth, up an average of 1.7
percent per year, compared to the national average increase of 0.6 percent
per year. The city proper continued to grow until 1960, when it reached its
maximum population of 808 thousand. The fastest growth, however, was
in the suburbs. Both the national government and the city government
began what was to become an impressive commitment of resources to
increase dramatically the rate of housing construction. By the early 1960s,
Sweden had the highest rate of housing construction in Europe. One way
chosen to speed up construction was to concentrate on building apartments
and to begin exploring the efficiencies of industrialized housing for apartment construction. Plans incubated before the war, including the plan for
the T-Bana, Stockholm's subway, and for high density centers near subway stops, were refined. Vällingby and then Farsta were built as the first
models of planned satellite center development.[16] (See fig. 2.4.)

The land bank was a key factor in Stockholm's ability to carry out its
plans efficiently and rapidly and to make housing available at a reasonable
price. During the 1940s and 1950s, Stockholm was leasing land within its
borders for development and buying land mostly outside its borders to
hold for future development.

Up until 1956, land acquisition continued to be the responsibility of the
city Real Estate Commission. This commission is headed by a member of
the city council, elected by the city council; the six other members of the
commission represent all of the political parties holding seats in the city
council. The commission's job was to find land, negotiate the price to be
paid, assemble the funds to pay for the land, supervise preparation of

FIGURE 2.4. Housing at Vällingby, Sweden (photo by Michael L. Strong)

building sites, choose developers for major projects, and allocate the city's housing quota among sites. In 1954, the city bought a private building company, STRADA, and, in 1956, designated it the city's company for purchase of land. All shares of STRADA are held by the city, and it is managed by a board of five, whose members include the city's real estate and finance commissioners. Although STRADA's purchases must be approved by the Real Estate Commission, as a quasi-independent company it can move fast and act without public debate on its acquisitions.

As the suburban municipalities grew bigger and stronger, they became unwilling for Stockholm to annex large chunks of their territory. In 1949 the last major annexation took place (except for the 1966 annexation of part of Järvafaltet, but Järvafaltet had been owned by the national government and used as a military training ground, so the circumstances governing its acquisition and annexation were atypical). The end of annexation as a politically acceptable prelude to development was the first failure in the city's long-time *modus operandi*, but few at the time foresaw its future financial implications. From 1958 on, the voluntary Greater Stockholm Planning Association, which was comprised of twenty-three municipalities including the city of Stockholm, influenced the location of development through its housing program.

The National Housing Board annually proposes to Parliament how many housing units shall be built with government aid. Since over 90 percent of the housing construction receives some measure of government aid, the government's annual decision essentially controls the rate of construction. Once the total has been fixed, the board allocates the units among the twenty-four provinces (administrative divisions of the national government whose boundaries are the same as those of the counties).

The Greater Stockholm Planning Association assumed the role of negotiator for its members with the provincial office of the National Housing Board, seeking as large an allocation as possible in light of the Stockholm area's acute housing shortage. Once the total was agreed upon, the association allocated the units among the member municipalities. All political parties were represented on the committees setting the allocation. Therefore, by the time the allocation is agreed upon, there is no need for public debate on it in the municipal councils.

Once the city received its allocation of housing units, it subdivided the funds among the builders. In a typical year—1961—45 percent of the gross floor area to be built was allocated to private builders, 45 percent to the five municipal building companies, and the remaining 10 percent to three cooperatives. It has been alleged that, for decades, Stockholm has had a quota for allocating the right to build housing, based on the distribution of seats in the city council among the various parties.[17]

With annexation no longer acceptable, Stockholm needed a new approach to develop its large suburban holdings. It started making agreements with suburban municipalities in which it owned land to develop housing there to be occupied partly by city residents and partly by residents of the municipality. Between 1959 and 1968, the city made ten such agreements.

Several legislative changes were enacted during the two decades studied here that affected land banking. In 1946,[18] owners of farm land were prohibited from selling their land to nonfarmers without specific authorization from the county agriculture board. The farmhouse and adjacent land were exempted from this requirement. The intent of this law was to keep land in farming by preventing speculators from purchasing it and causing a general escalation in farm prices.

In 1947,[19] The Building and Planning Act restricted dense development to areas shown for such use on municipally adopted detailed plans. (Dense development is that which requires public services such as roads, water, and sewers.) The law also authorized municipalities to require landowners to dedicate land for public use, such as for roads, parks, or public buildings, provided that these public uses will benefit the landowner. Since neither the law nor its implementing regulations specify how much land may be demanded in dedication, this is a matter that is negotiated between the landowner and the municipality. This act limited owners of land other than that planned for dense development to the construction of low-density, single-family housing. Like the farm sale law, its effect was to hold down land prices except in areas planned for dense development. No compensation was payable to landowners affected by either law.

In 1949,[20] the preexisting Expropriation Act was amended to permit municipalities to condemn land for urban uses and then to lease it for development. The municipality was permitted to resell the land only if it could show that the condemned owner was unable or unwilling to develop it within a reasonable period and with housing at a reasonable price. A municipality wishing to expropriate first gave notice to the landowner and offered what it thought a fair price. If the landowner did not accept the price offered, a real estate court fixed the value. Either party could appeal the amount awarded. Only when the expropriation price had been paid did the municipality get possession of the land.

These condemnation rights have proven most useful as a threat to induce landowners to sell by a negotiated agreement. The courts' long delays and substantial awards to the condemnees deterred the municipalities from widespread condemnation of land. Stockholm, for instance, couldn't reach an agreement with the owner of 1,260 acres at Sätra so, in 1955, it requested court approval to condemn. The court gave its consent in 1956, but the condemnation price was not fixed until 1961, and the city did not get possession until then.

In 1952,[21] the number of municipalities in Sweden was reduced from 2,365 to 904. In concept, though not in actuality, each municipality was to have at least three thousand people, to make possible the more efficient provision of services. This consolidation of municipalities began to strengthen the position of some suburbs vis-à-vis Stockholm.

In 1953,[22] the 1907 Lease Act was amended to alter substantially the terms of municipal land leases. First, under the new law, the term of the lease became indefinite. However, a municipality could give notice of its intent to end the lease, after sixty years for residential properties or twenty years for commercial and industrial properties, if it could prove that it needed the land. In such a case, the municipality paid the value of all buildings on the site at the time of termination of the lease. If the lessor municipality did not terminate the lease after the first sixty or twenty years, depending on the type of land use, it could not act to terminate again until another forty years had passed for residential properties or twenty years for commercial and industrial properties. Second, the law prohibited the municipalities from limiting the lessee's power to transfer the rights he enjoyed under the lease. Third, the municipalities were authorized to adjust rent terms every twenty years on residential leases and every ten years on other leases. The rent basis was the value of the site at the beginning of the lease term.

These revisions helped both lessors and lessees. The lessee was placed in a better position to mortgage his interest in the land, because the likelihood of termination of the lease was reduced substantially. The lessor municipalities were at last able to recoup some of the rise in land value, even though only at twenty- or ten-year intervals.

In 1959,[23] the Building and Planning Act was amended to require municipalities to establish building and planning committees authorized to issue building permits only where proposals are in accord with an officially adopted detailed plan.

The total result of these changes in the law was to give municipalities a more powerful position than previously in the control of land prices and development locations. Development could occur only where planned; this held down the price of land planned for farming or other low-density use. The expanded power of eminent domain helped the municipalities negotiate favorable terms when they wished to acquire land for development.

### The Sixties Boom

Growth and prosperity fueled Stockholm's land acquisition boom of the 1960s. So did passage of a new capital gains tax law, which sent landowners flocking to the city real estate office to sell land under the far more favorable provisions of the old law before the 1 January 1968 effective date of the new law.

By the 1960s, Sweden had acknowledged that it had a population distribution problem. Too many people were moving to the three largest metropolitan areas of Stockholm, Gothenburg, and Malmö, threatening small municipalities with declining levels of service and a consequent declining ability to attract new settlers. To counteract this, the government, in 1964, adopted a national location policy to make regional economic growth more equal.

At the same time, in and around Stockholm a conflict surfaced between people's housing preferences and the high-rise, high-density development preferred by the planners to maximize accessibility to jobs, shops, and open space and to speed construction. More and more people wanted single-family housing, a land-consumptive use.

National growth in the 1960s averaged 0.9 percent per year, up from 0.6 percent per year in the 1950s. Most of this growth was due to a net immigration that ranged from ten thousand to forty-six thousand annually. The immigrants gathered in the biggest metropolitan areas, where jobs were going begging, and added to the already severe pressure for housing construction. Greater Stockholm, an area somewhat smaller than Stockholm County, grew from 1.15 million to 1.3 million during the decade, for an annual growth rate of 1.3 percent. Even though growth in the city proper had peaked in 1960, city council continued to feel a commitment to provide a good living environment for the region's new residents. Much of the land bought prior to World War II already was developed or planned for development. With much more growth anticipated—perhaps in conflict with the national location policy—and with the evident desire of current residents to spread out on more land, city council endorsed a vast new land acquisition program.

At the time there was no other unit of government financially able and politically ready for such an undertaking. The 1960 regional plan for the period 1960–1990 had been ratified by the king, but the plan was advisory only. Further, there was no regional government in existence to implement it or to oversee its implementation by local governments.

Torsten Ljungberger, for decades one of the principal architects of Stockholm's land program, said of the 1960s purchases: "It is intended that by these large acquisitions of land the city of Stockholm will in future be able to take part in the further development of Greater Stockholm. These land purchases . . . have also insured the future of the recreational areas that are needed as part of forthcoming urban development."[24]

Municipalities at this time had four sources of financing for land acquisition: (1) their own revenues; (2) government loans, primarily from the National Pension Insurance Fund; (3) bank loans; and (4) bonds, which could be issued only with the approval of the National Bank of Sweden. Stockholm's funds came one-third from bank loans, one-third from municipal revenues, and one-third from the sale of bonds. Municipal revenues came principally from the municipal income tax, whose rate in 1964 was 14.5 percent of taxable income. By 1968, the rate had risen to 17.5 percent. Approval by the National Bank of the sale of bonds turns in part on the strength of the market for such bonds. In 1968, the city was able to market bonds at an interest rate of 6.25 percent. Customary terms for redemption of the bonds were from five to fifteen years.

Stockholm's most important single acquisition of the time was the result of a joint venture with four other municipalities. The national government no longer needed its military training field at Järvafältet, five miles from the center of Stockholm, so Stockholm, Solna, Sundbyberg, Sollentuna, and Järfälla bought thirteen thousand acres, paying eleven cents per square foot ($4,800 per acre, or six kroner per square meter). Many thought that the national government demanded an exorbitant price. Unquestionably, it was much more than the two cents per square foot (or $870 per acre) average on other acquisitions at this time.

The initial plan for Järvafältet called for a population of 100 thousand, so concentrated that one-third of the land would be permanent open space. Stockholm, on its thirty-nine hundred acres, was to provide housing for thirty thousand people and also to build a regional supercenter, Hansta, able to compete in its attractions with downtown Stockholm. For various reasons, including dissension among the five participating municipalities and the doubtful Skärholmen, the biggest center built by Stockholm until then, the initial plans have since been much altered and the plan for Hansta has been abandoned.

Järvafältet was by no means the only major purchase. Total acquisition rose from 2 acres in 1960 to 20,948 acres in 1967. Both, admittedly, were unrepresentative years. The average for 1960–1967—9,414 acres per year—perhaps gives a fairer picture.

Once the city is ready to develop some of its land, it builds roads and foot paths, installs sewerage, water, and other utility systems, and creates parks. Then it offers the development sites for lease. The rent charged is calculated to include a pro-rata share of the interest being paid by the city on its borrowings for land acquisitions, the cost of the infrastructure, and the cost of municipal administration. It can be adjusted where the developer faced unusually difficult site conditions. The rent charged does not depend on the actual costs for a given site; it is equalized for all development of a particular sort. Land leased for single-family detached houses and institutional uses such as churches and schools is priced by the size of the tract. In 1967, for sites up to 6,000 square feet, the annual rent was $0.04 per square foot. The lease price for sites to be used for row houses, apartments, offices, and parking garages was based on the amount of buildable floor area. Also as of 1967, these sites leased annually for $0.09 per square foot for apartments and $0.16 per square foot for offices. Commercial sites were leased at market value. Industrial sites were also leased at market value, although special terms could be offered to lure particularly attractive industries. As of 1967, 390 acres have been leased for industry.

According to a recent study by G. Max Neutze, raw land costs constitute only 1 percent of the monthly rent of an apartment.[25]

In 1963, Stockholm received $5.4 million and in 1966, $4.6 million in income from its leases. In 1963, the city spent $3.2 million on land acquisition and was the only municipality in Sweden to receive more in rents than it was paying for acquisition.[26] Such a comparison of income and outgo is misleading if stated without qualification. Most important, with the exception of commercial and industrial sites, the city never has set its lease rates with the aim of turning a profit. On the contrary, its goal has been to make housing sites available as cheaply as possible. For this reason, the income covers only borrowing costs, site development costs, and administration, and so cannot be looked at as a set-off against new expeditures. It is true that the city has viewed its land reserve as a sound capital investment, continually appreciating, portions of which could from time to time be sold at a profit.

The 1960s saw the culmination of the land bank program as it had evolved since 1904. At the same time, major changes were taking shape that would alter significantly the future character of the program.

The national government created several advisory commissions to investigate land policy questions and then enacted a number of new laws in response to recommendations of the commissions. As is customary in Sweden, the commissions were composed of a mix of members of Parliament, civil servants, and outside experts. In addition to the new laws of the 1960s, further municipal consolidation and creation of a strong county government were on the horizon for the early 1970s.

The laws of 1946 and 1947, which had been intended to halt speculation in land not planned for dense development, had not proven sufficient. As the standard of living rose, more and more Swedes bought land for single-family housing, either for full-time residences or for vacation homes. Around the metropolitan areas prices rose and much scattered site development occurred. By the late 1960s, the city was paying between $4,800 and $7,200 per acre for land, up dramatically from the $870 per acre average of a few years before.

One response was the Nature Conservancy Act of 1964.[27] This law authorized county administrative boards to designate all land within 984 feet (300 meters) of lake, river, and sea shorelines as land open to public access. However, if a municipality subsequently planned any of such areas for dense development, those areas automatically were dropped from the county's regulated open space area. The county administrative boards could also designate private lands as nature reserves and regulate use of such land.

The cumulative effect of the land use laws is that a landowner is entitled to compensation only for regulations that pose a grave impediment to his present use of the land. He no longer is entitled to undertake even sparse development. For example, a person might have bought a piece of land in the country, contemplating the building of a vacation home. If that land were then placed in a nature reserve, with no development allowed, the county would not owe the landowner any compensation for the loss of the right to sparse development. In situations in which the landowner believes that he is entitled to compensation, he must initiate the demand, much as in American inverse condemnation proceedings. The national government, through its Nature Conservancy Board, as of 1973, had a fund of $1.8 million from which to reimburse landowners for restrictions on land use.

Controlling land prices by regulation was one aspect of the government's response. The other was to make it easier for municipalities to buy land. In 1964, municipalities were authorized to invest money in other municipalities.[28] In 1966, the expropriation law was amended so that possession of the land passed as soon as the request to expropriate was approved.[29] In 1967, municipalities were given the right, under certain circumstances, to acquire state land for development.[30] Municipalities, proceeding in the same manner as for expropriation, apply to the crown for approval of the condemnation of the state land. If the application is approved but the parties fail to agree on the price or other terms, the issue is referred to the state's Municipal Land Commission, whose decision is final. Also in 1967, municipalities were authorized to revise their residential lease term every ten years, instead of every twenty years as before.[31]

A 1964 commission report[32] recommended that municipalities buy land ten years in advance of development in order to obtain it at a low enough price. Then, so that eventual price rises could accrue to the municipality, the commission recommended that the land be leased rather than sold for development. While Stockholm had been doing this for years, most municipalities had not because of lack of funds. For them, rapid turnover of a revolving fund was the only source of money to buy land. Suburban municipalities, particularly, had too little income to enable them to spend funds year after year to accumulate a stockpile of land for later development.

One outcome of this commission report was the establishment of a national loan program to assist municipalities to buy land and lease it for development. Government loans became available, starting in 1966, to cover 95 percent of the site value, as determined by the national government through its National Housing Board. The board uses comparable sales to arrive at the site value. Since the state fixes the amount that it will loan toward the purchase of a site, this effectively controls what municipalities can pay for land. Land purchased under this program can only be leased. The state loan is repaid over forty years. Interest is charged at the normal market rate. No principal payments are levied during the first ten years of the loan term.

In 1968, another state loan program for municipal land purchase was initiated. This program is also run by the National Housing Board and provides loans for land acquisition where the land is to be sold for housing. Loans are available regardless of whether the land is bought by voluntary sale, expropriation, or, after 1968, by preemption. Loans are repayable in ten years but in the first two years of the loan term, principal payments can be waived.

Concern over rising land prices continued. A 1966 study[33] of the real estate market in twelve counties found that the price index for open land had risen from 100 in 1957 to 117 in 1963. This increase was somewhat higher than the general price index increase and occurred despite the various rather stringent land use controls.

Another government commission report, in 1966,[34] proposed two laws that would increase dramatically the government influence over land transactions. The first proposal was that municipalities should have a first option on all land offered for sale. The second proposal was that the capital gains tax on land should be increased materially. Parliament responded favorably to both proposals and 1967 became a landmark year for land use legislation.

The "Law of First Option"[35] gives municipalities a right of first refusal on all land or land leases offered for sale and needed for future development. Small sites under three-quarters of an acre worth less than $40,000 are exempt from the law, as well as some sales between relatives. The law works as follows: when a seller and buyer have agreed upon a price, the buyer must notify the municipality in which the land is located of the terms of the agreement and request transfer of title. The municipality then has three months in which to preempt the buyer on the same terms. One municipality may preempt land in another municipality if that municipality so agrees.

The capital gains tax law,[36] which, since 1928, had imposed no tax on sales of land held for more than ten years, was made much more severe. Under the 1967 law, the full amount of the gain on short-term sales—those of land held less than two years—is taxable as ordinary income. For sales of land held for two or more years, 75 percent of the gain is taxable as ordinary income. There are some deductions and adjustments, but the tax still is stiff. Both individuals and corporations receive a standard $100 deduction on long-term gains. The gain can be adjusted as follows:

1. Improvements up to $600 per year may be added to the base value
2. The base value and the cost of improvements may be corrected for changes in the value of the kronor by using an index set annually by the National Tax Bureau
3. If there is a house on the site, the base may be increased by $600 per year for each year that the taxpayer owned the house
4. Business realizing a gain can defer it by placing the funds in a real estate replacement reserve
5. Long-term losses from land sales can be deducted from capital gains and may be carried forward for six years

Small wonder that landowners besieged real estate offices in Stockholm and other municipalities so that they could sell their land under the provisions of the old law.

### A Tale of Three Towns

Most current development in the Stockholm region is taking place on publicly owned land in suburban municipalities. The ownership and tenure patterns vary. Stockholm may own the land and develop it in cooperation with the municipality in which it is located. In some instances the suburban municipality may be the sole owner of the development land; in others, the municipality and private developers each may own part of it. Sixteen of the twenty-three municipalities in Stockholm County lease land for development.[37] Some other municipalities sell all of their development sites, and sometimes the decision to sell or lease depends upon the intended use of the land or the wishes of the purchaser.

The land bank programs in three Stockholm area municipalities— Botkyrka, Märsta, and Täby—will be described to give some sense of the range of approaches and of the common threads. The Norra Botkyrka development is a cooperative enterprise between Stockholm and Botkyrka, the two landowners. Märsta, now merged into the municipality of Sigtuna, is an expanded town beyond the suburban fringe in which ownership of the land to be developed has been split between the municipality and two cooperatives. Täby is a suburban municipality where virtually all development has occurred on municipal land.

The rapid growth experienced in each of these municipalities has been intended and planned for, at both the regional and local levels. All are served by expressways and commuter rail lines. Botkyrka and Täby soon will be linked to Stockholm by subway. All foresaw development and started buying land a decade or two in advance, as opportunities offered and municipal budgets permitted. Märsta, with the smallest population and least income, also encouraged two cooperatives, HSB and Riksbyggan, to buy land. Only Botkyrka has used the National Housing Board's program for land acquisition—and regrets it. The consensus among all three municipalities is that the program saves a municipality no money and, further, restricts its freedom in the price set for the sale or lease of land. Whether or not they borrow from the National Housing Board for land acquisition, all three municipalities are affected by the board's control. Almost all of their housing construction is subsidized in part by the board, and the board's loan values are shaped by what it judges to be a fair price for the developer to have paid for the land.

Land prices for purchases made from 1950 on have averaged about the same in Märsta and Täby ($1,410 per acre and $1,150 per acre, respectively). Half of the land at Norra Botkyrka had been bought long in advance of development. The rest was bought in the late 1960s, shortly before construction began, at an average price far higher ($3,500 per acre) than that paid in Märsta and Täby.

In disposing of land for housing, both Märsta and Täby sell in order to recoup their investment and pay off their loans. At Norra Botkyrka, Stockholm and Botkyrka agreed to lease all land. Botkyrka is not receiving sufficient income from its leases to pay the interest on its land acquisition loan.

All three municipalities are eager to attract industry, and the terms and rates are subject to bargaining pressure from potential industrial customers.

The municipalities all overbuilt high-rise apartments. Whether this was due to pressure from the National Housing Board, to a local miscalculation of demand, or to a combination of both factors, many apartments were vacant in 1973. The vacancy rate was 10 percent in Norra Botkyrka, 7 percent in Märsta, and 2.5 percent in Täby; all of these municipalities have responded by placing a new emphasis on single-family housing construction. Norra Botkyrka, with the highest vacancy rate, was least able to respond quickly to alter its construction program. Not until 1975 were over 50 percent of the housing units being built single family. Täby and Märsta have been under much less immediate pressure. By 1972, Täby had converted to 100 percent single-family housing construction and Märsta to entirely single-family housing or two-story apartment construction.

As table 2.3 shows, as of 1970, all three municipalities had about one-third of their housing stock in single-family units. This was about typical for the suburbs; the 21 percent single-family housing figure for Stockholm County includes the city of Stockholm, with its very low 10 percent. As of 1970, this also was about the split for housing construction throughout Sweden—namely, 69 percent multifamily housing, 9 percent row housing, and 22 percent single-family detached housing. The table also shows the projected decline in construction for the county as a whole during the mid-1970s, as well as the declining share for the city of Stockholm.

Along with the demand for much more single-family housing, the residents of Botkyrka and Täby have expressed concern over the loss of open space and the pervasiveness of growth. As in many other Stockholm area municipalities, the "Green Wave" has led local politicians to reconsider the desirability of growth. A few years ago there was widespread agreement that more growth was good for the Stockholm region. Today many are dubious. Hjalmar Mehr, Governor of Stockholm County, believes that between 75 and 80 percent of the municipalities now are revising their plans to slow or deter growth.[38]

### Botkyrka

The development of Botkyrka is illustrative of the cooperative arrangements entered into by Stockholm and outlying municipalities in which it owns land. Botkyrka lies immediately to the southwest of the city. It already is linked to Stockholm by an expressway and a commuter railroad. In 1975, the T-Bana opened the first of four stations to be built there, providing another rapid link to the center city.

TABLE 2.3. Housing Construction: Amount and Type

| Housing Construction | Year | Stock-holm County | Municipalities | | | |
|---|---|---|---|---|---|---|
| | | | Stock-holm | Bot-kyrka | Märsta | Täby |
| Existing housing units | 1970 | | | | | |
| % multifamily | | 79 | 90 | 64 | 67 | 66 |
| % one- or two-family | | 21 | 10 | 36 | 33 | 34 |
| Housing units built | 1965 | 17,773 | 5,907 | 290 | 481 | 952 |
| | 1966 | 17,339 | 4,523 | 213 | 116 | 591 |
| | 1967 | 18,981 | 5,869 | 497 | 477 | 691 |
| | 1968 | 24,324 | 8,565 | 765 | 539 | 1,129 |
| | 1969 | 24,290 | 9,313 | 866 | 755 | 552 |
| | 1970 | 23,023 | 7,191 | 1,195 | 872 | 656 |
| | 1971 | 23,775 | 5,541 | 3,316 | 805 | 310 |
| | 1972 | 22,385 | 2,889 | 4,406 | 459 | 322 |
| New units in one- or two-family houses | 1968 | | | | | |
| Number | | 5,127 | 1,031 | 124 | 132 | 240 |
| % | | 21 | 12 | 16 | 24 | 21 |
| | 1969 | | | | | |
| Number | | 5,710 | 1,312 | 219 | 200 | 237 |
| % | | 24 | 14 | 25 | 26 | 43 |
| | 1970 | | | | | |
| Number | | 6,119 | 883 | 299 | 362 | 126 |
| % | | 27 | 12 | 25 | 42 | 19 |
| | 1971 | | | | | |
| Number | | 5,710 | 868 | 504 | 196 | 101 |
| % | | 24 | 16 | 15 | 24 | 33 |
| | 1972 | | | | | |
| Number | | 5,727 | 847 | 640 | 72 | 322 |
| % | | 26 | 29 | 15 | 16 | 100 |
| Housing units planned | 1973 | 19,940 | 4,634 | 2,740 | 597 | 324 |
| | 1974 | 18,695 | 6,287 | 977 | 243 | 588 |
| | 1975 | 19,175 | 6,183 | 1,325 | 185 | 587 |
| | 1976 | 14,934 | 3,146 | 1,062 | 170 | 710 |
| | 1977 | 14,431 | 1,957 | 495 | 275 | 770 |

SOURCE: National Housing Board, Stockholm, Sweden

Botkyrka is growing at an enormous rate, as planned. From a base of 10,700 inhabitants in 1960, it was expected to reach 75,000 in 1975. Part of this growth is attributable to two municipal mergers—the first, in 1971, with Grödinge, which added 3,500 people, and the second, in 1974, with Salemstaden, which added another 12,600 people, but new development accounts for most of the growth. By 1977, the period of peak construction was expected to be over (see fig. 2.5). Development will then taper off to some five hundred or six hundred dwelling units per year, down from the high of forty-four hundred units built in 1972.

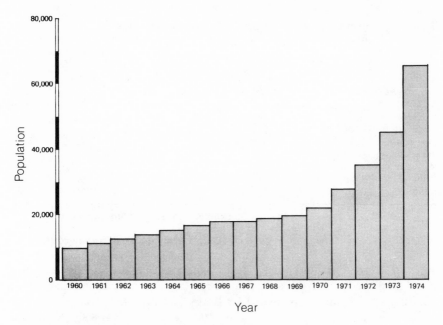

FIGURE 2.5. Botkyrka population, 1960–1975

SOURCE: Adapted from P. O. Sandquist, Botkyrka Real Estate Office, letter, 1973

The most intensive development is taking place in Norra Botkyrka, along the shore of Lake Mälaren. Botkyrka and Stockholm entered an agreement, in 1965, covering the conditions under which they would undertake joint development of Norra Botkyrka. They formed the Botkyrka Stockholm Housing Company to be directly responsible for execution of the project. Each made a commitment to acquire the additional ground needed, acting through STRADA. They agreed to split the cost of site preparation for multifamily housing. Sixty-five percent of the infrastructure was to be paid by Stockholm, 35 percent by Botkyrka. Stockholm was to lend Botkyrka money when Botkyrka found itself unable to raise funds elsewhere. The cost of development was projected to be $375 million (see table 2.4). Both municipalities agreed to leave sites at the same rates. The land was allocated as in Stockholm: 45 percent to public companies, 45 percent to private enterprise, and 10 percent to cooperatives. Since 75 percent of the housing built until 1974 was multifamily, and since all of that housing construction has received National Housing Board subsidies, it is the National Housing Board that has in fact controlled those lease rates. Industrial and commercial sites have been leased at market value.

Stockholm already owned over 700 acres at Norra Botkyrka, having purchased the land at the turn of the century. Botkyrka had bought 541

TABLE 2.4. Projected Development Costs, Norra Botkyrka

| Type of Cost | Millions of Kronor | Amount | Source of Funds (in Millions of Dollars) | | |
| | | | Municipal Loans | Other Loans | Grants |
|---|---|---|---|---|---|
| General, Stockholm[a] | 160 | 32 | 32 | | |
| General, Botkyrka[b] | 285 | 57 | 50 | | 7 |
| Developers | 1,130 | 226 | | 226 | |
| Subway | 170 | 34 | 19 | | 15 |
| Water and sewer systems | 90 | 18 | | 18 | |
| Principal roads | 40 | 8 | | | 8 |
| Total | 1,875 | 375 | 101 | 244 | 30 |

SOURCE: Letter from J. H. Martin, Stockholm Real Estate Office, undated.
[a] Includes land and some infrastructure costs.
[b] Includes land, some infrastructure costs, and school and kindergarten costs.

acres in 1948. Pursuant to the 1965 agreement, through STRADA they bought up the rest of the site, using expropriation where necessary. Now 41.5 percent of the site is owned by Botkyrka and 58.5 percent by Stockholm. The average price paid between 1965 and 1968 was $3,500 per acre (4.2 kronor per square meter). Stockholm's total investment in land has been $5,269,000 and Botkyrka's $3,081,000. (See table 2.5.)

The Norra Botkyrka development has experienced a number of problems, some typical of development today throughout the metropolitan area, some unique to Botkyrka.[39] Since all of the sites at Norra Botkyrka are being leased, both Stockholm and Botkyrka were eligible for loans toward acquisition costs under the National Housing Board loan-lease program. Botkyrka did apply but now questions the desirability of the loan-lease program. First, in accordance with board policy, the municipality must borrow for site and infrastructure costs on the private market and then seek to cover borrowing costs with the National Housing Board loan. Botkyrka did borrow from a bank at 7.5 percent interest, with the principal repayable in fifteen years. The National Housing Board loan covered only 95 percent of the site cost. Further, it restricted the municipality to a maximum interest rate of 6.5 percent, which it may charge the builders leasing land for development. This doesn't cover Botkyrka's borrowing costs.

Development costs are proving a heavy burden for both Botkyrka and Stockholm. It is reported that "furthermore, various social benefits have cost considerably more than was computed because of unexpected development of the household and income structures."[40] The income tax rate in Botkyrka in 1973 was 23.40 percent of a person's net income, a very onerous burden for the residents. Botkyrka is being forced to sell rather than lease land that it owns holds elsewhere in the municipality in order to boost current revenues.

TABLE 2.5. Principal Acquisitions at Norra Botkyrka

| Place | Acquiring Municipality | Year | Hectares | Acres | Swedish Kronors per Square Meter |
|-------|------------------------|------|----------|-------|----------------------------------|
| Norsborg | Stockholm | 1899 | 178 | 440 | 0.05 |
| Slagsta | Stockholm | 1908 | 124 | 306 | 0.13 |
| Alby | Botkyrka | 1948 | 219 | 541 | 0.35 |
| Hågelby | Botkyrka | 1965 | 85 | 210 | 2.22 |
| Hallunda | Stockholm | 1967 | 116 | 287 | 6.0 |
| Älvesta | Botkyrka | 1967 | 106 | 262 | 2.62 |
| Skrävsta | Botkyrka | 1968 | 68 | 168 | 3.2 |
| Fittja | Stockholm | 1968 | 89 | 220 | 6.5 |
| Brunna | Stockholm | 1968 | 60 | 148 | 4.8 |
| Total | | | 1,045 | 2,582 | |

SOURCE: P. O. Sandquist, Botkyrka Real Estate Office, letter, 20 Oct. 1972.

Stockholm doesn't receive any of the income tax revenues from the development on its land. Its leases aren't covering its costs and, in addition, it has loaned somewhere near $100 million to Botkyrka. The cost is so high that officials are unwilling to be precise either about it or about the prospective return on the investment. It is highly doubtful that Stockholm can continue to afford altruism in the form of cooperative agreements such as that with Botkyrka.

Some years ago Botkyrka attracted the headquarters office of the Alfa-Laval company. With two thousand employees, the company was a choice source of tax revenue. More recently, Botkyrka has not been so successful in marketing its industrial land. Municipalities to the north of Stockholm, like Täby, have been coming out on top in the competition to woo new industry. As evidence of this, the market value range of industrial sites in Botkyrka has dropped from $1.80 to $2.80 per square foot.

The market demand for apartments has plunged virtually everywhere. Although all apartments built in Norra Botkyrka were sold or rented when completed, as of the fall of 1973, the vacancy rate was 10 percent. In response, 36 percent of the housing units built in 1974 and 55 percent of those built in 1975 were to be single family. (See fig. 2.6.) That means further construction of a vast number of apartments, very possibly more than the market will absorb.

Last, the residents of Botkyrka, having seen what the future holds in the way of prospective development, don't like it all that well. In 1973, the Social Democrats had been in power locally for fifty-four years. Responding to the pervasive "Green Wave" sentiment, the voters rejected them and put the Center party in power. Given the advanced state of development at Norra Botkyrka, little change other than a shift to more single-family housing construction in the final stages is likely to occur there. Elsewhere in the municipality there may well be an increased reluctance to permit

FIGURE 2.6. Single-family housing, Botkyrka, Sweden (photo by Michael L. Strong)

high-density development, or even any development at all. One might argue that Botkyrka already has more than its fair share of the metropolitan area's intensive development, and this is a point of view with which many Botkyrka residents would agree.

### Märsta

Märsta, like Norra Botkyrka, has had a substantial number of development problems. However, thanks to innovative and thoughtful municipal leadership, it seems pointed toward future success after a decade of difficulties. Märsta's major growth occurred in the 1960s. Now there has been sufficient time—and sufficient inclination—to reflect on what went wrong and to design a different future for the community's next growth phase in the late 1970s.[41]

Märsta is twenty-five miles north of Stockholm. Although there are a commuter railroad and an expressway that provide excellent access to Stockholm, Märsta still lies beyond commuter range for most people. It was a small, slowly growing rural community of thirty-five hundred people until 1959, when the national government decided to build Sweden's largest airport, Arlanda, within the municipality.

The government and the Regional Planning Association favored substantial expansion of Märsta to provide a town convenient to the airport as a home for many of the three thousand people to be employed at Arlanda. Professor C.-F. Ahlberg, Director of the Regional Planning Association (now the director of regional planning for the Stockholm County Council), designed a plan shaped by transportation links and topography. Four hills intersected by two valleys give Märsta its particular character. The railroad follows one valley, and roughly parallel to it was the route of the proposed expressway that would link Arlanda to Stockholm and Uppsala. Professor Ahlberg's plan called for the eastern hill, located between the railroad and the expressway route, to be devoted to industry and for the other three hills to be developed for quite high density residential use. Development was to start on the northern hill, adjacent to the existing railroad station. The plan envisioned the eventual development of a commercial center in the valley at a central point between the hills. When that occurred, the railroad station was to have been relocated to the commercial center.

From the beginning, everyone sought to make Märsta more than an airport-support community. It was hoped that some people who worked in and around Stockholm would wish to settle there and that industries, including some relying on air freight, could be attracted to the industrial site.

Construction of housing and of a neighborhood shopping center adjacent to the railroad station started in 1962. Later, starting in 1966, two thousand apartments were built on the second hill. The housing on both hills was almost exclusively multifamily, including some ten-story point block towers on the hilltops and many ranks of low-rise apartment buildings on the lower slopes and near the railroad station. The developers provided few amenities, and the municipality few community facilities.

From the start, Märsta received disparaging publicity. It was the first dense, high-rise–dominated development so far out in the country. People driving along the highway to Uppsala saw it and criticized it. Märsta filled up with Arlanda employees, but little industry and few Stockholm people came. Some of those who did come had social problems and had had trouble finding housing elsewhere.

The Social Democrats were in power in Märsta from 1964 to 1967, when most of the development was taking place. In large part as a reaction to what had been built, the residents voted the Liberals into power in 1968, and they began a review of planning and development in Märsta. Power shifted to the Center party in 1971, but a Liberal was elected head of the council and the planning process initiated by the Liberals continued.

The feeling was shared widely that past development had been at too high a density with too little attention to the provision of amenities. To plan for the future, the municipal council and Stig Gunnerfeldt, head of the

Real Estate Office, determined that the citizens of Märsta should have an active role. A two-hundred-family cross-section of the municipality's residents was invited to work with five planning firms hired to develop alternative plans. The families were divided into groups, and each group was linked with a planning firm. Together, they formed planning teams. The citizen members of the planning teams were paid for the time they spent attending meetings with the professional planners. When all of the teams' plans were finished, they were presented at public meetings and debated.

After hearing the views of the residents, the municipal council made several decisions. Most fundamental, Märsta should not try to be a bedroom commuter town but should try to provide jobs in the municipality for its residents. The national government had refused to pay to move the railroad station to the location initially proposed for the town center, and Märsta lacked the money to move it. Given the decision not to try to be a commuter town, the location of the railroad station became less important and freed the town to relocate the planned center. It was decided to shift the center to between hills one and two and to leave the fourth hill undeveloped. After making these fundamental policy decisions, first priority was given to providing new services to hill one, including recreation areas, day care centers, teen centers, and small shops.

Planner Ralph Erskine, one of the five planners initially engaged, was awarded the job of continuing to work with local residents to develop three alternative detailed plans for the completion of development at hill two. One directive he and his team received was to mix housing types and to use high-rise buildings sparingly for visual emphasis. Another was to plan for small local schools for the elementary grades. By the fall of 1973, the three alternative plans were ready for public discussion. The planning process has taken a number of years, yet it has engendered a high level of public participation and has led to widespread consensus on a desirable future for Märsta.

Throughout this planning period, Märsta's situation has not remained static. In 1971, it merged with Sigtuna, a historic and charming town bordering Lake Mälaren. Because Sigtuna is a major tourist attraction and enjoys such a favorable reputation, its name was retained for the merged municipalities. By 1973, Sigtuna's population was 27,156, of which approximately 20,000 are located in Märsta. Sixty percent of the Arlanda workers live in Sigtuna, most of them in the community of Märsta. Eighty firms provide fifteen hundred jobs at the Märsta industrial park. The largest firm employs two hundred people.

In 1973, there was a 7 percent vacancy rate in the apartments that constitute 70 percent of Märsta's housing stock. As housing vacancies around Stockholm have increased, commuters have left Märsta to be nearer their jobs. Some apartment dwellers have shifted to the new single-family and two-story multifamily housing that Märsta has been building recently. Many of these vacant apartments are owned by the municipality's building company, Märstabostäder, and by cooperatives. The National Housing Board is absorbing some of their loss on the empty units.

There will be a new influx of residents because Arlanda is expanding substantially. By 1983, the government predicts that six thousand people will be working there, and, as in the past, it is expected that many of the newcomers will settle in Sigtuna.

Only a small proportion of the land in Sigtuna—5.3 percent—is owned by the municipality and Märstabostäder. However, most of the municipal land is in the area lying between the towns of Sigtuna and Märsta where future development is planned. In addition, local affiliates of two of the largest national development cooperatives, HSB and Riksbyggan, own substantial amounts of land.

Neither Märsta nor, since the merger, Sigtuna has used either of the National Housing Board loan programs for land acquisition. Some land is being bought through the Law of First Option. In some instances Sigtuna intervenes and preempts the private buyer; on other occasions the prospective seller, knowing of the law, contacts the municipality before offering the land on the private market.

The municipality has been buying land for the land reserve, for recreation, and for immediate development since 1957, while the housing cooperatives' purchases began in 1963. All purchases in the 1950s cost less than $785 per acre (1 kronor per square meter). In the 1960s, Märsta paid between $650 and $2,175 per acre (0.85–2.95 kronor per square meter) and the cooperatives between $1,300 and $2,435 per acre (1.86–3.10 kronor per square meter). Prices for the three purchases in the early 1970s were much the same.

Residential land is sold, either to Märstabostäder or to a private builder. The municipality cannot afford to lease the land because it needs the sale revenues to pay off its loans. Commercial land is leased. Industrial land is offered for sale or lease at the industry's option. The recent sale price of industrial land has been $0.73 per square foot (40 kronor per square meter), way below the $1.80–$2.00 per square foot being sought by Botkyrka. Currently, leasing is more popular with industry since it does not tie up capital. The lease terms are forty years at 7.7 percent for the first ten years on a base price calculated at $0.73 per square foot. Sigtuna is considering cutting the industrial land price to $0.18 per square foot (10 kronor per square meter) as part of a concerted effort to attract new industry to Märsta.

Ninety-five percent of all housing built at Märsta has received National Housing Board construction loans. Märstabostäder has had unusual success in holding costs well below the National Housing Board loan values at its three most recent developments. One development, consisting of 250 single-family houses, was built under Märstabostäder's supervision by two private developers, and the houses and lots then were sold. This project cost 8 percent less than the loan value. The land at the second and third projects, also single-family houses developed by private companies, has been retained by Märstabostäder. Costs at these projects were 10 and 14 percent under loan value. This remarkable achievement has been attributed to careful, accurate planning by the municipality and its building company.

### Täby

Täby is as close as one can come in the Stockholm region to an unalloyed success story. One could say "To those who have shall be given," but that would fail to acknowledge the high level of ability among members of the municipal council and their professional staff that has contributed to Täby's skill in attracting the development it sought. Municipal landownership has been a vital link between planning and development, and the financial health of the municipality has enabled it to buy almost all large tracts coming on the market. Täby has its problems and disappointments, but the overall record there is the envy of many other municipalities.

Täby began its slow evolution from farm to suburban community in 1906, when building of single-family houses for well-to-do Stockholm commuters began. A commuter railroad made it a short trip to downtown Stockholm, ten miles away, and gradual development at Täby was a natural extension of the handsome residential suburbs nearer to the city. Täby remained a politically conservative community. Until the 1950s its flavor was rustic. At that time it was clear that Täby, favored by accessibility and social preference, would be a major target for growth and that it was up to the municipality to plan posthaste for its future. The regional plan projected an expressway passing through the town roughly parallel to the commuter railroad. Stockholm and Täby agreed that the T-Bana should be extended to Täby.

Already in the 1940s and early 1950s a few large tracts of land had been brought for the municipal land bank. Next, the municipality developed a plan for intensive development, including a regional commercial center and industrial park, accessible to the railroad, T-Bana, and proposed expressway.[42] More acquisitions occurred in the 1960s, through the Näsby Company, a private real estate company bought by Täby that operates much as STRADA does for Stockholm. By the mid-1950s, Täby was ready for design competitions for development of a few of the sites it had previously acquired. Land was sold, and high-rise construction began to alter

TABLE 2.6.  Täby Housing, 1955–1969

| Project Name | Number of Multifamily or Single-Family Units | Landowner | Year Acquired | Sold to | Year Development Began |
|---|---|---|---|---|---|
| Täby Storcentrum | 3,000 MF | municipality | 1950 | private company / cooperative | 1964 |
| Näsbydal | 930 MF | municipality | 1950 | cooperative | 1957 |
| Grindtorp | 1,648 MF | municipality | 1950 | cooperative | 1960 |
| Näsbypark centrum | 1,208 MF | municipality | 1950 | municipal company / private company | 1955 |
| Hägernäs | 800 MF | private | | | 1957 |
| Viggbygärdet | 529 MF | private | | | 1966 |
| Norskogen | 200 SF | municipality | 1950 | private company | 1957 |
| North Ellagård | 350 SF | private | | | 1956 |
| South Ellagård | 190 SF | private | | | 1967 |
| Ankaret | 30 SF | state | | | 1967 |
| Ost Vallabrink | 142 SF | municipality | 1961 | private individuals | 1966 |

SOURCE: Interview with Councilman Göran Elgfeld and Mr. Månsson, Town Planner, 2 November 1973.

forever the community's sylvan character. Between 1955 and 1969, 9,027 dwelling units were built—8,115 apartments and 912 single-family houses. Overall, 75 percent of the housing (25 percent of the single-family and 85 percent of the multifamily housing) was built on land that had been owned by the municipality.[43] (See table 2.6.)

It is Täby's practice to try to buy all private land coming on the market.[44] By 1973, it owned 80 percent of the remaining undeveloped land, all purchased by negotiated agreement. This was estimated to be enough land for the next fifteen years' development needs. All remaining owners of substantial tracts are aware that Täby is a prospective purchaser. Mr. Göran Elgfeld, one of three members of the municipal council who also is a full-time municipal employee, believes that the expropriation law is not fair to landowners and wishes to avoid using it. He finds it unwieldy for the municipality as well. In 1968, Täby requested national government approval of the condemnation of twenty-five acres for general development purposes. As of 1973, they still had not received an answer and had bought 80 percent of the land by negotiation. Since all costs in an expropriation proceeding are paid by the expropriator, Täby finds it cheaper and quicker to pay 25 to 30 percent in excess of the market price and avoid expropriation.

The cost of land has varied from $395 per acre to $2,850 per acre between 1945 and 1973. The purchases have been few enough in number

TABLE 2.7. Major Täby Land Acquisition, 1946–1972

| Year | Site | Acres | Area (in hectares) | Cost (in millions of kronor) | Kronors per Meter$^2$ |
|------|------|-------|--------------------|------------------------------|------------------------|
| 1946 | Valla | 259 | 105 | .230 | 0.22 |
| 1950 | NFAB[a] | 1,289 | 522 | 7.300 | 1.40 |
| 1955 | Hägernäs | 543 | 220 | 1.620 | 0.74 |
| 1959 | Karby | 610 | 247 | 1.234 | 0.50 |
| 1961 | Brody | 325 | 132 | .657 | 0.50 |
| 1961 | Hägerneholm | 792 | 321 | 7.216 | 2.25 |
| 1963 | Skogberga | 403 | 163 | .975 | 0.60 |
| 1963 | Skålhamra | 583 | 236 | 1.500 | 0.64 |
| 1967 | Löttinge | 632 | 256 | 9.728 | 3.80 |
| 1970 | Vågsjö | 584 | 237 | 5.322 | 2.25 |
| 1972 | Hagby | 1,666 | 672 | 10.600 | 1.58 |
| Total | | 7,686 | 3,111 | 46.382 | |

NOTE: Purchases given are those in excess of 100 hectares of land made by the municipality of Täby or its companies.

[a] Purchase of a holding company whose assets consisted of 522 hectares of land in central Täby.

and widely enough spaced so that one suspects that individual site characteristics and development potential, rather than the overall land market, have been the primary determinants of price. Land that originally cost approximately $8 million is currently worth $14 million. (See table 2.7 and map 2.2.)

When Täby buys land, it will take over any outstanding mortgages and go to a bank to borrow the rest of the purchase price. Loans are for terms of from five to ten years, and the interest rate either may be fixed for the term of the loan or subject ot annual adjustment. About 80 percent of Täby's loans are at a fixed interest rate. In periods of low interest rates, obtaining a guarantee of a fixed rate costs a little more than taking a chance on the flexible rate. Täby has not floated bonds for land acquisition, because traditionally the Riksbank has been disinclined to approve such bonds for any municipality except Stockholm. Nor has Täby used either of the National Housing Board's land acquisition loan programs, believing them to be no cheaper than bank loans.

Residential land is sold following competitions for development of sites. The municipality specifies the desired density, housing mix, and selling price and then seeks proposals. It also withholds from sale all land needed for parks, schools, and other community facilities. Unlike Stockholm, Täby calculates its actual costs for a given site in determining what the selling price should be, although the price then may be adjusted upward or downward if this seems reasonable. Täby seeks to recover all of its costs, adjusted for inflation, and, if feasible, a small profit.

Land for the regional center was sold, because Täby needed the income.

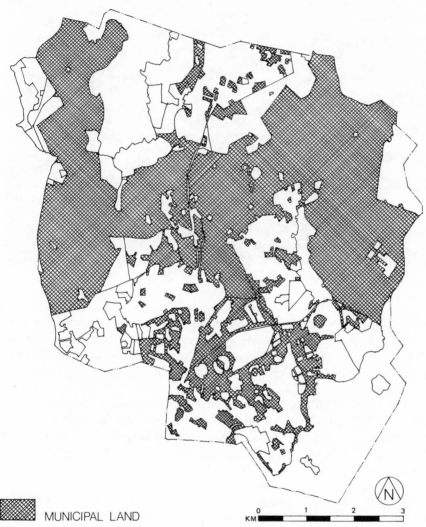

MUNICIPAL LAND

KM

0    1    2    3

MAP 2.2.  Täby municipal land

SOURCE: Adapted from Täby stadsarkitektkontor, *Inventeringskarta över Täby Kommun* (map) (1973)

Industrial land is offered for sale or lease at the industry's preference. (See fig. 2.7.)

Although Täby generally has been highly successful in competing for industry, it has a $4.5 million investment in land, roads, and sewers for one industrial area, Hägernäs, for which it has yet to receive national government approval. The regional plan showed industrial use for this general area, so Täby moved fast to prepare detailed plans and build

FIGURE 2.7. Täby center, Sweden (photo by Michael L. Strong)

roads. The provincial office of the national government approved the location but, after two years' consideration, rejected the detailed plan because of a disagreement over the location of an arterial road. The national government supported the province, and Täby now is negotiating to change the plan.

After years of building primarily high-rise apartments, Täby has had a surfeit. With a population of forty thousand the residents want growth to slow down. In 1973, there were 250 vacant apartments, and, recognizing the turn away from apartments, by 1972, construction had shifted to 100 percent single family housing. Most of the housing was developed on lots of ten thousand square feet or less. Some are row or chain houses.

While the municipality is financially healthy, people are concerned over the loss of woods and fields, and over the sense of having become a highly urban suburb.

### Dispersion and Disaffection

The 1970s have brought further changes in attitudes toward urban development and the means to control it. The national government has deepened its resolve to control the locus of development. It has begun to implement the national location policy, it has restricted even further the private property owner's rights to develop, and it has increased substantially the funding of the National Housing Board's loan program for public land acquisition. At last the government has recognized the pressure for single-family housing and has altered the single family to multifamily ratio of the National Housing Board annual housing program to reflect some of this demand.

The Stockholm region acknowledged the commonality of its interests by supporting the creation of a regional government and granting it broad powers to acquire land and to control development. Then, as political dominance shifted to the suburbs and as the actuality of urbanization seeped into the suburban consciousness, there was a retrenchment. The regional government has not been allowed to exercise many of its powers, and the surburban municipalities have begun to compete with one another for the choicest development morsels. The merits of growth have come into question. This reevaluation of growth benefits comes just as the national government has decided that the Stockholm region's growth should slow so that other areas may expand instead.

The city of Stockholm suddenly became aware that it had lost its dominant position. Population was declining, industry was moving out, and revenues were down. Formerly "the big, bad, rich city," in the words of a prominent Stockholmer, so rich and powerful that it didn't need help from the national government, Stockholm began to wonder how it could afford to develop its vast extraterritorial holdings. Turning them over to the regional government seemed the answer until the disaffection of the suburban municipalities from regional control became evident. Stockholm's most recent developments, Tensta and Rinkeby, have hardened the resolve of many other municipalities to maintain local control over what is built.

The suburban municipalities are coping with growth with moderate success. They are short of money and unable to provide many needed community facilities. They cannot afford to buy all of the land that they will need for future growth. Of most concern, parochial attitudes are developing that in the long run will be inimical to the interests of the region.

It is a time of reconsideration for all of the Stockholm region. The assurance and drive of the city in the 1950s and 1960s have faded. There has been a popular rejection of much that the city has built or proposed recently. The suburbs recognize their new power but have yet to decide what sort of a future they want for themselves or how vital regional cooperation will be.

## The National Framework

The government has moved to exert more national control over urban development both by direct controls and by the increased use of its financial powers. The land use control laws passed up through 1968 gave very strong powers to the municipalities and some powers—as in the case of the Nature Conservancy Act—to the national government. Some subsequent laws, particularly changes in the expropriation law, have strengthened the position of the municipalities even more, but some have shown a new will of the national government to influence the direction of urban growth.

For instance, in the early 1970s Parliament passed a series of laws to implement the location policy articulated in 1964. The intent of the policy was to bring about greater equality among all regions of the country, while at the same time stimulating economic growth and efficient use of resources. Twenty-six primary centers have been designated for growth, and thirteen of these have been selected to receive central government administrative jobs to be relocated from Stockholm. Under a 1971 law, six thousand jobs were selected for relocation and, under a 1973 law, four thousand more jobs were added to the list.

Firms planning new or substantially expanded facilities in the Stockholm, Gothenburg, or Malmö metropolitan areas must consult with a national government agency about the possibility of locating elsewhere before they can obtain a building permit. Some loans and grants are available for firms willing to locate in areas targeted for growth, as well as some grants to train employees for the firms. These last two measures have not had notable success, and the government is considering the adoption of more effective controls on industial location.

Encouraging growth elsewhere implies discouraging it in the three major metropolitan areas. For Stockholm County, the national government proposes a 1980 population of 1.6 to 1.675 million people. Without national intervention, it has been projected that 50 percent of Sweden's growth during the 1970s would occur in the Stockholm metropolitan area and 80 percent in the Stockholm, Gothenburg and Malmö areas combined.

The Stockholm region has grown more than twice as fast as the nation as a whole in recent decades. From 1930 to 1965, growth averaged 1 7 percent per year. This has increased the region's share of Sweden's population from 7 percent in 1870 to 20 percent in 1970. The 1970 regional plan projected growth between then and 1985 at 1.9 percent per year, for a 1985 total of 1,950,000. However, if the national government's location policies succeed, the Stockholm region would be held to the 1970 20 percent share of the national population, which would mean a growth rate of 1 percent per year.

Actual population figures are somewhat confusing because of changes in the definition of the region. Until the mid-1960s, reports generally used figures for an area called Greater Stockholm that did not include all of Stockholm County. Later, Stockholm County became the commonly used area for regional data. Then, in 1971, some boundary adjustments with neighboring Uppsala County caused further changes in the area defined as the Stockholm region. A 1971 population figure for the region was 1,486,144.

While the national government has had only limited success with its industrial incentive program, it has another potential tool for restraining the Stockholm area's growth. The National Housing Board could cut the number of housing units allocated to the region and, by so doing, effectively limit residential construction.

Over the years, the government consistently has sought measures that would hold down the price of land. Now that pressure for single-family housing has increased, this becomes more important. On the average, Sweden has been building forty dwelling units per acre in multifamily housing but only sixteen units per acre in single family. If there is to be a major shift to single-family housing development, more land will be needed.

Several proposals and legislative amendments in the 1970s have furthered the objective of controlling land prices. A government advisory commission proposed in 1972 that all housing receiving National Housing Board loans be located on public land.[45] Since 90 percent of residential construction does receive such loans, this would virtually eliminate competition from private investors in the land market. It would be a significant but not enormous change from current practice. For the 1971–1975 period, municipalities projected that between two-thirds and three-quarters of housing would be built on public land.[46]

The commission also proposed that the National Housing Board's land acquisition loan fund for land to be leased be increased from its 1972–1973 level of $17 million ($15 million appropriated and $2 million repaid on outstanding loans) to $50 million per annum. This level of funding would enable municipalities to buy enough land for approximately 70 percent of all housing construction. It also was proposed that the loans be coordinated with the board's allocation of housing units. While this would not force unwilling municipalities to buy or build, it could be used to limit growth in the three big metropolitan areas. The commission felt that all save the largest cities were still hampered in their efforts to buy land because they lacked both income and buying power.

There continue to be problems with the lease-loan program. Essentially, the difficulty is that the national government expects municipalities to participate with it in subsidizing housing construction but that many municipalities find this too great a burden. The National Housing Board, acting through its county offices, determines site value and loans ninety-five percent of this at market interest plus 0.25 percent for administrative costs. During 1973, this totaled 7.25 percent. Before the loan is granted, the municipality must have borrowed on the private market to obtain acquisition funds, often paying a higher than market rate on a larger sum than the National Housing Board loan. The board in effect determines the maximum price at which the municipality may lease to developers who receive the board's construction loans. Often, the lease income does not cover repayments of the National Housing Board loan. There is a further limitation on income under leases, whether to housing developers with National Housing Board loans or to anyone else. Although the site lease-hold law has been amended to provide for an indefinite lease term,[47] the law continues to permit rent revisions only at ten-year intervals. Further, current value at the start of the lease term is the rent basis. Under conditions of inflation and/or rising land values, this means that the municipalities are receiving less than market value for their leases in all but the initial years of the ten-year terms.

There is yet another problem, one that is a matter of custom rather than law. The lease rate, conceptually though not in practice, is supposed to cover the interest that the municipality must pay on its land acquisition loans plus administrative costs. It does not cover amortization of the principal. The theory of this is that the land is an asset whose value constantly is appreciating; therefore, if necessary at some point, selling the land would more than cover the repayment of the principal. However, the municipality is in the position of paying interest and principal on the loans, public or private, that it has taken out to finance the land purchase. This means that general revenues must be used to cover the gap between lease income and payments due. Under the National Housing Board lease loan program, the principal must be repaid over forty years.

Given these various problems, the future of site leasing is unclear. As Peter Heimbürger has said, "Clearly site leasehold has become a political issue and opinions often tend to toe the party lines, which has not been conductive to a balanced discussion."[48]

The loan program for acquisition for lease nonetheless has increased steadily in scale from $6 million initially to $15 million in 1972–1973. Demand has outstripped the available funds. Between 1966 and 1972, thirty-nine municipalities borrowed $160 million to buy land and then leased enough land for the construction of 123,180 dwelling units. Many municipalities are denied the right to sell bonds by the Riksbank and so have no alternative to the National Housing Board programs[49] in financing land acquisition.

As of 1973, fifty-two municipalities were leasing land, thirty-one for both residential and industrial development, eight for residential uses only, and thirteen for industrial uses only. Between 1971 and 1975, 20 percent of all housing construction was expected to occur on leased land.[50]

Changes in the expropriation law have made it cheaper and easier for municipalities to acquire land. These changes have, as well, made it a very risky gamble for private entrepreneurs to invest in land. Prior to 1972, expropriation could be used only where land was needed for a specific urban use. Under the new law,[51] expropriation is permitted of "land that in view of future development is required for urban building development." This is interpreted to mean land that will be needed within the next twenty years. No longer, as under the 1949 law, can the owner avoid expropriation by showing a willingness to develop. In addition, surrounding land that would rise in value because of the prospective development may be expropriated, as may leasehold interests.[52]

Also under the new law, the price paid in expropriation is the market value of the land ten years prior to expropriation, determined by looking at comparable sales. This sum is corrected for changes in the value of the kronor. The law presumes that any rise in value in land during that decade was due to the anticipation of a change in use and to public investments, and takes the view that the owner should not be compensated for this. The landowner has the burden of proving that the increased value is attributable to something else. During a transition period that will end in 1981, any rise in value that had accrued as of mid-1971 will be paid. The past reluctance of municipalities to expropriate because of overly generous court awards to landowners has been acknowledged and resolved by this new law.

However, many local governments, particularly the fast-growing suburbs, complain that they have the power but not the means to acquire land reserves. They are dependent primarily on the local income tax for their revenues, and many feel that that is already as high as people can bear. The income tax is far and away the most important local tax. The total yield from it exceeds that from the national income tax. Both taxes are collected by the national government, with the local tax being returned to the municipality or county where levied.

In 1971, local governments spent $8.6 billion. Of this, $4.5 billion was raised by local taxes, $1.6 billion by other local revenues, $0.5 billion by borrowing, and only $2 billion, or under 25 percent, came from the national government.

The national income tax is progressive, with the rate increasing from 10 percent on a taxable income of $3,000 or less to a maximum of 37 percent on a taxable income of $30,000 or more. Since 1968, as previously mentioned, capital gains are treated as ordinary income. Individuals may not deduct their local tax payments in calculating taxable income for national tax purposes but corporations may. Corporations pay a flat 40 percent of taxable income to the national government. The income and net wealth taxes together provide 40 percent of the national government's revenue.

The local income tax rate is set by each municipality or county and is a flat rate for all individuals and corporations. There is no maximum local tax rate set by law, but elected officials are sensitive to the otherwise heavy tax burdens carried by their constituents. In 1973, the average municipal rate was 24 percent of the taxable income.

A corporation pays local income tax where it "has a permanent establishment or owns real property." If a corporation has several locations, its income will be allocated among them. If a corporation or individual owns real property, a presumed income is imputed, calculated currently as 2 percent of the assessed value.[53] Corporations occupying their own property do not have this presumed income imputed to them, but individuals do. If the actual income, less deductions, is higher, the owner must report the actual income.

One serious problem for rapidly growing municipalities is that the local income tax is not collected until two years after new residents or enterprises move in. There is, therefore, a lengthy gap between the time when the municipality must borrow to buy land, improve sites, and put in the infrastructure and the time when tax revenues begin to be received from the newly developed sites. The national government, in 1971, moved to help the municipalities by making available an advance on local income tax revenues expected in the coming year.[54]

The national government has taken one further step to strengthen municipal governments. As of 1 January 1974, the number of municipalities was reduced from the 1,000 existing since 1952 to 260. The minimum population of a municipality now is 8,000, with the median population 15,000. All municipalities now have an urban center, and the government hopes that all can provide an adequate level of services. In the Stockholm region, the municipal merges mandated by law have fostered the desire for local autonomy and the sense that the individual municipalities may be strong enough to plot their own courses without help or interference from Stockholm.

### The Stockholm County Council

Before describing the Stockholm County Council and its functions, it may be well to distinguish it from the roles of the Greater Stockholm Planning Authority and of the county administration of the national government.

Around 1950, when the city of Stockholm had spilled over its boundaries, the national government and local people began using an area described as Greater Stockholm for planning and statistical purposes. This area did not include five municipalities in Stockholm County, but it did include those most heavily populated (see map 2.3). The National Housing Board recognized the Greater Stockholm Planning Authority and allocated housing units to it for suballocation, a procedure that continues today. Since 1968, there has been a common housing queue for this area, so that a resident of Stockholm may seek vacancies in Täby, for example. Each municipality may reserve up to 20 percent of the housing it builds for those of its residents in greatest need, but the rest must be available on an equal basis to the residents of Greater Stockholm. Since 1971, the housing agency for Greater Stockholm also has allocated the municipalities' contribution to housing construction. In 1973, Stockholm's share was $8.7 million for housing in the city and $4 million for housing in the suburbs. Thus, while planning and land use functions now reside in the Stockholm County Council, the Greater Stockholm Planning Authority retains a dominant voice in housing matters.

At the county level, there are two operating governments—the county arm of national government (Länsstyrelsen) and the county council (Landsting) (see fig. 2.8). The governor and the county boards, representing the national government, review plans, collect taxes, and distribute national investment. In effect, the governor and his administration speak for the nation, while the county council attempts to speak for the metropolitan area.

The Stockholm County Council was created in 1971,[55] empowered to act much as the municipalities act in the areas of planning, land acquisition, land use controls, and taxation. The county council has 149 elected members, an executive committee of 17, and a 7-person committee of commissioners chosen by the executive committee. With a majority of the population, the suburbs have more seats than Stockholm on the county council. However, the city elects by far the largest single contingent.

Other than in Stockholm County,[56] regional planning by the county councils is voluntary. Construction and management of hospitals and the administration of some social welfare programs and some educational activities are common roles for the county councils. Their limitations are self-imposed, since the law grants them virtually all of the powers of the municipal government.

Stockholm County, by agreement with its member municipalities, levies an income tax that, in 1973, was 9 percent of taxable income. Most of the revenues from this tax were passed on to the municipalities as grants.

Stockholm County has taken over the construction and operation of the T-Bana System. Those who feel that the T-Bana has fallen markedly behind schedule in serving the newly developed areas tend to blame the county administration.

City officials had foreseen that the new county council would move eagerly to adopt as its own the city's commitment to provide decent hous-

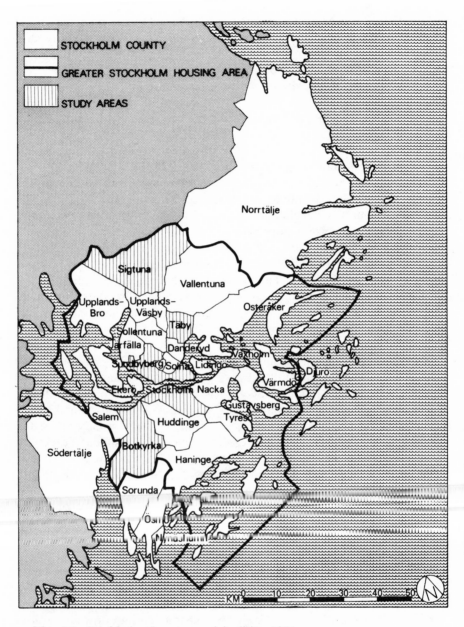

MAP 2.3.  Stockholm County municipalities, 1971

SOURCE:  Adapted from Thomas Atmer, letter, 1978

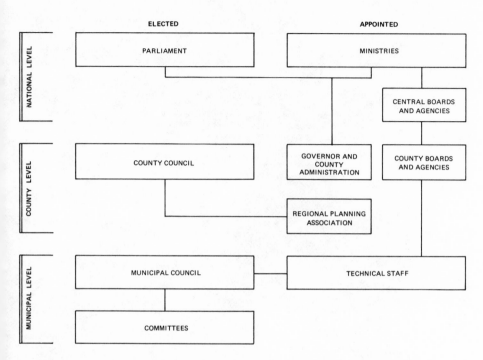

FIGURE 2.8. Swedish government structure

ing for all, using public land as a key element in policy implementation. The city, generously, was prepared to turn over much of its land to the county council for development. It also ceded to Terreno, the land acquisition company formed by the county council, the role of land banking for the region. In fact, the suburbanites were determined that the county should not be active in land acquisition and development. Such an outcome would give the individual municipalities too little control over the use of land within their borders. Therefore, they have permitted the county officials to buy land for public facilities, such as hospitals, subway stations, and parks, but not for a land reserve. The detail map of public land holdings in the central portion of Stockholm County is evidence of the small role played so far by the county council (map 2.4). Those powerful Stockholm politicians who lobbied enthusiastically for the creation of the county council must now wonder at their miscalculation either of the balance of power or of the basic concerns of those who would hold power in the county council. Torsten Ljungberger, dean of the city's land bank program, sees no hope for the county council as the land bank agency for the region and believes that Stockholm must reconstitute itself as in the past.[57]

MAP 2.4. Land ownership, 1970 (modified detail of map 2.1)

SOURCE: Adapted from Stockholm County Office, *Markägoförhållander*
[Land ownership situation] (map) (Stockholm, 1970)

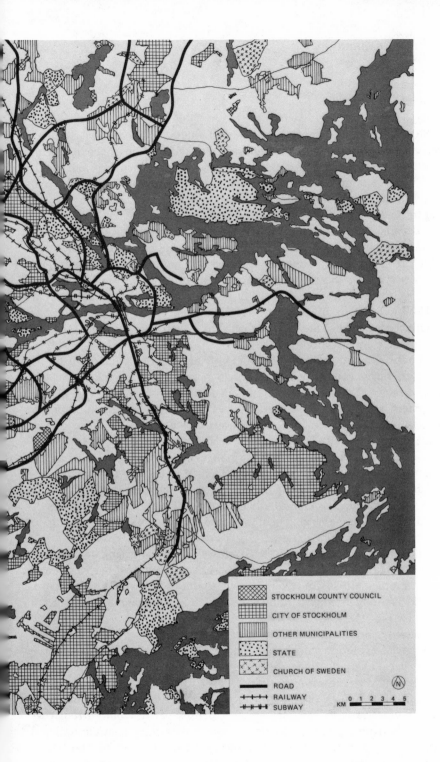

STOCKHOLM COUNTY COUNCIL

CITY OF STOCKHOLM

OTHER MUNICIPALITIES

STATE

CHURCH OF SWEDEN

ROAD

RAILWAY

SUBWAY

KM  0 1 2 3 4 5

*Stockholm Today*

Stockholm only recently has realized that it is no longer rich. As people and jobs have moved to the suburbs, the city has been left with aging structures, each needing more in the way of maintenance and yielding less revenue than before. Although the income tax rather than the real property tax is Stockholm's principal revenue source, its financial plight is similar to that of many American cities.

For decades Stockholm provided leadership and initiative in planning for growth, buying land, and making decent housing available at prices all could afford. Suddenly, all this has changed. No more land is being bought for the reserve, and the terms of the city's lease program are being challenged. Apartment vacancies have shot up from an average of 1.8 percent from 1967 to 1971 to 7.7 percent in 1972, evidence that not everyone has been satisfied with what Stockholm provided. Much is in flux, but it is too soon to predict the direction of changes.

Stockholm entered the decade owning 40 percent of the land within its borders, or thirty square miles, plus two hundred square miles of land outside the city limits. This was enough land for many years of future development and for regional parks to serve the growing population, so there was no need for further acquisitions on the scale of those in the 1960s. However, the city foresaw the need for some public body to step in and acquire key sites in areas nearly ripe for development. This could be the municipality in which the land was located. The city's leaders, however, had hoped it would be the county council that would act. When the council was created, Stockholm still had over 50 percent of the county's population, but this soon changed; with the change went the capacity to dominate county council decisions.

Another rude shock was the 1973 refusal of the Riksbank to approve Stockholm's request to sell some bonds. Stockholm long had been the envy of other municipalities for its record of success in gaining such bank approval. The city's reduced financial strength is thought to have been a major reason for the Riksbank rebuff.

Regrettably, it is impossible to trace the role of land banking in the city's financial evolution. Stockholm's borrowings for land purchases have been, for decades, part of general borrowing to finance various city operations. There is no account in the city budget to show, from year to year, how much of the city's outstanding debt is allocable to land purchases. The city's practice is to pay for capital expenses partly from current revenues, partly from the sale of bonds to cover borrowings from the national government or private sources, and partly from the sale of short-term notes to cover other borrowings. Amortization provisions vary from loan to loan. On occasion, bonds are paid off by the proceeds from the sale of new bonds. Even though one cannot segregate land transactions, it is possible to show that the city's revenues from its leases are at a lower interest rate than it is paying on its loans. The city always has held to the view that it should not profit from its investments, including land, but opinion has fluctuated over time and is dependent on an individual's politics and job as to whether the return from public land should cover land-related costs or be subsidized from other city revenues. For decades, by not attempting to cover the cost of amortizing principal, the latter view prevailed. "Real estate operators are not regarded as a source of revenue. . . . Any profits in the accounts would be regarded as evidence that rents could be lower."[58] Whether they actually did or not, lease revenues were supposed to have covered interest costs, site planning, ground improvements, infrastructure, and administrative costs, but never principal costs.

One must not overlook the fact that many of the lease rates were set for sixty years, so that what might have been a reasonable rate in 1910 was far from reasonable when the lease expired in 1970. Peter Heimbürger has calculated that a residential lease of 7,700 square feet was priced at $36 per year in 1915, $308 per year in 1968, and $692 per year in 1973.[59] Fifty-five percent of Stockholm's residents live on leased land. Stockholm holds twenty-four thousand leases in the city and two thousand leases in the suburbs. Of these twenty-six thousand leases, seventeen thousand were entered into with sixty-year terms. Since the law was not changed to establish twenty-year residential terms until 1953, some of the sixty-year leases won't expire until 2013. The twenty-year leases won't expire until 1988, since the ten-year residential leases came into being in 1968. These long-term, fixed-rent lease provisions result in obvious inequities among lessees, and they also lead to the city's receiving ridiculously low income from many properties.

The city currently is debating what policy to establish for leases coming up for renegotiation of rates as well as for new leases. In 1973, the Real Estate Office decided to base lease rates on the market value of land. For new residential leases, the average cost of raw land at Botkyrka and Järvafältet would be used. For renegotiated residential leases, 70 percent of assessed value would be used. For commercial, nonprofit, and industrial leases, market value, as evidenced by recent sales either in the city or in nearby municipalities, or expropriation awards would be used. The rate charged on the base would be 5.1 percent for residential properties, 16 percent for industrial sites, and 9 percent for other uses. However, at the time that this decision was made, government loans were running at 7.25 percent, and the weighted average lease rate was less than this.

The financial office of the city views the past and present lease policies as ruinous and politically motivated. Its staff proposes using the market value, adjusting it annually with a price index, and setting the rate at the city's borrowing rate. A committee is looking into the question, well aware that, in the words of one prominent official, "the lease program is a religion with many people. They don't want to look too closely at the facts for fear of what they might find." The essential question that the city must resolve is whether lease rates should cover land costs or whether the city's general revenues should continue to be used to subsidize these costs. In 1973, it was estimated that there was an $8 million gap between lease income and interest due on loans to cover land investments,[60] so the question is not an insignificant one.

One of the most fascinating unresolved questions is that of who will develop Stockholm's vast suburban holdings and who will pay for this development. There is near unanimity that the city can't afford another Botkyrka, but the alternatives remain to be explored. The county council could be invested with new strength by its members, the municipalities could bargain with Stockholm to buy sites, or the national government could assume a larger share of the costs. Stockholm, in a total rejection of past philosophy, could sell sites to the highest bidder, but this seems the least probable alternative. Growth may slow in the region, either as a result of national government policy or market tendencies, but there will still be a considerable volume of development, much of it at lower densities than in the past. Therefore, there is little question but that there will be a demand for much of the city-owned land.

APPENDIX

Cost of Living and Kronor/Dollar Exchange, 1914–1974

TABLE 2.8. Cost of Living and Kronor/Dollar Exchange, 1914–1974

| Year | Cost of Living Index | Swedish Kronor per Dollar | Year | Cost of Living Index | Swedish Kronor per Dollar |
|------|------|------|------|------|------|
| 1914 | 100 | 3.80 | 1944 | 234 | 4.20 |
| 1915 | 115 | 3.86 | 1945 | 233 | 4.20 |
| 1916 | 130 | 3.50 | 1946 | 234 | 3.92 |
| 1917 | 164 | 3.13 | 1947 | 240 | 3.60 |
| 1918 | 232 | 3.09 | 1948 | 252 | 3.60 |
| 1919 | 268 | 3.96 | 1949 | 256 | 4.04 |
| 1920 | 269 | 4.93 | 1950 | 259 | 5.18 |
| 1921 | 231 | 4.46 | 1951 | 300 | 5.18 |
| 1922 | 187 | 3.83 | 1952 | 324 | 5.18 |
| 1923 | 174 | 3.77 | 1953 | 328 | 5.18 |
| 1924 | 174 | 3.76 | 1954 | 330 | 5.18 |
| 1925 | 177 | 3.73 | 1955 | 339 | 5.18 |
| 1926 | 171 | 3.74 | 1956 | 356 | 5.18 |
| 1927 | 169 | 3.73 | 1957 | 372 | 5.18 |
| 1928 | 170 | 3.73 | 1958 | 388 | 5.18 |
| 1929 | 168 | 3.73 | 1959 | 381 | 5.18 |
| 1930 | 163 | 3.73 | 1960 | 407 | 5.17 |
| 1931 | 158 | 4.02 | 1961 | 416 | 5.17 |
| 1932 | 155 | 5.43 | 1962 | 436 | 5.16 |
| 1933 | 151 | 4.66 | 1963 | 449 | 5.20 |
| 1934 | 152 | 3.86 | 1964 | 463 | 5.16 |
| 1935 | 155 | 3.97 | 1965 | 486 | 5.17 |
| 1936 | 157 | 3.91 | 1966 | 518 | 5.17 |
| 1937 | 161 | 3.93 | 1967 | 540 | 5.17 |
| 1938 | 165 | 3.98 | 1968 | 550 | 5.17 |
| 1939 | 169 | 4.17 | 1969 | 566 | 5.18 |
| 1940 | 190 | 4.20 | 1970 | 605 | 5.19 |
| 1941 | 215 | 4.20 | 1971 | 650 | 5.11 |
| 1942 | 232 | 4.20 | 1972 | 689 | 4.76 |
| 1943 | 235 | 4.20 | 1973 | | 4.37 |
| | | | 1974 | | 4.41 |

SOURCE: Thomas Atmer, Head of Division of the Stockholm Town Planning Department, provided annual conversion rates from kronor to dollars, as well as a cost of living index for Sweden during this period.

NOTES

1. Much of the information here, as well as in subsequent sections, is derived from the excellent master's thesis, "Municipal Land Reserves in Sweden: Key to Planning Success," written by Shirley S. Passow in 1969.

2. Heimbürger, in his thorough, detailed report, "The Use of Municipal Land Ownership As an Instrument in Influencing the Structure of Urban Development: Sweden's Experience," further describes Swedish tenure practices prior to the twentieth century.

3. Freund, "Swedish Public Domain," p. 119.

4. Passow, "Municipal Land Reserves," p. 52, quoting from an interview with Yngve Larsson.

5. Stockholm City Planning and Building Office, "Land Acquisition and Leasehold System."

6. Interview with Hjalmar Mehr, now governor of Stockholm County and, from 1958 to 1966, finance commissioner of Stockholm City Council.

7. SFS [Svensk Författnings Samling] 1928: 370.

8. SFS 1907.

9. Heimbürger, "Site Leasehold in Sweden," p. 1.

10. Heimbürger, in "Site Leasehold in Sweden," p. 30, quotes the city council as saying:

> "the cost price to the City corresponds to the market value to which the City has contributed through its development and its previous constructions. . . . The City may not, however, figure as a speculator in new, unmerited appreciations deriving from the enterprise of individuals or their mutual competition. The City should therefore endeavor to find a golden mean in the fluctuating market value, which no doubt is most often to be found in lower reaches of that value."

11. Ljungberger, "Land Policy and Development."

12. Stockholm City Planning and Building Office, "Land Acquisition and Leasehold System," p. 3.

13. Heimbürger, "Site Leasehold in Sweden." See this article for details on redemption provisions.

14. Passow's data for 1904–1967 were used for this calculation ("Municipal Land Reserves," pp. 9, 10).

15. Ibid.

16. See Strong, Planned Urban Environments for details about the planning and development in Vällingby and Farsta.

17. Hanson, Stockholm Municipal Politics.

18. SFS 1946.

19. SFS 1947. 385.

20. SFS 1917: 189, as amended by SFS 1949: 663.

21. SFS 1952.

22. SFS 1907: 1734, as amended by SFS 1953: 415.

23. SFS 1959: 612.

24. Ljungberger, "Land Policy and Development," p. 6.

25. Neutze, "Land and Land Use Planning."

26. Heimbürger, "Site Leasehold in Sweden."

27. SFS 1964: 822. Naturvårdslag [Nature conservation]. The act also provides for national parks and for protection of some species of plants and animals.

28. SFS 1964. Lex Bollmora [the law that allows Stockholm to act as a developer in other municipalities].

29. SFS 1966.

30. SFS 1967: 878.

31. SFS 1967: 869.

32. SOU [Sveriges Offentliga Utredningar] 1964: 42.
33. Carlegrim, "Real Estate Market."
34. SOU 1966: 23, 24.
35. SFS 1967: 868.
36. SFS 1967: 748–755, amending SFS 1928: 370. Realisationsvinst [Capital gains tax].
37. According to the National Housing Board, Botkyrka, Huddinge, Järfälla, Nacka, Södertälje, Sollentuna, Solna, Stockholm, Sundbyberg, Tyresö, Upplands-Bro, Upplands-Väsby, and Värmdö all lease.
38. Interview, 13 Nov. 1973.
39. Comments about Botkyrka's development are from an interview with P. O. Sandquist and Sven Ivar Jansson, 8 Nov. 1973.
40. Höjer and Ljungquist, "New Residential Areas in the Stockholm Region," p. 19.
41. Much of the information about Märsta comes from Stig Gunnerfeldt, Planner, Sigtuna Municipality.
42. See Strong, Planned Urban Environments, for further details about the Täby center plans.
43. Hovinen, "Land Tenure and Residential Development."
44. Information about Täby's current land practices is from an interview with Councilman Göran Elgfeld and Mr. Månsson, Town Planner, 2 Nov. 1973.
45. SOU 1972: 40.
46. Heimbürger, "Municipal Land Ownership."
47. SFS 1970: 994.
48. Heimbürger, "Site Leasehold in Sweden," p. 37.
49. Ibid., During 1970, loans for the purchase of land for resale totaled $7.7 million.
50. Heimbürger, "Site Leasehold in Sweden."
51. SFS 1971: 122.
52. SFS 1972: 719.
53. For a more detailed discussion, see Neutze, "Land and Land Use Planning."
54. SFS 1971: 13.
55. SFS 1971: 156.
56. SFS 1969: 215.
57. Interview on 13 Nov. 1973, translated from Swedish by Christina Engfeld.
58. Neutze, "Land and Land Use Planning."
59. Heimbürger, "Site Leasehold in Sweden."
60. Interview with Ingrid Riddarstrand, city attorney's office, 12 Nov. 1973.

## PERSONS INTERVIEWED

Carl F. Ahlberg, Director of the Stockholm Regional Planning Commission, repeated discussions in October and November 1973

Thomas Atmer, head of Research and Long Term Planning, and Stefan Strom, Stockholm City Planning Commission, 16 October 1973

Curt Berg, Stockholm Real Estate Board, 30 October and 14 November 1973

Arne Bergkvist, Järva Development Company, 6 November 1973

Harry Bernhard, Deputy Director General, National Housing Board of Sweden, 31 October 1973

Goran Elgfeld, Councilman, and Mr. Mänsson, Town Planner, Täby, 2 November 1973

Stig Gunnerfeldt, Planner, Sigtuna Municipality, 9 November 1973

Per Holm, Professor of Regional Planning, Technical High School, 23 October 1973

Sven Jönsson, Vice Managing Director, STRADA, 29 October 1973
Torsten Ljungberger, STRADA, 13 November 1973
J. H. Martin, Stockholm Real Estate Board, 26 October 1973
Hjalmar Mehr, Governor of Stockholm County and, from 1958 to 1966, Finance
Commissioner of Stockholm City Council, 13 November 1973
Ingrid Riddarstrand, an attorney for the City of Stockholm, 12 November 1973
P. O. Sandquist and Sven Ivar Jönsson, planners, Botkyrka Municipality, 8
November 1973
Goran Sidenbladh, now retired, long-time Stockholm city planning director, 22
October 1973
Sten Wickbom, head of legal section, Ministry of Physical Planning and Local
Government, and Rolf Stromberg, 25 October 1973

### REFERENCES

Anton, Thomas J. *Governing Greater Stockholm: A Study of Policy Development and System Change*. Berkeley and Los Angeles: University of California Press, 1975.
Atmer, Thomas. "Transport Lines between Planned Communities and the Central City in the Greater Stockholm Area." Paper prepared for Urban Environment and Land Use Sector Group, Organization for Economic Cooperation and Development, Paris, 1972.
Bagstevold, Kjell. "How Much Can the Plan Influence the Development?" Stockholms Lans Landsting, paper 1972–09–05. Mimeographed.
Carlberg, E. Casten. Untitled paper for 1973 International Federation for Housing and Planning Congress. Theme 1, 1:D5–9. Mimeographed.
Carlegrim, Erik. "Real Estate Market, 1957–1963." National Institute for Building Research, Report 10:1966.
Freund, Rudolf. "Squandering the Public Domain in Sweden, 1820–1870." *Journal of Land and Public Utility Economics* 22 (1946): 119–30.
Hanson, Bertil Lennart. *Stockholm Municipal Politics*. Cambridge, Mass.: Joint Center for Urban Studies of the Massachusetts Institute of Technology and Harvard University, 1960.
Heimbürger, Peter. "Site Leasehold in Sweden." Paper prepared for National Board of Urban Planning. 1974.
————. "The Use of Municipal Land Ownership As an Instrument in Influencing the Structure of Urban Development: Sweden's Experience." Paper prepared for the Organization for Economic Cooperation and Development, Paris, 1973.
Höjer, Jan, and Ljungquist, Sture. "Organization and Financing of New Residential Areas in the Stockholm Region." Report to the Organization for Economic Cooperation and Development, n.d. Mimeographed.
Hovinen, Gary R. "Land Tenure and Residential Development in Greater Stockholm." Ph.D. dissertation, University of Minnesota, 1971.
Land Policy Commission. "Kommunal Markpolitik" [Municipal land policy]. Report 1. 1964.

Land Value Committee of 1963. "Markfrogan I ach II" [The land questions 1 and 2]. 1966.

Ljungberger, Torsten. "Land Policy and Development." In *Stockholm, 1919–1969*. Stockholm: Stockholm City Real Estate Board, n.d.

Neutze, G. Max. "Policy Instruments in the Urban Land Market: Analysis and Conclusions." Paper prepared for the Organization for Economic Cooperation and Development, Sector Group on the Urban Environment, U/CHG/73.474, September 1973. Summary Report, U/ENV/73.21, September 1973. Final report entitled "The Price of Land and Land Use Planning: Policy Instruments in the Urban Land Market." Organization for Economic Cooperation and Development. Paris, 1973.

Norr, Martin; Sandels, Claes; and Hornhammar, Niles. *The Tax System in Sweden*. Stockholm: Skandinaviska Enskilda Banken, 1972.

Ödmann, Ella. "Some Views on Land Ownership in Urban Planning and Housing Production in Sweden." *Geoforum* 13 (1973).

Ödmann, Ella, and Dahlberg, Gun-Britt. *Urbanization in Sweden*. Stockholm: National Institute of Building and Urban Planning Research, 1970.

Pass, David. "Vällingby and Farsta: From Idea to Reality." Ph.D. dissertation, Stockholm, 1969.

Passow, Shirley S. "Municipal Land Reserves in Sweden: Key to Planning Success." Master's thesis, Columbia University, 1969.

Romberg, Roberta V., and Vitarello, James D. "The Law As a Positive Framework for Future Development." Mimeographed. Stockholm: University of Stockholm, School of Law, 1971.

Skandinaviska Enskilda Banken. *Some Data about Sweden*. Sodertalje: Skandinaviska Enskilda Banken, 1972.

Stockholm City Planning and Building Office. *The City of Stockholm's Land Area, 1970*. Stockholm, 1970.

————. "Land Acquisition and Leasehold System in Stockholm." Stockholm, December 1967. Mimeographed.

Stockholms Stadsbygnadskontor. *Stockholm Urban Environment*. Stockholm, 1972.

Strong, Ann Louise. *Planned Urban Environments: Sweden, Finland, Israel, the Netherlands, France*. Baltimore: The Johns Hopkins Press, 1971.

Sweden. Ministry for Foreign Affairs and Ministry of Agriculture. "Urbanization and Planning in Sweden." Paper prepared for the United Nations conference on the human environment, Stockholm, 1972.

Sweden. Ministry of Labour and Housing and Ministry of Physical Planning and Local Government. *Planning Sweden*. English summary of *Priserna På Jordbruks-Fastigheter*, 1967. Stockholm: Allmanna forlaget, 1973.

Sweden. National Central Bureau of Statistics. *Agricultural Real Estate Prices, 1967*. Stockholm, 1969.

Sweden. National Housing Board. *Municipal Land Policy in Sweden*. Stockholm: The National Swedish Institute for Building Research, 1970.

# 3

# Land Banking
# in the Netherlands


### Achievements, Problems, and Prospects

For decades it has been the customary practice of most Dutch municipalities to buy land a few years in advance of development, prepare it for development, and then sell or lease the actual development sites, retaining a substantial portion of the land for roads, parks, and community facilities. Land banking has been the first step toward plan implementation, making it possible to provide housing sites in an attractive setting at moderate cost and to develop land in an efficient and orderly manner. There also has been an intent, poorly realized, to garner for the municipality increases in land value.

In 1971, 83 percent of the land offered for development was acquired from municipal land development enterprises. Of this land, 31 percent was leased rather than sold to the developer. The land development enterprises buy an average of eleven thousand acres yearly. Another eleven thousand move into development or permanent municipal holdings for public purposes. Therefore, the municipalities are buying at a rate consistent with development demands.

Land need not be acquired far in advance of need, since it is valued according to current use, holding down carrying costs. Because landowners recognize that little, if any, opportunity for speculation exists and are persuaded that municipalities pay a fair price for land, there is general

100

acquiescence to municipal proposals. In 1971, for instance, only 4 percent of the acquisitions required recourse to eminent domain. On the average, prices ranged from $9,000 per acre (seven guilders[1] per square meter) in rural municipalities to $22,000 per acre (seventeen guilders per square meter) in cities of 100,000 or more. These prices include the value of land for its current use, the value of structures, and compensation for consequential damages, and they run between two and three times farmland value.

A further benefit of the system of payment of compensation for land based on current use rather than potential future use is that owners of land planned for continued use as farms know that they have not been discriminated against economically as a result of the restriction of their land to farming.

Loans for land acquisition come from the Bank for Netherlands Municipalities or, for subsidized housing, from the national government. Although the bank is a joint endeavor of state and local government, the state determines how much the bank may lend, to whom, and for what purposes. Therefore, although municipalities initiate land banking endeavors, they cannot come to fruition without state approval.

For the Netherlands as a whole, land acquisition cost accounts for 15 percent of the sale or lease price. In areas below sea level, where much fill and drainage are needed, land accounts for only around 5 percent of the disposition price. In 1969, prices for residential land ranged from a low of $31,000 per acre (twenty-four guilders per square meter) in small cities to an average of $111,000 per acre (eighty-five guilders per square meter) in Amsterdam, Rotterdam, and The Hague, the three largest cities. Industrial land prices ranged from a low of $21,000 per acre (sixteen guilders per square meter) to an average of $69,000 per acre (fifty-three guilders per square meter) in the three large cities.

There is much variation among the municipalities and among different land uses as to whether land is sold or leased and whether the municipality profits, breaks even, or loses money on its land bank transactions. The predominant intention seems to be to make a small profit; since there is no profit on land disposition for subsidized housing, this must come from private housing, commercial, and/or industrial uses. However, some municipalities choose to run their land banks at a loss, while others have this result whether or not they so intend.

In general, people are satisfied with the Dutch land banking system, and there is no move to change it. While I admire what has been achieved, I believe that there are existing and incipient problems that call for resolution.

The Dutch purport to vest the municipalities with the principal decision-making power in the area of growth management. Yet, in fact, the municipalities cannot borrow to buy land without provincial and state approval. The state does have national growth management policies that could be implemented, in part, through the approval process for municipal acquisitions and municipal borrowing. Land acquisition loans for subsidized housing similarly could be granted or withheld dependent on the desirability, from a national perspective, of development in a particular municipality.

Municipalities are dependent on the state for 90 percent of their revenues, and many regularly run a considerable deficit. The state could encourage or require selected municipalities or all municipalities to alter their land disposition terms so as to realize the increase in value of the sites over the years and thus increase municipal revenues. To date, it has not taken this initiative.

Last, the question of what units of government—central cities, suburban municipalities, and/or newly formed regions—should be responsible for land banking in the future demands thoughtful consideration. It is a fact that many central cities, saddled with debt and resented by their smaller neighbors, are not going to continue buying land unless given increased revenues and broader powers. So far, some suburban municipalities have managed land bank programs successfully while others have been short of money and management skills. If they are to have principal responsibility in the future, they will need greater assistance from the state. Alternatively, if the national government should conclude that its growth policies can best be fostered by regional agencies, it will need to create such agencies and establish their roles in relation to that of municipal government.

As in the Stockholm region, metropolitan expansion has brought increasing power to the suburbs. It is for the national government to evaluate whether this power is likely to be used in a manner compatible with national interests and, if so, to reinforce the suburban municipalities and, if not, to lodge greater power elsewhere. Dutch planners, government officials, and politicians hold a range of views on this issue but have yet to make it a matter of extended, public debate. The time is ripe for such a debate and for national leadership.

### The Origins of Dutch Land Banking

The Dutch began land banking in 1896 in Amsterdam, a few years before the Swedes. The immediate reasons for instituting land banking in the Netherlands were different from those that motivated Stockholm and other Swedish cities, yet underlying national values were comparable.

Two related factors provided the impetus for land banking. First, the principal cities were entering a period of extremely rapid growth. Amsterdam, after a decline in the late eighteenth and early nineteenth centuries, had completed construction of the North Sea Canal in 1874. This stimulated the growth of shipping and industry. Rotterdam's port was expanding rapidly. The Hague was also receiving a share of the large migration of workers from the farms to the cities. The powerful Liberal party, many of whose members were merchants, endorsed municipal land acquisition as the sole way in which enough housing could be provided to meet the needs of the influx of newcomers. So, while provision of workers' housing was the dominant motive for land acquisition, the generating factor was inmigration to the cities rather than emigration as in Sweden.

Second, since most of the land to be developed was below sea level and consisted of a layer of peat averaging sixty to seventy feet in depth, extensive and expensive site improvements were needed before construction could start. Given a preexisting, intricate national system for drainage of land below sea level,[2] it is hardly surprising that it was considered more appropriate for the public sector than the private to acquire land and prepare it for development.

Consistently from 1900 until today, the Netherlands and Sweden have shared similar social values. Both countries have always viewed public real estate programs as a means of furthering the public interest, and both have seen the public interest as including adequate housing and a decent living environment for all.

The land acquisition practices of the large Dutch cities prior to World War II were roughly parallel. Land was bought as it came on the market if the price was attractive. If the land were outside the municipal borders, it might or might not be annexed, depending on both political and planning considerations. The Hague, for instance, in 1900 and 1920, annexed substantial areas that included large municipally owned tracts. Amsterdam's last major annexations were in 1923.

Whether land was sold or leased for development varied from city to city. Amsterdam always leased its land. From 1896 to 1915, it leased on a seventy-five-year term, at the end of which the structures as well as the site were to belong to the city, without payment of compensation. With a high rate of growth—doubling from 230 thousand to 460 thousand in forty years—the municipal council thought that the benefit of the anticipated sharp rise in land values should accrue to the public. However, there was some reluctance on the part of potential lessees to give up all claim to compensation should the lease be terminated, so, in 1915, the city switched to a perpetual lease with terms of fifty years. The lease rate was 4 to 6 percent of the land value, adjusted every five years for changes in the value of the guilder. The basic rate could be revised only at the end of a term. If the municipality terminated the lease, compensation was payable for structures.

*Legislation Affecting Land Banking*

Soon after land banking was launched as a municipal undertaking, several laws were passed that affected Dutch planning and development.

The Housing Act of 1901, which was in actuality both a housing and a planning act, required municipalities with a population in excess of 10,000 to prepare extension plans for land adjoining built-up areas and to submit these plans to the provincial government for approval. The plans allocated sites for development as well as for such open space uses as agriculture, natural area preserves, and shaping development. Land included within an approved expansion plan could be bought by the municipality for improvement prior to development.

By a 1901 amendment to the Compulsory Purchase Act of 1851,[3] if a municipality were unable to negotiate a voluntary purchase of land needed for housing, that land could be acquired by eminent domain. The act was amended again in 1908, to authorize eminent domain for all land shown in an expansion plan as intended for development. Use of eminent domain by Dutch cities dates back to the Middle Ages, when rulers would issue letters patent to municipal councils enabling them to condemn sites for waterworks, fortifications, and expansion. One Dutch planner has noted:

Of old, the Dutch have been familiar with the idea that far-reaching measures must be taken by the authorities in consequence of the necessity to guard the country against inundation. This circumstance has probably contributed to the fact that expropriation in the Netherlands is more readily accepted than in most other countries.[4]

Since 1789, the Constitution has provided that eminent domain might occur only where there is a public necessity and upon payment of full compensation. Implementation of an approved extension plan is assumed to be an act of public necessity, so eminent domain for this purpose requires only an order of a municipal council, confirmed by a royal decree. Eminent domain for roads, railroads, canals, docks, and airports, is also by royal decree. Other eminent domain actions require that Parliament pass an Act of Utility declaring that there is a public necessity.

In an eminent domain proceeding, if the municipality and the seller are unable to agree on the purchase price, three court-appointed experts recommend a price to the court. There is no appeal from the court's decision as to the amount of the award. The 1851 act states that "by allowing appeal, one would only encourage proscrastination and proceedings without adequate grounds."

Since 1920, the municipality has been entitled to ask the court for immediate possession of the property being condemned. Interest at the rate of 5 percent is payable when the compensation award finally is made.

Implementation of the Housing Act of 1901 reflects a Dutch attitude toward public control of land use that has remained consistent over the years. The municipalities have enjoyed strong public support for land acquisition and for the use of eminent domain where a voluntary approach fails. Land acquisition has been used only for land planned for development. Municipalities have not considered purchasing land planned for open space uses other than public parks, since limitation to such uses by plan and without compensation was considered fair and equitable.

### Financing Land Acquisition

Land banking began at a time of declining municipal financial capability. Until 1865, municipalities had been autonomous in their power to raise revenues and had relied extensively on excise taxes. This was thought to impede the free movement of goods, so, gradually, the national government took control over the taxing power. The municipalities then found it increasingly difficult to borrow for public acquisition and site improvement.

In 1914, the Association of Netherlands Municipalities founded the Municipal Credit Bank, with the intent that most of the 1,120 municipalities then in existence should subscribe to shares. The capital was to be used for municipal loans. Regrettably, by 1916, only thirty-seven municipalities had joined, paying in the paltry total of $14,000.

Concluding that the initial concept wouldn't work, the Association of Netherlands Municipalities sought national participation and, in 1922, reorganized the bank under the still current name of the Bank for Netherlands Municipalities. This time, the national government put up half of the capital, and the government's Central Bank agreed to discount municipal promissory notes. In addition to the national government, there are 740 shareholders, including provinces, polder boards, and other public bodies as well as municipalities. Each member holding at least twenty-eight shares receives six votes; the state, even though it invested half of the capital, has only six votes.

The bank is governed by a board consisting of the minister of internal affairs and the minister of finance, acting ex officio, two people nominated by the Association of Netherlands Municipalities, four people who are members of the colleges of burgomaster and aldermen[5] of the member municipalities, and three people chosen from the population at large. The board is elected at a meeting of shareholders.

Since the reorganization in 1922, the bank has been the principal source of funds for municipal land acquisition.

### Current Conditions

Since World War II, almost all development in medium and large Dutch metropolitan areas has occurred on land previously acquired by a municipality. For many years after the war there was a severe housing shortage, the municipal governments saw public land acquisition as an important means of speeding up housing construction and keeping housing costs down.

The great need of extensive areas for the building of houses and other necessary buildings after the war, has brought home to most Municipalities that they should aim unswervingly at acquiring the required real estate in time and as much as possible in large areas, forming one uninterrupted whole, after which the Municipalities themselves, either calling in the assistance of building-contractors or not, take the opening-up in their own hand. . . . In executing all the works themselves, the Municipalities have the control of the speed[y] opening-up [of] the area, and the possibility that certain parts, from speculative considerations, would lie fallow for a shorter or longer period, has been done away with. For the purpose of the Municipality is not to make profits, but to supply the existing needs as adequately as possible.[6]

As housing pressures have eased in the 1970s, there has been a modest increase in private development on private land, but this still remains a small share of total development activity. In 1971, 83 percent of development was on land bought or leased from municipalities. Leasing is becoming increasingly important, particularly in the larger municipalities. In 1971, 31 percent of the municipal land offered for development was leased. Altogether, in 1963, some 10 percent of the country was in public ownership. A substantial portion of this was new polder land created by the national government. Initially, all of this land, whether used for farms or urban uses, remained in public ownership. Currently, some is being offered for sale. Leasing of municipal land has become increasingly common since 1963, so the percentage of land in public ownership has undoubtedly increased.

Landowners have accepted the fact that if their land is planned for development it will be purchased by a municipality several years prior to development. There is no need for public purchase many years in advance of development in order to avoid speculative prices, for it also is accepted that a fair purchase price is one equal to farm value plus moving, resettlement, and, possibly, retraining expenses, plus compensation for the disruptive effect of moving. The total price is from two to three times the farm value. A fair price is not thought to be what an owner might have been able to obtain had the land been sold to a private developer. Landowners whose land is planned for continued low-intensity uses do not clamor for compensation for denial of the right to develop, since neighbors whose land is acquired for development do not reap a speculative harvest.

Developers accept the land banking role of the municipalities to such an extent that frequently they buy attractive sites, sell them to a municipality for a nominal sum, and then lease or buy them back for development after the sites are ready. One large developer, the Empeo group of the Bredero Company, looks ahead about five years and determines likely sites for residential, commercial or industrial use, consults with the municipality where a site is located as to the compatibility of the company's objectives with those of the municipality, and, if the municipal response is favorable, buys the land. It then sells the land to the municipality for the nominal sum of one guilder. Alternatively, when the land is planned for housing the municipality may negotiate the purchase, with Empeo putting up the money. In either case, the municipality agrees to prepare the land, put in improvements, and then lease or sell the land to the company for development. If housing is to be built, there will be an agreement as to the split between subsidized, partly subsidized, and private units. Empeo favors working with municipalities for two reasons: it assures that the sites chosen by the developer will be included in the municipalities' development plans, and it contributes to the social objective of keeping both aided and private housing costs down.[7]

If a private entrepreneur risks buying land without municipal approval, the municipality may not include the land in its development plan. One Utrecht builder paid $0.18 per square foot (six guilders per square meter) for land, intending to create a lake and adjacent commercial recreation area. The local development plan was changed so that this was not a permitted use, and the land value plummeted to $0.03 per square foot (one guilder per square meter).

Alternatively, a municipality may expropriate a developer's land if, in its view, the proposed residential development will not provide an appropriate social mix. Such action was recently upheld on appeal on the ground that, since the developer could not by law build low-income housing and therefore obtain a proper social balance, it was proper for the municipality to expropriate and develop the site.

The Dutch approach to land banking is calm, low key, and rational. For them it has worked extremely well. Whether it will continue to do so depends on several factors, chief among them what governmental entities will control urban fringe development and what funds will be available for land acquisition. The divergence of interests between central cities and suburban municipalities and the financial problems of the central cities have strong parallels to conditions in Sweden and the United States.

*Growth*

One constant factor underlying the commitment to municpal land acquisition has been growth. The Netherlands is one of the most urban, most densely populated countries in the world. The 1900 population was 5.1 million, of which 66 percent was urban, that is, in municipalities with a population of 5,000 or more. In 1950, the population had risen to 10 million, of whom 85 percent were urban. Thirty-one percent of the people lived in municipalities with populations in excess of 100,000. By 1969, despite some success in promoting emigration, the population had risen to 12.8 million; 91 percent of the people then lived in urban areas, and 58 percent lived in agglomerations in excess of 100,000. As in other developed countries, the major cities have been losing population while people spread out into the suburbs. (See fig. 3.1 and map 3.1.) For the Netherlands this is a particularly serious problem. The nation, as a result of widespread hunger during World War II, has a commitment to agricultural self-sufficiency. There simply is not enough land to accommodate the wishes of a growing population for single-family detached housing and to assure the desired farm yield.

With one of the world's lowest death rates—7 per 1,000 people in 1971—and a birth rate that year of 20 per 1,000 people, the Netherlands in 1971 projected an annual increase of 1.5 percent and a population in the year 2000 of ± 16 million. Since then, due in part to the widespread use of contraception, the projection has been revised downward to around 16 million. Already, 7 percent of the land is developed; this would double by 2000 according to current projections.

The Randstad is the area subject to the greatest development pressure. Roughly defined, it is part of the provinces of North Holland, South Holland, and Utrecht, and it includes the Netherlands' four biggest cities, Amsterdam, Rotterdam, The Hague, and Utrecht (see map 3.2). More than one-third of the population lives there on 5 percent of the land.

The government has enjoyed modest success in diverting growth to other areas of the country,[8] but its battle to retain substantial open space at the center of the Randstad continues. The cooperation of the small municipalities on the inner and outer edges of the Randstad is essential. Even if most development occurs on land acquired by the larger municipalities, scattered development in some small municipalities, depending on the location, can impinge seriously on open space objectives.

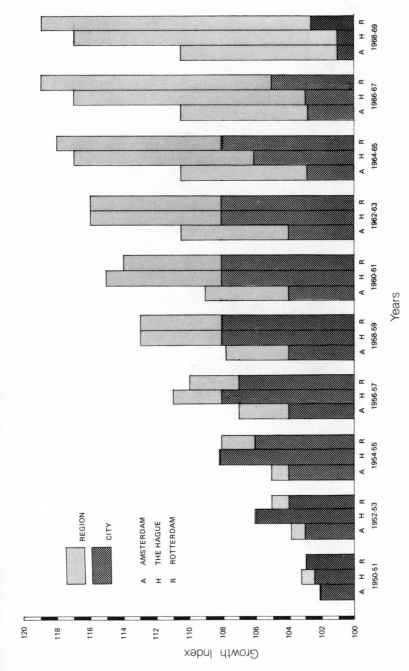

FIGURE 3.1. Growth patterns in the Randstad

SOURCE: Adapted from Netherlands, Ministry of Housing and Physical Planning, "The Randstad: The Urbanized Zone of the Netherlands," mimeographed (The Hague: Information Service, 1970)

< 100 PERSONS PER SQ KM

100-200 PERSONS PER SQ KM

200-600 PERSONS PER SQ KM

600-1000 PERSONS PER SQ KM

> 1000 PERSONS PER SQ KM

0  10  20  30  40  50
KM

MAP 3.1.  Population density, 1975

SOURCE: Netherlands, Lower Chamber, session 1975–76, nos. 1–2.

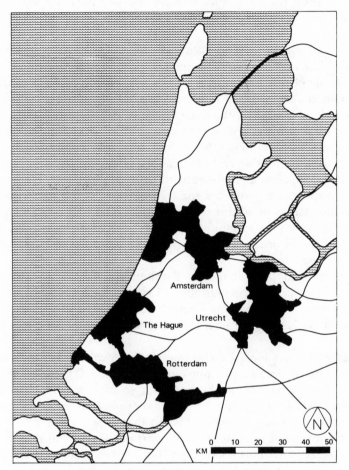

MAP 3.2.  Major urban areas of the Randstad

SOURCE: Adapted from Netherlands, Ministry of Housing and Physical Planning, "The Randstad: The Urbanized Zone of the Netherlands," mimeographed (The Hague: Information Service, 1970)

*Planning*

Because the heart of the Randstad is subject to such intense development pressure, the planning and land acquisition powers of the small municipalities, the central cities, regional agencies, the provinces, and the national government are put to their greatest test there. Recent events suggest the need for more and stronger regional planning and for more direct ways for the national government to implement its policies.

*National Planning.* The policy of the national government is that there should be little further development in the center of the Randstad so that its farmland will continue to provide open space amenity to the more than 4 million nearby urban residents. Instead, the government wishes to encourage development on the outer fringe of the Randstad and elsewhere in the country in a pattern termed concentrated deconcentration. It has sought to implement this and other policies primarily by persuasion.

The minister of housing and physical planning does have a direct means of achieving municipal compliance with national objectives. He or she can issue an order to the provinces for transmission to the municipalities to take specific actions in accord with stated national policies. This power is now used to secure the location of facilities such as highways. Presumably the minister could order that certain land be allocated to agriculture, but this has not been done.

A look at some scattered new development in much of the central Randstad leads to two conclusions: (1) municipalities have seen it as coinciding with their economic interests to plan for further development, and (2) the national government has not acted to prohibit such development.

The burgomasters have a direct interest in growth in that their salary is determined by the size of the municipal population. The salaries of other municipal employees are established with relation to the burgomaster's salary. Establishing a different basis for compensation would be one small step the national government could take to alter growth pressures.

One illustration of reluctance on the part of the national government to intervene directly to affect municipal development objectives while still trying to carry out national policies was the 1968 decision to buy much of the land on the south side of the New Waterway and between the south wing and the Amsterdam–North Sea Canal wing of the Randstad. Had there been national intervention in the municipal planning process to insist that the land be planned for open space uses, this state purchase would have been called for only insofar as the land was to be used for public recreation.

*Regional Planning.* The provinces have developed a number of regional plans. If completed soon, these plans may be used as a basis for rejecting proposals in municipal plans.

The Ministry of Internal Affairs, after consultation with the Ministry of Housing and Physical Planning, has developed a proposal that the country be divided into twenty-six regions and that these regions be given some power to implement their plans. There has been one rather unsuccessful prototype of a nationally constituted regional planning authority. In 1964, to stimulate efficient development and intermunicipal cooperation in part of the Randstad, Parliament created the Rijnmond (Rhine estuary) Public Corporation.[9] Twenty-four muncipalities along the New Waterway, ranging in size from municipalities with fewer than 2,000 residents each to the city of Rotterdam with approximately 675 thousand people, were designated members and directed to plan for port and industrial development and for related housing, open space, waterways, roads, and water and air pollution control. The law provides that, upon completion and acceptance of a plan by the corporation and its approval by the province, the member municipalities will be required to implement the plan. While this would appear to be a powerful tool for coordinating and concentrating development, as of 1974, ten years after enactment of the enabling law, the Rijnmond Public Corporation did not have an agreed upon plan.

The Eindhoven region recently has enjoyed some success with regional planning. Several other metropolitan areas, including Utrecht, Delft, and The Hague, have been making tentative efforts. The fears harbored by some of the small municipalities of central city domination have been a major impediment to the development of effective regional planning agencies. Observing this, the executive branch of the national government has concluded that national leadership is needed to bring such planning into being and to achieve its implementation.

*Municipal Planning.* Municipalities, acting under the Physical Planning Act of 1962, may prepare a municipal master plan. If they fail to adopt a master plan after a request from the province to do so, the province may prepare and adopt a master plan binding on them.[10] Municipalities must prepare a development plan for non-built-up areas and may prepare such a plan for built-up areas. The development plan must be adopted by the municipal council and submitted to the province for approval, modification, or rejection. There is a limited right of appeal from the provincial decision to the national Council of State, which advises the crown on a decision. Only those who either filed a formal objection to the adoption of the plan or objected to amendments made at the time of adoption may appeal. If the crown rejects a plan, the municipality must amend the plan in accordance with the crown's objections. In this way, by reponse rather than initiative, the national government can exercise a limited influence on a central Randstad municipality's desire for development. Once adopted, a development plan has a binding effect on the use of land.

The plans for the municipality of Naaldwyk illustrate the gap between national policy for the open areas of the Randstad and local preferences.

Naaldwyk is a town of twenty-three thousand people located in the province of South Holland midway between the New Waterway and the Hague. In 1960, the province prepared a regional plan for seven municipalities, including Naaldwyk. The plan, to which the municipalities were given little opportunity to contribute, called for keeping much of the land in pasture. The municipalities filed objections with the Council of State, alleging that the land would provide an adequate return only if used for horticulture and greenhouses. The crown agreed, and today much of the land is covered with hundreds of greenhouses producing flowers. While this is an agricultural use, it does not provide the open space amenity contemplated by the national government.

There is also urban growth in Naaldwyk. The town is buying seventy acres from twenty-nine separate owners, at the high price for the Netherlands of between $0.15 and $0.21 per square foot (five and seven guilders per square meter). On this land, in accordance with its development plan, Naaldwyk intends to have one thousand homes built, using a mix of row houses and four-story apartments. The land will be prepared for development and then sold at cost to two nonprofit housing associations. The acquisition cost is expected to be approximately 60 percent of the sale price, an atypically high proportion.

The central cities still can and do buy land for development in neighboring municipalities, but to a lesser extent than formerly. Because annexation has not been politically acceptable since World War II, the development must accord with the plans of the outlying municipality and must receive provincial approval. This is not always forthcoming. The cities and their architects are known to prefer high-density, high-rise construction. Many people have a strong antipathy to such development, finding it monotonous, inhuman, and lacking in a sufficient mix of services and activities. Nationwide, forty thousand apartments stood vacant in 1973, reflecting popular rejection of high-rise housing.[11] The city-suburban government split in housing preference has led some suburban municipalities to reject city development proposals and others to negotiate for a lower density more in keeping with the wishes of their residents. Furthermore, many central cities no longer have the financial capability to acquire large suburban holdings and are ready to cede this role to the areas in which growth is occurring.

## Land Banks

Land banking is largely, but not exclusively, the responsibility of land development enterprises. These organizations exist in the majority of Dutch municipalities, including 115 out of 118 municipalities with a

TABLE 3.1. Municipal Land Acquisition, 1965–1971

| Year | Number of Transactions | Area Acquired | | Average Price[a] | |
|------|------------------------|---------------|-------|------------------|---------|
| | | 1,000 m² | Acres | Per m² | Per Acre |
| 1965 | 3,480 | 55,049 | 13,920 | 4 florins | $ 5,227 |
| 1966 | 4,756 | 46,394 | 11,732 | 5.6 | 7,318 |
| 1967 | 4,666 | 39,244 | 9,924 | 6.5 | 8,494 |
| 1968 | 4,960 | 41,318 | 10,448 | 6.6 | 8,625 |
| 1969 | 5,092 | 39,116 | 9,891 | 7.7 | 10,062 |
| 1970 | 5,182 | 44,538 | 11,262 | 9 | 11,761 |
| 1971 | 4,802 | 38,818 | 9,816 | 8.9 | 11,631 |
| Total | | 304,477 | 76,993 | | |

SOURCE: Netherlands Central Bureau for Statistics.
[a] These prices include structures and consequential damages, if any.

population of 20,000 or more. As of 1970, they held 204 thousand acres (82,600 hectares), which they were in the process of preparing for sale or lease for development. The larger municipalities have far larger stocks of land, while the smaller municipalities, as a group, are currently acquiring more.

Acquisition and disposal each have run at about eleven thousand acres per year, but, of the land passing out of the land development enterprises' hands, over half has gone into other municipal accounts for such public uses as roads, schools, and parks. Generally, land is sold at a small profit, and the cost accounts for no more than 15 percent of the sale price. This is due to the exceptionally high cost in the Netherlands of preparing sites for development.

*Acquisition.* The prices paid by municipalities for land rose rapidly from 1965 to 1971, while the number of transactions and the acreage acquired remained more or less constant after 1966. For the Netherlands as a whole, the average price paid per acre for land, any existing structures, and consequential damages rose from $5,227 in 1965 to $11,631 in 1971 (forty thousand guilders per hectare to eighty-nine thousand guilders per hectare). All municipalities together have purchased an average of eleven thousand acres yearly (see table 3.1).

The price of land bought by the municipalities during this period rose considerably more rapidly than the gross national product per capita. The sale price of land acquired from municipalities rose at a rate approximately parallel to land acquisition prices, while the sale price of private land rose somewhat faster. The cost of home building has, on the contrary, risen less rapidly than the gross national product. (See table 3.2.)

TABLE 3.2. Indices for GNP, Land, and Housing

| | | Price of Land per Square Meter | | | |
| Year | GNP per Capita | Raw Land Bought by Municipalities | Developed Sites Bought from | | Cost of House Building |
| | | | Municipalities | Others | |
| 1965 | 100 | 100 | 100 | 100 | 100 |
| 1966 | 108 | 152 | 121 | 134 | 106 |
| 1967 | 117 | 167 | 144 | 170 | 106 |
| 1968 | 128 | 214 | 156 | 217 | 113 |
| 1969 | 142 | 242 | 190 | 242 | 127 |
| 1970 | 155 | 226 | 193 | 242 | 141 |
| 1971 | 172 | 231 | 235 | 291 | 159 |

SOURCE: Netherlands Central Bureau for Statistics. The GNP index is from an OECD report on the Netherlands, cited in G. Max Neutze, "The Price of Land and Land Use Planning: Policy Instruments in the Urban Land Market," report (Paris: Organization for Economic Cooperation and Development, 1973).

There are considerable variations in purchase patterns depending on the size of the municipality. Rural municipalities and towns with fewer than 10,000 people buy over one-half of the land. Predictably, the land they buy is cheaper than that bought by the larger municipalities. Their purchase prices averaged $9,149 per acre (7 guilders per square meter) in 1971, compared with $11,502 per acre (8.8 guilders per square meter) for satellite municipalities, $17,514 per acre (13.4 guilders per square meter) for cities of 50,000–100,000, and $21,958 per acre (16.8 guilders per square meter) for cities over 100,000. All of these prices are for land and buildings combined. All land in the Netherlands is used intensively and farm holdings are small, so most acquisitions include structures as well as land.

Only 4 percent of the purchases made between 1965 and 1971 were by eminent domain. Eminent domain may be used only after a municipality has tried and then unable to reach an agreement with a landowner for a voluntary purchase. In eminent domain cases, the municipal council passes an order of taking, giving an opportunity for the filing of objections, and then submits the order to the crown for approval. The three appraisers charged with determining market value are, by law, required not to include the value attributable to a site because of its anticipated future use. Location and the ease with which a site may be developed are factors considered in fixing market value. In no case may a value lower than farm value be set. In those cases in which the municipality dominates the land market, determination of market value is particularly difficult.

In addition to payment for land and structures, compensation also includes consequential losses, such as moving expenses, the termination of a business if moving is not feasible, losses realized on the sale of stock or equipment, and any decrease in value of remaining property. "In actual fact this value is often so much higher than the agrarian value that the amount received by the owner of land purchased compulsorily yields as much or more in interest than he used to earn from his farm."[12]

If a business can't survive a move, the common court practice is that the owner is paid the anticipated annual revenue for thirteen or fourteen years multiplied by ten, less the interest anticipated on the capital sum and less the estimated future earnings of the owner. Tenants, often farmers unable to find other land available for lease, are compensated in similar manner. Tenant compensation is calculated as anticipated annual income multiplied by seven or eight for land without buildings and by eight or nine for land with buildings, less the same corrections applied to the compensation of owners of businesses.

Once the appraisers submit their recommendation to the court, the court must make an award within twenty-one days. Eminent domain cases take priority over all others. The law permits appeals solely for errors of law.

Most land bought by municipalities is bought by land development enterprises. In 1970, 481 of the then 913 municipalities[13] had created such entities, including all but three of the municipalities with 20,000 or more people. There are two land bank (grondbedrijf) associations, one for Amsterdam, Rotterdam, The Hague, and Utrecht, and the other, the Association of Land Banks of Moderate-Size Municipalities, for cities in the 100,000 to 200,000 population range. Each of these associations meets informally to discuss common problems of acquisition, financing, and disposition of sites.

*Land Holdings.* Much of the data pertaining to municipal land holdings is available only with reference to the land development enterprises. Therefore, the data exclude land owned by those municipalities lacking such agencies and, for municipalities with land development enterprises, land bought and held by general municipal government.

The total land holdings of the land development enterprises amounted to 204,000 acres in 1970. The larger the municipality, the more land, on the average, it tends to possess. Unfortunately, the available data are not disaggregated in such a way as to make it possible to determine whether the rapidly growing municipalities are also the municipalities adding to their stock of land at the greatest rate. (See fig. 3.2 and table 3.3.)

The larger the municipality, the greater the proportion of the stock of land that is subject to long-term lease, suggesting that the smaller municipalities have a greater need to turn over land and recover their investment. Of the municipal land not subject to long-term lease, all classes of municipalities have approximately half of their stock ready for building and half awaiting preparation.

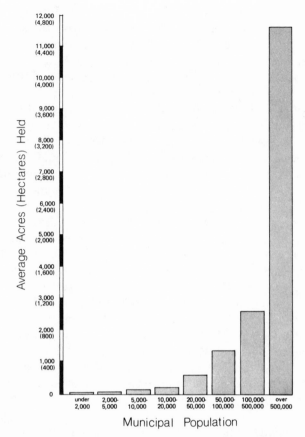

FIGURE 3.2.  Average land holding by size of municipality, 1970

Three percent of the land development enterprises—those representing municipalities of 100,000 population and over—hold one-third of the land. Since the enterprises that are the largest land holders are also agencies of the biggest municipalities, it is not surprising that their land carries a book value equal to 48 percent of that of all land held by the enterprises. (See table 3.4.)

*Disposition.* An increasing share of land going into development comes from municipal land banks; in 1965, the municipal share was 64.5 percent and, by 1971, it had reached 83.2 percent. Leasing by municipalities had been increasing slowly between 1965 and 1970. Then, in 1971, it spurted to a high of 31 percent of all land going into development. (See table 3.5.)

If one takes eleven thousand acres per year as the average acquired by

TABLE 3.3. Land Development Enterprise Holdings, 1970

| Municipal Size | Number of Municipalities | Number of LDEs | Other | | | | | | | | Total | |
|---|---|---|---|---|---|---|---|---|---|---|---|---|
| | | | Under 25-Year Lease | | Ready for Construction | | Building Sites | | Unprepared Land | | | |
| | | | Hectares | Acres | Hectares | Acres | Hectares | Acres | Hectares | Acres | Hectares | Acres |
| 500,000 and over | 3 | 3 | 2,293 | 5,664 | 5,611 | 13,859 | 308 | 761 | 5,974 | 14,756 | 14,186 | 35,040 |
| 100,000–500,000 | 11 | 11 | 891 | 2,201 | 5,367 | 13,256 | 1,191 | 2,942 | 4,232 | 10,453 | 11,681 | 28,852 |
| 50,000–100,000 | 26 | 25 | 1,077 | 2,660 | 6,397 | 15,801 | 474 | 1,171 | 6,108 | 15,087 | 14,056 | 34,719 |
| 20,000–50,000 | 78 | 76 | 234 | 578 | 8,866 | 21,899 | 2,349 | 5,802 | 7,586 | 18,737 | 19,035 | 47,016 |
| 10,000–20,000 | 163 | 132 | 97 | 240 | 4,977 | 12,293 | 1,448 | 3,577 | 6,674 | 16,485 | 13,196 | 32,595 |
| 5,000–10,000 | 226 | 158 | 75 | 185 | 3,418 | 8,442 | 1,037 | 2,561 | 4,053 | 10,011 | 8,583 | 21,199 |
| 2,000–5,000 | 263 | 64 | 9 | 22 | 326 | 1,793 | 117 | 289 | 898 | 2,218 | 1,750 | 4,322 |
| Less than 2,000 | 143 | 12 | | | 28 | 69 | 32 | 79 | 201 | 496 | 261 | 644 |
| Total | 913 | 481 | 4,676 | 11,550 | 34,990 | 87,412 | 6,956 | 17,182 | 35,726 | 88,243 | 82,748 | 204,387 |

SOURCE: Netherlands Central Bureau for Statistics.

NOTE: Some land under long-term lease is removed from jurisdiction of the Land Development Enterprise and administered by the general services branch of the municipality. Such land is not shown in this table.

TABLE 3.4. Distribution of Land Development Enterprise Holdings, 1970

| Total Holdings | Number of LED's | Percentage of Land Held | Percentage of Book Value |
|---|---|---|---|
| 2,470 acres (1,000 hectares and more) | 14 | 33 | 48 |
| 247–2,470 acres (100–1,000 hectares) | 154 | 53 | 40 |
| Less than 247 acres (less than 100 hectares) | 313 | 14 | 12 |
| Total | 481 | 100 | 100 |

SOURCE: "Statistics of the Municipal Land Development Enterprises, 1970."

Dutch municipalities, then the acreage disposed of by land development enterprises in 1969 would suggest that the municipalities are running about constant with their needs. This would not be so if there were a commitment to reduce much further the private share of the land market or if there is a further decline in the density of the land being developed. Fifty-two percent of the land disposed of in 1969 went to other municipal accounts, predominantly for streets, schools, and other public uses. Only 29 percent went to residential uses, yet that land accounted for 63 percent of the price paid. Residential uses are charged a higher rate than industrial uses for such municipal services as streets and sewers, but within a particular use category the rates are evenly distributed. (See table 3.6.)

There is considerable variation among Dutch municipalities as to whether land is sold or leased at a profit. The 1969 sale prices, including a capitalized price for land leased, are much higher for the larger municipalities than for the rest. Residential land in Amsterdam, Rotterdam, and The Hague sold[14] for an average of $111,095 per acre (eighty-five guilders per square meter) and industrial land for $69,271 per acre (fifty-three guilders

TABLE 3.5. Sources of Land for Urban Development, 1965–1971

| Year | Acquired from Municipalities | | Acquired Privately |
|---|---|---|---|
| | By Purchase | By Lease | |
| 1965 | 56.8% | 7.7% | 35.5% |
| 1966 | 69.0 | 3.2 | 27.8 |
| 1967 | 66.6 | 6.3 | 27.1 |
| 1968 | 65.4 | 6.8 | 27.8 |
| 1969 | 71.6 | 8.4 | 20.0 |
| 1970 | 69.8 | 10.5 | 19.7 |
| 1971 | 52.2 | 31.0 | 16.8 |

SOURCE: G. Max Neutze, "The Price of Land and Land Use Planning: Policy Instruments in the Urban Land Market," report (Paris: Organization for Economic Cooperation and Development, 1973), citing *Monthly Construction Statistics* (January 1973).

TABLE 3.6. Disposal of Land by Land Development Enterprises, 1969

| Intended Use | Sold | | Leased[a] | | Allocation to Municipal Use | | Total | | Percentage of Area | Percentage of Price |
|---|---|---|---|---|---|---|---|---|---|---|
| | Hectares | Acres | Hectares | Acres | Hectares | Acres | Hectares | Acres | | |
| Industrial | 351 | 867 | 50 | 124 | 24 | 59 | 425 | 1,050 | 9 | 12 |
| Residential | 1,177 | 2,907 | 38 | 94 | 100 | 247 | 1,315 | 3,248 | 29 | 63 |
| Streets | | | | | 1,178 | 2,910 | 1,178 | 2,910 | 26 | 1 |
| Recreation | 79 | 195 | 8 | 20 | 246 | 608 | 333 | 823 | 7 | 3 |
| Other, including schools | 488 | 1,205 | 14 | 35 | 810 | 2,001 | 1,312 | 3,241 | 29 | 21 |
| Total | 2,095 | 5,174 | 110 | 273 | 2,358 | 5,825 | 4,563 | 11,272 | 100 | 100 |

SOURCE: "Statistics of the Municipal Land Development Enterprises, 1970."
[a] 25 years or longer

per square meter). In cities from 20,000 to 500,000 people, residential land sold for between $52,280 and $62,736 per acre (forty to forty-eight guilders per square meter). Residential land in smaller cities sold for between $31,368 and $44,438 per acre (twenty-four to thirty-four guilders per square meter). Industrial land outside the three big cities ran between $20,912 and $44,438 per acre (sixteen to thirty-four guilders per square meter).

On occasion, municipalities enter into a construction lease with developers and then, on completion of the buildings, sell or lease the land to the occupant. This procedure is used to control the price at which the land will pass to the user.

Statistics on acquisition and disposition prices show that land accounts for only a small portion of municipal costs. Figure 3.3 indicates that, for rural land, on the average land runs at 15 percent of all costs prior to sale or lease. For the two urban fringe developments of Slotermeer and Bijlmermeer it was even less—6 percent and 5 percent, respectively.

Since the central government subsidizes up to 40 percent of the cost of preparing sites for development and since the government is concerned with keeping site costs down, it sets a limit, by region, at which municipalities may market their land. In establishing this limit, the government takes into consideration the regional market value of raw land. The municipalities stick within this overall limit but offer sites at different prices for different uses.

### Municipal Finance

Although it is up to the municipalities to initiate action to buy land and, having bought it, to decide whether to lease or sell it, no municipality's program would be possible without state approval and funding. Therefore, it is ultimately the state that decides how extensive the municipal land bank program will be.

Since 1964, essentially the sole source of funds for municipal land acquisition has been the Bank for Netherlands Municipalities. Its loans are state controlled, and, recently, with many municipalities running large deficits, the state has rejected some requests to borrow for land acquisition.

In the Netherlands, taxes have not been used as a tool to affect land use. As one commentator recently noted:

The Netherlands has had remarkable success in slowing the rate of increase of urban land prices by bringing unimproved and agricultural properties into urban use at a rate roughly corresponding to demand. This has been done

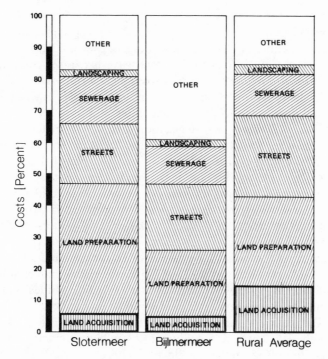

FIGURE 3.3. Distribution of land acquisition and site preparation costs

SOURCE: Adapted from Chambres d'Agriculture, "La Loi d'Orientation Agricole," mimeographed (January 1977)

almost exclusively by public planning and land acquisition, rather than through taxation.[15]

Nonetheless, it is useful to review briefly the sources of local revenues in order to clarify the reasons for dependence on the Bank for Netherlands Municipalities.

*Municipal Income.* In 1972, municipal expenditures totaled 15 percent of national expenditures, and, as has been typical in recent years, 90 percent of the municipal funds came from the state. These funds take the form of general and special grants.

Fifty percent of municipal revenues come via the general grant, which is paid out of the state's municipal fund. This fund is fed by a variety of state-levied taxes. The general grant is distributed to the municipalities by means of a formula that includes the number of inhabitants, size, density of the built-up area, and costs of social services. Forty percent of the municipal revenues comes from direct state grants, made for special purposes. These grants may be made using the same formula for a similar group of municipalities or may earmark funds for a specific project.

The municipalities have raised revenues from several sources: a series of local taxes, including a road tax, a waterways tax, a sewerage tax, a dog tax, and an entertainment tax; profits from locally run utilities; and income from land. The real property tax was of no significance. It was collected by the state and distributed to the municipalities, but its yield was very small. However, as of 1970,[16] new legislation made it a potential source of municipal income. No later than 1 January 1979, or sooner if municipalities elect, many of the small local taxes and the preexisting real property tax expire. Instead, for all but agricultural land, both landowners and renters will pay a tax based on imputed income. For residential property, value will be calculated as the annual rent or imputed rent multiplied by a coefficient ranging from ten to twenty. Owners and renters may be subject to different rates on the same basis, as may different classes of owners.

In recent years, revenues have not covered the spending of a substantial number of municipalities. In 1971, 37 percent of the municipalities had a budget deficit. In 1972, while the number of municipalities with a deficit had declined to 30 percent, the total amount of the deficit had increased slightly. The four largest cities have the largest deficits; as of 1972, Amsterdam's deficit was $45 million (123 million guilders), Rotterdam's was $20 million (55 million guilders), Utrecht's was $10 million (26 million guilders), and The Hague's was $8 million (21 million guilders). Transportation and education are the largest deficit items.

Amsterdam has chosen to sink more and more deeply into debt on the assumption that the state should and will bail it out. As of 1973, the state had offered to contribute enough additional money to cut the annual gap between revenue and expenditure in half and, in return, had demanded that Amsterdam cut its level of services and lower some of its standards. Amsterdam was holding out for a better deal. The city argues, for in stance, that its extraordinarily costly new subway is warranted because it will provide rapid and efficient service to people living in the newly developing outskirts. Therefore, the city says that it should not be required to pay half of the subway's cost.

*Financing Land Acquisition.* There are four possible sources of money for municipal land acquisition: municipal revenues, loans from the state, loans from the Bank for Netherlands Municipalities, and loans from commercial sources. Since the revenues of many municipalities are inadequate to meet ongoing municipal needs, let alone cover land purchases, and since the state has exercised its power to bar municipalities from borrowing from any source other than the Bank for Netherlands Municipalities, the bank and the state are virtually the sole sources of funds.

The state regulates all municipal borrowing for land acquisition. The first step is to seek provincial approval to borrow money. This approval is then submitted to the minister of internal affairs for state approval. If the province denies a request, which it does on occasion if it believes that the municipality is overextended, the municipality may appeal the denial to the Council of State. There is a further constraint on municipal borrowing: Parliament annually sets a limit on the total sum that may be borrowed for capital purposes. In addition to obtaining approval to borrow, municipalities with a population of less than 100,000 must have the approval of the provincial government to buy or sell land.

Once a municipality is authorized to borrow, the Bank for Netherlands Municipalities must lend.[17] The bank receives a monthly notice from the minister of internal affairs stating how much money may be lent. If it has insufficient funds to meet all approved loan requests, the provinces set priorities and the minister of internal affairs directs the bank to loan in accordance with these priorities.

The minister of internal affairs and the minister of finance have the power to declare, because the capital market is tight, that municipalities may borrow only from the bank. Such a restriction has been in effect since 1964. In the late 1960s, the bank was authorized to loan $30 million (80 million guilders) per month. By 1973, the sum had risen to $67 million (180 million guilders) per month, of which $11 million (30 million guilders) was earmarked for land acquisition and site preparation.

Prior to 1964, loans were for ten years with principal payments deferred for the first five years. Currently, loans are for twenty-five years and carry constant principal and declining interest payments. The interest rate is the current commercial rate at the time of the loan. No prepayment is allowed during the first ten years of the loan. During years eleven through fifteen, a municipality may prepay with a 1.5 percent penalty and during years sixteen through twenty-five, with a 1 percent penalty. The board of the bank sets the loan terms.

As of 1971, the long-term debt of the municipalities totaled $7 billion (19 billion guilders), of which 72 percent was owed to the bank. Dutch municipalities are responsible for a large share of the national debt; for instance, in 1965, Amsterdam's debt alone was 13.4 percent of the national debt.

The bank raises funds on both the private and the public capital markets. On the private side, it turns to institutional investors such as insurance companies, pension funds, and commercial banks. On the public side, it sells bonds, recently for twenty-five-year terms.

The state lends money for land acquisition solely for Housing Act construction. Loans under this program are for seventy-five years at market interest and cover 100 percent of the land cost.

## Central City Land Banks

A brief look at the land banks of the four largest cities and of one medium-sized city, Tilburg, shows comparable commitment to the concept of land banking but considerable disparity in results. All five cities have engaged in land banking for decades, and all have exercised a virtual monopoly on development sites within their borders. All of the cities except Tilburg have run out or before long will run out of land and do not anticipate annexing new land.

Amsterdam and Rotterdam show the most divergent results of the four big cities. Amsterdam, except for one instance of acquiescence to a state request, has not been buying land extraterritorially, has no open land left to buy within its borders, and appears to be operating its reserve, all of which is leased, at a loss. Rotterdam still has some vacant land within its borders and continues to buy there but also has been buying land, under intermunicipal agreement, in thirty-seven other municipalities. The price it pays has the lowest ratio to farmland value of the five municipalities—2 times farmland value compared to 2.5 or 3 times farmland value for the others. It breaks even on residential sales and profits from commercial and industrial leases.

Tilburg's situation is illustrative of older cities located away from growth areas. In an effort to bolster its faltering economy by attracting new industry, Tilburg intentionally operates its land bank at a loss.

Several issues are raised by the status of land banking in these five cities. Some are municipal questions, but more require state policy decisions. The Dutch cling to the view, which seems mythical to me, that most decision making that affects development occurs at the municipal level. In deference to that perspective, I will address first the issues that may perhaps be resolved at the local level.

As with the Swedes, a major motivation for the Dutch in instituting land banking was the desire to provide a decent living environment for all. Making sites available at a low price was one way of realizing this objective. Therefore, the rental or sale price was calculated to cover costs. Leasing, at different times in different cities, came to be seen as a means by which the city could also benefit from rising land values. However, some cities—for example, Amsterdam and, to a lesser degree, The Hague—have not altered the rate provisions of their leases to enable them to capture increments in land values. It cannot be argued that maintaining the same base rate for twenty-five, fifty, or seventy-five years is an equitable means of subsidizing housing, since the rate paid by two lessees of comparable sites will vary widely, dependent on the year in which each lease was signed.

There does not appear to have been adequate exploration of the contribution to municipal revenues that the land bank could and should make and in what proportions this contribution should be levied on various land uses.

Another major issue over which the central cities can exercise some control is the extraterritorial extension of land banking. Rotterdam's achievement of entering into cooperation agreements with thirty-seven other municipalities proves that it can be done and, apparently, done profitably for all concerned. Yet the statistics on land acquisition show that many suburban municipalities have chosen to engage in land banking on their own and have found the means to do so. Both in the Utrecht and Rotterdam areas there have been efforts to create regional agencies that could exercise the land bank functions, but these efforts have yet to bear fruit. Future land banking in the Netherlands could follow any or all of these models—central city acquisition in outlying areas, acquisition by individual suburbs, or regional acquisition. It is unlikely that state land banking, except for the polders, would become an acceptable alternative. With the major cities running out of land within their borders and with the prevailing opinion that land banking is a desirable public function, it is time for an evaluation of the economic, sociological, and political implications of each of the above three models for future action.

The national government should participate in this evaluation. Since it has a national growth policy and, in effect, controls municipal land banking through its approval or disapproval of requests to buy or sell land and requests for loans from the Bank for Netherlands Municipalities, it should have an acute concern for what composition of political units will be seeking to carry out land banking in the future.

The state also has a direct interest in municipal lease or sale terms. The large municipalities all run substantial deficits and assume that the state will save them from insolvency. The state is already the prime source of municipal revenues. Should it be state policy further to underwrite municipal budgets from general revenues? Should some selected municipalities, or all municipalities, be urged or required to earn more from their land revenues? This is an inadequately explored means of implementing the national growth policy.

Another source of state leverage that does not appear so far to have been related to growth policy is the Housing Act loan basis. In determining what is a reasonable price to pay for land and for improvements in different parts of the country, the state could add as an element the comparative desirability of stimulating growth.

With the winding down of the acquisition programs in three of the four major central cities, the Netherlands is at a point at which the future directions of land banking are unclear. An articulation of the issues and choices at the national level is timely.

## Amsterdam

Barring unforeseen developments, Amsterdam's land acquisition program is at an end.[18] Since municipal land is leased, the city will continue to be engaged in land banking, but the reserve will remain about as it is today. The city's last annexations were in 1923, and the land now constituting the city is largely developed. The only large current project is Bijlmermeer, an area expected to house one hundred thousand people by 1985. Although Bijlmermeer is located outside Amsterdam's borders, the city accepted responsibility for it at the state's request. Whether or not Bijlmermeer will be annexed to the city is to be decided by Parliament soon. The current view in Amsterdam is that the city has fulfilled its land acquisition responsibilities, an attitude that has been shaped in part by the resistance of suburban municipalities to city acquisitions and in part by the city's increasingly parlous financial condition. (See map 3.3.)

When Amsterdam did buy land, its procedure was to start acquiring tracts as soon as work began on an extension plan. The city paid approximately three times the farm value for the land, and, on the average, land constituted 2 percent of the completed development cost. All land is leased. "As was decided by City Council in 1966 by an overwhelming majority, the only well-planned manner of distributing building sites prepared by the city is by the continued use of the leasehold system."[19]

In principle, the original rent is set at somewhere between 4 and 6 percent of the cost of buying and preparing the site. This base, however, varies with the purpose for which the site is leased and is an overall average. Social housing sites are leased for fifty-year terms, with rents subject to adjustment by reference to the "net home product" as published by the Central Bureau of Statistics. Residential sites for private development are leased at prices that vary with location and development cost but that average $0.09 per square foot (three guilders per square meter). These housing leases have been perpetual since 1915, while commercial and industrial leases have been perpetual since 1966. The lease can be terminated only on a finding by city council that to do so is in the public interest. Commercial and industrial land is leased at a current rate of between $0.24 and $0.30 per square foot (eight to ten guilders per square meter). The rent is adjusted every five years by reference to the net home product index. The adjustment coefficient is published in the *Gemeenteblad* (city gazette) in the year prior to its effective date. Between 1958 and 1970, the adjustments ranged from +1.1 percent to +1.3 percent. The rent may be adjusted for changes in the value of the site only once every fifty years. This adjustment is determined by three experts, chosen by the city and lessee by mutual agreement. If such agreement is not forthcoming, the

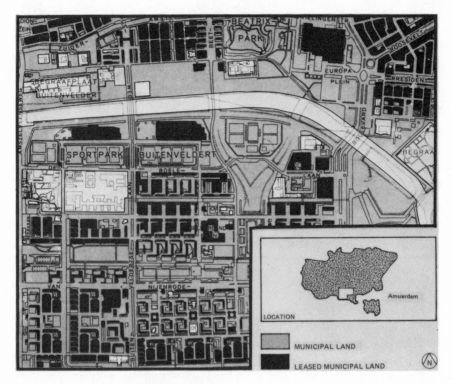

MAP 3.3. Public lands in Amsterdam

SOURCE: Adapted from Eigendomstoestand Gemeent, *Dienst P. W. Amsterdam, sector Grondbedrijf* (map) (Amsterdam, 1973)

city chooses one, the lessee chooses one, and together these two experts pick a third.

G. Max Neutze has observed of the Amsterdam leasehold system that "the method . . . has the merit of simplicity but is neither very efficient nor very equitable."[20] As in Stockholm, by failing to adjust the base rate at frequent intervals to reflect changes in site value, the city has given many lessees a windfall and simultaneously denied itself a fair return on its investment. Particularly given its present very large debt and continuing deficits, Amsterdam might well consider revising the rate provisions of its leases.

### Rotterdam

Rotterdam's situation with respect to land banking diverges considerably from that of Amsterdam.[21] First, the city proper is not fully built up,

TABLE 3.7. Rotterdam Land Holdings, 1963–1972

| | Land Held | | | | | |
|---|---|---|---|---|---|---|
| | In the City* | | Outside the City | | Total | |
| Year | Hectares | Acres | Hectares | Acres | Hectares | Acres |
| 1963 | 9,100 | 22,500 | 2,900 | 7,200 | 12,000 | 29,700 |
| 1964 | 9,300 | 23,000 | 3,300 | 8,200 | 12,600 | 31,200 |
| 1965 | 10,000 | 24,700 | 4,300 | 10,600 | 14,300 | 35,300 |
| 1966 | 10,300 | 25,400 | 4,600 | 11,400 | 14,900 | 36,800 |
| 1967 | 12,000 | 30,000 | 3,200 | 7,900 | 15,200 | 37,900 |
| 1968 | 12,200 | 30,100 | 3,300 | 8,200 | 15,500 | 38,300 |
| 1969 | 12,300 | 30,400 | 3,300 | 8,200 | 15,600 | 38,600 |
| 1970 | 13,000 | 32,100 | 3,400 | 8,400 | 16,400 | 40,500 |
| 1971 | 13,000 | 32,100 | 3,400 | 8,400 | 16,400 | 40,500 |
| 1972 | 13,100 | 32,400 | 3,300 | 8,200 | 16,400 | 40,600 |

SOURCE: Data provided by Rotterdam City Planning Commission
* Including Hook of Holland

and so land acquisition within its borders continues. Second, the city does buy land outside its borders. Third, residential land is sold, and leasing of other land is a recent innovation.

For the decade 1963–1972, land holdings within the municipal borders have increased gradually and steadily, while holdings elsewhere have remained about constant, declining from approximately 30 percent to approximately 20 percent of all holdings. During this period Rotterdam owned land in thirty-seven other municipalities. The total land held rose from 29,700 acres (12,000 hectares) in 1963 to 40,600 acres (16,400 hectares) in 1972 (see table 3.7). Both inside and outside of Rotterdam some land was sold off and other land acquired during the decade, so that the stock of land held varied from year to year. The largest extraterritorial acquisition was for port development at Rozenburg, while other large acquisitions were for reservoirs to serve the region, recreation, and residential development.

Rotterdam's normal acquisition routine begins simultaneously with work on an extension plan. Such plans customarily are for an area to house approximately twenty thousand people. People whose land will be included in the plan are contacted and invited to negotiate the sale of their land. At the same time an expropriation plan is prepared and offered for public comment. The plan and comments are sent to the minister of housing and physical planning, who makes a recommendation to the Council of State, which, in turn, advises the crown. The crown approves the expropriation plan. By this time, about 75 percent of the landowners will have agreed to a voluntary sale. For the others, a separate expropriation action is required for each parcel. If the city is in a hurry, it may request early possession and receive this approximately six months after commencing the expropriation action. Otherwise, possession passes after the court receives expert testimony and sets a price for the land. Because the municipality pays all court costs, including lawyers' and experts' fees, and because the process consumes several years, Rotterdam, like other municipalities, tries to avoid expropriation.

In Rotterdam, where the city controls the land market, the experts can only approximate market value. Since any private developer would be competing with the city, whose interest is to keep prices low, the market value for private land would be affected. This fact results in relatively low expropriation awards. Land sold for agriculture runs between $0.03 and $0.05 per square foot (1 to 1.5 guilders per square meter), while expropriation awards, for land only, excluding improvements, run between $0.06 and $0.08 per square foot (2 to 2.5 guilders per square meter). Rotterdam finances all of its land acquisition by means of loans from the Bank for Netherlands Municipalities.

Land planned for residential use is sold. However, this includes only the land to be occupied by the structures or, for single-family houses, by the structures and their private gardens. All streets and open spaces remain municipal property. The city builds no housing and sells most of its sites to nonprofit associations who receive Housing Act subsidies for land and improvement costs as well as for the housing itself. The sale price is set with the intention of enabling Rotterdam to break even. At Ommoord, one of Rotterdam's newer areas, land was sold at $6,300 (17,000 guilders) per house site and $3,700 (10,000 guilders) per apartment on the average. (See figs. 3.4 and 3.5.)

Land planned for port, industrial, and commercial uses is leased on long-term, indefinitely renewable leases. Until 1970, industrial land was sold, but then the city concluded that it would be more profitable to lease it. The city renegotiates lease rates every five years.

When Rotterdam wishes to buy land extraterritorially, it approaches the other municipality and proposes that they cooperate on preparation and implementation of an extension plan. If the other municipality concurs, Rotterdam starts buying land even before a formal cooperation agreement is signed. When the extension plan is ready, the other municipality will submit it for provincial and state approval and will also submit an expropriation plan. When expropriation is necessary, the other municipality will act and then sell the land to Rotterdam. Many municipalities welcome Rotterdam's cooperation and initiative because they lack the managerial or financial capability to act on their own. Further, Rotterdam has established its credentials by succeeding with its own program.

FIGURE 3.4. Cottages for the elderly, Pendrecht, the Netherlands (photo by Michael L. Strong)

FIGURE 3.5. Ommoord, the Netherlands (photo by Michael L. Strong)

## The Hague

The Hague's situation vis-à-vis land banking lies somewhere between that of Amsterdam and Rotterdam.[22] It no longer has any farmland left within its borders. However, it is buying some land in neighboring municipalities and it is proceeding to develop under cooperation agreements similar to those described for Rotterdam. About one-third of The Hague's land is in public ownership; there used to be more, prior to sale for development.

Land acquisition is financed from current revenues, loans from the Bank for Netherlands Municipalities, and state loans under the Housing Act. Since 70 percent of The Hague's housing built since World War II is social housing, the state's role in financing land acquisition has been considerable. Acquisition costs average about 10 percent of the city's investment in preparing sites for development.

Once the sites are ready, they may be sold or leased. Industrial land, bought for $0.12 to $0.18 per square foot (4 to 6 guilders per square meter), with an investment of $1.20 per square foot (40 guilders per square meter) in site improvements and infrastructure, may be sold for between $3 and $4.50 per square foot (100 to 150 guilders per square meter), yielding a nice profit. Commercial land is likely to be leased at a profit, although some sites are sold. Social housing sites are leased. Since 1910, private housing sites generally have been leased. The term is for from thirty to seventy-five years, with the seventy-five-year term most common. There is no right of renewal. The rental rate is fixed for the entire lease term. It is based on actual costs for land, site improvements, infrastructure, and administration, with a profit included where possible, with the rate set at the average interest that has prevailed over the prior five to ten years. In 1973, this rate was 8 percent.

## Utrecht

Utrecht did achieve one post–World War II annexation.[23] After thirty years of unsuccessful negotiation with neighboring municipalities, it turned to Parliament, seeking annexation authorization so that the city would have space on which to provide needed housing. Parliament approved the legislation in 1954, and Utrecht's population jumped from 180 thousand to 225 thousand as a result of the annexation. As soon as the annexation had been approved, Utrecht began buying all land that would be needed for development. In almost all cases, the purchases were by voluntary agreement, with the city paying from $0.12 to $0.15 per square foot (four to five guilders per square meter), compared with a farm value of around $0.06 per square foot (two guilders per square meter). Today there remain only two undeveloped tracts of land in Utrecht, one planned for nine hundred homes and the other for thirty-five hundred. Both are ownd by the municipality. Once they are built up, that will mark the end of the city's acquisition and site preparation program.

Until August 1973, land owned by the city was sold when ready for development. Now, for the small amount of land remaining, leases will be used.

## Tilburg

Tilburg is an old, established, medium-sized city. It is located to the south of the Randstad, outside the area of rapid urban expansion. Its land bank activities differ from those of the four large cities in that land development proceeds slowly, much land still is available within the city's borders, and the city is willing to lose money on its land operation in an effort to lure new enterprises.[24]

Tilburg lies only a few miles north of the Belgian border. It was a site of nineteenth-century industrial expansion, which, for Tilburg, meant the manufacture of woolen textiles and of shoes. The municipality's population, which peaked at 180 thousand prior to World War II, is now down to 150 thousand, but is predicted to grow to 165 thousand by 1985. The industrial buildings are obsolete, unemployment is a continuing problem, and attracting new industry is difficult because of more favorable tax conditions in nearby Belgium.

The municipal government has been fighting to overcome these problems by redevelopment, active solicitation of new industry, and a vigorous land bank program. Since 1959, two thousand homes and many run-down factory buildings have been demolished to make way for a new central shopping area with a handsome municipal theater, municipal offices, a railroad station, parking, a pedestrian shopping street, and a circumferential access road. Two 300-acre (120-hectare) industrial parks have been created on the outskirts, and the state, backing Tilburg's efforts, has contributed 50 percent of the cost of plant construction.

All development is on land bank sites. The municipality now owns 2,700 acres (1,100 hectares) out of a total area of 20,000 acres (8,000 hectares). About one-half of the municipality is built up, so that there is ample land within its borders for further expansion, should there be a demand.

Tilburg began acquiring land around 1920 on a small scale, with no political opposition, and has continued ever since. Today, about $3 million (8 million guilders) is spent yearly on land. The procedure is similar to that described for Rotterdam. Over 90 percent of Tilburg landowners sell voluntarily, so there is little recourse to eminent domain. Farm value in Tilburg is between $0.02 and $0.03 per square foot (0.8 to 1 guilder per square meter), and the city pays $0.06 to $0.09 per square foot (2) to 3 guilders per square meter) for the land.

Because Tilburg is above sea level, on solid ground, site improvements are less costly than in most of the Randstad. Therefore, as is true of similarly situated land elsewhere in the Netherlands, land costs account for approximately 15 percent of all site costs.

Industrial sites are sold below cost. Commercial sites and sites for private housing are sold at cost. Social housing sites are leased for seventy-five years, but the municipality has been losing money on these leases since the state has refused in its loans to cover in full Tilburg's costs. This is a problem comparable to that in Amsterdam. Tilburg believes that it is necessary to provide a certain level of amenity, particularly in parks and landscaping, to attract residents, while the state views these costs as more than "reasonable." This is particularly serious for Tilburg, because 90 percent of the housing construction is social housing. As in much of the rest of the country, there is strong pressure to build more single-family houses. Until the late 1960s, the split in construction in Tilburg was 50-50, but, in response to public opinion, current building now is 65 percent single family. Almost all of the single-family construction is row housing.

All in all, Tilburg loses money on its land bank. For 1971–1973, the loss is estimated at $1.5 million (4 million guilders). Tilburg has accepted this loss as a means to a stronger economic base, but there is an incongruity between its position and that of the state in setting "reasonable" bases for loan terms under the Housing Act. If the state does wish to stimulate concentrated deconcentration, it will need to choose further fiscal means to aid cities like Tilburg.

NOTES

1. Throughout this chapter, the 1973 conversion rate of 2.7 guilders per dollar has been used. Thus, 1 guilder per square meter = $0.93 per square foot, or $1,307 per acre. In the text, figures have been rounded.
2. See Strong, *Planned Urban Environments*, pp. 209–18, for a fuller description of Dutch water management systems.
3. Act of 28 August 1851 (stat. bk. 125).
4. Morée, "Town Planning and Real Estate Policy," speech on Netherlands and Rotterdam real estate policy, mimeographed.
5. The burgomaster heads municipal government and is appointed by the crown; the aldermen are chosen by and from the municipal council. Together they administer the municipal government.
6. Rutgers, "Municipal Real Estate Policy."
7. Interview with P.J.P. Bernelot Moens, Empeo, 23 November 1973.
8. See Strong, *Planned Urban Environments*, pp. 253–61, for details.
9. Stat. bk. 427, 5 November 1964.

10. The Housing Act of 1901, as amended, has been replaced by the Housing Act of 1962 and by the Physical Planning Act of 1962 (stat. bk. 1962, sections 286 and 287, stat. bk. 1964, sections 220, 221, and 334, effective 1 August 1965). The new housing act is significant in that it acknowledges a government responsibility to assure the provision of sufficient housing.

11. Interview with Professor G. F. Witt, Professor de Haan, and Lecturer D. L. Rodrigues Lopes, Delft University of Technology, 5 December 1973.

12. "Town and Country Planning and Compulsory Purchase in the Netherlands," mimeographed, p. 12. (No author, publisher, or date is available.)

13. In 1946, there were 1,015 municipalities. By 1974, acts of Parliament had merged a number of municipalities, so that the total number had declined to 843.

14. In cases of lease, the rent was capitalized.

15. Grimes, "Urban Land and Public Policy," p. 31.

16. Act of 24 December 1970.

17. Comments on the operation of the Bank for Netherlands Municipalities are from an interview with Deputy Director J. Hoftÿzer and H. Beets, 10 December 1973.

18. Interview with Dr. H. Oosterhuis and Mr. Homan, Public Works Dept., City of Amsterdam, 29 November 1973.

19. "Leasehold in Amsterdam." No publisher or date. Mimeographed.

20. Neutze, "Land and Land Use Planning."

21. The principal source of information about Rotterdam's land bank program is staff of the Rotterdam City Planning Commission, including C. M. Briët, L. J. Berink, H. J. Willemsen, and E. J. Boorsma-Worst.

22. Comments on The Hague are from an interview with A. B. Schrader and D. Douma, The Hague City Hall, 20 November 1973. Mr. Schrader is the chairman of the Association of Directors of Land Banks (Grondbedrijf) of Large Municipalities.

23. The Utrecht discussion is based on an interview with Mr. Harteveld, a member of the Utrecht municipal council and of its executive committee, 23 November 1973.

24. Interviews with Anthony Scheffer, former director of the Tilburg Land Bank and former president of the Association of Land Banks of Moderate-Size Municipalities, and J.D.A. Strÿers, Director of Public Works, Tilburg, 20 November 1973 and 3 December 1973.

## PERSONS INTERVIEWED

P.J.P. Bernelot Moens, Empeo Group of Billiton, 13 November 1973

L. M. Briët, head of land acquisition section; L. J. Derink, deputy head, financial administration and land development calculation section; H. J. Willemsen, head of information office; and E. J. Boorsma-Worst, member of information office, Rotterdam City Planning Office, 28 November 1973

Mr. Harteveld, member of Utrecht Municipal Council, 23 November 1973

Deputy Director J. Hoftÿzer and H. Beets, Bank for Netherlands Municipalities, 10 December 1973

De Savornin Lohman, attorney, Ministry of Housing and Public Property, 6 December 1973

Dr. H. Oosterhuis, economist, and Mr. Hamon, surveyor, City of Amsterdam, Public Works Department, Real Estate Section, 29 November 1973

Mr. Samson, attorney, and J.W.N. Droog, Ministry of Housing and Physical Planning, 19 November 1973

Antony Scheffer, former director of the Tilburg Land Bank and former president of the Association of Land Banks of Moderate-Size Municipalities; and

J.D.A. Strÿers, Director of Public Works, Tilburg, 20 November 1973 and 3 December 1973
A. B. Schrader, and D. Douma, Municipality of the Hague (070) 624121; Room 3210, Stadhuis, 20 November 1973
Professor Jacobus P. Thijsse, former director, Institute of Social Studies, The Hague, November 1973
Professor G. F. Witt, Professor de Haan, and Lecturer D. L. Rodrigues Lopes, Delft University of Technology, 5 December 1973
Town clerk, head of public works department, representative of building association, director of builders, Naaldwyk, 6 December 1973

REFERENCES

Amsterdam. Department of Public Works. *Town Planning and Ground Exploitation in Amsterdam.* Amsterdam: Public Works Service, 1967.
Bank for Netherlands Municipalities. *Verslag over het boekjaar, 1972.* The Hague: Bank for Netherlands Municipalities, 1973.
Bommer, Jan. *Housing and Planning Legislation in the Netherlands.* Rotterdam: Bouwcentrum, 1967.
Burke, Gerald L. *Greenheart Metropolis.* London: Macmillan, 1966.
Canaux, Jean, and Nicholas, Yves. "Land Problems in Town Planning." Paper prepared for the Council of Europe, Strasbourg, 13 March 1968.
Grimes, Orville. "Urban Land and Public Policy: Social Appropriation and Betterment." International Bank for Reconstruction and Development, Bank Staff Working Paper no. 179. May 1974.
Netherlands. Ministry of Housing and Physical Planning. "The 'Randstad': The Urbanized Zone of the Netherlands." Mimeographed. The Hague: Information Service, 1970.
———. "Townplanning and Redevelopment in the Netherlands." Mimeographed. The Hague: Information Service, 1970.
Neutze, G. Max. "The Price of Land Use Planning: Policy Instruments in the Urban Land Market." Report for the Organization for Economic Cooperation and Development. Paris, 1973.
Rutgers, J. "Municipal Real Estate Policy in the Netherlands." Mimeographed lecture. Rotterdam: Town Planning Department, 1971.
Simons, D. "The Netherlands." *Studies in Comparative Local Government* 4, no. 1 (Summer 1970).
Streefland, N. "Choosing a Basis for Taxation of Real Estate." Paper presented to International Association of Assessment Officers, Chicago, August 1973.
Strong, Ann Louise. *Planned Urban Environments: Sweden, Finland, Israel, the Netherlands, France.* Baltimore: The Johns Hopkins Press, 1971.
Tankirk, H. J. "The Position and Function of the Council for Municipal Finance in the Netherlands." *Local Finance* 1, no. 3 (July 1972).
Union of Netherlands Municipalities. "The Institution of a Public Authority for the Rhine Estuary Area." Mimeographed. n.d.
Witt, G. F. *Gemeentelijk Grondbedrijf* [Municipal land ownership]. Delft: Delft University: 1969.

# 4

# France: A Recent Convert to Land Banking

## Land Banks in a Private Property System

Land banking in France occurs in a context of attitudes toward private ownership of land that is far closer to that prevailing in the United States than to that in Sweden and the Netherlands. For this reason alone, the shift in France over the past two decades to an ever increasing commitment to land banking and the range of experimentation there with all aspects of land banking are of particular relevance to the United States.

The introductory chapter of this book described the origins and evolution of the American commitment to private determination of the use of land. French thought followed a parallel course over the same period of time. The French Declaration of the Rights of Man, issued in 1789, said, "Whereas property rights are sacred and inviolable, no man could be deprived of them save for reasons of public need, expressed in legal form, and subject to proper compensation, paid beforehand."[1] The Civil Code of 1804 was a clear and total abandonment of the preexisting feudal concept of property, and emphasized: "Property is the right to enjoy and to dispose of things in the most absolute manner, provided that the use made of it is not prohibited by law or regulations."[2] From these points of departure, the French have developed a resistance to being told by the government what to do with their land that differs little from American landowners' behavior. French and American landowners also share an expectation of profiting from the unearned increment in land.

As Edgard Pisani, former minister of agriculture and of public construction, said:

May God forgive me, but I have the impression that the enemy, our enemy, is not the aristocracy but the bourgeoisie: it is not feudal property concepts, but the property concepts of the French Revolution and of the Civil Code. . . . In fact, property is for us a fundamental value and a cardinal virtue; it should be inscribed on the facades of our public buildings with the same emphasis as equality, and well ahead of liberty and fraternity.[3]

What set France on a course toward land banking some twenty years ago was not a widespread shift in popular beliefs but a different and more urgent set of pressures on land than those in the United States at that time. Growth in France had been minimal over the century from 1850 to 1950, with the population increasing by only 4 million. Suddenly, the growth rate turned upward and, between 1950 and 1970, the population increased by 9 million. Part of this increase was as a result of the repatriation of residents of former French colonies.

Rural outmigration was late in coming to France; as recently as 1950, only 50 percent of the population lived in cities of 2,000 people or more. Then, as people finally left the farms, cities grew at an average rate of 2.7 percent annually. Growth was unevenly distributed, with the Paris region and the southeast under great pressure while some other regions lost people. In the cities there was an acute shortage of housing, as a result of the damage or destruction of 2.5 million dwelling units during World War II and the failure until the mid-1950s of housing construction to approach an acceptable rate. In the rural areas inheritance laws had led to the splintering of holdings such that many farmers owned too little land, and, often, what land they had consisted of a number of small parcels spread out over too large an area for efficient use.

The government responded to these acute problems of growth and change by instituting national land use planning to set policies for the location of urban growth and national economic planning to establish economic growth targets. National investment was the principal means of implementing these plans. There was, at the time, little local land use planning or regulation that could be related to national planning.

In 1958, given the absence of effective local land use controls, the government decided to create a new control mechanism for major development that could be used to implement its growth policies. By that time there was substantial state aid for infrastructure and housing, and the state was sensitive to the fact that its assistance was fostering land speculation, which, in turn, was responsible for increasing housing costs. Land costs in the 1950s were rising three times as fast as construction costs. Robert Arrago[4] noted:

These incendiary prices reinforce residential segregation, thus accentuating the disparity and rigidity of social classes, standing in the way of realizing urbanization plans, adding to the cost of public works, and slowing the implementation of housing policy. In a word, they contribute to the growth of individual and collective frustrations.[5]

The then minister of public construction,[6] Albin Chalandon, observed:

The principal enemy of urbanism is the Frenchman's attachment to ownership of land. In this realm, one must navigate between reefs without looking for a perfect solution, because there is none. . . . A "municipalization" or, more precisely, a "collectivization" of land of a progressive and rational sort, which is the only definitive solution of the problem, is too utopian to wish to realize instantaneously.[7]

The government's first foray into design of a system of land use controls that could halt speculation while still leaving most land subject to little regulation met with considerable success and was the inspiration for several later systems. The concept was as follows: municipalities anticipating substantial growth should select locations for intensive rapid development to receive much of that growth; those locations should be designated priority urbanization zones; state and local infrastructure funds should be channeled to the zones; and land prices there should be controlled by a combination of public preemption power and purchase. The preemption power was one of the two essential elements of the system. Any land in the zone that was offered for sale could be preempted by the municipality with the price fixed at the land's value one year prior to the designation of the zone. Also essential to success was the availability of funds to enable municipalities to preempt often enough so that landowners would learn that the power was real.

Awareness that one could be preempted led to a willingness to negotiate sales of land at a fair price, either to municipalities or directly to developers for construction in accord with the plans for the zone. The municipalities had the power of condemnation as a back up, but it was seldom needed.

The state contributed to the realization of the zones in a number of ways It directed its land acquisition, infrastructure, and housing funds to them, mostly in the form of subsidized loans, it provided technical support through land appraisals and reviewing the economic feasibility of proposals, and it assisted in the formation and guidance of local companies to carry out development of the zones. These companies were another innovation, since they were formed by a combination of public and private shareholders, with the municipality always holding a majority interest.

Many municipalities responded to the enabling legislation and formed priority urbanization zones. The concept was well regarded, but its implementation alone was quite inadequate to cope with speculation. For instance, in the early 1960s land costs constituted 26 percent of the price of housing in the Paris region, even though most of the housing being built there consisted of high-density, high-rise apartments. The Ministry of Public Construction issued a warning:

The speculative increase in land prices has disastrous results, economic, social, and political. Through its very excesses, it could lead us to question the right of property, even if the latter remains the symbol and one of the best guarantees of individual liberty. The rapid increase in population and the related expansion of urban areas . . . involve a far-reaching redistribution of land and a considerable volume of transactions in conditions where demand is far in advance of supply.

It is not to be wondered at if this disequilibrium creates a certain pressure on prices, but the increase becomes an abuse when it derives from malfunctioning of the real estate market, from uncoordinated demand or the systematic withholding of supply. The public authorities, when they buy, service, or use land themselves, play a role in this respect that can be and ought to be decisive.[8]

The National Assembly concurred and, between 1960 and 1968, authorized several additional programs that expanded significantly the role of the public sector in land use control. These newer programs departed from the original model in a variety of respects; among the innovations were provisions for rural land preservation zones, long-term holding zones, land acquisition by private nonprofit and profit-making companies, valuation at market price at the time of preemption, and disposition by lease or subject to easements. The right of preemption is a constant in all but one of the systems, as is state participation, both financial and technical.

Experience with public designation of development or nondevelopment zones followed by limited public or publicly authorized land acquisition in order to control future use of the land has been positive for the most part. There have been some problems. Sufficient funds have not always been available when needed for land purchase. Politics have intervened so that at times zones that are less than ideal have been designated for development, and intensive development has been allowed and infrastructure provided outside the development zones. Private market housing has been difficult to attract to the development zones because of the concentration there of subsidized housing for people of modest and moderate income. Nonetheless, by 1971, the government was sufficiently committed to the concept of land acquisition to limit speculation and to control land use that the National Assembly, in approving the sixth national plan,[9] committed the state to spend $330 million (1.65 billion francs) to foster the acquisition of land reserves during the 1971–1975 period that it was in effect. The plan specifically urged that land be bought early, before much development value had settled.

France has responded to the prevailing sentiment for private control of land by designating large areas as zones in which acquisition could occur but then restricting actual purchase to the lands more critical for development, farming, or resource protection. This approach results in a rough sort of equity that dampens the grosser excesses of speculation while still leaving the bulk of land transactions in private hands.

### Land Banks and Land Use Controls

There is a current effort in France to affect the use of all land in urban areas by requiring enactment of zoning-type regulations. Because few municipalities have adopted these regulations so far, it is too soon to say whether the extent of uncompensated control over land use that the enabling legislation foresees them as achieving will be realized. Municipalities either may continue to drag their feet, adopting nothing, or may adopt regulations that are not stringent enough to bring about the location of development and the preservation of open space in accord with their own plans. In the meantime, both large-scale development and the preservation of open land are occurring through reliance on the land bank programs.

The six land bank programs that are described in this chapter have no characteristics common to all. They differ as to: whether the intended land use is urban, open, or a combination of both; whether they may be established by municipalities, departments,[10] regions,[11] the state, public authorities, and/or private agencies; their level of activity; whether they have a right of preemption; and how their land acquisitions are funded. About the only generalization possible is that, in one way or another, the state is important to the success of all of the programs and it exercises some influence on their decisions. Because it is important to understand and compare the approaches of all six programs, they have been summarized very briefly in table 4.1, before being described in greater detail in this and the following section of the chapter. This section provides an overview of the enabling laws and regulations and of the general operation of the programs. The final section is a review of how the programs actually function, using the Marseilles region as a focal point.

There is so much complexity within and variation among the programs that the summary here is likely to be most helpful if used first as a quick introduction and then returned to for a capsule review following a study of the details provided about each of the programs.

### Plans[12] and Plan Enforceability

As in the United States, local land use planning is a quite recent undertaking, one that was first instituted in the larger cities and metropolitan areas and that has not yet spread to many of the smaller municipalities. By law, all urban municipalities with 10,000 inhabitants or more were to have had plans in effect as of 1 January 1975. In reality, few of the municipalities met this deadline, but most had plans in process; by 1 January 1976, 19 percent had adopted them. Enforceable regulations to implement the plans are being adopted much more slowly. Also as of 1 January 1976, only 5 percent of the municipalities required to do so had enacted zoning controls.

As plans have become more widespread and as planning procedures have been refined, permission to develop increasingly has been tied to conformity with plans. There have been three stages of this linkage between plans and development permits. First, permits were loosely related to but not dependent on planning. During this period, which began at the end of World War II, building permits were a prerequisite for development,[13] with public as well as private development subject to the permit process.

The second stage began with a 1958 decree[14] that called for three types of plans: (1) master plans for urbanization, (2) detail plans for urbanization, and (3) summary urbanization plans for the smaller of France's thirty-eight thousand municipalities. The law called for these plans to be adopted or rejected by the municipal council of the affected municipalities following a public hearing. After approval, the plans then were subject to approval by the departmental prefect. A plan rejected by the municipal council still could be approved by joint order of the minister of public construction and minister of interior. The master plan was a long-term plan for a large area—a city, a metropolitan area, or a small region—that described desired land use and density in a general sense and specified the locations of major transportation and utility systems. The master plan also could indicate sites to be reserved for open space or for large-scale public development. If the land was shown as reserved for public use, the owner could demand that the public purchase the land within three years of the demand or else forfeit the right of acquisition.[15] The detail plan was more precise, applied to a smaller area, and was prepared when development was imminent. Building permits were to be granted based on its specifications. Many local governments did not adopt these plans, and, to protect its interests, the national government enacted a regulation to limit the granting of building permits. It provided: "When, by reason of their importance, their location, or their influence, projects would conflict with land use objectives reflected in regional economic and social development plans and national directives concerning development, building permits can be refused or granted subject to special conditions."[16]

The 1958 planning structure merits mention, not for its successes, but for its shortcomings. Pierre Raynaud, Secretary General of the Interminis-

TABLE 4.1. French Land Bank Programs

| Program Classified by Future Land Use | Year Instituted | Sponsor | Scale of Program | Preemption Power | Funding[a] |
|---|---|---|---|---|---|
| *Development* | | | | | |
| ZUP (priority urbanization zone) | 1958 | Municipality(ies). Development often by public-private corporation | At peak in late 1960s: 57,000 acres (23,000 hectares) and 28% of annual housing construction in zones. Most land in zone purchased | Right of preemption at land value 1 year prior to zone designation | Loan subsidized by FNAFU. Six-year term, amortization deferred 3 years. 1974 interest: 3.5–3.75% |
| ZAC (planned development zone) | 1967 | Any level of government or public authority. Acquisition and development often by private corporation | Almost 1,000 zones under development and over 500 more planned in 1975. Most land in zone purchased | No preemption unless in a ZAD. Two-year moratorium until zoning adopted | Public acquisition: FNAFU loan as above. Private acquisition: up to 50% of land cost by MATELT loan for 6 years with amortization deferred 3 years |
| *Open space* | | | | | |
| SAFER (farm acquisition) | 1960 1962 | Nonprofit company of farm organizations and farm lenders | Buys 12% of farm land on market each year | May preempt at current market value. Must resell with 15-year farm covenant | Loans from National Bank for Farm Credit up to 15 × SAFER capital + reserve. 1974 terms: 5 years at 4.5%. State subsidy. Fee charged to |

| | | | | | subdivision in zone |
|---|---|---|---|---|---|
| (...esque zone) | 1961 | state | France in 1974. Little of this to be acquired | preempt at current market value. No ZAC allowed in ZCP | |
| *Development and/or open space* | | | | | |
| ZAD (deferred development zone) | 1962 | Municipality(ies); state | Zones covered 1% of France in 1974. Some land acquired, much later released from zone | Preemptive right for 14 years at land value 1 year prior to zone designation | Antispeculation: FNAFU loan. Land bank: 25% local; up to 75% CAECL loans. 1974 terms: 15 years at 8.25%. Some direct state acquisition |
| Regional Council Land Bank | 1973 | Municipal or department initiative, regional approval | Small | No | Regional taxes, borrowing |

[a] The total loan funds available in 1974 for land acquisition from the principal state accounts were $16 million (80 million francs) through FNAFU and $40 million (200 million francs) through CAECL. Loans advanced by both of these agencies originate with the Central Savings Bank, the largest lender in France and the principal source of funds for plan implementation.

terial Mission for Languedoc-Roussillon, said of plans developed under the 1958 law:

The principal criticism in recent years of the urbanization plans is that they evolve so slowly that construction is held up awaiting their completion yet, once they are approved, the plans often have been overtaken by new imperatives that came into being during the study period. Hardly is their content known before revision begins.

Moreover, those plans actually adopted provide very imperfect information to administrators and landowners as to the building capacity of sites. The law concerning land use is imprecise and often unforeseeable, which leaves room for arbitrary decisions, slows construction, and favors speculation.[17]

The then minister of public construction voiced similar criticisms:

By an intellectual process that one can well understand, the pioneers of planning have tried to organize urban development through plans limited to a definition of long-term objectives. Since these plans are prepared *without any budgetary constraint*, these theoretical and unreal documents very often are utopian.

Operational planning now seeks to add programming to these schemes. . . . Ambitious, complex, and slow, this planning would have ended in blocking construction if general recourse to the variance had not acted as a safety valve. But case by case variances lead to subjectivity.[18]

Recognition of the 1958 law's unwieldy procedures, the lack of specificity of the master plans, delays in enactment, and the absence of priorities led to major legislative revisions in 1967. The Land Law of 1967[19] inaugurated the third and current stage of local planning and plan enforcement. Currently, numbers of planners question whether it has served planning objectives any better than its two predecessors. The 1967 law substituted the Schéma Directeur d'Aménagement et d'Urbanisme (SDAU), or Master Schematic Plan for Land Management and Urbanization, and the Plan d'Occupation des Sols (PLS), or Land Use Plan, for the master plan and detail plan.

An SDAU is described in the law as a middle-term, or thirty-year, schematic study for an urban area. It is mandatory for municipalities in urban areas with a population of 10,000 or more. A total of 9,616 municipalities with a population of 35.9 million people have been directed to prepare SDAUs. The 1972 target date for enactment of the SDAUs was moved back to 1975, but few municipalities met that deadline either. Only twelve SDAUs, for municipalities with a total population of 3.1 million, had been approved prior to 1 January 1975. However, one year later fifty-one SDAUs covering 1,788 municipalities with a population of 8.9 million had been adopted, so progress was being made.

The regional prefect has primary responsibility for obtaining municipal participation in the preparation of the SDAU. The prefect is charged with setting up a commission composed of the staffs of the departmental offices of the national ministries and elected officials of the municipalities in the urban area. Representatives of professional groups with skills to contribute are invited to work with the commission. A commission's work results in the production of a report that must include: (1) an analysis of the current situation and of prospective economic and demographic development in a regional context; (2) a statement of land use objectives and their justification, including the future relationship between urbanization and rural land management and the optimal use of existing and predicted major public construction; (3) the principal phases of the realization of the objectives; (4) a generalized map of future land use; and (5) a map or maps showing planned urban expansion and renewal, principal open spaces, sites to be protected, and principal public construction including infrastructure.[20] After comment and revision, the report is submitted to the municipal council for a formal opinion. Approval power is vested in the regional prefect or, in specified circumstances, in the Council of State.

The SDAU is an understanding between the local and national governments and is not binding on third parties. Once the SDAUs are in force, the law requires that Zones d'Aménagement Concertées (ZACs), or Planned Development Zones, major public acquisition for land banks or other purposes, and major public infrastructure construction be compatible with their land use objectives. The law also provides that a public agency acquiring a land reserve must "manage it as would a good father of a family."[21]

The POS, although termed a land use plan by the French, is analogous to the American system of zoning. A POS is required for municipalities in an urban area of over 10,000 people, for municipalities affected by a major catastrophe, for municipalities affected by other special circumstances, or upon the order of the prefect. For those areas in which a POS is required but that are not subject to an SDAU, a Plan for Rural Land Management (PAR, Plan d'Aménagement Rural)[22] must be prepared. These plans are similar in concept to the SDAU and, like it, must be respected by the regulatory provisions of the POS.

As of 1 January 1976, 8,378 municipalities with a population of 39.3 million had been directed to undertake work on the POS; only 418 municipalities with a population of 1.3 million had completed this work. The POS is prepared jointly by state and municipal officials and consists of: (1) a report that shows its compatibility with the SDAU if there is one, and that sets forth principles for economic and demographic change and public construction; (2) maps showing floor area ratio (Coefficient d'Occupation des Sols, or COS) districts, zones where infrastructure and other public construction warrant immediate development, nondevelopment zones including zones intended to remain undeveloped and zones not currently ready for development, zones presenting particular hazards to development, boundaries of particular areas such as Picturesque Zones, various categories of development zones, including Priority Urbanization Zones (Zones à Urbaniser par Priorité, or ZUPs), Deferred Development Zones (Zones d'Aménagement Différée, or ZADs), and ZACs, and utility easements; and (3) provisions (under French law they are administrative easements) spelling out permitted uses. There is no compensation for these provisions, although limitations on development in the various non-development zones are constrained by a law[23] that fixes one acre (4,000 square meters) as the maximum lot size that may be required for a structure.

The POS not only is binding on third parties, but it becomes so as soon as it is published rather than upon approval by the prefect. No development permits are to be granted unless in accord with the POS.

The major question posed by the POS concept is whether the French people will accept the degree of uncompensated regulation upon which it is premised. Olivier Guichard, while minister of public construction, expressed a positive view in 1973:

I believe it reasonable to foresee a future in which the development zone is used more selectively and in which it is replaced by the provisions adopted through land use plans that will protect agriculture from all urban intrusion while making possible its modernization and transformation.

Others, myself included, are dubious. So far, municipalities have been wary of applying the POS to limit the right to develop or have been ready to grant relief from its restrictions. The granting of eighty thousand building permits over the past five years in parts of the Paris region zoned as rural is one of many reasons for skepticism.

The remarks of a member of the municipal council of Le Tholonet, a rapidly developing suburb of Aix-en-Provence, aptly describe the situation of local officials.

The municipal council is approached by those who wish to protect all or almost all land, by others who wish no restrictions on the right to build—given a market, this clearly is very tempting—and by those who wish their land be open for development while others' land is protected. This situation is extremely uncomfortable, the more so because the POS is set by a commission composed of three municipal elected officials and representatives of the ministries of Agriculture, Public Construction, and Cultural Affairs and that, as a last resort, it can be imposed by the prefect on his signature alone. One must foresee, and foresee reasonably. . . . It is necessary to choose the solution that suits the greatest number.[24]

Max Falque, a resident of Le Tholonet and an environmental planner, also has questioned their equity:

Everything occurs as if the allocation of land values was by lottery. With 15 million landowners that means an equivalent number of tickets, which would constitute a record. Up to this point one could say that the procedure is one of proven popularity; no political platform has ever challenged the national lottery or trifacta. However, the dice are loaded. The planners lack the innocence of the big wheel and the ticket holders are able to alter their numbers. To do that, one only need have enough influence to obtain a change of zoning. In other words, the lottery would be honest if one believed in the perpetuity of land use plans. This is neither possible nor desirable because planning is but the reflection of socioeconomic conditions whose rapid evolution characterizes the contemporary world."[25]

The situation has become even more complex with the authorization, in 1976, of the transfer of development rights. A columnist for *Le Monde* who regularly writes about development issues observed, "The idea is ingenious but dangerous. In our law, urbanization easements cannot be paid for. . . . Isn't one going to nourish an illusion in the minds of landowners, encouraging them systematically to demand development rights on their land?"[26]

### Regulation and Acquisition of Land: The Zs

The success of the POS in enforcing plans thus remains an open question. There has, however, been extensive experience since 1958 with another approach to plan implementation, referred to colloquially as the Zs. Zs most commonly are development or deferred development zones— ZUPs, ZADs, or ZACs—but alternatively may be Picturesque Zones— Zones à Caractère Pittoresque, or ZCPs—where protection of the natural, historic, or esthetic character of the countryside or of specific sites is the objective.

As of 1975, construction was under way in almost one thousand development zones, and over five hundred more were planned or under study. The execution of plans for all types of Zs turns upon extensive land acquisition that may be either by voluntary negotiation, preemption in all but ZACs, or condemnation. The combination of controls applicable in the Zs, their linkage to local and state spending for infrastructure and development, and their involvement of the private sector provide a system unique to France. In the context of an individualistic society eager to protect private investment in land, it is a system that has been reasonably successful. Where it has not worked, this often has been due to a less than wholehearted commitment to the underlying planning principles and/or to inadequate funds at the time payment is due.

*ZUPs.* ZUPs were the earliest type of development zone, initiated in 1958,[27] to direct and time growth while restraining speculation. Although they now have been largely supplanted by ZADs and ZACs, many principles governing their organization, finance, and operation have remained constant. Therefore, an examination of the ZUP mechanism in some detail provides a basis for subsequent discussion of the other zones. The following review defines the ZUP, describes who is responsible for its designation and development, specifies how land acquisition and disposition occur, outlines sources of funding, and summarizes data on the use of ZUPs.[28]

ZUPs are zones designated by local government(s) for short-term development; they must include a minimum of 500 dwelling units and may include other types of land use. Land designated as a ZUP usually is publicly acquired, prepared for development, and then resold to private builders.

The enabling legislation for ZUPs states that they are intended to: (1) create rational development patterns and provide agreeable living conditions, particularly for people of moderate income; (2) coordinate the financing of land acquisition and development; (3) centralize construction of infrastructure; and (4) unify administrative responsibility for development areas spread over more than one municipality.

It was the further intent of the law that scattered development outside the ZUP should be discouraged. One mandate and one permissive device to channel development to ZUPs were included in the law. Any development in excess of 100 dwelling units that required public expenditure for infrastructure could be built only in a ZUP. In addition, municipalities were authorized to deny permission to develop small projects elsewhere if infrastructure was lacking and ZUP sites were available.

ZUP designation is requested by a municipality, or, if the site is located in more than one municipality, by all municipalities having jurisdiction over portions of the site. Approval is granted by the departmental prefect if fewer than 10,000 dwelling units are involved and by the Ministry of Public Construction for larger projects.

Once designated, ZUPs usually are placed under the charge of nonprofit companies known as SEMs (Sociétés d'Economie Mixte, or Public-Private Companies), which are joint undertakings of the public and private sectors.[29]

An SEM's capitalization must be at least $50,000 (250,000 francs). A minimum of 50 percent and a maximum of 65 percent of the capital must be subscribed by local government(s). Other subscribers may include departments, agencies of the state, moderate rent housing companies, chambers of commerce, savings banks, and housing associations. SEMs are managed by administrative councils of from three to twelve members, chaired by a person chosen by the participating local government(s).

SEMs were designed specifically to build large-scale urban developments. They are a preferred alternative to public-sector development because they provide a more flexible administrative structure. In addition, they allow both local and national governments to participate in policy decisions affecting specific projects. However, local and state development objectives are not always compatible, and provision for joint participation in an SEM gives no assurance that conflicts will be resolved. Since the state controls much of the funding for development projects, it has an influence disproportionate to the number of shares it may hold.

The state's power over SEM actions is not limited to its ability to grant or withhold funds. In addition, the departmental prefect—or the regional prefect if the SEM crosses department lines—is authorized to call and participate in meetings of the administrative council and may exercise a temporary veto over any action. The veto becomes permanent if confirmed within one month by the appropriate minister. This veto power gives the prefect a role in fundamental decisions of the SEMs.

An SEM often is inexperienced with development, and for this reason will turn to one of two national companies, Central Company for Public Construction (Société Centrale pour l'Equipement du Territoire, or SCET) or Subsidiary Company for Renewal and Land Development (Société Auxiliaire de la Rénovation et de l'Equipement Foncier, or SAREF),[30] for technical assistance and for help in the management and financing of its projects. Not all ZUPs are developed through SEMs, and not all SEMs rely on SCET or SAREF for aid, but an SEM-SCET relationship is the most usual pattern.[31] In 1968, SCET-affiliated SEMs produced some 120 thousand dwelling units (see fig. 4.1); 82 thousand, or 68 percent, were located in ZUPs. These 82 thousand dwelling units constituted 20 percent of the housing built during that year.

SCET is technically a private corporation, but in actuality the state exerts control over it through the Central Savings Bank (Caisse des Dépôts et Consignations, or CDC). In 1967, the Central Savings Bank created a holding company, SCDC (Société Centrale d'Aide au Développement des Collectivités, or Central Company for Local Government Development Assistance), for its various subsidiaries that provide technical assistance to local governments. The capital subscription of SCET after creation of this holding company is shown in table 4.2.

SCET has been characterized by the government as "a corporation that functions under the aegis of the administration in a spirit of public service."[32] It is a limited dividend corporation that may pay a maximum rate of 6 percent. Its governing administrative council consists of one representative of each of the shareholders, the president and the executive director of the corporation, and four mayors. The financial community and local governments thus have direct representation on the administrative council. The council also has nonvoting members, including representatives of

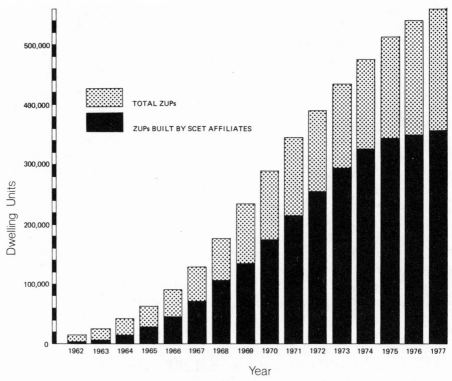

FIGURE 4.1. Housing construction by SCET-affiliated SEMs

SOURCE: Adapted from Société Centrale pour l'Equipement du Territoire, Département d'Aménagement, Yves Boddaert, to Max Falque, 21 August 1978

TABLE 4.2. SCET Shareholders

| Company | Capital Subscription | | |
| --- | --- | --- | --- |
| | Dollars | Francs | Percentage |
| SCDC | 2,040,000 | 10,200,000 | 51 |
| Central Savings Bank | 1,003,000 | 5,015,000 | 25 |
| National Bank | 239,200 | 1,196,000 | 6 |
| Land Bank of France | 239,200 | 1,196,000 | 6 |
| National Bank for Farm Credit | 239,200 | 1,196,000 | 6 |
| National Bank for State Markets | 239,200 | 1,196,000 | 6 |
| Bank of France | 200 | 1,000 | |
| Total | 4,000,000 | 20,000,000 | 100 |

SOURCE: Société Centrale d'Aide au Développement des Collectivités.

several ministries, the national planning commission, (Délégation à l'Aménagement du Territoire et à l'Action Régionale, or DATAR), and the prefect of the Paris region.

The state has several ways of exercising influence—through its holdings in some of the SCET shareholders, through its nonvoting members of the council, and through its power of approval of the people chosen to be the president and executive director of SCET and of the four mayors chosen to serve on the council.

The distribution of shares in SCET is a good clue as to its primary function, which is to be an intermediary between the SEMs and the principal sources of development financing. SCET helps the SEMs by offering good financial planning plus access to lenders. The Central Savings Bank and the other lenders benefit from this by having greater assurance as to the safety of their investments.

The agreement between an SEM and SCET is likely to provide for administrative services, legal advice, and financial planning. SCET will acquire a few shares in the SEM and will assign some of its staff to the SEM for the duration of the agreement. Its fee is 3.5 percent of the total cost of the project. François d'Arcy has evaluated the SEM-SCET structure as it has contributed to the realization of ZUPs and comes up with a mixed appraisal from both local and state officials.

A questionnaire sent to mayors of 141 cities with populations over 30,000 was completed and returned by 65 of them. Thirty-three had had an SEM-SCET project, 15 had had an SEM project not affiliated with SCET, 16 had had no SEM project, and 1 did not provide a responsive answer. Some of the questions and answers[33] are given in table 4.3.

Thus, many local governments have depended on SEMs and SCETs to create their ZUPs, often because they lack adequate technical or administrative staff. However, many are concerned that creating an SEM and having it contract with SCET is likely to result in some loss of local control. D'Arcy quotes a mayor of a city of fifty thousand who holds a negative view:

The question posed is whether a local government retains project control if it turns to SCET or a similar company for help. To this question, based on information I was able to obtain before undertaking our ZUP, I answer: no. The fact that the local government holds a majority interest in the stock of the SEM alters nothing. The SEM will have its own administrative staff, research office, and working capital. In reality, if the local government calls in SCET it in effect gives up its right to disagree, and there is a real triumph for technocracy.[34]

The prefects, although appointees of the state, have a different perspective from that of the state's central administration. They have considerable

TABLE 4.3. Municipal Evaluation of ZUP Management

| Question | Number of Respondents |
|---|---|
| Is it normal to create a SEM to develop a ZUP? | 25 |
| Or should very big cities develop their own ZUPs? | 11 |
| Or should all medium-sized cities develop their own ZUPs? | 26 |
| Can a municipality using a SEM-SCET structure maintain sufficient control of the project? | |
| Yes | 39 |
| No | 25 |
| No response | 3 |
| Do you think that a SCET-aided project costs more than one undertaken by a municipality? | |
| Yes | 32 |
| No | 24 |
| No response | 9 |
| Local governments hold the majority of the stock in SEMs; is this an important means of control? | |
| Yes | 50 |
| No | 12 |
| No response | 3 |
| If your answer was yes, does intervention of SCET in SEM management reduce possible local control? | |
| Yes | 20 |
| No | 28 |
| No response | 2 |
| What would you think of putting some mayors on the SCET administrative council?[a] | |
| Necessary | 27 |
| Desirable | 21 |
| Would have no practical outcome | 13 |
| No response | 4 |

SOURCE: François D'Arcy, *Structures Administratives et Urbanisation* (Paris: Berger-Levrault, 1968).

[a] The questionnaire was distributed before the four mayors were added to the SCET administrative council.

power over decisions of the SEMs and since the mid-1960s, when the ministries established department-level staffs under the prefects, have had the ability to provide a range of technical services as well. For instance, since 1966, staff members of the Departmental Office of Public Construction (Direction Départementale d'Equipement, or DDE), the Land Administration, and the treasurer–paymaster general have served as technical advisers on SEM administrative councils. The prefects also have some ability to assist the SEMs in obtaining short-term loans. Therefore, there exists a certain degree of rivalry between the prefects and SCET as to who can best serve the SEMs.

According to d'Arcy, officials of the central government judge SCET as having been successful and indispensable. Prior to its creation, the state had failed to establish a means of coordinating local development with state and private financing. There was too much centralization of ZUP reviews and too little coordination of funding decisions. As a Ministry of Public Construction report commented:

After the euphoria of the first years, one gradually perceived that it wasn't sufficient to create many ZUPs, but that it was necessary to have the financial means to acquire land and equip it. The administration, having undertaken too many projects, couldn't follow through properly on them all.[35]

SCET was able to offer flexibility, a degree of removal from the state bureaucracy, central responsibility, and speedier results. As d'Arcy concludes, it was the prior incoherence of the state's actions in financing large-scale development that made SCET essential and that was the source of its power.[36]

The ability to acquire all land in a ZUP at a nonspeculative price and then to carry out its development in accordance with publicly adopted plans provides a powerful means of directing urbanization. Public acquisition, usually carried out through an SEM, may be by voluntary purchase, preemption, or condemnation. Voluntary purchase is most common, since the existence of the preemption and condemnation powers is enough to persuade most owners to negotiate sales.

The legal device of a public right to preempt private market sales[37] has been developed by the French to serve as an effective damper on land prices. As applied in ZUPs, any landowner who wishes to sell and who has an acceptable offer must notify the municipality in which the land is located of the offer and its terms. The municipality, or more usually the SEM if one has been designated as developer for the ZUP, then has two months to preempt the buyer. Whoever holds the preemption right must notify the prefect as to whether the right will or will not be exercised. If it is not exercised, the prefect has a further period of one month to preempt on behalf of the state. The right of preemption exists for four years after the creation of the ZUP and may be extended for an additional two years.

A key feature of preemption under this law is the avoidance of payment for a publicly created development value. Compensation is calculated on the existing use value of the land preempted measured one year prior to the designation of the ZUP, rather than the market value at the time of the preemption.

If a landowner refuses to sell to the municipality or SEM voluntarily and does not attempt to negotiate a private sale and so provide an opportunity for the use of the preemptive right, condemnation is the remaining alternative. The first step is to obtain a Declaration of Public Utility (Déclaration d'Utilité Publique, or DUP). Since 1967, there has been no question but that the public purpose includes land acquired for land banks. The state, local governments, urban communities, urban districts, and groups of local governments that are competent in urban planning are authorized to acquire real property, if need be by condemnation, in order to form land reserves with a view to extending agglomerations, providing for open space surrounding these agglomerations, or creating new towns or tourist resorts. Therefore, for ZUPs and other Zs there is little problem in obtaining the approval of the DUP. When there is an SDAU, acquisition may take place only in order to carry out that plan.[38] Since 1958, the law has stated that land condemned for a development zone may be resold to a private developer.

Condemnation law has undergone several revisions in recent years with respect to the basis for valuation. As of 1935, the law specified that any increase in value due to the anticipation of a public project was not to be included in the condemnation award. The law was amended in 1962 as follows: (1) it reaffirmed the above 1935 provision and stated that value added by the expectation of regulatory change should also be excluded; (2) it shifted the date of valuation to one year prior to the hearing on the DUP from valuation as of the date of the award;[39] and (3) it specified that the award should be based solely on the land's value for currently permitted uses.[40] The 1962 law was not enforced, because the expropriation judges found it unfair to remove the value added by expectations of public action when landowners whose property was not expropriated could sell for a price that included this value. Public pressure led to a modification in 1965: the valuation date became the date of establishing the amount of the award, but the valuation was based on the existing use value of the property one year prior to the DUP hearing.[41] This change was intended to preserve from the 1962 act the screening out of use value changes occasioned by the announcement of the taking but at the same time to protect the landowner from losses due to inflation between the time of valuation and the time of payment. A companion bill, passed on the same day, provided that valuation in preemption proceedings should be carried out exactly as in condemnation,[42] except that the date for establishing existing use value is one year prior to designation of the ZUP.

The law, if applied as intended, does protect the public from paying for values that it has created. However, there is a certain injustice in that this gain can be realized in private market transactions. As Arrago says: "The law of 10 July 1965 penalizes heavily those who are expropriated because neighboring landowners can realize freely the development value denied to the expropriated. . . . Such provisions are contrary to the constitutional principle of the equality of citizens in relation to public expenses."[43]

Appraisal of the value of the land is the responsibility of the Land Administration,[44] which handles appraisals for all public purchases save those of the Central Savings Bank and its subsidiaries and purchases below an amount set by the minister of economics and finance. The Land Administration is under the jurisdiction of the state's Tax Office and has staff in each department who answer to the departmental prefect.[45] Values are set by site visits and by reference to comparable sales, with data obtained from the Land Administration's detailed and up to date records of all property transactions and tax assessments. There is no stated methodology for separating out value attributable to public actions, and Arrago, among others, sees this as a troublesome problem.

Since 1957, the most complex appraisals have been carried out by an elite corps of inspectors working out of the Paris central headquarters. These inspectors are expected, by the example of their appraisals, to disseminate national perspectives on valuation to the inspectors working at the department level.

Once an inspector has placed a value on land, the appraisal is submitted by the departmental director of the Land Administration to the central office, which then issues acquisition approval to the SEM or local government. Although the Land Administration is a state agency establishing values for public purchases, there is widespread agreement that it operates in a fair and objective manner.

Acquisitions are subject to a second state control, this one with respect to economic viability. The Commission for the Control of Land Projects (La Commission de Contrôle des Opérations Immobilières) is headed by a member of the Council of State appointed by the prime minister; like the Land Administration, staff work in each department is under the prefect, while the central office in Paris coordinates department work. The staff's task is to review comments on the economic aspects of acquisition proposals, received from such sources as mayors, prefects, planning offices, and the Land Administration, and to prepare a report from a neutral perspective. Since the state is the source of much of the funding for land acquisition, this report is intended to provide an independent judgment, free from the biases of local proponents.

Once the Land Administration has determined the land value and the Commission for Control of Land Projects has prepared its report, the SEM or public agency makes an offer. In the case of a preemption, if the price offered is equal to the price that the seller was prepared to accept on the private market, the seller may not refuse the offer. Otherwise, he or she has one month to accept the offer, request condemnation, or withdraw from the market. Silence on the part of the seller is deemed to be a withdrawal from the market.

There is a widespread consensus that court awards on condemnation are overgenerous, contribute to rising land prices, and are not in accord with the intent of the law. As Arrago comments:

The judges often appear to forget that Article 544 of the Civil Code, which confers virtual sovereignty over his land to the owner . . . was drafted during an epoch (the eighteenth century) when individualism triumphed. . . . This liberal and individualistic tendency of the code, favoring the most extreme individual property rights, has been changing since the mid-twentieth century, during which time property has become a social function and the rights of the individual are considered to be subject to limitation on behalf of the public interest.[46]

Parfait offers a further explanation:

All would be perfect if the estimates of the Land Administration inspectors were accepted . . . by the land judges and if there weren't, in some cases, discrepancies of up to 200 percent. This anomaly results . . . from a sort of rivalry between functionaries of the administrative and judicial branches. . . . Article 21 imposes on the court a series of directives that must form a brake on speculation [but] . . . these rules . . . are applied very narrowly by judges of the court concerned about protecting private property.[47]

High court awards encourage sellers to have recourse to condemnation and discourage municipalities from its use.

One heralded advantage of the right of preemption is that the public gains immediate control over land yet need not pay for this control by acquisition until landowners seek to sell. Unfortunately, there are factors that inhibit the ideal operation of this system. Land may be needed quickly, long before an owner wishes to sell. This situation calls for the use of eminent domain and enough funds in hand to make payment. Alternatively, a number of landowners may band together, seek prospective buyers, and demand preemption before the public planned to acquire their land, knowing that sufficient public funds are not available and that as a result they will be able to sell for whatever the market will pay. A successful response to both of these situations turns upon ready availability of funds. Given the complex nature of the funding process, funds often have not been at hand when needed.

Development of a financial plan is probably the most vital service that the SCET staff renders to the SEM. For a ZUP, a budget is prepared that shows both the purpose for which funds are needed and the sources of funding. There are five purpose categories: land acquisition, primary, secondary, and tertiary viability, and general expenses. Primary viability includes those facilities that tie the ZUP to its metropolitan area, secondary viability includes facilities that serve residents of the ZUP in general, and tertiary viability includes private facilities, such as parking and gardens for individual residents. The mix of funding by developers, local governments, the state, and lending institutions and the availability of subsidies depends upon the category of purpose for which the funds are needed. The sole funding discussed here is that for land acquisition.

Municipalities may buy with their own funds, but rarely do these suffice. They are not allowed to float bonds for land acquisition, but they may borrow on the private market. However, the rate paid may not exceed a rate set monthly by the government. Funds seldom are available at or below this rate. This leaves agencies of the state as the prime sources of loans or grants.

State funds for land acquisition, as well as for other ZUP needs, are granted only after completion of a several-stage approval process. First, the sum needed must be included in the budget of the regional prefect. This budget is the means of implementing the regional sector of the national economic and social development plan.[48] The regional budget must be approved by the Fonds de Développement Economique et Social (FDES), a national intergovernmental agency headed by the minister of finance and economic affairs. Other members of FDES are the ministers of interior, public construction, industry and commerce, education, agriculture, and social affairs, and the heads of the National Planning Commission, Land Bank, and Central Savings Bank. National plan perspective is contributed by an interministerial committee concerned with land acquisition for development zones.[49]

Once the budget lines for the ZUP are approved by FDES, funds can be allocated. The Central Savings Bank is the principal source of loans for land acquisition in ZUPs. It requires local government guarantees on most of its loans to SEM, reducing the likelihood of default and increasing the continuity of repayment to help the bank's rate of return. The principal sum of the loan is based on an estimate of the price that the SEM will receive for the land on resale. The loans to the municipalities or SEMs often receive an interest subsidy from the National Fund for Land Management and Urban Planning (Fonds Nationale d'Aménagement Foncier et d'Urbanisme, or FNAFU).[50] Since 1964, the loans have been for terms of no more than six years. Amortization of the principal is delayed for three years on five- and six-year loans and for lesser periods on shorter term loans. As of 1974, the Central Savings Bank interest rate of 7 percent could be subsidized by FNAFU[51] to bring it down to 3.5 or 3.75 percent to borrowers.[52]

The time required to process an application may be four to six months. If an SEM needs money to pay for land before the loan is received it must borrow either from private banks or SCET for the interim, backed by a municipal guarantee.

SCET offers another type of financial service to its participating SEMs. Any SEM that has temporarily uncommitted funds received with the assistance of SCET may place them in a pool of SCET-SEM funds at the Central Savings Bank, which lends them to other SEMs for short terms.

Once the land in a ZUP has been purchased and the infrastructure installed, the SEM offers sites for sale or lease. Sale has been the more common practice except for the city of Lyons and La Défense, the major office development project adjacent to Paris. FDES has a formula for setting the price that covers costs of acquisition, improvements, and administration. The Land Administration, the prefect, and the departmental director of the Ministry of Public Construction all must be consulted by the SEM and have a right of approval over the prices to be set for sites for various uses. Sites for government-subsidized moderate income housing are priced lower than sites for private market housing. As Jamois notes, this policy led to difficulties in selling the private market sites:

Private developers hesitate to undertake unsubsidized housing projects in ZUPs because, first, they must pay a price for land that is, if not higher, at least often the same as the price for land at the center of metropolitan areas and, second, they must consider client preference, which often evinces little desire to buy relatively expensive housing on the outskirts of a city and in areas for the most part inhabited by people of modest income.[53]

As of 1966, 173 ZUPs had been designated, covering 56,810 acres (23,000 hectares). Fifty-three percent of the land in the ZUPs was already in public hands. Development in these ZUPs was planned to include 754 thousand dwelling units. The number of dwelling units planned per ZUP ranged from the legal minimum of 500 up to 23,000. Actual annual housing construction in ZUPs had risen to 116 thousand units by 1967, or about 28 percent of all housing construction during that year. Forty percent of this construction was by SCET-affiliated SEMs. (See fig. 4.2.)

Although the power to establish development zones had been used widely, the desired antispeculative effect on other urban fringe land did not materialize. Between 1958 and 1964, urban land prices rose by 20 percent per year nationally and by 25 percent in the Paris and Lyons urban areas. By 1975, only 116 ZUPs were still under development, and no new ones were contemplated.

Jamois, commenting on the success of ZUPs, concluded that many were doomed to fail because political pressure had caused the choice of unsuitable sites, sometimes sites where there was insufficient demand for housing and sometimes sites poorly serviced by public facilities.

*ZADs.* ZADs were authorized in 1962,[54] four years after ZUPs, to be the second weapon in the French antispeculative arsenal. Areas designated as ZADs lie in the path of development projected to occur ten to fifteen years in the future. The intended use of the ZADs often is unspecified or unknown, but designation is authorized where there is considered to be a need to restrain land prices. In 1971,[55] the purposes for which ZADs may be designated were expanded to include acquisition of land for the establishment of land banks.

ZADs often serve as pre-ZUPs or pre-ZACs in that they are designated for large areas well in advance of need of the land for development; then, when development is timely, the zone is partly or wholly redesignated as a

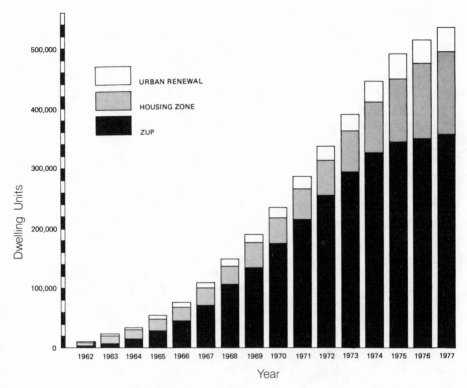

FIGURE 4.2.  Housing in ZUPs

SOURCE:  Adapted from Société Centrale pour l'Equipement du Territoire, Département d'Aménagement, Yves Boddaert, to Max Falque, 21 August 1978

ZUP or ZAC. In a similar manner, ZADs serve as holding zones for major public works projects such as expressways, ports, and airports.

Land included in a ZAD may later be determined to be most desirable used as open space or for low-density development. In this case it is released from the ZAD designation after sufficient other land had been acquired for development and the danger of speculation has passed.

ZADs are created in much the same manner as ZUPs. The power to designate a ZAD is vested as follows: (1) with the departmental prefect in response to a request from one or more municipalities; (2) with the minister of public construction if the holder of the right of preemption is to be the state or specified public authorities or if the proposed ZAD crosses departmental boundaries; or (3) with the Council of State if there have been negative comments from the affected municipality or municipalities. While the state can create a ZAD, local initiative is encouraged and preferred.[56] If the danger of speculation is particularly severe, a prefect, in response to a municipal request, can create a provisional ZAD for a three-year term pending approval of a conventional ZAD.

Upon designation, a right of preemption comes into being that binds the landowner for fourteen years.[57] The right of preemption also exists in the provisional ZAD and may be exercised by the prefect. If there has been a provisional ZAD, its three-year term is counted as part of the total fourteen-year preemption period for the ZAD. The preemption price, as in ZUPs, is the existing value of the land one year prior to designation, valued as of the time of preemption. Certain involuntary transactions, including eminent domain, passage of title through an estate, and awards in bankruptcy, are exempt from the right of preemption.

The fourteen-year preemption period is made less onerous for the landowner by an escape provision. One year after designation of a ZAD, any affected landowner may demand that the holder of the right of preemption buy the land, either at a mutually agreeable price or by condemnation. The holder of the right of preemption then has six months in which to proceed. If the land is acquired, payment must be made within six months either of the decision to acquire at the asking price or of the settlement of the condemnation price. If the right of preemption is not exercised, the landowner may demand the retrocession of all rights to the property, which then may be sold free of any preemptive right. If land in a ZAD becomes part of a ZUP, the operative date for purposes of determining land value is one year prior to designation of the ZAD.

Since more than twenty times as much land has been placed in ZADs as in ZUPs—1,358,500 acres (550,000 hectares) were in ZADs as of 1974—adequacy of financing has become an ever more critical issue. As Parfait observes, inability to buy land

is uniquely the consequence . . . of the legislator who gives the state and local governments a right . . . and refuses to give them a means of using it. Shouldn't one, each time an order issues establishing a ZUP or ZAD, inscribe in the local government or state budget . . . the credits necessary for implementation of the right of preemption?[58]

The state's target is to have 2.47 million acres (1 million hectares), or 2 percent of the total land area, in ZADs by 1980. Unless adeqaute funds are available for land assembly, designation will be a vain act. The state has recognized the merit of Parfait's criticism and has acted to make more money available. Whether the funding is sufficient remains to be seen.

In 1972, regional prefects were given responsibility for developing regional programs (Groupe Interministériel Foncier, or GIF) to relate land acquisition needs to available funds. They were directed to consult with the departmental prefects and then to project how much land was expected to be placed in ZADs in 1973 and up until the end of the sixth plan in 1975. Next, they were to estimate the funds needed for proper use of the right of preemption in existing ZADs and in ZADs likely to be created. These regional programs must be updated annually. After reviewing the programs from all of the regions, the Interministerial Land Group[59] notifies each regional prefect of the region's loan allocation, which the prefect then suballocates by department. Since 1972,[60] there have been two types of state loans authorized, one for each category of ZAD acquisition—the antispeculative purchase and the land bank.

Preemptions by local governments or public authorities for the purpose of restricting speculation are eligible for FNAFU-subsidized loans[61] under the terms previously described for ZUPs. The loan sum available for these subsidies was doubled from $8 million (40 million francs) in 1971 to $16 million (80 million francs) in 1972. Preemptions by the state or prefects are funded through another FNAFU account.[62]

For land banks, principally in ZADs, the state provided $40 million (200 million francs) in loan funds in 1971 and again in 1972, 1973, and 1974. Funds for the loans come from the Central Savings Bank and are placed with the Bank to Assist Local Governments with Public Construction, or CAECL (Caisse d'Aide à l'Equipement des Collectivités Locales, created in 1971), which administers the loans. Municipalities apply to the regional representative of the Central Savings Bank, who submits recommendations to CAECL after consulting the prefect and the Departmental Office of Public Construction. If the proposed acquisition affects more than one department, the regional prefect must be consulted. If the loan is approved, CAECL advances the funds. In 1974, the interest rate was 8.25 percent. The loan term is fifteen years, and amortization of the principal is not deferred. The land bank loans are solely for long-term holdings; land that is expected to be equipped with infrastructure within six or seven years is specifically excluded. The local government is expected to provide at least 25 percent of the acquisition cost.

If the state acts to preempt, its acquisition is funded through FNAFU. Under special circumstances, FNAFU may advance money for land bank acquisitions. Figure 4.3 shows the structure of acquisitions in ZADs for land subject to preemption. While preemption is not widespread, the government asserts that, on an average, land is purchased at half the price that would be demanded without the power to preempt.[63]

To a much lesser extent, acquisition of land in ZADs to constitute land banks may be by direct state action or by state grants to local governments. The Central Savings Bank invests part of its funds in land intended for future development and seeks a return on the investment of approximately 8 percent per year. The Ministry of Public Construction provides funds both for land bank and open space acquisition. In 1974, the

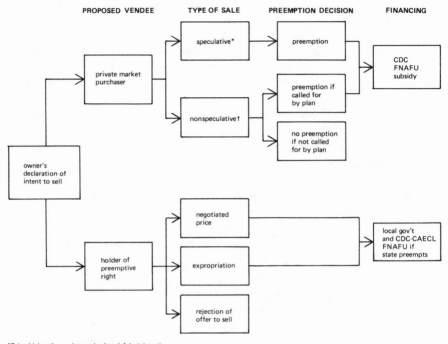

PROPOSED VENDEE    TYPE OF SALE    PREEMPTION DECISION    FINANCING

*Price higher than value set by Land Administration
†Price equal to or lower than value set by Land Administration

FIGURE 4.3. ZAD acquisition of land subject to preemption

SOURCE: Adapted from Max Falque, SOMI, Aix-en-Provence, letter, 1974
* Price higher than value set by Land Administration
† Price equal to or lower than value set by Land Administration

amounts, respectively, were $77,000 (367,000 francs) and $7 million (35 million francs).

An example from the Paris region illustrates some of the difficulties associated with ZADs, as well as reasons why the public sector finds it necessary to turn to them. The Land and Technical Agency of the Paris Region, the AFTRP, is responsible for providing sites for over 100,000 dwelling units each year, as well as for buying land to provide accompanying open space. In 1969, the AFTRP sought and obtained the designation of a 138,200-acre (56,000 hectare) ZAD covering parts of forty-five municipalities located between Paris and Chartres.[64] (See map 4.1.) An autoroute linking Paris to Chartres and Orléans was expected to be located somewhere in the ZAD, and the area was undergoing rapid urban expansion as well. The SDAU shows two areas within the ZAD, namely, the Valley of Chevreuse and the plateau overlooking it, as agricultural open

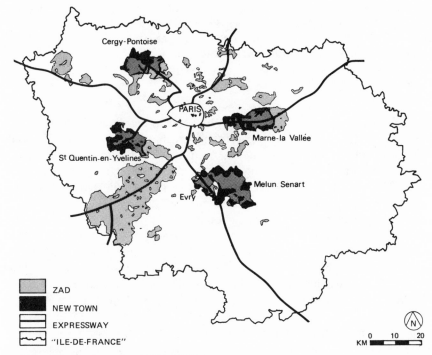

MAP 4.1.  Paris region ZADs, 1974

SOURCE: Adapted from Préfecture de la Région d'Ile-de-France, Institut d'Aménagement et d'Urbanisme de la Région d'Ile-de-France, *La Région d'Ile-de-France en
bref* (Paris, 1977), p. 18

space. In 1974, the duke of Luynes and Chevreuse decided to sell two
tracts of fields and woods in this area, totaling 3,389 acres (1,372 hectares), to Lazard Bank. The AFTRP, which holds the power of preemption
in the Paris region, preempted the sales. At that time there was no POS,
and one was not expected to be completed until 1976. Lazard Bank had
offered $7.6 million (38 million francs) for the land, or $2,243 per acre
(27,697 francs per hectare). The Land Administration valued one tract of
1,359 acres (550 hectares) at $2.9 million (14.5 million francs), or 85
percent of the owner's asking price of $3.4 million (17 million francs). In
attacking the preemption, the duke said that the action showed:

a lack of confidence in the state and its regulations. . . . The government says,
"I am buying because I am weak next to the power of the bankers." I don't
understand why M. Guichard[65] didn't solemnly declare, "This land is protected; I will allow no variance." At this rate it will be necessary to buy all the
sensitive sites in France—half the country. . . . Lazard Bank controls some
insurance companies; it must have some land reserves. This is a good invest-

ment since it has been proven that the value of rural lands rises, particularly when the lands are open. I know M. David Weill, the president of the bank well; he is a childhood friend. He came hunting at my grandmother's. If I had thought for one second that he intended to sell randomly in the valley, I never would have signed the agreement. . . . I certainly will not accept the price offered by the Land Administration.[66]

If the POS had been in effect and if it had shown the duke's land in a farm use zone, would the AFTRP have found preemption necessary? Theoretically not, but the duke's comments accurately reflect the public sector's skepticism about its own regulations, a skepticism that, for many, extends to the POS as well as the SDAU. As the duke points out, the price of open land keeps rising, making it an excellent investment; the price does not keep rising because the land grows good potatoes.

   *ZACs.*[67] The ZAC is an umbrella category established in 1968 to embrace all of the previously created development zones, including ZUPs, industrial zones, housing zones, and urban renewal zones. It is distinct from the ZAD, which is a deferred development or holding zone.

   ZACs have two stated objectives: (1) to offer land for development that has been properly equipped with public services, and (2) to organize major metropolitan development projects so that they occur in the right place at the right time with adequate financing. This description applies equally well to ZUPs. The principal difference is that ZACs are likely to feature private-sector participation at the project scale, rather than at the subdivision scale as previously. In fact, the desire to achieve broader and earlier private investment was a major force behind enactment of the ZAC legislation. Frequently, contracts are entered into for private companies to acquire the land, install the infrastructure, and carry out the development.

   In describing the provisions that govern ZACs, much of what has been said about ZUPs remains applicable. Where the laws and regulations have changed, in general the ZUPs are still governed by the previous provisions.

   ZACs may be initiated by the state, a department, a municipality, an urban community, or a public authority. Designation of ZACs is by the minister of public construction, who has delegated part of this power to the prefects. Since 1970,[68] prefects approve the designation of ZACs, other than ZUPs and urban renewal zones; where the applicant is a municipality, a department, or a nonstate public authority, the zone will provide fewer than 10,000 dwelling units, no unusual subsidy is required, and, where relevant, the regional prefect endorses the program for major public works. If the state or a department seeks to create a ZAC, it must consult the municipality or municipalities in which the ZAC would be located. If it fails to obtain their approval, the state or department may designate the ZAC only upon obtaining a joint order from the ministers of public construction and interior, or, if the affected area has a population in excess of 50,000, by decree of the Council of State.[69]

Once a ZAC has been designated, the power to prepare detailed plans, to acquire land, to install infrastructure, and to develop the site may be exercised by the public body that applied for the designation, by some other public body on the request of the applicant, by an SEM, or by contract with a private company. If execution of the ZAC is to be by a private company, the contract must be approved by a joint order of the ministers of public construction and interior or, if the contract is of a form approved by the Council of State, by the prefect.[70]

ZACs must conform with SDAUs but, instead of being governed by the POS, are subject to their own Plan for Development of the Zone, or PAZ (Plan d'Aménagement de la Zone). However, the goals of the POS and PAZ must be compatible. Furthermore, the desire of local governments to create ZACs is being used as an incentive to bring about their adoption of the SDAU and POS. A 1974 Ministry of Public Construction regulation provides:

With the intent of inciting local governments to accelerate approval of the SDAU and publication and approval of the POS, and to establish ZACs only if they are compatible with them, . . . from this point on I establish the following conditions for creation of ZACs: (1) Where there is a POS but no SDAU, a ZAC may not be established outside the urban zones or future urban zones of the POS; . . . (2) if the POS has not been made public, the designation of ZACs will be deferred until publication; (3) municipalities in which neither an SDAU nor a POS has been adopted . . . shall have no ZAC designation that includes housing.[71]

The PAZ consists of maps showing the principal streets and future land use, regulations to apply within the ZAC, and, sometimes, provisions governing esthetics. Accompanied by the construction program and a description of proposed financing, the PAZ is submitted to the prefect for approval. In many instances a public hearing must precede the approval.[72]

There is no right of preemption in a ZAC, other than for ZUPs. However, if the ZAC is located within a ZAD, as is often the case, the preemptive rights of the ZAD may be exercised. In addition, any public body that initiated the creation of a ZAC may enact a two-year moratorium on construction within the ZAC. After this period, if no PAZ has yet been adopted, any refusal to issue a building permit for construction creates a right in the landowner to demand that the public body buy the land within three years. If a PAZ has been adopted, the permit shall issue if the application is in accord with the PAZ and shall be denied if it is not.

The regulations governing the acquisition of land in a ZAC by condemnation depend on whether the organization carrying out the development is public or private.[73] If the developer is an SEM and is essentially public, the local government where the ZAC is located has the legal authority to condemn land. However, the regulations specify that condemnation should not be used for more than 5 or 10 percent of the total area and that the future use of the land should be for a public purpose. The regulatory limitations on public-sector condemnation arise from a concern for public opinion. If large amounts of land are taken from one private owner by a local government and, after improvement, are resold to other private owners, this would lead to objections. In the words of the regulation, "it is not to be doubted that massive use of expropriation would be, in this case, inopportune."[74]

If the land developer is from the private sector, condemnation is authorized for land needed for realization of the ZAC and frequently is used extensively as the only way to assemble land speedily. Landowners are to be paid promptly and construction should be completed within six years. A private-sector developer may negotiate with the local government to assume the costs of infrastructure construction in lieu of paying the usual infrastructure tax.[75]

Public-sector developers of ZACs except for urban renewal zones may apply for advance loans for land acquisition.[76] The loans are from the Central Savings Bank and receive an interest subsidy from FNAFU. If the ZAC designation was of a type delegated to the departmental prefect, then the prefect may approve these loans subject, of course, to the total amount of FNAFU-subsidized loan funds allocated to the department by the regional prefect. Other eligible ZAC developers must seek the loans through the Ministry of Public Construction. Loans solely for land acquisition and up to one-half of the total land acquisition cost may be granted after the designation of the ZAC and before a provisional financing plan has been adopted. These loans may be for four or five years with amortization deferred for two years or, at most, for six years with amortization deferred for three years.

*Picturesque Zones.*[77] Ever since 1930,[78] France has had legislation to protect significant sites, particularly places of historic and architectural importance. In 1959, the application of this law was extended to cover large natural areas, either rural or urban, to be protected as woods or open space.[79] In 1960, these areas were designated Sensitive Zones (Zones Sensibles),[80] and over the next two years various regulations were issued for the administration of such zones. In 1961, in a related move, the Finance Law established the Departmental Open Space Tax (Redevance Départementale d'Espaces Vertes, or RDEV)[81] to be levied on all development in Sensitive Zones, with the revenue earmarked for open space acquisition or maintenance. A new zone, the ZEP, or Zone d'Environnement Protégé, was created in 1977.

All of this legislation and the accompanying regulations are precursors to the current legislation and regulations providing for Picturesque Zones. This term encompasses all of the previously designated areas, such as Sensitive Zones, areas surrounding national and regional parks, and classified architectural or historical sites. As of 1974, there were seven hundred Picturesque Zones affecting parts of nine thousand municipalities and covering one-third of the nation.

Development is not barred in Picturesque Zones, but it is subject to more stringent regulation to assure its compatibility with the outstanding characteristics of a zone. In addition to the regulation of development, the public interest is protected by a right of preemption[82] and by the Departmental Open Space Tax, which taxes the development allowed to provide funds for the purchase of compensating reserves.

The government's stated purpose for authorizing Picturesque Zones was as follows:

The government and part of the public are more and more preoccupied with avoiding the deterioration of the countryside and with obtaining quality architecture, well integrated with urban or natural sites. Continual vigilance of public authorities, better communication with builders, and the creation among the public of greater sensitivity to esthetic issues are necessary to achieve this. . . . This is why the law of 16 July 1971 instituted "Picturesque Zones."[83]

The zones may be created wherever the quality of sites and the threats to them may warrant. Their provisions do not replace the SDAU or POS, if they exist, but should be incorporated in them. If there is no POS, the departmental director of public construction proposes the designation of a zone to a study group consisting of the departmental director of agriculture, the architect of buildings of France, and the regional representative of the Ministry of the Environment. Local governments also may initiate the designation. The boundaries are fixed and the designation made by the prefect.

The study group develops provisions that, typically, recommend how construction may be fitted into the site and what external characteristics, such as size, colors, and roof style, it should have. Special restrictions appropriate to the site also are recommended. The provisions are based on a file that must include three items: a report justifying the need for the creation of the zone, a map of the proposed zone, and a list of recommendations for the site. "The recommendations must be concrete, illustrated by graphics, written in simple language that is readily understood and not techincal."[84]

The material in the file is sent to the affected municipalities along with a notice of a public hearing to be held within three months. This hearing may coincide with the hearing required for the adoption of a POS. After the hearing, the file and accompanying comments are sent to the prefect, who issues an order creating the zone. The order must be posted at the municipal offices, published among the official acts of the department, and published in two newspapers of general circulation in the department. Revisions are made in a similar manner.

If the Picturesque Zone provisions are incorporated in a POS, then the binding effect of the POS will prevent inappropriate development. Where there is no POS, building permits may incorporate special conditions. ZACs are not to be created in Picturesque Zones.

The right of preemption,[85] which was created initially for Sensitive Zones, now is applicable to Picturesque Zones. The minister of public construction can issue an order designating all or any part of a Picturesque Zone as an area within which the department may preempt private market sales. The order is issued after the minister solicits advice from the general council of the department and from the municipal councils of affected municipalities. Accompanied by a map of the area subject to preemption, it is filed at the municipal office of each affected municipality. Notice of the order is widely posted, advertised, and distributed, to notaries among others.

The prefect must be notified of all sales subject to preemption. Within two months, the department must notify the would-be seller either that it renounces the right to preempt, that it will preempt according to the seller's terms, or that it proposes a different set of terms. If the department's terms are unacceptable to the seller, a price can instead be set by the expropriation court. If the department chooses not to preempt, the sale must be according to the terms originally described. If the department does wish to preempt, the seller has one month to accept the price offered, go to court, or renounce the sale. If the court sets the price, the prefect then has one month to notify the seller either that the department renounces the right to preempt or that it will preempt at the court-established price. Payment must be within two months of the decision to acquire, whichever form it may take. Any sale in violation of the preemption provisions is void.

The Departmental Open Space Tax is used to finance land acquisition in the Picturesque Zones. This tax originally was authorized in 1961, for all areas included in Sensitive Zones. It may be used for the acquisition of open space either by negotiated purchase, preemption, or condemnation. The tax falls due at the time of subdivision approval for all subdivision occurring after 24 December 1960 and at the time of the initial construction on each lot for subdivisions approved after 1 January 1951 and prior to 24 December 1960.

The tax has two elements. There is a fixed charge of $100 (500 francs) per lot, which the general council of the department has the right to increase up to $200 (1,000 francs) per lot. In addition, there is a levy of 1 percent of the fixed charge for each 1,100 square feet (100 square meters) or fraction thereof of lot area in excess of 22,000 square feet (2,000 square meters). For example, for a lot of 44,000 square feet (4,000 square meters), or approximately one acre, in a department using the maximum charge, the tax would be: $200 (1,000 francs) + $2 (10 francs) x 20 = $240 (1,200 francs). A number of types of subdivision are exempt from the tax. These include subdivisions for nonresidential purposes, subdivisions by public agencies not for industrial or commercial purposes, and subdivisions for moderate rent subsidized housing.[86]

### Other Land Bank Acquisitions

The Zs are the principal mechanism for creating land banks. There are three additional, diverse approaches to land acquisition that complete the range of land bank tools. These are direct intervention by the state, purchase and resale by state-assisted corporations committed to farmland preservation, and regional financing of local and departmental land acquisition.

Direct state intervention is not carried out as part of an ongoing program, and, therefore, does not have policy, administrative, and financial dimensions that can be outlined. Several examples of its use to acquire large amounts of land rapidly will be described in the section of this chapter on the Marseilles region.

The farmland preservation program has been operating successfully since the early 1960s. A total of 1.7 percent of the land of France had been bought, improved where necessary, and either resold or was awaiting resale for farm use as of 1975. This land constitutes a private reserve of farmland. The program was designed with the assistance of farm organizations and farm lending institutions, and it has continued to enjoy their support and participation ever since. Its only shortcoming is that of inadequate capitalization to carry out acquisition at the rate considered desirable.

The newest land bank program is that of the regional councils. Regional councils are authorized to levy a few modest taxes and to borrow to finance their programs. Many have given top priority for the use of their revenues to funding land acquisition by municipalities and departments. While the program is modest, if offers local governments a new source of funds for constituting land banks.

*Farmland Preservation.* France has had a long-term commitment to the improvement of farm productivity and to the encouragement of the family farm. The country is blessed with a large stock of high-quality farmland, from which it regularly derives an export surplus. The farm problems to which government policy and programs have been directed are those of inefficient farm holdings, the exodus of young people, low farm income, and, more recently, competition for land from developers and rapidly escalating land prices.

French national economic plans all have stated specific targets for the agriculture sector, and legislation has been enacted to foster the achievement of these targets. Public acquisition of farmland for resale to people who make a commitment to the continuation of farming is one aspect of a larger farmland preservation program that also includes reparceling, subsidized loans, retirement income payments, and tax relief.

Private, nonprofit organizations called SAFERs (Société d'Aménagement Foncier et d'Etablissement Rural, or Company for Land Management and Rural Organization) are an active force in the farmland market, buying an average of 12 percent of the agricultural land offered for sale each year, making improvements to the land where desirable, and then reselling it to the people anxious to remain in or begin farming. A key feature of the SAFER enabling legislation is the organization's power to preempt other purchasers. Unlike preemption in the development zones, the SAFER pays the market value as of the time of preemption. Since 1962, 16 percent of all SAFER purchases have been by preemption. In many other instances, sellers offer to sell to SAFERs voluntarily, knowing that a sales agreement with another purchaser can be preempted. Therefore, the existence of the power to preempt, whether or not it is used, has a considerable effect on farmland sales.

Farming is a more significant factor in the economy of France than in that of the United States. A larger share of the land is farmed than in the United States—52 percent compared to 49 percent—and a much larger share of the population is engaged in farming—12.9 percent compared to 3.4 percent, both as of 1972. Also as of 1972, agriculture contributed 5.7 percent of the French gross domestic product, more than twice the 2.7 percent for the United States. The value of French agricultural exports consistently has exceeded the value of agricultural imports; in 1972, the net of exports over imports was $1 billion.[87]

Meat, milk, and eggs account for over one-half of the value of agricultural produce. In 1975, their total contribution was 55 percent, while grains contributed 15 percent, wine 9 percent, and other crops 21 percent.

Although the number of people engaged in agriculture remains high, it has been declining rapidly. Between 1954 and 1968, 2.25 million people ceased farming. The rate of decline of males working on farms was 3 percent per year from 1954 to 1962 and 3.8 percent per year from 1962 to 1968. To the extent that the exodus from farming leads to a more

TABLE 4.4. Distribution of Total Number of Farms by Size of Farm

| Size of Farm | | | | | |
|---|---|---|---|---|---|
| Acres | Hectares | 1955 | 1967 | 1970 | 1975 |
| 0–12.5 | 0–5 | 37.6% | 29.7% | 31.0% | 30.3% |
| 12.5–50 | 5–20 | 43.2 | 42.1 | 38.2 | 33.4 |
| 50–125 | 20–50 | 15.8 | 21.8 | 23.3 | 26.1 |
| 125–250 | 50–100 | 2.6 | 5.0 | 5.8 | 7.9 |
| 250 and over | 100 and over | 0.8 | 1.4 | 1.7 | 2.3 |

SOURCE: SCEES, Ministry of Agriculture.

TABLE 4.5. Distribution of Farm Area by Size of Farm

| Size of Farm | | | | | |
|---|---|---|---|---|---|
| Acres | Hectares | 1955 | 1967 | 1970 | 1975 |
| 0–12.5 | 0–5 | 6.1% | 3.6% | 3.2% | 2.4% |
| 12.5–50 | 5–20 | 36.0 | 27.3 | 23.5 | 18.3 |
| 50–125 | 20–50 | 33.8 | 37.5 | 38.0 | 37.5 |
| 125–250 | 50–100 | 14.9 | 18.8 | 20.8 | 24.6 |
| 250 and over | 100 and over | 9.2 | 12.8 | 14.5 | 17.2 |

SOURCE: SCEES, Ministry of Agriculture.

efficient farm size for the remaining farmers, stimulus to young people to enter or stay in farming, and higher income levels, it is desirable and, in fact, is encouraged by government subsidies in the form of early retirement payments to older farmers and loans to young farmers. However, as of the 1970 agricultural census, there were still many more old than young farmers—8.2 percent were under thirty-five and 17.3 percent were sixty-five or older. Despite years of national commitment to raising the income of farmers relative to that of the rest of the labor force, little change has occurred. Farm income indeed has risen, but no faster than other income. In 1974, net income per capita after taxes was $2,454 for farm proprietors, $1,227 for farm laborers, $4,626 for professional workers, and $1,584 for laborers.

The government has had greater success in stimulating an increase in the size of farms and in its reallotment program to achieve a more efficient structure of farm parcels. Over the twenty years from 1955 to 1975, while total farmland remained at around 75 million acres (30.4 million hectares), the average size of farms rose from 33 acres (13 hectares) to 53 acres (21 hectares). Tables 4.4 and 4.5 show the shifting distribution of the number of farms and of farm area.

While almost one-third of all farms are still less than 12.5 acres (5 hectares), the amount of farmland in such small holdings had declined to

2.4 percent by 1975. Consistent with government policy to encourage medium-sized family farms, the number of large farms and the acreage in such farms have remained modest, although showing a steady increase. As of 1975, only 6 percent of French farms were categorized "industrial" as compared to "family."

Due to former laws governing inheritance, many farm holdings consist of a number of small parcels, scattered over a several-mile radius. In 1970, there were 1.46 million farm parcels with approximately 4 million owners.[88] This pattern led to inefficient use of the land and of the farmer's time. To overcome this problem, in the 1950s the government instituted a program of reparceling. Local and department officials work with farmers to develop plans to reallocate holdings so that each farmer receives land of equivalent value to what he formerly held but in larger, contiguous parcels. Since the program began, 22 million acres have been reparceled. In recent years, an average of 865 thousand acres (350 thousand hectares) have been affected yearly.[89]

As farmland prices rise it becomes increasingly difficult for farmers to compete with speculators and other nonfarm investors. Frequently, as in the United States, land that is of high value for farming also is highly desirable for urban development or for second homes. Increases in farmland prices recently have been running at 13 percent per year, with the average price rising from $243 per acre (3,001 francs per hectare) in 1960 to $640 per acre (7,909 francs per hectare) in 1970 and $1,080 per acre (13,338 francs per hectare) in 1975. These averages mask enormous disparities among regions and between urban fringe and rural areas. For instance, the intensely cultivated and highly productive fruit and vegetable lands of Provence are under tremendous pressure from developers and were selling for up to $8,000 per acre (98,800 francs per hectare) in 1974. Of all farmland sold in recent years, 22.5 percent has been sold to nonfarmers, 17.7 percent has been sold to new farmers, and 11.5 percent has passed through the hands of an SAFER.[90]

The principal laws enacted in response to the need to modernize agriculture were the farm laws of 1960[91] and 1962.[92] The goal of the Farm Law of 1960 was "to promote and favor family farming able to make the best use of modern technology."[93] Both laws sought to advance this goal by increasing the size of small farms, reducing the agricultural population selectively, and increasing farm productivity.

Several concerns underlay Parliament's passage of these farm laws:

1. By 1960, much of rural France was being depopulated. While more of the new urban residents were coming from villages and towns than from farms, substantial declines in the farm population were continuing. Frequently it was the young people who were leaving the farms

2. Many farm holdings were inefficiently small and/or widely scattered
3. The urban population was beginning to exercise a preference for lower density development, often consuming good farm land as a result
4. The gap in income between farmers and many other sectors of the labor force was increasing

Specific programs to implement the goals and objectives of these two laws included the reparceling program already discussed, various forms of subsidies, income payments, tax relief, and public land acquisition.

Subsidies often take the form of reduced interest on farm loans. The Farm Bank (Crédit Agricole) lends at rates of interest that vary with the purpose of the loan. For instance, young farmers and farmers who have completed development plans for the modernization of their farms may borrow at 4 or 4.5 percent interest, as compared to 7 percent for ordinary farm loans. Most farmland purchase and farm improvement loans originate with the Farm Bank. In 1972, the Farm Bank lent $500 million (2.5 billion francs) for farm purchases; this sum covered 52 percent of such purchases that year.[94]

The 1962 law created a fund for farm assistance (FASASA, the Fonds d'Action Sociale et d'Amélioration des Structures Agricoles) in the Ministry of Agriculture. The principal payment program under this fund offers retirement income to farmers who agree to sell their farms and move elsewhere. Under this program, from 1964 to 1975, over 20 million acres were sold by older farmers, either to young farmers getting established or to other farmers wishing to enlarge their holdings. Farmers participating in the retirement income program also benefit from a 60 percent reduction in the value-added tax on land sales.[95] Since the tax is at the rate of 17 or 18 percent of the value added, the saving can be significant.

Farmland acquisition for the purpose of keeping land in farming under the 1960 law was entrusted to the newly authorized SAFERs.

The provisions of the Farm Law of 1960 pertaining to land banking were enacted two years after legislation authorizing land banking for purposes of urbanization[96] and are modeled on the earlier provisions in some respects. Acquisition by preemption was authorized by the Farm Law of 1962, both in order to promote rational reallotment of farm tracts and to assure that fair prices are paid for farmland.

Two measures of the success of the farmland acquisition program are the amount of land acquired and resold to farmers and the number of farmers aided. From 1964 to 1975, over 2 million acres (810,000 hectares) of farmland were bought and over 1.7 million acres (688,000 hectares) were resold for farm use. In recent years, SAFER has bought an average of 12 percent of all agricultural land sold. Through the land assembly program fifty-seven thousand farmers enlarged their holdings, six thousand young farmers were established in farming, eight hundred farm-ers moved to new sites, and four hundred farmers whose land had been expropriated for nonfarm use were relocated on a new farm.

The following pages summarize the farmland acquisition provisions of the farm laws of 1960 and 1962, discussing sequentially the form of organization selected, acquisition by purchase or preemption, management and resale, and financing. Experience with SAFER is then described in brief.

The Farm Law of 1960 authorized the creation of nonprofit companies, called SAFERs, to buy and sell farm land. An SAFER could be formed to serve either a single department or several departments jointly. In response to the law, SAFERs were established in all but a few departments of France. Although not required by the law, all of the SAFERs elected a corporate form of organization. Ninety percent of their capital was sub-scribed by local farm organizations and farm lending institutions and 10 percent by a national company of farm organizations and farm lenders called SCAFR (Société Centrale d'Aménagement Foncier Rurale, or Central Company for Rural Land Management). The largest capitalization, for SAFERs either covering five departments and/or located in areas of particularly high land prices, ranged from $250,000 to $400,000 (1.25 million francs to 2 million francs). The average capital subscription was $200,000 (1 million francs) and was for SAFERs covering three depart-ments. While these sums are small, the SAFERs use their capital as re-volving funds and receive national government assistance. By law, the subscribers receive 5 percent interest on their shares.

Although SAFERs are private corporations, control of their activities is divided between the shareholders and the national government, somewhat in the manner of state-franchised utilities in the United States. The share-holders have voting rights in proportion to their stock subscription, up to a maximum of 5 percent of the votes. Each SAFER has a general assembly consisting of members of farm organizations, farm banks, SCAFR, and another national organization. Members of the general assembly elect a maximum of twelve people to the administrative council that directly over-sees the SAFER. National government control is exercised through two government commissioners, who are representatives of the ministries of Agriculture and of Finance and Economic Affairs. Customarily, the gov-ernment commissioners for an SAFER are the director of the Departmental Office of Agriculture and the departmental director of fiscal affairs of the Ministry of Finance and Economic Affairs. All projects involving $20,000 (100,000 francs) or more must have the prior approval of the government commissioners, as must any project involving the exercise of the right of preemption. If a government commissioner opposes a project, then the SAFER has one month in which to appeal to the minister who appointed that commissioner. SCAFR, with a capitalization of $700,000 (3,500,000 francs), assists the SAFERs by providing financial, accounting, legal, and technical assistance.

An SAFER may acquire land either by voluntary sale or by preemption. The right of preemption has been used in 16 percent of all acquisitions, and its existence is considered a vital part of SAFER powers. The right of preemption was not granted without a legislative struggle. Edgard Pisani, the then minister of agriculture, commented recently about the SAFERs:

> They were, and they remain for some, a lively menace to private property. The most significant debate at the time of their creation was relative to the right of preemption. . . . Although in truth a modest reform, . . . one nevertheless heard from all sides that "the eternal order of the fields" was menaced. . . . If the government had not had a disciplined majority, the text would not have been adopted.[97]

An SAFER may buy any farmland on the open market or it may offer to trade some of its land for other land in order to assemble more efficient tracts. It learns of the availability of land from notaries, farmers, the press, and its own staff. Once it decides to make a bid, it is in open competition with any other bidders for the land.

It is also possible for an SAFER to acquire by right of preemption, exercised when a farm owner seeks to sell. The farm organizations promoted amendment of the farm law to make preemption possible, because they believed it a necessary additional power in the effort to keep good land in agriculture. The SAFER requests the prefect to designate a given area as subject to the right of preemption for farm use. No land in a development zone (ZUP, ZAD, or ZAC) and no land in an SDAU or a POS shown as intended for urban uses may be included. The prefect must seek the advice of farm organizations concerning the proposed designation and then submits a recommendation to the minister of agriculture. If the recommendation is favorable, the minister publishes a decree designating the area. The decree is published among the legal notices in newspapers, posted at municipal offices, and mailed to notaries. People selling farmland are deemed to have notice of it, and any sale without prior notice to SAFER is void. The right of preemption is granted for a three- to five-year term and may be renewed. About 60 percent of agricultural land is subject to an SAFER right of preemption.[98]

Some sales and transfers are exempt from the right of preemption. No exchanges between farmers, sales to close relatives, sales to a farmer or tenant farmer whose land has been expropriated, or sales to an adjacent farmer are subject to preemption.

Tenant farmers have a right of preemption superior to that of SAFER.[99] In addition, rights of preemption held by the state and by other public bodies have priority over the SAFER's preemptive right.

An owner who wishes to sell, who has a prospective buyer, and whose land is subject to a right of preemption must notify the SAFER and the tenant farmer if there is one, by registered mail, of the intent to sell, the proposed sale price, the conditions of sale, and the name of the proposed buyer. Preemption by SAFER must occur within thirty days of notification, either at the seller's price or by request to the court to fix the price. Between notification of an intent to sell and SAFER's decision to preempt, the seller can reconsider and decide not to sell. If SAFER accepts the offering price, the seller is bound; if SAFER obtains a court determined price, the seller can back out of the sale but must pay the expenses of setting the price.

Once land has been acquired, the SAFER determines whether it is in need of improvements prior to resale. If improvements are needed, the SAFER will do the work. This work may include drainage, irrigation, construction of berms, planting of windbreaks, afforestation, or restoration or construction of buildings.

While holding the land, the SAFER is likely to place it under short-term lease for farming. Land may be held for five years, or under special circumstances for ten years, before being sold. The usual time of holding land is between six and eighteen months. During this period, the SAFER is likely to be acquiring adjacent parcels to assemble a larger and more efficient tract, contacting nearby farmers who may wish to buy the land or trade some distant parcel for it, and seeking out farmers, such as sons working a too-small holding with their fathers, who wish to set themselves up in a new location.

Sales are primarily but not exclusively to farmers. Old structures and poor land may be sold to nonfarmers for second homes. There is an enormous demand for such properties in some parts of the country. Already 2.8 million French households have access to a second home. Some land may be determined more suitable for forest use. Some land may be ceded to or exchanged with land of public agencies for parks, reservoirs, roads, and other public uses. In most instances, however, the sale is to a farmer. Frequently there is competition for the land. Which farmer should be chosen as the purchaser is a subject to which the SAFERs give considerable attention. The objective is to sell the land, not to the highest bidder, but to the person who will benefit most as a farmer by its acquisition. Favored by the law are farmers with too little land, farmers willing to exchange their present tracts for more efficient holdings, farmers whose land had been condemned for a public purpose, and young farmers anxious to establish themselves. The land must be sold rather than offered on a long-term lease, but, to help farmers lacking enough capital to buy, the SAFER can sell to a group of people (the Groupement Foncier Agricole, or Agricultural Landowning Group) wishing to be corporate owner-lessors of a farm. The SAFER must consult a technical advisory committee of representatives of farm organizations and administrative agencies and obtain approval from the government commissioners prior to signing an agreement of sale.

The successful purchaser must agree to farm the land for fifteen years, personally and/or with his family. During this period the land may not be sold or subdivided, except under exceptional circumstances with the SAFER's approval. This fifteen-year limit is a weakness of the program. The SAFERs, with government subsidies, act with the intention of preserving agricultural land, yet, at the end of the fifteen-year term, the purchaser is free to sell the land for development.

The administrative costs of SAFERs are paid for in part by a charge on sales. The state subsidy is 2 percent of the cost of all acquisitions and of the revenue from all sales. The charge to purchasers is 2 percent of the acquisition cost, 2 percent of the sale price, and 6 percent of the cost of any improvements made by the SAFER.

The acquisition program is aided by loans from the National Bank for Farm Credit. An SAFER may borrow from one of the bank's regional branches up to fifteen times the capital and reserve holdings of the SAFER. The terms are five years at a subsidized interest rate, which, in 1976, was 4.5 percent. The bank deducts a small amount from this loan to fund its loan guarantee.

The developmental offices of the Ministry of Agriculture may pay up to 40 percent of the cost of improvements to land and buildings.

A farmer purchasing from an SAFER also may receive help from the National Bank for Farm Credit. The farmer may borrow either up to 80 percent of the purchase price or a maximum sum of $30,000 (150,000 francs) for thirty years at 4.5 percent interest.[100] The exact amount of the loan turns upon a number of factors, including whether the farmer is to be newly established or is adding to a prior holding, the farmer's age, the size of the tract, and the quality of the land. The farmer may obtain a second mortgage of up to $30,000 (150,000 francs) at 7 percent interest.

The level of activity of SAFERs has varied considerably by region, as can be seen in map 4.2. The north, northeast, and alpine regions have been relatively inactive. The north and northeast are level or gently rolling, fertile areas where tracts tend to be large, reallotment is not needed, and farming is holding its own very satisfactorily. In the alpine departments, on the other hand, little land is suited to farming. There, the government's concern is with providing help to prevent too great depopulation. Bordeaux, Burgundy, Gascony, and the Languedoc-Roussillon regions all have had very high levels of SAFER land investment.

For the nation as a whole, SAFERs, in 1970, bought 13 percent of farmland on the market and 21 percent of such farmland that was subject to preemption.[101] About one-third of the purchases were from farmers

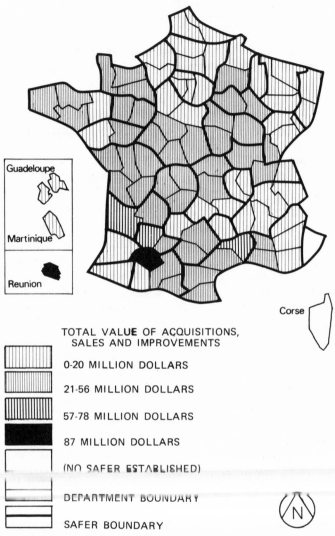

TOTAL VALUE OF ACQUISITIONS,
SALES AND IMPROVEMENTS

|||||||| 0-20 MILLION DOLLARS

|||||||| 21-56 MILLION DOLLARS

|||||||| 57-78 MILLION DOLLARS

■ 87 MILLION DOLLARS

(NO SAFER ESTABLISHED)

DEPARTMENT BOUNDARY

SAFER BOUNDARY

MAP 4.2. Activity of SAFERs to 1976

SOURCE: Adapted from Chambres d'Agriculture, "La Loi d'Orientation Agricole,"
mimeographed (January 1977), p. 23

who had accepted government retirement income payments. SAFERs offer
them a ready market. Purchases have been averaging a little under two
hundred thousand acres (eighty-one thousand hectares) per year, and
sales by SAFERs in the last few years have caught up with this rate, as can

TABLE 4.6. SAFER Purchases and Sales, 1964–1975

| Year | Purchases | | Sales | |
|---|---|---|---|---|
| | Acres | Hectares | Acres | Hectares |
| 1964 | 155,000 | 62,750 | 52,500 | 21,300 |
| 1965 | 117,500 | 47,600 | 72,500 | 29,400 |
| 1966 | 145,000 | 58,700 | 100,000 | 40,500 |
| 1967 | 155,000 | 62,750 | 135,000 | 54,700 |
| 1968 | 182,500 | 73,900 | 145,000 | 58,700 |
| 1969 | 200,000 | 81,000 | 160,000 | 64,800 |
| 1970 | 182,500 | 73,900 | 157,500 | 63,800 |
| 1971 | 197,500 | 80,000 | 177,500 | 71,900 |
| 1972 | 207,500 | 84,000 | 202,500 | 82,000 |
| 1973 | 195,000 | 79,000 | 207,500 | 84,000 |
| 1974 | 182,500 | 73,900 | 180,000 | 72,900 |
| 1975 | 192,500 | 78,000 | 177,500 | 71,900 |
| Total | 2,112,500 | 855,500 | 1,767,500 | 715,900 |

SOURCE: "La Loi d'Orientation Agricole."

be seen in table 4.6. Cumulative operations of the SAFERs from 1964 through 1975 are shown in figure 4.4.

The price paid by SAFER runs less than the average price of farmland, because the SAFERs tend to stretch their funds by avoiding the high-price, urban-fringe farmland. In 1970, for instance, SAFERs paid an average of $500 per acre (6,175 francs per hectare) for their purchases, while the national average farmland price was $640 per acre (7,900 francs per hectare).[102]

SAFER activity has led to very little litigation. In 1970, only 1.1 percent of all purchases involved litigation, and 60 percent of those actions were brought by the SAFERs. Over the years almost two-thirds of all judicial decisions have supported the actions of the SAFERs.

The conclusions shared by several commentators are that the SAFER structure and operation are sound but that the scale of need for SAFER investment has not been matched by fiscal resources.

Bernard Collet, Director General of SCAFR, observed: "After fifteen years of activity, SAFER has not become a sclerotic organization, but it is at a crossroad; it has failed to achieve the target of acquiring 250 thousand acres (100 thousand hectares) yearly, and it must diversify and extend its arena of action."[103]

A report for the organization for Economic Cooperation and Development concludes:

SAFER activities . . . have a definite stabilizing effect on the agricultural land market, since their resale prices, which are comparatively low, are taken as reference prices for the region. Land market statistics established on the basis of sales notifications received by the SAFERs are also a [sic] great value for a

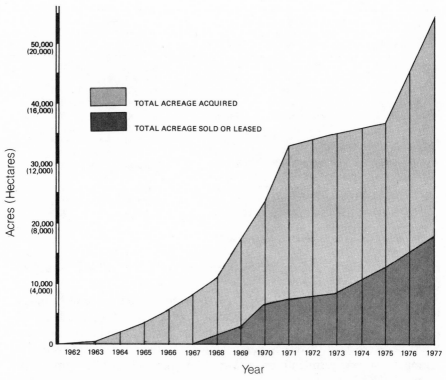

FIGURE 4.4. SAFER cumulative purchases and sales, 1962–1975

SOURCE: Adapted from Chambres d'Agriculture, "La Loi d'Orientation Agricole," mimeographed (January 1977), p. 21

proper understanding of the structure and functioning of this market. On the other hand, it should be observed that SAFER action is sometimes criticised. Most of the criticism stems rather naturally from the delicate nature of their intervention, which touches closely on important personal interests. It is equally natural that some mistakes have been made, especially during a running-in period.[104]

A third source observes that the intent of the law is to encourage the wise use of natural resources but that the means provided for implementing the law are inadequate. Further, the farm laws failed to foresee the difficulties of controlling nonagricultural uses of land in agricultural areas or the scale of land speculation that has occurred.[105]

*The Regional Councils.*[106] The newest land bank program is that funded by the regional councils. Regional assemblies first were proposed by de Gaulle to provide some decentralization of governmental decision making, but the proposal was rejected in a 1969 national referendum viewed by the voters as a test of de Gaulle's general popularity. This was only a temporary setback. Four years later regional councils came into being[107] and, with the adoption of their first budgets in 1974, began to function. These budgets showed tnat land acquisition, partly for open space and partly as a reserve for later development, was the top priority for many of the nation's twenty-one regions. It is possible that the regional councils may be able to act as catalysts to coordinate several of the pre-existing land acquisition programs in order to respond more effectively to this broadly recognized need for land reserves.

The regional councils are legislative bodies whose membership consists of representatives of the other three levels of government—members of the National Assembly[108] from the region, representatives of the general councils of the departments in the region, and representatives of the larger municipal councils in the region. There is some sentiment for altering representation so that it would be by direct election in order to increase people's sense of relation to the region.[109]

The regional council, acting as a legislative body to set policy and determine budgets, functions in coordination with the Economic and Social Committee and the regional prefect to form the Regional Public Authority (EPR, Etablissement Public Régional). The Economic and Social Committee is the regional equivalent of the state-level Economic and Social Council. It draws members from the principal economic, social, professional, family, educational, cultural, scientific, and sporting organizations of the region. It is consulted on all regional proposals and offers its advice. The regional prefect, among other functions, is the executive officer of the regional council.

The regional councils have three types of funding by which to support their programs. The state transferred to them the right to collect the tax on driver's licenses, an annual charge of twelve dollars (sixty francs) per person. They also are authorized to levy an additional millage on three existing taxes, but the total income from these three taxes to the Regional Public Authority may not exceed a per capita maximum set each year.[110] The third source of revenue is borrowing. The regions have considerable autonomy in determining program priorities and in allocating their funds. While the Regional Public Authorities may not buy land for their own account, they may make grants to departments and municipalities for land acquisitions. The authority creates an administrative review process for grant applications and, by regulation, specifies its criteria for judging these applications.

While the amounts of money available for land acquisition are small, this is a grant program so that the recipients are not under pressure to turn over the land and obtain a return in order to pay back a loan. Much of the land being purchased is intended either for continued open space or for medium-term land reserves.

### Focus on the Marseilles Region

All of the government's innovative land bank legislation has been tested in the Marseilles region. This region provides an excellent focus for consideration of the efficacy of the various laws and programs, both because of its diversity of experience with land banking and because the acquisitions have been carried out against a background of intense growth pressure.

Within the spectrum of experience are acquisitions for new towns, resort towns, urban expansion, port and industrial development, farms, and open space; acquisitions by means of preemption, voluntary agreement, and condemnation; and acquisitions carried out by different levels of government, sometimes in conjunction with one another and/or the private sector. Most of these programs have been spurred on by a sense of urgency arising from widespread urbanization and constantly rising land prices. These conditions have led to a greater than normal willingness to experiment with new approaches.

For the purpose of this illustrative review of land bank projects, the Marseilles region is defined, rather loosely, to include the Marseilles metropolitan area, the municipalities surrounding the Etang de Berre, Fos, and other areas within the Department of Bouches-du-Rhône. The coastal area of Languedoc-Roussillon, which lies to the west of the Marseilles region, also is included for the purpose of describing its land bank program for resort new towns (see map 4.3). Since the discussion centers on projects within the Department of Bouches-du-Rhône, a few figures describing population growth and changes in land use there and within the Marseilles metropolitan area will provide a context. (See map 4.4.)

In 1968, the population of the Bouches-du-Rhône was 1.471 million; of this total, 92 percent—1.35 million people—was concentrated in the Marseilles metropolitan area. One million people lived within the city proper. The growth rate then was 2.7 percent per year,[111] 0.5 percent due to natural increase and 2.2 percent due to inmigration and immigration. This growth rate was more than double the 1.2 percent growth rate for France as a whole. The projected population for the year 2000 in the Bouches-du-Rhône is 3.5 million, with 2.3 million people, or 66 percent of the population, expected to live in the Marseilles metropolitan area. The city's population already had peaked and, by 1975, had dropped to 915,000. Over half of the growth is expected to occur outside the Marseilles metropolitan area.

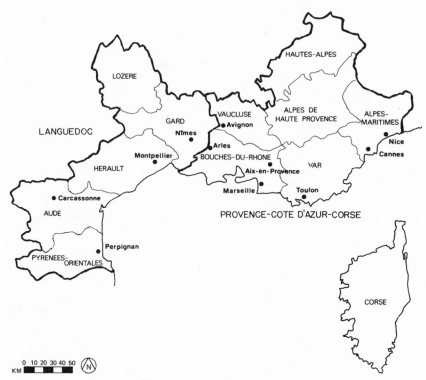

MAP 4.3.  France's Mediterranean coast

Land is being converted to urban use at a rapid rate. Of the department's 1,309,000 acres (530,000 hectares), only 38 percent, or 494,000 acres (200,000 hectares), was still in open space, agricultural, or forest use as of 1970. Approximately 12,400 acres (5,000 hectares) of these open lands are sold yearly, and only 3,700 acres (1,500 hectares) remain in rural uses after the sale.[112] Therefore, almost 2 percent of the stock of undeveloped land is being converted each year. The competition for land is felt ever more keenly, and there is increasing acceptance of the need for public acquisition to assure that the land is used for its planned purpose, be that crops or houses.

The concept of the development zone has gained wide support as a means of plan implementation, although the roles of the public and private sectors in the development zone have changed since ZUPs were instituted in the late 1950s. The right of preemption, first tested in the development zones, has proven valuable both for the acquisition of specific tracts and as a constraint on prices. Its use has been extended to several other programs, including farmland acquisition by SAFER and open space acquisi-

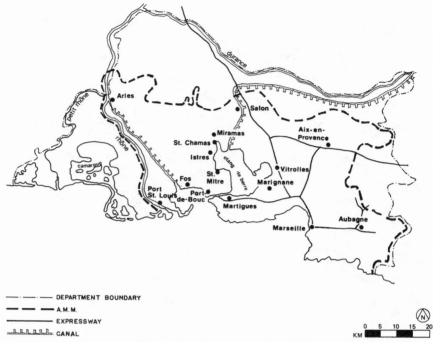

MAP 4.4. Bouches-du-Rhône

SOURCE: Adapted from Ian B. Thompson, *The Lower Rhône and Marseille* (Oxford University Press, 1975), pp. 6, 33

tion in Picturesque Zones by the department. State initiative, while often resented at the local level, has been a critical element in the success of acquisition strategy for several of the larger projects. State financial participation, in the form of direct acquisition, grants, or loans, has been essential for most of the programs.

What has been lacking to date is regional coordination of the planning and acquisition. There have been too many actors and programs vying for attention and funds. The regional council, with its early commitment to land banking as a necessary tool for the implementation of plans, may become the needed coordinator and intermediary with the agencies of the state.

All six programs in which advance land acquisition plays an integral part are active currently in Bouches-du-Rhône. They are being used for acquisition for general urban development (the Zs), port and industrial development, new towns, farmland preservation, preservation of environmentally sensitive zones, and municipal and departmental land reserves. Not all of the acquisitions can be described as being for land banks, since in some instances the specific future use is known at the outset and the land immediately is committed to that use. However, the acquisitions combine to form a mosaic of land purchase and retention, resale, or lease for the purpose of plan implementation.

The following description of activities in the department is illustrative rather than comprehensive. Unfortunately, the available data are not always comparable among the programs. One cannot say, therefore, how much land has been acquired in the department over a given period of time either for land banks or for stated uses. A few comparisons do provide a sense of the order of magnitude of the acquisitions and expenditures of the various programs.

Looking first at land acquired for some form of urbanization, the Zs are the principal source of activity. The most significant figure for the development zones is that enough land is now in ZACs to accommodate approximately half of the yearly construction of subsidized housing. Since 80 to 90 percent of all housing built receives some subsidy, land in ZACs can meet at least 40 percent of the demand for housing sites. Much of this land was placed in ZADs before the ZACs were created, so that it is subject to the power of preemption. Sites for the new towns and expansion of existing towns at the Etang de Berre encompass 34,600 acres (14,000 hectares) of ZADs; as of 1977, 3,745 acres (1,516 hectares) of this land had been purchased for three new towns, at an average price of $5,700 per acre (70,000 francs per hectare). At Fos, where a vast port and industrial complex has been built, 18,000 acres (7,200 hectares) of largely marshy coast were bought without reliance on the Zs, mostly for between $320 and $640 per acre (4,000 to 8,000 francs per hectare). Extensive use of leases of land bank land has occurred both at the Etang de Berre and Fos.

Three programs are contributing to land acquisition for continued open space or rural use. SAFER has been buying an average of 11 percent of the farmland offered for sale each year and, from 1972 through 1975, had purchased a total of 6,477 acres (2,622 hectares), all of which is resold to farmers subject to a covenant for fifteen years' continued farm use. The Departmental Open Space Tax had, as of 1972, made possible the purchase of 9,530 acres (3,857 hectares) of environmentally sensitive land to be kept permanently in a natural state. The newest program is the land reserve program of the regional council. As of the end of 1976, the regional council had funded or was considering proposals from eighteen Bouches-du-Rhône municipalities for the acquisition of 1,704 acres (690 hectares) for land banks, parks, open space, and community facilities. The average cost of this land was estimated at $1,309 per acre (16,401 francs per hectare), of which the regional council grants would cover an average of 81 percent.

*The Zs*

Development zones have been and continue to be the most commonly used tool for land assembly. Creation of a ZUP, ZAD, or ZAC provides long-term control over the use of land. Theoretically, this control affords the public sufficient time and leverage to implement plans without calling for immediate, widespread public purchases. The experiences of Marseilles[113] and Aix-en-Provence[114] suggest that political pressure and lack of adequate funds at critical junctures can impede or imperil successful application of the theory.

Of the three zones, ZUPs are passé, ZADs cover extensive areas, and ZACs enjoy widespread current use. The Departmental Office of Public Construction has exerted pressure on municipalities wishing to designate ZACs to locate them on land not planned for agriculture or open space, to provide developers a fair chance to participate in the calculation of their costs, and to include state-aided housing in them. In 1973, for instance, over one-half of the state-aided housing built in the Bouches-du-Rhône was located in ZACs. The municipalities have found that, by involving private landowners and developers in the planning and acquisition process for ZACs, it has been possible to trade off somewhat higher development densities for private contributions to the cost of infrastructure and other public facilities. In addition, the private sector has proven able to build more quickly and more efficiently than the public sector, thus enabling it to pay more for land than the municipalities could afford. This is advantageous in obtaining tracts by voluntary negotiation, thus avoiding the necessity of obtaining a DUP and proceeding through condemnation.

*Marseilles.* The city of Marseilles and the five bordering municipalities that constitute the Marseilles urban area are short of developable land. Of the total urban area of 311,470 acres (77,000 hectares), 37,050 acres (15,000 hectares) consist of mountains or cliffs planned for permanent open space, and 24,700 acres (10,000 hectares) already are urbanized at high densities.[115]

The city's situation is the tightest of all. As of 1974, only about 2,470 acres (1,000 hectares) of easily developable land remained within the city limits. Although the city's population has peaked, this land is attractive to developers, prices are high, and there is much pressure on politicians to alter plans so as to increase permitted density. Given the shortage of buildable land, the state over the years has urged the city to place much of this land in development zones so as to control the timing of development and use of the land. Marseilles's first ZUP was created in 1960, close on the heels of the 1959 adoption of the Marseilles master plan. This ZUP, of 333 acres (135 hectares), was planned for 7,250 dwelling units, or thirty-two to forty units per net acre (80 to 100 units per net hectare), in order to cover high acquisition and improvement costs. These costs totaled $2,400 (12,000 francs) per dwelling unit, while elsewhere a developer could buy land for $1,200 to $1,600 (6,000 to 8,000 francs) per dwelling unit and spend only $400 to $600 (2,000 to 3,000 francs) per dwelling unit on improvements, ending up with a total cost of between $1,600 and $2,000 (8,000 and 11,000 francs) per unit, or less than in the ZUP. Land costs everywhere in the city were high; between 1954 and 1963, they rose over fivefold to an average of $31,000 per acre (36 francs per square meter),[116] while in comparison the construction cost index doubled. Improvement costs outside the ZUP were lower because the developments were small—less than 300 dwelling units—and, therefore, exempt from many of the city's requirements for infrastructure and dedication of land for roads, schools, and parks.[117] The city further handicapped itself in the first ZUP by building 4,000 units of moderate income housing there and charging only $2,000 (10,000 francs) of its actual $2,400 (12,000 francs) per unit cost against each unit. The remainder was added to the per unit sale price for private-sector housing and thus further increased the housing price differential between the ZUP and other areas.

The city soon found itself caught in a dilemma. It had the legal right to refuse all requests for development of more than 100 units outside the ZUP, yet to meet demand it needed to build at the rate of 8,000 dwelling units per year, more than the total final capacity of the ZUP. In 1966, it did create another ZUP of 1,900 acres (760 hectares), planned for 30,000 dwelling units, and bought most of the land in both ZUPs. The city also created several ZADs totaling around 12,350 acres (5,000 hectares). However, its purchases in them of 1,976 acres (800 hectares) did not begin to meet the demands for land for development. (See map 4.5.)

The city did not purchase more land for two reasons: lack of money and other priorities for the available funds. The state's Central Savings Bank did not provide enough loan support and the city was unable to increase its two-thirds share.[118] The state does not require the city to earmark loans granted as to particular types of land acquisition. As part of the city's five-year capital program, it proposes various types of acquisition and requests a state loan subsidy. The state's commitment usually is not forthcoming until two years of the five-year period have elapsed. Once the subsidized loans are approved, the state leaves their allocation largely at the city's discretion.

Of the funds available for land acquisition—for the 270-acre (110-hectare) solid waste disposal site north of the Etang de Berre, for hospitals, roads, schools, and development parks—Marseilles thought it essential to allocate a substantial amount annually to purchase land for open space. The Calanques, the dramatic cliffs that drop abruptly to the Mediterranean on the city's southern flank, have received top priority (see

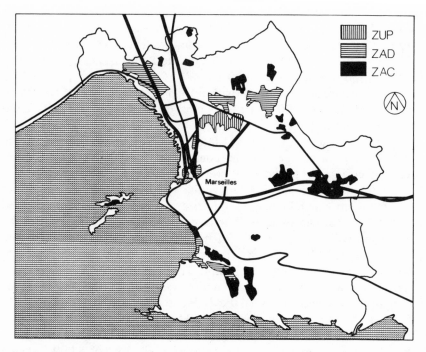

MAP 4.5.  Marseilles ZUPs, ZADs, and ZACs

SOURCE: Adapted from Délégation à l'Aménagement du Territoire, *Languedoc-Roussillon* (1967), p. 8

fig. 4.5). Marseilles is committed to preventing development of this rugged and unspoiled area, and over half of the 12,350 acres (5,000 hectares) is now in public ownership. Some land there has been purchased by right of preemption under the ZCP law.

The city has established DUPs in order to be able to finwhich land threatened with imminent development counter to its plans. The 2,470 acre (1,000-hectare) site of a new university campus at Luminy is one such instance.

Condemnation has proven very costly, and, therefore, has been avoided where possible (see table 4.7). In addition, the condemnation process takes from one to three years, thus forestalling development. Immediate possession on condemnation is authorized only for expressways.

Failure to acquire enough land after designation of ZUPs and ZADs has had unfortunate consequences. Because the city did not have an adequate reserve to accommodate development, and because it would have been politically suicidal, the city council was never able to deny permission to develop outside of the Zs. It did not acknowledge that failure to bar other

FIGURE 4.5. Picturesque Zone, Les Calanques, Marseilles, France

TABLE 4.7. Marseilles Condemnation Awards

| | ZUP 1 | | Central Market Station | |
|---|---|---|---|---|
| | Dollars per Acre | Francs per Square Meter | Dollars per Acre | Francs per Square Meter |
| City offering price | 7,970 | 9.15 | 13,070 | 15 |
| Award of land judge | 23,120 | 26.8 | 19,600 | 22 |
| Award of court of appeal | 31,080 | 35.6 | 35,290 | 41.2 |

SOURCE: Data provided by Marseilles Metropolitan Area Planning Agency

development would make it impossible to carry out plans for the ZUPs. Yet it was hardly surprising that these other areas competed successfully with the ZUPs for private development. For reasons already mentioned they were, in general, cheaper to develop. Further, as more and more state-aided moderate income housing (Habitation Loyer Modérée, or HLM) was built in the development zones at high density, the private sector became less and less willing to invest there. Eventually, ten thousand units of high-density HLM housing were built in one ZUP, and social problems began to proliferate.

The smaller ZADs in built-up, declining areas, such as Ste. Barbe in the Arab Quarter, the St. Charles railroad station, and the southern terminus of the expressway, have been successful. In these locations the landowners had no other potential purchasers and received what they thought to be a fair price. Elsewhere, especially in the northeastern part of the city where some two thousand landowners were subject to ZADs, land prices outside the ZADs kept rising, again because the city was unable to restrict development, and political opposition to the ZADs began to mount. On the eve of the 1971 municipal election, Mayor Gaston Deferre promised a tumultuous throng assembled to protest the zones that, if the socialists were reelected, the zones would be abandoned but for the expressway site. Following a socialist victory, the city council officially voted to drop the ZUPs and ZADs, except for a few ZADs that were redesignated as ZACs. This action was not within the city council's power, since formal designation of the zones rests with the minister of public construction. However, since the city has not acted to exercise its right of preemption in the zones, they continue to exist only on paper.

The ZACs have not encountered these problems. They are numerous but comparatively small and have the advantage of private entrepreneurial backing. Several of those under development are planned for shopping centers and offices.

*Aix-en-Provence.* Aix, as many other municipalities, has worked in succession with ZUPs, ZADs, and ZACs. While there have been difficulties, caused in part by a surge of growth occurring sooner than projected, the serious antagonisms that arose in Marseilles have been avoided and the development created has been reasonably successful.

Aix has been one of the more delightful cities of southern France. Its springs and fountains made it a green oasis long before irrigation reached Provence. Its university has enhanced its cultural life. The beauty of its natural setting, adjacent to Mont Ste. Victoire, and of its old quarter long have drawn artists and writers. Once rapid development reached the Marseilles region, Aix was certain to be affected. It has been more fortunate than many of its neighbors in that, given its attractions, it has drawn a larger share of the affluent. Also, it has many less skilled newcomers, including a large community of North Africans.

In 1960, Aix moved to respond to this growth by seeking the creation of a 160-acre (65-hectare) ZUP. In 1962, the Ministry of Construction approved the ZUP and a DUP enabling condemnation so that the city could move rapidly to acquire land. The city then was projecting a population of over 80,000 by 1970 and over 90,000 by 1975, a growth rate comparable to that for the Marseilles region. It estimated that, at twenty-four dwelling units per acre (sixty dwelling units per hectare), it should establish a land reserve of 670 acres (270 hectares), one-quarter in renewal areas, one-quarter in the ZUP, and one-half in a ZAD, which it then requested the ministry to approve. This approval was granted in 1964.

Development occurred sooner than anticipated due to the French exodus from Algeria. The 1966 census revealed that Aix already had one hundred and three thousand people, and the projection for the year 2000 was raised to two hundred thousand. The ZUP couldn't meet even immediate needs and, worse, because those able to pay had bid up housing prices elsewhere, the city chose to build only subsidized housing in the ZUP. This created sharp social stratification between those living inside and outside of the ZUP. Although the ZUP is conveniently located, reasonably attractive, well served by shops, and has substantial office space, all of which brings in workers, many feel that there is a stigma attached to living there. (See fig. 4.6.)

This history influenced events at the ZAD, called Jas de Bouffan. The city was concerned about its ability to proceed rapidly enough to acquire land and prepare it for development. In 1967, it sought to have the ZAD redesignated as a ZUP. The prefect agreed in 1968, but warned the city that financing would be very difficult. To attract builders to the new ZUP, the prefect recommended levying an improvement tax on development elsewhere. The city concurred and levied a 1 percent tax in 1968, which it raised, in 1969, to 2 percent for moderate rent housing and 3 percent for other construction. Meanwhile, it was developing plans for Jas de Bouffan to have a substantial office component, a large shopping center to divert

FIGURE 4.6. A game of *boule* in the Aix-en-Provence ZUP, France (photo by Michael L. Strong)

pressure from the crowded center of Aix, and good public transportation, since the site is just beyond the Aix circumferential expressway. There are to be 5,140 dwelling units at 24 per acre (60 per hectare) net, with a floor area ratio of 0.3. The public facilities will have a floor area ratio of 0.2 and will include a stadium, hospital, schools, and playing fields.

Acquisition began in 1968, and, in 1969, the city sought a DUP for the entire zone. The site consists of many small parcels, the largest being only forty-two acres (seventeen hectares). The DUP proved necessary, because a lawyer encouraged many property owners to force the city to condemn, in hopes of obtaining higher prices. About 60 percent of the sites were condemned—a very high percentage in comparison to other acquisitions by Aix—but the judges have awarded the same amounts as paid under voluntary purchase. On an average, this has been $10,000 per acre (13 francs per square meter), plus 25 percent for related expenses.

Later, the departmental office of the Ministry of Public Construction suggested that it might be wiser for Aix to seek a transformation of the ZAD into a ZAC, rather than a ZUP, because of the difficulties the city would face in financing so much land acquisition and site preparations so quickly. Aix agreed, its SEM prepared a new proposal, and the area became a ZAC in 1970.

The land acquisition costs are estimated at 5.6 million (28 million francs), financed in full by loans from the Central Savings Bank and CAECL. Infrastructure and public improvement costs are estimated at $13.4 million (67 million francs). It is estimated that resale of development sites will yield $14.8 million (74 million francs), and if the developers' contributions are $2.4 million (12 million francs), then the deficit will be $1.6 million (8 million francs). The state is expected to pick up 60 percent of the deficit, with the city paying the remainder.

Aix hoped to attain a much more diversified mix of housing at Jas de Bouffan, but outside events again have led to a predominance of subsidized housing. At the time that sites were available for development, capital was virtually unobtainable for private housing and, consequently, most of that being built is subsidized.

Aix also has several small ZADs in the old quarter of the city. One is to be renewed as a merchandise distribution center. Another, where many North Africans live in crowded conditions, is being renewed by the rehabilitiation of existing structures. When a building comes on the market, the city does not preempt if it is in fair condition and has toilets and running water. This is in order to avoid widespread evictions of the immigrant tenants. When the city does preempt, it turns the building over to the moderate rent housing program for rehabilitation or, where unavoidable, for demolition and new construction. To pay for these acquisitions, Aix borrowed $7.2 million (36 million francs), mostly on the private market at 7.75 percent.

### Large-Scale Land Banks:
### Languedoc-Roussillon and Fos–Etang de Berre

The state has initiated a number of land development projects of national significance. Because of the scale of the projects, early acquisition of land at nonspeculative prices was critical to their success. Advance knowledge of the state's development intentions would have inflated overall acquisition costs astronomically. Therefore, planning and proceeding with an acquisition process that maintained secrecy was an important element of the projects. Other key elements were obtaining adequate funds when needed and designing a working relationship among the state, the local government, and the private sector.

Two of the earliest and largest of these projects are located to the west of Marseilles. Languedoc-Roussillon and Fos–Etang de Berre both illustrate the state's approach to the land acquisition process. Both have been successful with respect to the elements stated above: the necessary land was acquired at prices uninflated by the state's development plans, adequate acquisition financing was secured, and new functional relationships for the execution of the projects were formed. The success with which secrecy was maintained and speculation avoided did lead at Languedoc-Roussillon to widespread bitterness about the prices paid. This reopened a question that remains fundamental and unresolved both in France and the United States: is the landowner entitled to some share of the unearned increment in value attributable to public action?

The Languedoc-Roussillon project is vast, multicentered resort development extending along the Mediterranean Sea from the Spanish border on the west to the marshes of the Camargue on the east. The Marseilles metropolitan area lies further east, beyond Fos. During the early stages of Languedoc-Roussillon, the state acquired some ten thousand acres (4,000 hectares) of land at an average price of thirteen hundred dollars per acre (1.5 francs per square meter). Initial purchases to establish market price were carried out in secret through a straw party. Next, in 1963, widespread experimentation began with the new ZAD technique; at one point sixty thousand acres (24,700 hectares) of Languedoc-Roussillon were placed in ZADs to avert speculation. Because many key sites had been purchased prior to the creation of the ZADs, the right to preempt was used infrequently. DUPs were relied on where there was a need to condemn. A novel form of public agency, temporary in nature and designed for rapid action, first was tested at Languedoc-Roussillon and proved efficacious enough to serve as the model for later coastal development projects.

Fos is a new port and industrial complex planned to rival such European ports as Rotterdam and Hamburg. Like Languedoc-Roussillon it was initiated in the early 1960s. At Fos, some eighteen thousand acres (seventy-two hundred hectares) were bought at prices ranging from $320 to $640 per acre (0.4 to 0.8 francs per square meter). The state and the Marseilles Chamber of Commerce and Industry cooperated on planning for Fos, and both provided funds for land acquisition. Land is held by the Marseilles Port Authority, a public-private company with participation by the state, the local government, the chamber, labor, and port users. Once the port infrastructure was in place, almost all sites were leased. As of 1970, income from the sites had covered one-quarter of the $310 million (1.55 billion franc) acquisition cost.

At the Etang de Berre, the residential and commercial support area for Fos, reliance has been on a blanket use of ZADs. Much of the 34,600 acres (14,000 hectares) in these zones is also subject to DUPs, in order to make rapid land assembly possible. Land acquisition agencies have made extensive use of the right of preemption, acquiring over 2,300 acres (948 hectares) in this manner between 1968 and 1974. State loans, either at low interest or at no interest for leased land, have been the other key element enabling public agencies to buy as needed.

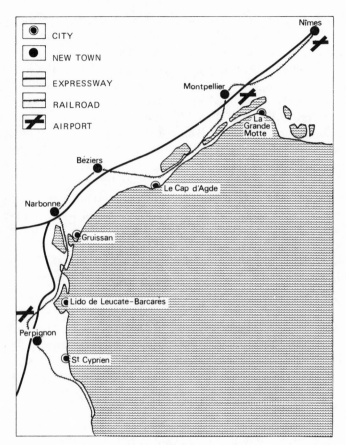

MAP. 4.6.  Languedoc-Roussillon new towns

SOURCE: Adapted from Max Falque, SOMI, Aix-en-Provence, letter, 1978

*Resort New Towns: Languedoc-Roussillon.*[119] To initiate the Langue-doc-Roussillon development, the state, during the 1960s, bought almost ten thousand acres (four thousand hectares) of land at a reasonable price, using the then current range of legal controls in combination with an administrative structure designed for the exigencies of the project. As it became timely, the state handed over development sites to SEMs, which, with the aid of loans from the Central Savings Bank, built the infrastructure. They then sold tracts to developers, who built in accord with the plans that had been adopted. (See map 4.6.)

There had been thoughts of developing the Languedoc-Roussillon coast since the early 1950s. The region was economically backward and the country needed more coastal resorts to boost tourist income. The Riviera was approaching saturation and tourists of moderate income, both French and foreign, were choosing places other than France for their vacations. The French tourist balance of payments was declining steadily. Languedoc-Roussillon, although endowed with one hundred miles (160 kilometers) of sandy beach and over twelve miles (20 kilometers) of rocky shore, was attracting a relatively small share of the vacation trade. In 1962, for instance, it registered fewer than 700,000 vacation stays, in comparison with 2.2 million for the Riviera. There were good reasons for its comparative unpopularity: the coastal marshes were thick with mosquitoes, the trees were sparse, the winds were strong, and access was poor. Further, until the National Company for the Lower Rhône–Languedoc (La Compagnie Nationale du Bas Rhône–Languedoc) completed a number of projects in the 1960s, many places had a very limited water supply. Turning the Languedoc-Roussillon coast into an attractive tourist destination area would require a major commitment over a period of years.

In April 1962, the state decided to go forward with the project. Only those who would need to know in order to acquire the key tracts of land were told of the decision. Secrecy was deemed essential to hold down land prices. This was particularly important at Languedoc-Roussillon, because the goal was to create inexpensive to moderately priced accommodations that would attract both French and foreign vacationers. In the 1950s, French building site costs had risen four times as fast as construction costs. Land speculation at Languedoc-Roussillon could destroy at the outset the possibility of providing less expensive tourist opportunities.

After considerable debate among those few people charged with a decision, it was decided that a land bank would be created. Nationalization of the area was considered and rejected as antithetical to the widely held and deeply cherished belief in private property. ZUPs were thought inappropriate for such a large area. ZADs had just been authorized and had yet to be tested; therefore, they were not to be relied upon as the sole land use control. Nevertheless, taxes hadn't worked, "speaking practically, all of the systems to recover speculative value that have been adopted in France have failed."[120] The Dutch and Scandinavian successes with direct purchase of land persuaded the French that this should be the principal tool, with secondary reliance on ZADs. As Arrago observes:

The development of the Languedoc-Rossillon littoral led those responsible for it to experiment, on a large scale, with certain antispeculative measures, such as the creation of land reserves and deferred development zones. . . . Further, the use of two successive expropriation laws in the same vast and complex undertaking made it possible to make a better comparison of the advantages and disadvantages of each and to reveal the flaws of certain provisions, all of which undoubtedly constitute progress in the search for greater efficacy and equity at a time when recourse to expropriation is frequent.[121]

The government made several decisions early in the life of the project that guided planning and land acquisition:

1. There would be six tourist destination centers;[122] wherever possible, these centers would not be located where speculation already had occurred
2. Secrecy should be maintained until a large amount of land had been acquired
3. The project should not be hampered by linking it to fiscal reforms
4. Land acquired would be held for a moderate term
5. Condemnation should be avoided in the early stages because it would cause delay and publicity
6. Tracts varying by location, size, and other characteristics would be bought to provide multiple land value referants for later use in condemnation actions

As soon as the commitment to Languedoc-Roussillon was made, the Ministry of Public Construction was given an advance of $3 million (15 million francs) by FNAT to begin buying land. The usual appraisal and negotiation procedures were altered in several respects to achieve speed and preserve secrecy.

The National Company for the Lower Rhône–Languedoc was chosen to act as negotiator and apparent purchaser. The company had been active in the local land market for some years while building its water supply network, and therefore a series of further negotiations would not be suspect.

Appraisals were done by the Land Administration's elite corps of inspectors rather than by its staff at the department level. They had access to the extensive land transaction data of the National Company for the Lower Rhône–Languedoc and visited sites with the company employees who had been chosen to act as negotiators. The inspectors classified land by use, size, location, and special characteristics. Since much of the land was planted in vineyards, inspectors who were specialists in vineyard values did these appraisals, adding soil type, root stock, and weight of harvest to the factors considered for other land. For all land except large vineyards, comparable sale data were relied upon to develop an average price for each type of site. The value of vineyards of more than fifty acres (twenty hectares)—vineyards larger than needed to support a family—was arrived at by capitalizing income at the middle- or long-term borrowing rate of the National Farm Loan Bank. As soon as the appraisals were completed, they were submitted directly to Land Administration headquarters, bypassing the departmental director. The minister of public construction was notified as soon as they were approved.

Meanwhile, the Central Commission for Control of Land Operations had received a preliminary file for review. Within one week, it approved the purchase of almost five thousand acres (two thousand hectares) on condition that a full review of the file would follow.

Upon approval of the first phase of the project and of the related appraisals, the minister of public construction directed the company to acquire options at prices not to exceed the approved appraisals by more than 25 percent. The options were acquired in the name of the company or "for the account of those whom it may concern." The whole operation moved so quickly that the first options were in hand in May of 1962, a month after it had been decided to undertake the project. In Arrago's opinion, the authorization to offer up to 25 percent over the appraised price contributed greatly to the negotiators' success.

Within a year, options had been acquired and exercised on 3,100 acres (1,250 hectares) at prices averaging $130 per acre (0.15 francs per square meter) for swamp, $260 per acre (0.3 francs per square meter) for waste land, $2,600 per acre (3 francs per square meter) for the sites nearest existing development, and $640–960 per acre (8,000–12,000 francs per hectare) for good quality vineyards. These purchases established base prices for later negotiations and condemnation. With the prices a matter of record, secrecy no longer was necessary, and a permanent organization could be created to be responsible for the project.

A new organization was designed to meet the requirements. Its principal tasks were to articulate the project concept, acquire further land, and carry out major public improvements such as mosquito control and afforestation before conveying sites to SEMs.

The SEMs would be valuable at a later stage, offering decentralization of detailed planning through contracts with private consulting firms, infrastructure construction, and the marketing of development sites. In addition, and a matter of great importance, they would provide a structure for local participation. As Lepêtre comments:

The SEMs provided a supple link at the development and construction stage between the Parisian bureaucracy of the state and local interests by choosing prominent local politicians as their presidents. The president of the general council of the Hérault department, who was also a senator and mayor, was named president of the SEM for La Grande Motte, and the same type of prominent people were named for the other SEMs.[123]

During the early phases, however, the state determined that it wanted a large measure of control. Anticipating some local opposition, it wanted an organizational structure that would enable it to act regardless of local views. In addition, it sought to create an agency that, although temporary, would have high-powered staff with access to the upper ranks of the state bureaucracy. The agency was to place an emphasis on flexibility and initiative, since the project could be expected to present novel problems. The

Interministerial Mission for Tourist Development of the Languedoc-Roussillon Littoral (La Mission Interministérielle pour l'Aménagement Touristique du Littoral Languedoc-Roussillon) was created in 1963,[124] in response to these ideas. Its members were representatives of the ministries of Interior, Economics and Finance, Budget, Construction, Public Works, and Agriculture, and of the Tourist Commission; the regional prefect for Languedoc; and, when needed, the prefects of the four departments within the region—Gard, Hérault, Aude, and Pyrénées-Orientale. The representatives of the ministries were granted decision making power, so that actions voted on by the mission members did not have to be confirmed by each ministry. The prime minister appointed the president and secretary general of the mission. The president, M. Racine, was a leading civil servant who also served as chief of staff to the minister of interior and, later, to the minister of finance. His ability and contacts contributed much to the success of the mission. The mission was given a three-year life, subject to renewal, with a 1975 target date for completion of the project. In fact, due to the recession, work has proceeded more slowly than originally planned and, as of 1977, the mission still was active.

Once the mission was in existence, it exercised primary responsibility for planning and further land acquisition. Its budget at the Ministry of Finance was a global sum with no line items, thus giving the agency tremendous flexibility, as its need varied among the purchase of land, drainage, roads, afforestation, and other major improvements. A regional plan, prepared under contract by private consultants, was begun in 1963 and adopted in 1964, after comment by the general councils of the departments.[125] ZADs were created in 1963, and Languedoc-Roussillon became the prime locus for experimentation with the new technique. Acquisition continued, usually by negotiated purchase, sometimes by condemnation following a Declaration of Public Utility, and ocaasionally by right of preemption.

The regional plan was needed in a hurry to provide a sharper focus for land acquisition decisions and, it was hoped, to dampen speculation in the areas shown as remaining undeveloped. Prepared and adopted within six months, it prescribed future land use and density. The overall density for each resort town was calculated from the specification that half of the people should be able to use the beach at any one time.[126] The land use zones included areas for tourists, agriculture, woods, afforestation, nature protection, and industry. The maximum gross density for tourist accommodations was to be forty beds per acre (one hundred beds per hectare). In zones to be used for agriculture or woods, the landowner or tenant could build one private dwelling for his own use on a plot at least 200 feet (60 meters) on a side, or approximately one acre in area. Plots almost three times as large were required in zones with high tourist amenity.

Municipal plans remained in force insofar as they conformed to the regional plan; to the extent that they did not conform, municipalities were required to amend them. The regional plan had the same legal effect as the municipal plans, namely, that development not in accord with the plan was prohibited. Land shown on the plan as intended for future public use, either for roads or for community facilities, was excluded from this blanket statement. Owners of this land were entitled to demand that it be purchased from them within three years of the date of their demand. In fact, these demands generally were limited to situations in which an estate had to be settled or in which there was a partition of ownership.

Under French law, unlike American law, the land use control that comes into force on the adoption of a binding plan is an administrative easement in gross. No compensation is paid for this easement and there is no legal right on the part of the landowner to claim that there has been a taking. However, relief may be sought from the terms of the easement under procedures analogous to American zoning variances.[127] It was an awareness of the frequency and ease with which variances are obtained that led the Languedoc-Roussillon mission to be unwilling to rely on the binding force of the regional plan. Of particular concern were the six areas designated for development as tourist centers.

ZADs were established in three of the four departments to provide surer control. Not knowing how large a ZAD would be needed to provide protection against speculation, the mission chose to include very large areas, even though this constituted a degree of intervention in the private land market that added to local resentment. At that time ZADs were just coming into use; there were then only ten ZADs, covering thirty-five hundred acres (1,450 hectares), in all of France, in comparison to 136 ZUPs, covering forty-six thousand acres (18,500 hectares). Languedoc-Roussillon soon became the national leader in the use of ZADs, placing almost sixty-thousand acres (24,700 hectares) in these zones. ZADs of five thousand acres (2,000 hectares) were created around several of the tourist centers.

Acquisition proceeded, two-thirds of it by voluntary agreement. In 1963 and 1964, 2,500 acres (1,000 hectares) were purchased, financed by FNAFU loans. The Central Savings Bank and SCET, neither of which was subject to the double control of the Land Administration and the Commission for Control of Land Operations, helped by buying important parcels at several of the tourist centers and then turning them over to the mission. Some 1,250 acres (500 hectares) were acquired in this manner. By 1964, to discourage increases in land prices at the designated tourist centers, the mission began seeking DUPs to put landowners on notice that condemnation would be used if necessary. By 1966, more than 13,000 acres (5,429 hectares) was covered by DUPs. There was only one challenge as to whether a public purpose was to be served by the taking, and the administrative court upheld the mission.

Some land to be developed as part of the project was not acquired by the mission, provided that the owner agreed to comply with the plan and to pay the SEM an appropriate amount for the site improvements.

The right of preemption created by the ZADs was little exercised, largely because most would-be sellers abandoned their decision to sell when notified that their sale would be preempted. Between 1963 and 1966, there were 440 declarations of an intention to sell, 187 decisions to preempt, 163 withdrawals from the market, and only 24 preemptions. By 1966, the mission was ready to reduce the area in ZADs, in large part because most of the land needed for development had been acquired and resold to an SEM. With the SEMs about to begin marketing impoved development sites, the protection of the ZAD designation could be used on a more limited basis.

As of 1968, when the bulk of the land acquisition had been completed, $9,519,800 (47,599,000 francs) had been paid for land at Languedoc-Roussillon. This averaged out to $1,300 per acre (1.5 francs per square meter). The prices were higher at some of the tourist centers, reaching an average of $3,200 per acre (3.7 francs per square meter) at La Grande Motte and Leucate-Barcares. (See fig. 4.7.)

*Port-Related Development: Fos–Etang de Berre.* Fos is the immense new port and industrial complex spreading over some eighteen thousand acres (seventy-two hundred hectares) of coast west of Marseilles. If it fulfills French hopes, calling it the Mediterranean Europort will not be a misnomer.

Because Fos is not an isolated undertaking, a review of the approach to land acquisition and disposition there would be incomplete without similar consideration of nearby areas around the Etang de Berre, a large but shallow salt lake between Fos and Marseilles.

Planning and development have proceeded in several stages. Sequentially, since 1961, there have been a review of limitations on port development at the Etang de Berre, land acquisition and planning for port and industrial development at Fos, land acquisition and planning for further related development north of Fos, and land acquisition and planning for new town and residential development around the Etang de Berre. Development throughout the area has been marked by the frequent companions of rapid growth: pollution, confusion, interjurisdictional infighting, and a pronounced decline in the quality of the living environment. These serious shortcomings, however, are not the issue of this study and should not obscure the success, measured in time and cost, of the various means used to acquire land.

*Fos.* The decision to build a major European port at Fos responded to needs of both the state and the Marseilles area. For once, despite their different political orientations, the national government and the city government shared a common objective and worked together to advance it.

FIGURE 4.7.  La Grande Motte, France (photo by Michael L. Strong)

By 1961, other West European nations were competing vigorously for port trade; the Dutch at Rotterdam and the West Germans at Hamburg, particularly, were committed to further expansion of their already highly successful ports. The French government was prepared to invest enough to create one port designed to compete with the European leaders. Dunkerque had been rebuilt and was as fully developed as the government thought was warranted. After consideration, the government concluded that there were two choices: expand Le Havre or build an entirely new port at Fos at the mouth of the Rhône. The old port of Marseilles had no room for expansion, so if there were to be a major port in the Marseilles area, it would have to be built from scratch. The Gulf of Fos, 6.25 miles (10 kilometers) wide and 165 feet (50 meters) deep, was the best site on the French Mediterranean coast. Several factors tipped the balance in favor of Fos: the comparative locational advantage, the potential for stimulating other development, and the area's need for jobs.

There were already several large West European ports on the North Sea—Antwerp, Amsterdam, Rotterdam, London, Hamburg, and Le Havre among them. Serving Western Europe along the Mediterranean, there were only Genoa, Marseilles, and Barcelona, and Barcelona was not a major competitor. If the Rhine and the Rhône could be linked for shipping, there would be great potential advantage to a port at the mouth of the Rhône.

Marseilles had been designated a growth pole, an area selected by the state for major investment in order to divert pressure from Paris. Yet neither the port of Marseilles nor the nearby Etang de Berre could be expanded into a highly competitive, major port. Fos alone offered the opportunity of using port development to advance the growth pole concept. Three refineries were in operation at the Etang de Berre—BP, Shell, and Elf, a French company—and a pipline was planned to link this area to Lyons, Strasbourg, Munich, and Karlsruhe. Creating a port capable of receiving five-hundred-thousand-ton tankers could stimulate large-scale expansion of the petrochemical industry in the Marseilles area. Yet the Etang de Berre itself was not a prospect for further port development, being only twenty-six feet (eight meters) deep at its deepest point. Fos was adjacent and could provide a catalyst for expansion.

The port of Marseilles was losing business and was unsuited to redevelopment and expansion. Manufacturing, which consisted primarily of processing imported raw materials, also was sluggish in Marseilles. To compound the local economic problem, immigration to the area was high, particularly from North Africa. The need for new jobs was acute.

The Marseilles Chamber of Commerce and Industry actively promoted Fos from the start as an economic boon for the area. The city's political leaders were dubious at first, since Fos was thirty-eight miles (sixty kilometers) from Marseilles, but soon concluded that the chamber was right. Rotterdam's enormous success with Europort, at the mouth of the Rhine and a comparable distance from the crowded old port in the heart of the city, provided a tempting model of what might be achieved. In late 1961, senior representatives of the national government met in Marseilles with key local people and reached the decision to develop Fos. Land acquisition and planning began at once.

Fos at the time was mostly marsh, accessible only by boat, and used chiefly for hunting and fishing. About the only commercial activity was that of the Salins du Midi, which evaporated sea water to produce salt. The coastal strip, defined as extending inland to the winter high-water mark, was open to the public as part of the maritime public domain. Further inland was public land formed by alluvial deposits. Prior to 1963, this latter type of public land could be sold; subsequently the law was revised and the land became part of the inalienable maritime public domain.

Since the private land, at this time, had little commercial value, it was inexpensive, and the government was anxious to buy before prices rose in anticipation of development.[128] In January of 1962, the Central Savings Bank notified the Marseilles Chamber of Commerce and Industry that it had acquired an option on about 4,000 acres (1,619 hectares) at Fos for $640 per acre (0.8 francs per square meter).[129] The chamber responded by creating the Public-Private Syndicate for Planning and Development of

TABLE 4.8. Fos Area One: Proposed Land Use

| Item | Acres | Hectares |
|------|-------|----------|
| Industry | 10,374 | 4,200 |
| Wharves | 1,358 | 550 |
| Commercial | 1,088 | 440 |
| Municipal | 1,185 | 480 |
| Water | 2,668 | 1,080 |
| Miscellaneous | 1,130 | 460 |
| Total | 17,803 | 7,210 |

SOURCE: Service Promotion Industrielle, Port Autonome de Marseille, *Doing Business at Fos* (Marseilles: Service Promotion Industrielle, 1972).

Fos. Members were the chambers of commerce of Marseilles and Arles and the municipalities of Marseilles, Arles, Fos, and Port St. Louis. Other municipalities were invited to join but could not afford to subscribe to shares in the syndicate. The syndicate assembled funds sufficient to buy 2,500 acres (995 hectares) of the optioned tract. Forty percent of the cost was contributed by the state's Ministry of Public Construction and the rest was raised locally, mostly by the Marseilles chamber. The state bought the rest of the tract. Through a special mission, the state then purchased 8,200 acres (3,378 hectares) of marsh for $320 per acre (0.4 francs per square meter) from the Salins du Midi. After these two vast tracts had been acquired, only a few other large parcels—those in excess of 1,200 acres (500 hectares)—remained to be purchased. In addition, a considerable number of small parcels were needed. The state acquired some of these tracts through FNAFU and SCET and the syndicate bought others, occasionally by resort to eminent domain. In the few cases where eminent domain was used, the condemantion awards ranged from $800 to $1,000 per acre (1 to 1.25 francs per square meter).

In 1965, the state created a new public-private agency, the Port Authority of Marseilles, to complete the acquisitions, hold land, plan, develop, and manage Fos.[130] The port authority is directed by a board consisting of five representatives of the national government, two representatives of the local government, eight representatives of the chamber of commerce, seven representatives of port users, and two representatives of port employees. It designated the 17,800 acres (7,200 hectares) lying between the towns of Port St. Louis and Fos as Area 1. The proposed uses of the site are shown in table 4.8. (See map 4.7.)

FNAFU, SCET, and the syndicate sold their holdings in this area to the port authority, which received 80 percent of its acquisition funds from the Ministry of Public Construction. By this time the plans for Area 1 had taken form, and the initial work to create the port was under way. The

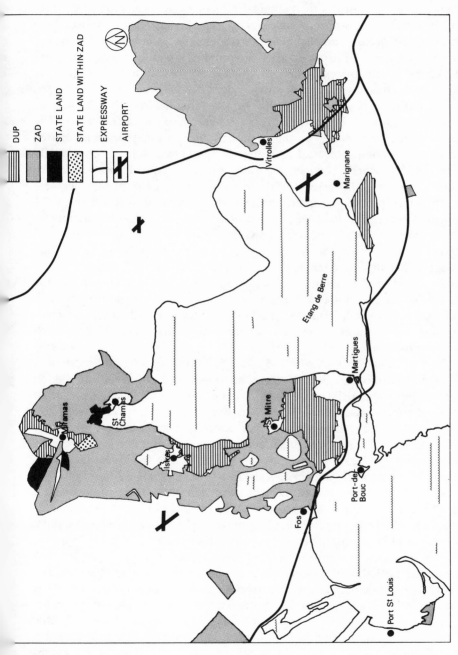

MAP 4.7. Fos–Etang de Berre ZADs and DUPs, 1976

SOURCE: Adapted from Mission Interministérielle pour l'Aménagement de la Région de Fos–Etang de Berre, *ZAD, January 76* (map) (Marseilles, 1976)

plans set new job targets for the mid-1970s of twelve thousand at the port and in related industry and sixteen thousand in the tertiary sector. Iron and steel, refineries, and chemicals were the major industries to be sought. Most housing for the expected sixty thousand new residents was to be built elsewhere, partly by expansion of the existing small towns around the Etang de Berre and partly by new town construction there.

Later, the Port Authority called for the creation of Area 2, west of Istres and north of Port St. Louis, as an additional industrial zone. The state created two ZADs in the area and the port authority purchased substantial amounts of land. Among the purchases were one of 1,100 acres (437 hectares) bought for $800 per acre (one franc per square meter), one of 4,500 acres (1,800 hectares) bought for $1,000 per acre (1.25 francs per square meter), and a truck farm of 1,200 acres (471 hectares) where the land was valued at $1,400 per acre (1.7 francs per square meter). While inflation, awareness of development plans, and greater suitability of the land for development all contributed to land values higher than in Area 1, there was one constraint on a further rise in land values. In the vicinity of Istres, and affecting much of Area 2, the state holds an avigation easement for planes using the large military airfield. The easement, which limits the height of buildings and chimneys, in combination with the noise from the jets keeps land values from rising as much as they would otherwise.

By 1970, the port authority had spent $12.4 million (62 million francs) on land acquisition for Fos. Of this, it had raised one-quarter, or $3 million (15 million francs), internally, through port charges and the sale or lease of development-ready sites. Two tracts were sold to steel companies; following these sales, the port authority adopted a lease policy. The lease terms are a minimum of eighteen years and a maximum of seventy years, with thirty-five years most customary. The lease rate for industrial sites is set for six years and then revised at three-year intervals by the use of the national construction cost index. The base rate is $0.026 per square foot (1.32 francs per square meter). The base year is 1953; in 1969, the index was 216. The base rate is multiplied by factors for size of tract, location, and the value of the particular industry to the port and region.

It is too soon for an appraisal of the success of Fos. There is much warranted criticism of inadequate provision for housing and inadequate aid to the municipalities confronted with a population influx. The little housing built at Fos proper has been described as "temporary barracks, swept by the wind, built in a desolate place in a corner of the industrial zone."[131] The expressways have disfigured some formerly beautiful countryside. Pollution, of air, land and water, is an unresolved problem. An almost constant yellow haze blankets the Etang de Berre and the smell frequently is foul. In addition, the city of Marseilles dumps some nine hundred tons of solid waste daily in the plain of Crau, just north of the Etang de Berre.

There are coordination problems and overlapping responsibilities among the port authority, the departmental office of the Ministry of Public Construction, the local governments, and MIAFEB (Mission Interministérielle pour l'Aménagement de la Région Fos–Etang de Berre), the agency for the development of Fos and the Etang de Berre. Gaston Deferre, the socialist mayor of Marseilles, laments that Fos is autonomous in name only, being controlled from Paris. The communist mayor of Port St. Louis in turn resents the port authority's power over Fos. The town of Fos is distressed by the air pollution that has accompanied development. One response has been to create yet another agency. In 1973, the Intermunicipal Syndicate for Coordination of Planning of the Fos Zone (Syndicat Mixte Intercommunal de Coordination pour l'Aménagement de la Zone de Fos) was formed. Its members include thirteen municipalities and the general council of the Bouches-du-Rhône, and its purpose is to coordinate land and development policies for the Marseilles-Fos region.

On the positive side, somewhere between 6,000 and 7,000 jobs had been created in some fifty firms at Fos by the mid-1970s. However, that achievement pales when contrasted with the thirty thousand people then out of work in the Bouches-du-Rhône. The port, by 1973, had overtaken Genoa, Antwerp, and Le Havre in tonnage of imports and exports, with petroleum accounting for the bulk of its trade. The docks also handled a substantial volume of bauxite, liquified natural gas, and container cargo. In 1975, 54 million metric tons of oil were refined at the Etang de Berre. The Solmer steelworks has a 3.5-million-ton output. The recent rate of growth of Fos has been greater than that of any of its competitor ports, including Rotterdam.

One can say that the land acquisition program moved rapidly and smoothly, evidencing considerable cooperation among the state, local government, and the private sector. Buying large tracts in advance of public awareness of development plans established market value; this, combined with the existence of the eminent domain power, made it possible to buy the land at reasonable prices. State initiative in providing the bulk of the funds for land acquisition, in authorizing direct state acquisition, and in transferring title to the port authority, with its shared state–local–private sector management, has been critical. So, too, has been the leadership exerted by the Marseilles Chamber of Commerce and Industry.

*Etang de Berre.*[132] Planners' goals for the communities situated around the Etang de Berre are that these communities should contribute to the vitality of Marseilles as a regional center and to the viability of Fos as an industrial and port facility by providing a good living enviroment and substantial employment for many of the region's inhabitants. In part this is to occur by the expansion of existing towns and cities, but much of the development is to be located in four or five new towns with populations ranging from 80,000 to 200,000.

Land acquisition for all types of development has followed development zone designation for the most part. Initially a few ZUPs were created, but primary reliance has been on ZADs and ZACs. In addition, substantial areas are covered by DUPs, establishing the right to use eminent domain. Virtually all of the land surrounding the Etang de Berre not already urbanized or used for military or commercial airfields has been placed in a development zone. The one exception is prime agricultural land, tracts of which remain near Marignane airport, the new town of Vitrolles, and the town of Port du Bouc. This land, on an average, is worth $8,100 per acre (10 francs per square meter) for farming, and it is planned for continued farm use.

The ZADs total 34,600 acres (14,000 hectares). The initial ZADs were created in 1967 and 1971, by the prefect in the name of the state, and were provisional. These ZADs became permanent in 1974, and offer a fourteen-year period, dating either from 1967 or 1971, for the exercise of the right of preemption. Several other ZADs have been created subsequently.

The DUPs were approved in 1972 and 1973. They overlap the ZADs to the extent of 2,700 acres (1,100 hectares) at Vitrolles, 4,000 acres (1,600 hectares) at Martigues, Port de Bouc, and Saint Mitre les Remparts, 3,600 acres (1,468 hectares) at Istres, and 800 acres (330 hectares) at Miramas. Because much of the land was scheduled for development in the near future, widespread use of the DUP was considered necessary. With the assurance that eminent domain was possible, acquisition could go forward rapidly. As of early 1977, 3,745 acres (1,516 hectares) had been purchased for three Etang de Berre new towns, Istres, Miramas, and Vitrolles.[133] (See figure 4.8.) The total cost of the acquisition for these three new towns as of that date was approximately $22 million (107 million francs), or approximately $5,700 per acre (70,000 francs per hectare). (See table 4.9.)

At the new town site of Vitrolles, enough land has been placed in ZACs to provide for the construction of a regional commercial center to serve three hundred thousand people and housing to accommodate fifteen thousand people. Acquisition there, even in the early 1960s, cost as much as $7,300 per acre (9 francs per square meter) for residential sites. The Vitrolles site is adjacent to the existing town of Vitrolles, with a 1976 population of twenty-two thousand, and close to Marignane airport and its surrounding industrial complex, all of which has contributed to the high land values.

Similar conditions have prevailed throughout the area. Land has been expensive because the new town sites are located adjacent to existing towns and in a heavily developed area. Choosing to locate new towns

TABLE 4.9. Public Land, Etang de Berre New Towns, 1977

| | New Town | | | | | | | | | | | |
| | Istres[a] | | | | Miramas | | | | Vitrolles | | | |
| | Area | | Cost | | Area | | Cost | | Area | | Cost | |
| Nature of Acquisition | Acres | Hectares | Dollars | Francs | Acres | Hectares | Dollars | Francs | Acres | Hectares | Dollars | Francs |
|---|---|---|---|---|---|---|---|---|---|---|---|---|
| Purchases financed by state loans to MATELT[b] (Budget Chapters 55-40, 55-41) | 973 | 394 | 4 | 22 | 291 | 118 | 2 | 10 | 1,272 | 515 | 7 | 34 |
| FNAFU, sections A and C[c] | 82 | 33 | 1 | 4 | 5 | 2 | | | 84 | 34 | | 3 |
| Subtotal | 1,055 | 427 | 5 | 26 | 296 | 120 | 2 | 10 | 1,356 | 549 | 7 | 37 |
| Purchases by EPAREB on its own account | 358 | 145 | 3 | 13 | 321 | 130 | 3 | 13 | 363 | 147 | 2 | 8 |
| Total | 1,413 | 572 | 8 | 39 | 617 | 250 | 5 | 23 | 1,719 | 696 | 9 | 45 |

NOTE: Data given is as of Mar. 15, 1977. Cost is in millions of dollars/francs. Where cost was less than 0.5 million francs or dollars no cost figure is shown, since rounding is to nearest million dollars/francs.

SOURCE: M. F. Gaston, Chief of the Land Division, EPAREB

[a] 183 additional acres (74 hectares) have been purchased and resold.

[b] MATELT is the Ministry for Planning and Development, Public Construction, Housing, and Tourism.

[c] FNAFU section A funds are for state purchase of lands planned for public uses. FNAFU section C funds are for state or local government acquisition by preemption.

FIGURE 4.8.  Istres ZAC, France (photo courtesy of M. Gaston, EPAREB)

around the Etang de Berre has meant not only that there was substantial preexisting development value but also that much of the land had been subdivided into small parcels. These factors made the right to condemn and to preempt essential. Between 1968 and 1972, preemption was used to buy some 1,900 acres (about 770 hectares) at a total cost of $4.9 million (24.3 million francs), or an average of $2,600 per acre (3.16 francs per square meter). (See table 4.10.)

Until 1973, land was bought by the Ministry of Public Construction through the Departmental Office for the Bouches-du-Rhône. Since then, EPAREB[134] (Etablissement Public d'Aménagement des Rives de l'Etang de Berre, or Public Authority for Planning and Development of the Banks of the Etang de Berre) has been charged with acquiring land and preparing sites for development. EPAREB is a public agency governed jointly by the

TABLE 4.10. Preemptions at Etang de Berre, 1968–1972

| | | | Source of Funds | | | | | | | |
|---|---|---|---|---|---|---|---|---|---|---|
| | FNAFU Loans | | | | | State Budget Chap. 55.40 Loans | | | | |
| | Area | | Cost | | | Area | | Cost | | |
| Year | Acres | Hectares | Dollars | Francs | | Acres | Hectares | Dollars | Francs | |
| 1968 | 2 | 1 | 10,000 | 50,000 | | 5 | 2 | 5,000 | 25,000 | |
| 1969 | 15 | 6 | 25,200 | 126,000 | | 25 | 10 | 61,200 | 306,000 | |
| 1970 | 10 | 4 | 25,500 | 127,500 | | 210 | 85 | 531,600 | 2,658,000 | |
| 1971 | 148 | 60 | 875,630 | 4,378,150 | | 1,370 | 555 | 2,983,204 | 14,916,021 | |
| 1972 | 91 | 37 | 145,200 | 726,000 | | 20 | 8 | 196,991 | 984,957 | |
| Total | 266 | 108 | 1,081,530 | 5,407,650 | | 1,630 | 660 | 3,777,995 | 18,889,978 | |

SOURCE: Data provided by Direction Départementale, Service des Domaines, Marseilles.

state and local governments of the Etang de Berre area. Its administrative council consists of five state representatives, designated by the minister of public construction, the minister of interior, and six local representatives, chosen by the member municipalities. The president, in 1974, was the socialist mayor of Vitrolles. The director of EPAREB is named by the minister of public construction after consultation with the administrative council and the regional prefect. Although the municipalities within EPAREB's jurisdiction have governments ranging from conservative to communist, their stands on development are shaped far more by local preferences than by party politics.

EPAREB has been acquiring land by preemption, voluntary purchase, and eminent domain. In those areas planned for new town development or for open space, the right of preemption has been exercised for almost all properties coming on the market. As of early 1974, EPAREB had preempted ninety sales covering 445 acres (180 hectares), paying $3,985,000 (19,925,000 francs), or $8,900 per acre (11 francs per square meter). Out of 2,342 acres (948 hectares) acquired by right of preemption between 1968 and early 1974, in only two instances did the sellers reject the state or EPAREB offer and turn to a land judge to set the price. Land planned for other uses is preempted only if EPAREB thinks that the sale price is so high that it would alter the going market value for land in that area.

Otherwise, land is bought by voluntary purchase, although EPAREB is prepared to condemn if there are holdouts. While there is much scattered opposition to the acquisitions, only in one location has there been organized opposition, led by a lawyer, which led to widespread refusal to sell and subsequent condemnation.

EPAREB is permitted to offer up to 10 percent above the Land Administration's estimate of land value. Any higher offer must be approved by the Land Administration before being made. Once a purchase agreement had been reached, it must be initialed by the Land Administration.

There are two sources of state loans for land acquisition for reserves for development within two to six years, and there is no maximum limit on the loan amount. Central Savings Bank loans are for a ten-year term at an effective interest rate of 3.1 percent. The actual rate is 6.5 percent, but a subsidy from FNAFU brings it down to 3.1 percent. Budget chapter 55–40 (until 1974 chapter 55.43) loans are available directly from the treasury but only where the publicly acquired land will be leased for development. These loans may be granted with no interest. Eighty-four percent of the Ministry of Public Construction loans for Etang de Berre new towns land acquisition were from the treasury, and these loans covered 61 percent of all land acquired by the ministry and EPAREB between

1968 and 1977. The leased land consists of sites for commercial centers and for government-assisted housing. Sites for other housing and for industry are being sold, and land planned for open space will be transferred to the Ministry of Agriculture for management.

### Farmland Preservation: The Bouches-du-Rhône SAFER[135]

A look at the Bouches-du-Rhône SAFER provides an impression of the context of opportunities and obstacles within which the SAFERs operate. The Bouches-du-Rhône SAFER has spent between $1 million and $2 million (5 million and 10 million francs) annually for land acquisition. This is about average for the nation. Land prices and development pressures, however, are far greater than average. With a growth of more than double that of France as a whole and an annual conversion of 2 percent of the open land to development, preservation of the prime farmland is increasingly difficult. Funds spent to buy farmland do not stretch as far as elsewhere, and the SAFER average price paid has risen from over $1,400 per acre (17,000 francs per hectare) in 1972 to over $2,000 per acre (almost 25,000 francs per hectare) in 1975.

The SAFER whose territory includes the Bouches-du-Rhône covers five departments[136] and, in 1974, was capitalized at $255,000 (1,272,000 francs). Its shares are held by forty ogranizations. It is anxious to increase its capitalization in order to expand the land acquisition program.

The SAFER's acquisition program is closely tied to departmental policies for the preservation of agricultural land. Several years ago, the Departmental Agricultural Office took the initiative to develop maps to recommend which land should be used for agriculture.[137] These maps were prepared by task forces for each of the thirteen areas in the department covered by SDAU and for three areas not included within an SDAU. The task force members included the staff of the Departmental Agricultural Office, representatives from the Departmental Public Construction Office, Departmental Office of Mines, OREAM (Organisme d'Etude d'Aménagement d'Aires Métropolitaines, Planning and Management Study Organization for Metropolitan Areas), and farm organizations. Their intent was to approach the problem of land use with urbanization, not agriculture, as the residual. Open land, whether or not currently in farming, was evaluated and what was considered important for agriculture was mapped for future agricultural use. In 1973, the Permanent Commission for Rural Land[138] approved the maps, and municipalities then were provided with copies of them.

These maps are advisory documents only, but they are being used by the municipalities in developing their POS and have increased awareness of the importance of preserving farmland. Although agriculture is a major land use in the department, municipal councils in the Bouches-du-Rhône are dominated by nonfarmers. As members of the municipal councils become increasingly sensitive to the financial burdens of urbanization, they are looking with considerable interest at the possible use of the POS to hold land in farming. While most farmers in the department earn a comfortable living from farming, many are not ready to relinquish the development value of their land. A POS that designates large portions of a municipality for continued farm use may meet with considerable resistance from members of the farm community. I attended a meeting called by the municipal council of Peyrolles to consider a POS that would have kept in farming large, flat, productive tracts along the Durance River that also had high value for industrial and residential development. Despite the pleas of the representatives of the departmental offices of Agriculture and Public Construction that urbanization would be better located elsewhere, the farmland owners were adamant that they wanted a land use designation that would enable them to sell for development, if they chose to do so.

With over half of the sales of farmland in the department for nonfarm purposes, SAFER cannot afford to wait for widespread adoption of the POS. In any event, there is no assurance that municipalities will reflect in their POS the recommendations of the Permanent Commission for Rural Land. Although farming is intensive and profitable in the Bouches-du-Rhône, with a long growing season and much irrigated land, sales for development are even more profitable. In many locations land prices are so high that the SAFER chooses not to spend its limited funds there. The prices that the SAFER does pay are highly variable, ranging from $400 per acre (5,000 francs per hectare) to $8,000 per acre (100,000 francs per hectare). The latter was the 1974 prevailing price paid at Aubagne, a rich truck garden area just east of Marseilles. The maximum is not set by law but by the SAFER's best judgment on the disposition of its resources. (See figure 1.9.)

SAFER activity in the Bouches-du-Rhône from 1972 through 1975 is displayed in tables 4.11 and 4.12. Table 4.11 shows SAFER purchases as part of the total market for farmland. All of the sales reported were subject to preemption by SAFER. As can be seen, most sales were of very small parcels of land—the mean size was under five acres (two hectares). These parcels generally were too small to be suitable for SAFER purchase for farm use. Exceptions were those parcels needed to assemble larger, more efficient holdings, or parcels whose high sale price would influence the land market. From 1972 through 1975, 54 percent of all agricultural land was sold for nonfarm purposes, 35 percent was sold to persons intending to continue farm use, and only 11 percent was sold to SAFER. This last figure is quite close to the 1970 national figure of 13 percent. Of

TABLE 4.11. Farmland Sales, Bouches-du-Rhône, 1972–1975

| Land Sales | 1972 | | 1973 | | 1974 | | 1975 | |
|---|---|---|---|---|---|---|---|---|
| | Acres | Hectares | Acres | Hectares | Acres | Hectares | Acres | Hectares |
| For nonfarm use | 11,251 | 4,555 | 10,920 | 4,421 | 5,518 | 2,234 | 4,441 | 1,798 |
| For farm use, other than to SAFER | 3,707 | 1,501 | 5,469 | 2,214 | 5,926 | 2,399 | 5,394 | 2,184 |
| To SAFER | | | | | | | | |
| Voluntary | 1,235 | 500 | 1,949 | 789 | 1,538 | 623 | 1,472 | 596 |
| By preemption | 124 | 50 | 49 | 20 | 69 | 28 | 40 | 16 |
| Total | 1,359 | 550 | 1,998 | 809 | 1,607 | 651 | 1,512 | 612 |
| Total | 16,317 | 6,606 | 18,387 | 7,444 | 13,051 | 5,284 | 11,347 | 4,594 |

SOURCE: "Bilan de l'activité des quatres dernières années," SAFER, Provence–Alpes–Côte d'Azur.

TABLE 4.12. SAFER Purchases and Sales, Bouches-du-Rhône, 1972–1975

| | Purchases | | | | | | Sales | | | | | |
|---|---|---|---|---|---|---|---|---|---|---|---|---|
| | | Area | | Cost (in millions) | | | | Area | | Revenue (in millions) | | |
| Year | Number | Acres | Hectares | Dollars | Francs | | Number | Acres | Hectares | Dollars | Francs | |
| 1972 | 57 | 1,359 | 550 | 2 | 10.1 | | 84 | 1,494 | 605 | 2.1 | 10.6 | |
| 1973 | 74 | 1,998 | 809 | 3.6 | 17.9 | | 99 | 3,095 | 1,253 | 3.4 | 16.8 | |
| 1974 | 102 | 1,608 | 651 | 3.4 | 17.2 | | 131 | 2,218 | 898 | 4.1 | 20.7 | |
| 1975 | 101 | 1,512 | 612 | 3.1 | 15.6 | | 133 | 1,447 | 586 | 2.9 | 14.6 | |

SOURCE: "Bilan de l'activité des quatres dernières années," SAFER, Provence–Alpes–Côte d'Azur.

FIGURE 4.9. Farmland conversion near Aix-en-Provence, France (photo by Michael L. Strong)

TABLE 4.13. Cumulative Income from the Departmental Open Space Tax, 1961–1972

| Year | Alpes-Maritimes | | Bouches-du-Rhône | |
|------|---------|--------|---------|--------|
| | Dollars | Francs | Dollars | Francs |
| 1961 | 27,114 | 135.570 | | |
| 1962 | 201,444 | 1.007.220 | 7,443 | 37.215 |
| 1963 | 394,404 | 1.972.020 | 19,618 | 98.090 |
| 1964 | 673,273 | 3.366.364 | 26,952 | 134.760 |
| 1965 | 934,107 | 4.670.534 | 47,163 | 235.815 |
| 1966 | 1,277,469 | 6.387.344 | 63,535 | 317.674 |
| 1967 | 1,445,957 | 7.229.784 | 73,919 | 369.595 |
| 1968 | 1,584,735 | 7.923.674 | 115,927 | 579.634 |
| 1969 | 1,760,093 | 8.800.464 | 164,966 | 824.829 |
| 1970 | 1,974,763 | 9.873.814 | 210,849 | 1.054.244 |
| 1971 | 2,315,529 | 11.577.645 | 239,534 | 1.197.669 |
| 1972 | 2,755,880 | 13.079.401 | 370,008 | 1.850.039 |
| Annual Mean | 227,990 | 1.139.950 | 33,637 | 168.185 |

SOURCE: Bouches-du-Rhône Préfecture, "Groupe d'Etudes Régionales," June 1973.

the 6,477 acres (2,622 hectares) bought by SAFER, only 4 percent was acquired by preemption. However, a much larger proportion of the transactions were made by preemption, indicating that the SAFER preempted more often in the acquisition of very small parcels. Also, preemption inquiries were initiated in more than ten times as many instances as resulted finally in preemption, suggesting that most landowners chose to sell voluntarily to the SAFER rather than to insist on preemption.

Table 4.12 shows SAFER acquisition and disposition of land. Acquisi-

tion and sale prices of SAFER land have risen from over $1,400 per acre
(18,000 francs per hectare) in 1972 to over $2,000 per acre (almost
25,000 francs per hectare) in 1975, for an average increase of 11 percent
per year. This table does not show when land sold had been acquired, or at
what price, or whether improvements had been made prior to resale. Also,
since the total income from sales of $12.5 million (62.7 million francs)
over the four-year period only exceeds the total expenditures of $12.1
million (60.8 million francs) for purchases by $400,000 (2 million francs),
it seems unlikely that the sale price reflects much of the inflation in the
price of land. If this is correct, and if there have been substantial expenditures for improvements, the revolving fund may require greater aug-
mentation than currently is being received from public subsidies, even to
maintain a constant rate of acquisitions. This is a problem faced throughout much of France. However, while acknowledging that funds are insufficient to meet acquisition goals, it is important to stress that SAFER has had
a significant impact on the use of farmland and that it enjoys the strong support of the farm community. Unlike the POS, the farmer receives market
value, including accrued development value, on sale. Also unlike the POS,
which is subject to change, the community knows that the farmer buying
from SAFER cannot change the use of the land for a fifteen-year period.

*Open Space Preservation:*
*Picturesque Zones in the*
*Bouches-du-Rhône and Alpes Maritimes[139]*

The law that initially authorized the creation of Sensitive Zones and
that now includes them in the broader category of Picturesque Zones
permits the designation of urban as well as rural areas. The response to
this law by the departments of Bouches-du-Rhône and Alpes Maritimes
shows how a different definition of types of land to be included leads to a
vast difference in boundaries and thus in revenues from the Departmental
Open Space Tax. The Bouches-du-Rhône mapped 1,262,000 acres
(511,100 hectares), or 18 percent of the land of the department, as Sensitive Zones (now Picturesque Zones) but excluded all cities (see map
4.8). The Department of Alpes Maritimes, on the other hand, mapped its
entire coast, including the cities of Cannes, Nice, Grasse, and Menton in
its 1,061,000-acre (429,400-hectare) Sensitive Zone. This amounts to 24.5
percent of the department's total area. The significant difference is not so
much in the greater land area mapped by Alpes Maritimes but in the fact
that most areas undergoing development are included. (See map 4.9.)
    Each department set its tax at the legal maximum of $200 (1,000
francs) per lot. By the close of 1972, the Bouches-du-Rhône had received

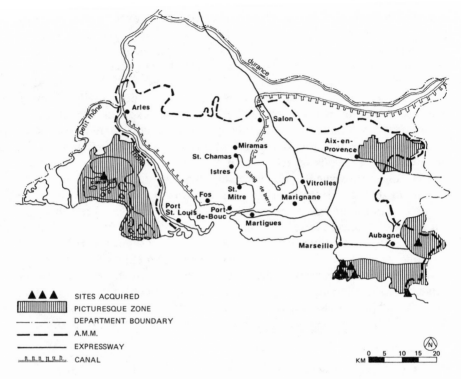

▲▲▲    SITES ACQUIRED

PICTURESQUE ZONE

—·—·—    DEPARTMENT BOUNDARY

— — —    A.M.M.

————    EXPRESSWAY

ᴖᴖᴖᴖᴖᴖ    CANAL

0  5  10  15  20
KM

Map 4.8.  Picturesque Zone, Bouches-du-Rhône

only $380,000 (1.9 million francs) from the tax, while the Alpes Maritimes had revenues totaling $2.74 million (13.7 million francs). Since the concept underlying the law is that development augments the preexisting need for open space, it is curious that a department should exempt from taxation those areas undergoing the most intensive development. If the Bouches-du-Rhône were to redefine its sensitive area to include such cities as Marseilles, Aix-en-Provence, Fos, and the communities of the Etang de Berre, departmental revenues for open space acquisition would rise dramatically.

Both departments have acquired many tracts of open space in recent years, but not solely by relying on the income from the Departmental Open Space Tax. (See table 4.13.) The Bouches-du-Rhône has purchased 9,530 acres (3,857 hectares), of which 6,860 acres (2,777 hectares) are in the marshes of the Camargue. The Alpes Maritimes has bought 795 acres (322 hectares). Anticipation of tax revenues has enabled the departments to borrow in order to buy as properties come on the market. Loan terms have been five to fifteen years at 5 to 7 percent interest. The six loans obtained by the General Council of the Bouches-du-Rhône have

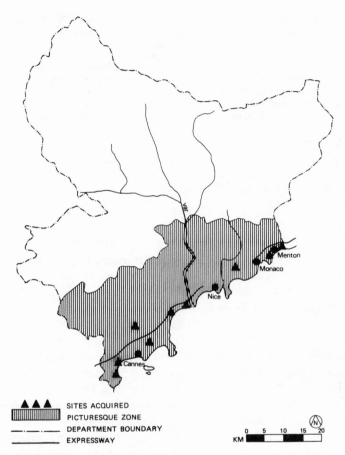

MAP 4.9.  Picturesque Zone, Alpes Maritimes

provided the total sum of $1.45 million (7.25 million francs), or almost four times the yield from the tax (see table 4.14).

Although this program is not, strictly speaking, a land bank program (because there is no intention that any of the land should be sold or leased for private purposes), the law is important for its linking of the demand for open space created by development with a tax to finance open space acquisition.

*Municipal and Departmental Land Reserves:*
*The Role of the Regional Council*

The Provence–Alpes–Côte d'Azur region includes the six departments of southeast France—Alpes de Haute Provence, Hautes Alpes, Alpes Maritimes, Bouches-du-Rhône, Var, and Vaucluse. As of 1976,

TABLE 4.14. Bouches-du-Rhône Borrowing for Open Space Purchases

| Year of Loan | Lender | Amount of Loan | | Rate | Term |
|---|---|---|---|---|---|
| | | Dollars | Francs | | |
| 1963 | group of local governments | 202,960 | 1,014,800 | 5% | 10 years |
| 1965 | group of local governments | 311,160 | 1,555,800 | 5% | 10 years |
| 1967 | group of local governments | 155,000 | 775,000 | 5.75% | 10 years |
| 1967 | savings bank | 115,540 | 577,700 | 5% | 10 years |
| 1971 | CAECL | 426,148 | 2,130,740 | 6% | 5 years |
| 1973 | savings bank | 240,000 | 1,200,000 | 7% | 15 years |
| | Total | 1,450,808 | 7,254,040 | | |

SOURCE: Bouches-du-Rhône Préfecture, "Groupe d'Etudes Régionales," June 1973.

after the 1975 census and accompanying reapportionment, there were 101 members of the regional council serving a population of 3.6 million. The 28 deputies and 15 senators held their seats by virtue of their election to the National Assembly. Thirty members had been designated by the departmental general councils and 28 members by those municipalities with over 30,000 inhabitants. The Bouches-du-Rhône, with 39 councilors, had the largest delegation and the Alpes de Haute Provence and Hautes Alpes, with 7 councilors each, had the smallest delegations. Initially the representatives of Alpes Maritimes refused to participate in the regional council and sought, unsuccessfully, a split of the region. They believed that the concerns of the Côte d'Azur with the promotion of tourism would not receive adequate attention, because the regional council would be dominated by representatives most strongly committed to the promotion of industrial development. The state did not accede to their demands, and now all departments participate actively in the work of the regional council.

The regional council has given highest priority to the creation of land reserves, both for immediate open space use and for future development. Since the regional council cannot acquire land, it makes grants to municipalities and departments to aid them in land acquisition. As of the close of 1976, the regional council had approved or was considering 83 grants for the acquisition of 3,902 acres (1,579 hectares). The grants would total $9 million (45.5 million francs), which would cover 81 percent of the acquisition cost.

*The Program of the Provence–Alpes–Côte d'Azur Regional Council.* The Provence–Alpes–Côte d'Azur Regional Council, which is dominated by a leftist majority, has chosen as its guiding principle "to act so that people live better in this region, but better in all respects."[140] In the longer time perspective of the seventh plan, the council is emphasizing the

TABLE 4.15. Regional Council Revenue Sources

| Item | Dollars | Francs | Percentage |
|---|---|---|---|
| Drivers' licenses | 2,080,000 | 10,400,000 | 9 |
| Gray cards | 1,492,000 | 7,460,000 | 7 |
| Property registration | 7,188,000 | 35,940,000 | 32 |
| Local taxes | 6,780,000 | 33,900,000 | 30 |
| Loans | 5,000,000 | 25,000,000 | 22 |
| Total | 22,540,000 | 112,700,000 | 100 |

SOURCE: Service de Presse, Conseil Régional de Provence–Alpes–Côte d'Azur, "La Région: Où va l'argent?," Marseilles, 3 November 1976.

alteration of the distribution of activities between the wealthy, heavily urbanized coast and the poorer, depopulated interior mountain areas; the improvement of the quality of the urban and rural environment; the amelioration of social conditions and the assurance of job security; and the development of ties throughout the Mediterranean basin. For now, five immediate priorities have dictated the annual budget allocations. Top among them is land investment, followed by environmental protection, communication, promotion of employment, and social assistance:

in refusing, vigorously, to accept responsibility for expenses legally the charge of the state—schools, to cite only one example—the regional council has resolved to avoid undertaking too many activities, which would scatter its efforts ineffectively, and to concentrate its efforts on fundamentals:

—the definition and the application of a land policy that limits speculation and anarchic construction;
—the safeguarding of jobs;
—social protection;
—environmental conservation;
—the promotion of economic development.[141]

To implement their programs, a number of regional councils have voted to levy the maximum tax allowed, but the Provence–Alpes–Côte d'Azur Regional Council has not, finding it too heavy a load for its constituents. Table 4.15 shows the distribution among the possible revenue sources[142] in the 1974 and 1975 budgets approved by the Regional Council of Provence–Alpes–Côte d'Azur. In each of these years the revenues raised were allocated as shown in table 4.16.[143]

The 27 percent of the budget spent for land acquisition is distributed in accord with policies set by the regional council. The council created a special land commission to study land policy and, based on the land com-

TABLE 4.16. Regional Council Spending

| Item | Dollars | Francs | Percentage |
|------|---------|--------|------------|
| Land acquisition program | 6,080,000 | 30,400,000 | 27 |
| Promotion of employment | 4,140,000 | 20,700,000 | 19 |
| Social assistance | 4,020,000 | 20,100,000 | 18 |
| Communications | 3,240,000 | 16,200,000 | 14 |
| Environment | 2,120,000 | 10,600,000 | 9 |
| FIAR | 1,720,000 | 8,600,000 | 8 |
| Administration | 888,000 | 4,440,000 | 4 |
| Miscellaneous | 260,000 | 1,300,000 | 1 |
| Total | 22,468,000 | 112,340,000 | 100 |

SOURCE: Service de Presse, Régional de Provence–Alpes–Côte d'Azur, "La Région: Où va l'argent?," Marseilles, 3 November 1976.

mission's recommendations, established four categories of reserves for which it will allocate funds for the purchase of land.[144] These are:
1. *Long-term land banks*. For this purpose, tracts beyond the area of current speculation will be bought and held, either for future urbanization or for protection of the natural environment. Properties must be at least twenty-five acres (ten hectares) in size, and preference will be given to those that can be opened for public use without much immediate expenditure or cost of upkeep.
2. *Land intended for housing or community facilities*. Priority will be given to land planned for moderate rent housing, playgrounds, and public parks.
3. *Land intended for industrial development*. Land will be acquired in small and middle-sized municipalities to assist them in attracting new industry. At least 12.5 acres (five hectares) will be required per tenant, to avoid creating cut-up, unmarketable industrial zones.
4. *Agricultural land banks*. Land for agriculture will be acquired after consultation with organizations concerned with the preservation of farm use.

The regional council has adopted the following cost-sharing formulas for grants to municipalities and departments for the above types of land acquisitions: for land banks and open space, from 70 to 90 percent of land cost; for housing and community facilities, from 60 to 90 percent of the land cost; for aid to farming, from 60 to 80 percent of the land cost; and for attraction of industry, from 50 to 70 percent of the land cost. The grants also are conditioned on the financial status of the recipient government.

The Regional Public Authority has established a thirteen-step grant application process.[145] The first three steps constitute the original application. The applicant municipality or department completes a form describing the size, location, ownership, proposed use, and estimated price of the land in question and agrees to use eminent domain if necessary to acquire the land. This form and accompanying information are sent to the departmental general council and to the departmental prefect. The president of the general council comments on the application and then forwards it to the president of the Regional Public Authority's land commission; the departmental prefect, after commenting, forwards the application to the regional prefect, who, in turn, transmits the material to the president of the land commission.

Steps four through ten consist of analyses and of the winnowing of the applications that fail to conform to the four categories of land that may be acquired. SCET is then requested to prepare summary files on those applications that are appropriate as to purpose. The land commission reviews these files, rejecting some applications at this stage. Those applications still under consideration are returned to SCET for further documentation, including an evaluation of land prices by the Land Administration. The land commission then makes its final decision and, for those applications that it recommends, directs the applicants to execute and submit to the departmental prefect a contract between the applicant and the Regional Public Authority, the minutes of the municipal or general council approving the contract, and a supporting file. The departmental prefect verifies this information and transmits it to the regional prefect.

The next step is the preparation by the regional prefect of a report to the regional council so that it may execute the contract and issue an order to allocate funds. The final two steps cover payment. The regional prefect notifies the recipient of the signing of the contract and the allocation of funds. Payment is made when the recipient either provides a certificate of purchase of the land and evidence of the financing of its share of the cost or, in the case of eminent domain, the expropriation order, a court order setting the price, and a certificate that financing has been obtained.

The proposed acquisitions, as of the close of 1976, were distributed unevenly among the six departments, both from the perspective of money to be spent and land to be purchased. As shown in table 4.17, 44 percent of the land proposed to be purchased was located in the Bouches-du-Rhône, although only 20 percent of the funds of the regional public authority were to be granted to applicants from that department. Conversely, only 17 percent of the land to be acquired was in the Var, where 34 percent of the funds were to be allocated. These disparities reflect the very great differences in land prices among the applicant municipalities; for example, land purchased or proposed for purchase in seven municipalities of the Alpes Maritimes would cost seven times as much, on an average, as the land to be purchased in the Bouches-du-Rhône municipalities. Given that the proposed acquisitions in the Alpes Maritimes include the purchase of land for subsidized housing by the rich coastal municipalities of Antibes, Cannes, and Menton, these high land prices are hardly surprising.

TABLE 4.17. Proposed Regional Public Authority Land Acquisition Assistance, 1976

| Department[a] | Number of Projects | Land to be Purchased | | Regional Public Authority Grants (in millions) | | Land Cost | |
|---|---|---|---|---|---|---|---|
| | | Acres | Hectares | Dollars | Francs | Dollars per acre | Francs per Square Meter |
| Alpes de Haute Provence | 10 | 200 | 81 | 0.5 | 2.4 | 2,988 | 3.69 |
| Hautes-Alpes | 14 | 180 | 73 | 1.0 | 5.0 | 6,883 | 8.50 |
| Alpes Maritimes | 7 | 222 | 90 | 1.4 | 7.0 | 7,773 | 9.60 |
| Bouches-du-Rhône | 18 | 1,707 | 690 | 1.8 | 9.2 | 1,054 | 1.33 |
| Var | 14 | 682 | 276 | 3.0 | 15.3 | 5,571 | 6.88 |
| Vaucluse | 20 | 911 | 369 | 1.3 | 6.6 | 1,765 | 2.18 |
| Total | | 3,902 | 1,579 | 9.0 | 45.5 | | |

[a] The data for the Bouches-du-Rhône are as of 31 Dec. 1976, while the data for the other five departments are as of 1 Nov. 1976.

Overall, land prices are estimated at an average of $2,307 per acre (2.88 francs per hectare). Most of the applications for grants were from small municipalities; many of them, particularly those located in areas of high land prices, would not be able to institute land reserves without the aid of the Regional Public Authority.

The municipalities must provide approximately 20 percent of the acquisition price. Since 1973, they have been able to raise this money by borrowing from a CAECL fund of $40 million (200 million francs) established solely to lend money for land bank purchases. The loans are for fifteen years at an interest rate of between 8.5 and 10 percent. While CAECL does provide a source of funds, the high interest rates discourage many municipalities from applying.

The enthusiastic response of the local governments to the regional council's land acquisition program has led members of the council to question the adequacy of potential funds to meet the demand. One possibility that the land commission of the regional council is considering is the purchase of easements rather than the fee. At the land commission's invitation, the planner, Max Falque, presented a proposal for development of an easement program. His proposal included the following comments:

Purchase of easements . . . must result in a more efficient use of public funds, a greater acceptance of public action by a people who are strongly attached to the concept of private property, and finally a better guarantee of the lasting protection of nature. . . . The POS envisions development prohibitions but these rarely will be absolute, and experience shows that over time they will not be respected, given pressure both from private land owners and needs of the public sector, as for expressways, industrial zones, or marinas. Fee acquisition is doubly costly, requiring payment both for purchase and for management. . . . Municipalities are well aware that management of large tracts of land costs dearly and that a peasant, without exception, manages the land better than the government. The first step is to determine the public purposes to be served by land to be subject to easements. All other uses, particularly those pertaining to the land's productivity, would remain at the owner's disposition. The contractual nature of the control and the fact that the public compensates the owner for the rights it obtains will assure stability.[146]

The proposal to undertake a study has been accepted and began in April 1977.

*Regional Council Participation in the Bouches-du-Rhône.* The Bouches-du-Rhône has the largest population of the six departments in the Provence–Alpes–Côte d'Azur region and, as has been noted, the largest amount of land so far proposed for participation in the land reserve program of the regional council.

Eighteen municipalities have sought regional council grants totaling $1,843,000 (9,213,000 francs), covering an average of 81 percent of the total cost of the land. With a few exceptions, the applicant municipalities are small or medium sized, and many are somewhat removed from speculative pressures. This explains in large part why the average estimated cost of the acquisitions in the Bouches-du-Rhône—$1,309 per acre (16,401 francs per hectare) as of the close of 1976—is so low in comparison to those in the Alpes Maritimes. The range of the acquisition cost, actual or estimated, was from $162 per acre (1,998 francs per hectare) for 459 acres (186 hectares) at Meyrargues for a land bank to $44,000 per acre (550,000 francs per hectare) for 15 acres (6 hectares) at Aubagne for a park. Meyrargues is a small city of 22,000 north of Aix-en-Provence, beyond the metropolitan area. Aubagne is the municipality of 281,000 adjacent to Marseilles where SAFER has paid its top price of $8,000 per acre (98,000 francs per hectare) for farmland.

Table 4.18 provides details as to the program in the Bouches-du-Rhône. Most of the applications are for fairly small tracts, with 13.5 acres (33.3 hectares) the median size. All of the applications are for acquisitions for land banks, open space, or community facilities.

The top priority given to land banking by the Regional Public Authority and the immediate, enthusiastic response to the authority's land bank program lead to several conclusions. First, there is a widespread consensus that control of the use of land is a vital public function. Second, land

TABLE 4.18. Land Reserve, Bouches-du-Rhône: Participation of the Regional Public Authority

| Local Government | Purpose of Acquisition | Area | | Cost | | Participation of EPR | | | Approval of the Land Commission | Approval of the Regional Council | Order of the Prefect | Payment |
|---|---|---|---|---|---|---|---|---|---|---|---|---|
| | | Acres | Hectares | Dollars | Francs | Percentage | Dollars | Francs | | | | |
| Gréasque | open space | 121 | 49 | 20,400 | 102,000 | 88 | 17,952 | 89,760 | 5/5/75 | 9/23/75 | 10/6/75 | 1/7/76 |
| Puy-Ste-Réparade | open space | 2 | 1 | 36,000 | 180,000 | 84 | 30,240 | 151,200 | 5/5/75 | 9/23/75 | 10/6/75 | 9/22/76 |
| Aix-en-Provence | playground | 5 | 2 | 81,000 | 405,000 | 83.6 | 67,716 | 338,580 | 6/16/75 | 11/22/75 | 12/20/75 | 6/23/76 |
| Meyrargues | land bank | 459 | 186 | 74,343 | 371,716 | 80.9 | 60,218 | 301,089 | 5/5/75 | 11/22/75 | 12/20/75 | 6/23/76 |
| Jouques | community facilities | 25 | 10 | 56,000 | 280,000 | 76.5 | 42,840 | 214,200 | 2/14/75 | | | |
| Peynier | land bank | 282 | 114 | 350,000 | 1,750,000 | 83 | 290,500 | 1,452,500 | 2/14/75 | 11/22/75 | 5/10/76 | 6/10/76 |
| Barbentane | land bank | 27 | 11 | 95,582 | 477,912 | 82 | 78,377 | 391,887 | 11/22/75 | 2/9/76 | 3/8/76 | |
| Simiane-Collongue | open space | 613 | 250 | 262,000 | 1,310,000 | 80 | 209,600 | 1,048,000 | 12/12/75 | | | |
| Peypin | open space | 82 | 33 | 48,055 | 240,279 | 84 | 40,367 | 201,834 | 12/12/75 | 2/9/76 | 3/8/76 | 10/21/76 |
| Bouc Bel Air | open space | 5 | 2 | 33,250 | 166,250 | 82 | 27,265 | 136,325 | 12/12/75 | | | |
| Lambesc | community facilities | 5 | 2 | 184,290 | 921,450 | 75.9 | 139,876 | 699,380 | 3/19/76 | | | |
| Allauch | open space | 5 | 2 | 166,000 | 830,000 | 82.4 | 136,784 | 683,920 | 6/4/76 | 7/3/76 | 7/19/76 | |
| Les Pennes-Mirabeau | playground | 2 | 1 | 50,544 | 252,720 | 76.5 | 38,666 | 193,330 | 6/4/76 | | | |
| Venelles | open space | 7 | 3 | 31,800 | 159,000 | 85 | 27,030 | 135,150 | 6/4/76 | | | |
| Pelissanne | open space | 30 | 12 | 13,415 | 67,075 | 86 | 11,537 | 57,685 | 7/16/76 | | | |
| Chateauneuf-les-Martigues | open space | 2 | 1 | 26,000 | 130,000 | 78 | 20,280 | 101,400 | 10/8/76 | | | |
| Aubagne | park | 15 | 6 | 660,000 | 3,300,000 | 82 | 541,200 | 2,706,000 | 11/26/76 | | | |
| Mallemort | public garden and park | 12 | 5 | 74,800 | 374,000 | 83 | 62,084 | 310,420 | 11/26/76 | | | |
| Total | | 1,704 | 690 | 2,263,479 | 11,317,402 | | 1,842,532 | 9,212,660 | | | | |

SOURCE: Regional Council, Provence-Alpes-Côte d'Azur, 31 Dec. 1976.

banking is accepted as one necessary tool to achieve this control. Third, the demand for funds for land acquisition will greatly exceed the budgetary capacity of the Regional Public Authority. This combination of pressure for funds for land acquisition against limited regional revenues could have positive consequences for the totality of French land bank programs. The Regional Public Authority could become the regional coordinator for the nationally assisted and nationally initiated land bank programs. This could be helpful to municipalities who now must deal with a number of bureaucracies, each with its own rules and criteria. It also could bring about more effective use of the various funds available for land acquisition. Coordination is needed; whether the Regional Public Authority will attempt to meet this need, and, if so, whether it will succeed, remains to be seen.

### APPENDIX

Abbreviations

AFTRP    Agence Foncière et Technique de la Région Parisienne, Land and Technical Agency of the Paris Region
AGAM    Agence d'Urbanisme de l'Agglomération Marseillaise, Marseilles Metropolitan Area Planning Agency
CAECL    Caisse d'Aide à l'Equipement des Collectivités Locales, Public Bank to Assist Local Governments with Public Construction
CDC    Caisse des Dépôts et Consignations, Central Savings Bank ('consignment' comes from deposit of notary fees)
CIAT    Comité Interministériel pour l'Aménagement du Territoire, Interministerial Committee for Planning and Development
COS    Coefficient d'Occupation des Sols, Floor Area Ratio
DAFU    Direction de l'Aménagement Foncier et de l'Urbanisme, Division of Land Management and Urban Planning
DATAR    Délégation à l'Aménagement du Territoire et à l'Action Régionale, Division for Land Planning and Regional Action
DDE    Direction Départementale de l'Equipement, Departmental Office of Public Construction
DUP    Déclaration d'Utilité Publique, Declaration of Public Utility (after written investigation and announcement by prefect, no oral hearing but written notice)
EPAREB    L'Etablissement Public d'Aménagement des Rives de l'Etang de Berre, Public Agency for Planning and Development of the Banks of the Etang de Berre
EPR    Etablissement Public Régional, Regional Public Authority

| | |
|---|---|
| FASASA | Fonds d'Action Sociale et d'Amélioration des Structures Agricoles, Fund for Social Action and Improvement of Farm Structures |
| FDES | Fonds de Développement Economique et Social, Economic and Social Development Fund |
| FIAR | Fonds Interministériel d'Aménagement Rural, Interministerial Fund for Planning and Development |
| FIAT | Fonds d'Intervention pour l'Aménagement du Territoire, Intervention Fund for Planning and Development |
| FNAFU | Fonds National d'Aménagement Foncier et d'Urbanisme, National Fund for Land Development and Urban Planning |
| FNAT | Fonds National d'Aménagement du Territoire, National Fund for Land Development |
| GIF | Groupe Interministériel Foncier, Interministerial Land Policy Group |
| HLM | Habitation Loyer Modérée, State-Aided Moderate Income Housing |
| MATELT | Ministère de l'Aménagement du Territoire, Equipment, Logement et Tourisme, Ministry of Planning and Development, Public Construction, Housing, and Tourism |
| MIAFEB | Mission Interministérielle pour l'Aménagement de la Région Fos–Etang de Berre, Interministerial Commission for Planning and Management of the Fos–Etang de Berre Region |
| OREAM | Organisme d'Etude d'Aménagement d'Aires Métropolitaines, Planning and Management Study Organization for Metropolitan Areas |
| PAR | Plan d'Aménagement Rural, Plan for Rural Land Management |
| PAZ | Plan d'Aménagement de la Zone, Zone Management Plan |
| POS | Plan d'Occupation des Sols, Land Use Plan |
| RDEV | Redevance Départementale d'Espaces Verts, Departmental Open Space Tax |
| SAFER | Société d'Aménagement Foncier et d'Etablissement Rural, Company for Land Management and Rural Organization |
| SAREF | Société Auxiliaire de la Rénovation et de l'Equipement Foncier, Subsidiary Company for Renewal and Land Development |
| SCAFR | Société Centrale d'Aménagement Foncier Rural, Central Company for Rural Land Management |
| SCDC | Société Centrale d'Aide au Développement des Collectivités, Central Company for Local Government Development Assistance |
| SCET | Société Centrale pour l'Equipement du Territoire, Central Company for Public Construction |
| SDAU | Schéma Directeur d'Aménagement et d'Urbanisme, Master Schematic Plan for Land Management and Urbanization |
| SEM | Société d'Economie Mixte, Public-Private Company |
| ZAC | Zone d'Aménagement Concertée, Planned Development Zone |
| ZAD | Zone d'Aménagement Différée, Deferred Development Zone |
| ZCP | Zone à Caractère Pittoresque, Picturesque Zone |
| ZEP | Zone d'Environnement Protégé, Environment Protection Zone |
| ZUP | Zone à Urbaniser par Priorité, Priority Development Zone |

NOTES

1. Article 17.
2. Article 544.
3. Pisani, *Utopie foncière*, pp. 10, 17.
4. Principal Tax Inspector, Land Administration.
5. Arrago, *Les Problèmes fonciers*, p. 38.
6. The ministry responsible for housing, infrastructure, land acquisition, and land use planning has undergone repeated changes in title and scope. It is currently the Ministry of Planning and Development, Public Construction, Housing, and Tourism, or MATELT. For simplicity's sake this ministry is referred to throughout as the Ministry of Public Construction.
7. Quoted in Parfait, *La Planification urbaine*, pp. 42–43.
8. Circular 63–36 of 10 June 1963.
9. Approved 15 July 1971.
10. Departments can be compared in scale to American counties. However, although they have an elected legislative body, they are administrative units of the state, administered by state civil servants headed by a prefect.
11. The twenty-one regions typically include several departments. Until 1973, when they were granted some degree of autonomy, they were wholly creatures of the state.
12. The focus here is on local land use plans. For a short description of the goals of French national economic planning, plans one through six, and of national land use planning, see Strong, *Planned Urban Environments*, pp. 313–51.
13. Ordinance, 27 October 1945, incorporated subsequently in article 84 of the 1954 Code of Development and Housing.
14. Decree 58–1463 of 31 December 1958, and decree 59–1089 of 21 September 1959.
15. Article 28, 1954 Code of Development and Housing.
16. Article 15, decree 61–1298 of 30 November 1961.
17. "Au service d'un aménagement national," *Urbanisme* 86 (Spring 1965): 21.
18. "Urbanism," paper of the minister of public construction and housing, June 1970, reprinted in Le Moniteur, *Les Zones d'aménagement*, 2nd ed. (April 1973), pp. 22, 23.
19. Loi d'Orientation Foncière, law 67–1253 of 30 December 1967 (Journal Officiel [J.O.] 3 January 1968); decree 69–551 of 28 May 1969 (J.O. 8 June 1969); modified by laws 69–1263 of 31 December 1969, 71–581 of 16 July 1971, and 72–575 of 5 July 1972 (J.O., respectively, 4 January 1970, 17 July 1971, and 7 July 1972).
20. Article 5, decree 69–551 of 28 May 1969.
21. Article 12, law 67–1253.
22. Article L. 121–1 of the Code de l'Urbanisme.
23. Law of 16 July 1971.
24. Remarks made December 1973.
25. Bulletin ACEAR 6, June 1975.
26. Michèle Champenois, in *Le Monde*, 10 April 1976.
27. Ordinance 58–1447 of 31 December 1958 (J.O. 4 January 1959); ordinance 59–693 of 3 June 1969; circular of 25 September 1969 (J.O. 3 October 1959); law 62–0848 of 26 July 1962 (J.O. 27 July 1962); decree of 7 November 1962 (J.O. 8 November 1962); decree of 30 May 1969 (J.O. 31 May 1969).
28. Major sources for this discussion are Jamois, *Les Zones à Urbaniser par Priorité*; d'Arcy, *Structures administratives*; and the invaluable source of laws, regulations, and commentary thereon, Le Moniteur, *Les Zones d'aménagement*.
29. SEMs were authorized initially in 1950. See decree 55–579 of 20 May 1955,

for the basic text, which later was amended and incorporated in the Code of Municipal Administration. *Peyrot* v. *Société de l'Autoroute Esterel–Côte d'Azur*, 8 July 1963, held that SEMs are governed by private law even though public bodies hold a majority of the shares.

30. SAREF is a subsidiary of an agency created by a number of banks and insurance companies.

31. The Paris region had special problems with speculation and political resistance to ZUPs. To counter this, the government, in 1962, created a special agency, AFTRP (Agence Foncière et Technique de la Région Parisienne, or Land and Technical Agency of the Paris Region), to implement ZUPs throughout the region.

32. Quoted in d'Arcy, *Structures administratives*, p. 38.

33. See ibid., pp. 281–91, for further details.

34. Ibid., p. 90.

35. Comité Central d'Enquête sur le Coût et le Rendement des Services Publics, "Rapport sur les missions, la structure, le fonctionnement et les moyens du ministre de la construction" (Paris, 1965), p. 63.

36. D'Arcy, *Structures administratives*, p. 152.

37. Ordinance 58–1447 of 31 December 1958; circular of 25 September 1959; law 62–848 of 26 July 1962 (J.O. 27 July 1962), as amended by law 65–561 of 10 July 1965 (J.O. 11 June 1965).

38. Law article L. 221.1, 67–1253 of 30 December 1967 (J.O. 3 January 1968); modified by laws 69–1239 of 31 December 1969, 71–581 of 16 July 1971, and 72–575 of 5 July 1972.

39. Ordinance 58–907 of 23 October 1958.

40. Law 62–848 of 26 July 1962.

41. Law 65–559 of 10 July 1965.

42. Law 65–561 of 10 July 1965.

43. Arrago, *Les Problèmes fonciers*, p. 108.

44. Les Domaines, governed by articles R18 and R19 of the state property code.

45. Decree 64–250 of 14 March 1964.

46. Arrago, *Les Problèmes fonciers*, p. 61.

47. Ibid., p. 40.

48. Ordinance 64–251 of 14 March 1964.

49. Circular 67–24 of 17 March 1967.

50. FNAFU was called FNAT (Fonds Nationale d'Aménagement du Territoire) before 1963.

51. The loan is called "fnafuable."

52. Letter circular of 14 January 1974 of MATELT; circular 74–422 of 6 August 1974 of the Ministry of Interior.

53. Jamois, *Zones à Urbaniser par Priorité*, p. 161.

54. Law 62–848 of 26 July 1962 (J.O. 27 July 1962); decree 62–1300 of 7 November 1962 (J.O. 8 November 1962); law 65–561 of 10 July 1965; circular 70–120 of 21 October 1970.

55. Law 71–581 of 16 July 1971; circular 71–102 of 9 September 1971. Various provisions of the law have been amended since 1972; for the most part only the most recent version is described here.

56. Circular of 7 November 1974, of MATELT.

57. Law 71–581 (J.O. 16 July 1971) extended the preemption period from eight to fourteen years.

58. Parfait, *La Planification urbaine*, p. 41.

59. Interministerial circular 72–100 of 30 June 1972.

60. Circular 72–137 of 23 August 1972.

61. Section C, chapter 32; interministerial circular of 17 April 1971.

62. Section C, chapter 31.

63. Minister, MATELT, in *Le Monde*, 27 May 1975.

64. Decree 62–479 of 14 April 1962.

65. Olivier Guichard, then minister of public construction.

66. Michele Champenois, in *Le Monde*, 30 January 1974.

67. Decree 68–1107 of 3 December 1968 (J.O. 10 December 1968); decree 69–550 of 30 May 1969 (J.O. 31 May 1967); circular 69–67 of 4 June 1969; circular 70–2 of 6 January 1970; decree 70–485 of 5 June 1970; circular 73–94 of 16 May 1973; circular 74–22 of 6 February 1974; and circular 75–36 of 18 February 1975.

68. Order of 27 November 1970 (J.O. 4 December 1970).

69. Code de l'Urbanisme, article R. 311–2.

70. Ibid., article R. 311–4.

71. Circular 74–22 of 6 February 1974 (J.O. 13 February 1974).

72. Code de l'Urbanisme, article R. 311. 9–311.20.

73. Circular 73–94 of 16 May 1973 of MATELT.

74. Ibid., section 5.1.

75. Circular 69–67 of 4 June 1969, section 112; TLE, or Taxe Locale d'Equipement.

76. Order of 30 May 1969 (J.O. 31 May 1969); circular 69–95 of 14 August 1969; circular 69–107 of 15 October 1969. These are FNAFU A-category subsidies.

77. Law of 16 July 1971 (article L.430–2 of the Code de l'Urbanisme); circular of 11 February 1974 (J.O. 3 March 1974).

78. Law of 2 May 1930.

79. Decree of 26 June 1959; modified by decree of 28 May 1968.

80. Ministerial directive of 1 October 1960.

81. Article L.142.2 to 142.4 of the Code de l'Urbanisme.

82. Article 65 of law 60–1384 of 23 December 1960.

83. Circular of 11 February 1974 (J.O. 3 March 1974).

84. Ibid., section 2.2.

85. Article L.142–6 to 142–17 of the Code de l'Urbanisme.

86. Article L.142–3 (a) of the Code de l'Urbanisme.

87. Service Central des Enquêtes et des Etudes Statistiques (SCEES, central service for inquiries and statistical studies) Ministry of Agriculture.

88. Institut National de la Statistique et des Etudes Economiques (INSEE), Economie et Statistique, March 1972.

89. Ministère de l'Agriculture et Ministère de l'Equipement, "Aménager l'espace rurale."

90. Chambres d'Agriculture, "La Loi d'Orientation Agricole."

91. Law 60–808 of 5 August 1960 (J.O. 7 August 1960); decree 61–610 of 14 June 1961 (J.O. 15 June 1961).

92. Law 62–933 of 8 August 1962 (J.O. 10 August 1962); modified by ordinance 67–824 of 23 September 1967 (J.O. 28 September 1967).

93. The same goal is reflected in directive 72–159 of 17 April 1972 of the European Economic Community.

94. Chambres d'Agriculture, "La Loi d'Orientation Agricole."

95. J.O. 13 March 1963.

96. Code de l'Urbanisme, article L. 211–1 to L. 211–8; article R. 211–1 to R. 211–11.

97. Pisani, *Utopie foncière*, p. 7.

98. Organization for Economic Cooperation and Development, "Structural Reform Measures in Agriculture."

99. Under a law passed on 13 April 1946, tenants who preempt may turn to a special court, the Tribunal Paritaire, on which other tenant farmers sit, to have the price of the land set. As in other preemptions, the owner can renounce the sale if the price is unacceptable.

100. J.O. 5 December 1969.

101. Organization for Economic Cooperation and Development, "Structural Reform Measures in Agriculture."

102. Ibid.

103. "Les S.A.F.E.R.," in Chambres d'Agriculture, "La Loi d'Orientation Agricole," p. 22.

104. Organization for Economic Cooperation and Development, "Structural Reform Measures in Agriculture," p. 122.

105. *Les Lois d'orientation à l'épreuve des faits.*

106. Comments on this section were received from J. P. Geoffroy, staff director of the Provence–Alpes–Côte d'Azur Regional Public Authority.

107. Law of 5 July 1972, creating regional councils as of 1 October 1973.

108. France's legislature is bicameral, consisting of the Senate and the Chamber of Deputies.

109. Jerome Monod, in *Le Monde*, 13 July 1977.

110. In 1974, it was three dollars (fifteen francs) per capita and, in 1977, sixteen dollars (seventy-eight francs) per capita.

111. California during the 1960s experienced the same rate of growth.

112. "Recensement général de l'agriculture," 1970–1971.

113. As recounted in interviews with Messrs. Bigo, Gallas, Guillermin, and Schudel of AGAM, Mr. Gamelin of SCET, and Mr. Georges LaCroix, General Director of Technical Services, City of Marseilles, January and February 1974.

114. Interview with Mr. Guy Crest, Deputy to the Mayor of Aix-en-Provence, February 1974.

115. The Marseilles metropolitan area is much larger than the urban area. It has 640,000 acres (260,000 hectares), of which 218,000 acres (88,000 hectares) remained in farm, forest, or open space use as of 1972.

116. Bigo, "L'Urbanisme." The range was from $4,360 per acre (5 francs per square meter) for open space to $1,306,800 per acre (1,500 francs per square meter) for center-city renewal land.

117. Law of 8 July 1957; decree of 31 December 1958. Under this law, Nice and Cannes on occasion require developers to contribute a money equivalent instead of land.

118. In 1963, this amounted to $7.12 million (35.6 million francs).

119. A major source for this discussion about Languedoc-Roussillon is Arrago, *Les Problèmes fonciers.* Comments on the text were received from Bernard Lepêtre, a former member of the staff of the Interministerial Mission for Tourist Development of the Languedoc-Roussillon Littoral. See Strong, *Planned Urban Environments*, for more information about planning and development of Languedoc-Roussillon.

120. Arrago, *Les Problèmes fonciers*, p. 56.

121. Ibid., p. 19.

122. From east to west, they were: La Grande Motte, Le Cap d'Agde, the mouth of the Aude River, Gruissan, Leucate-Barcares, and the coast from Canet to Racou. The development at the mouth of the Aude later was dropped from the plan.

123. Comments dated 14 April 1977.

124. Established by decree 63–580 of 18 June 1963.

125. Plan d'Urbanisme d'Intérêt Régional; decree 64–9 of 7 January 1964.

126. Communes in Hérault. Hérault

127. A derogation may be granted.

128. Much of the information about land acquisition comes from conversations held in January and February of 1974, with Mr. Mandron and Mr. d'Annella of the Chamber of Commerce and Industry of Marseilles and Mr. Sasia of the Marseilles Port Authority.

129. Terrain de la Feuillane.

130. Law of 29 June 1965, which created the Port Autonome de Marseilles.

131. Etienne Mallet, in *Le Monde*, 27 February 1974.

132. The sources of much of the information about the Etang de Berre were Mr. F. Gaston, a lawyer on the EPAREB staff responsible for land acquisition, and Mr. Gourdon, Departmental Director of the Land Administration. Comments, dated 1 April and 21 June 1977, were received from Gaston on a draft of this section.

133. Land also has been acquired by the municipalities of Fos sur Mer and Les Pennes Mirabeau for new town development.

134. J.O. 7 March 1973.

135. The information about the Bouches-du-Rhône SAFER was provided by Mr. Burdeyron, Director, SAFER, Provence–Alpes–Côte d'Azur.

136. The department of Alpes Maritimes, which is in the region, did not choose to join.

137. This information is drawn from an interview with Mr. Bonnier, Direction Départmentale de l'Agriculture, 17 January 1974.

138. Membership included representatives of the departmental offices of agriculture, public construction, and mines, MIAFEB, OREAM, the Chamber of Agriculture, the Departmental Federation of Farmers, the Department Center of Young Farmers, the Regional Farm Bank, the Federation of Agricultural Cooperatives, and the Canal de Provence.

139. Comments received from Jean Bonnier, Study Director, OREAM, June 1977.

140. Service de Presse, Conseil Régional de Provence–Alpes–Côte d'Azur, *La Région: Où va l'argent?*, 3 November 1976.

141. Ibid.

142. Ibid.

143. Ibid.

144. Service de Presse, Conséil Régional de Provence–Alpes–Côte d'Azur, *La Politique foncière de la région*, Marseilles, 5 November 1976.

145. Ibid.

146. Falque, "Recherches sur la maîtrise foncière," pp. 2, 3.

## PERSONS INTERVIEWED

André Bigo, Marseilles, 6 February 1974

Jean Bonnier, Director, Departmental Office of the Ministry of Agriculture, Department of Bouches-du-Rhône, 17 January 1974

Jean Burdeyron, Director, SAFER, Provence–Alpes–Côte d'Azur, 29 January 1974, 25 August 1976

Philip Chadbourn, U.S. Consul, Marseilles, January 1974

Guy Crest, advisor and attorney to the mayor of Aix-en-Provence, 11 February 1974

Guy D'Annella, Chamber of Commerce and Industry, Marseilles, 17 January 1974

Max Falque, Director of Planning, Société du Canal de Provence, 28 January 1974, 26 August 1976

Lucien Gallas, Director, AGAM, Marseilles, 6 February 1974

Yves Gamelin, Regional Director, SCET, Marseilles, 5 February 1974

Franck Gaston, attorney in charge of acquisitions, EPAREB, Vitrolles, 7 February 1974

—— Gourdon, Departmental Director, Service des Domaines, Marseilles, 5 February 1974

Guy Guillermin, Assistant to the Director, AGAM, Marseilles, 21 January 1974

Georges LaCroix, Director of Technical Services, City of Marseilles, 24 January 1974

E. C. Mandron, Department Head, Chamber of Commerce and Industry, Marseilles, 17 January 1974

François Perrin, attorney for OREAM, Marseilles, 21 January 1974
Bernard Sazia, attorney for Port Authority of Marseilles, 6 February 1974
—— Schudel, attorney for OREAM, Marseilles, 6 February 1974

REFERENCES

Arrago, Robert. *Les Problèmes fonciers et leurs solutions: Les Leçons d'une expérience: l'Aménagement du littoral Languedoc-Roussillon.* Paris: Berger-Levrault, 1969.
Association Normande d'Economie Rurale Appliquée. *Aménagement et agriculture.* Cahier 30. Caen: Association Normande d'Economie Rurale Appliquée, 1975.
Bec, Michael. "Essai de jugement critique sur la politique des Zones d'Aménagement Concertées." Mimeographed. University of Aix-en-Provence, 1974.
Bigo, André. *L'Urbanisme face au problème foncier.* 1968. No publisher.
Bornet, Bernard. *Tourisme et environnement: Faut-il souhaiter une concentration ou une déconcentration touristique?* Aix-en-Provence: Université d'Aix-Marseille, Centre d'Etudes du Tourisme, 1974.
Bosc, R. "La Politique des Zones d'Aménagement Concertées." Revue de la Direction Départmentale d'Equipement des Bouches-du-Rhône. 1973.
Boury, Paul, ed. *Les Zones d'aménagement, urbanisme régimentaire et opérationnel.* Paris: Le Moniteur, 1973.
Chambres d'Agriculture. "La Loi d'Orientation Agricole quinze ans après." Supplement no. 595–96. (January 1977).
Cultiaux, Didier. *L'Aménagement de la région Fos–Etang de Berre.* Paris: Documentation Française, 1975. Nos. 4164, 4165, 4166.
D'Arcy, François. *Structures administratives et urbanisation.* Paris: Berger Levrault, 1968.
Davidson, A. W., and Leonard, J. E., eds. *Urban Development in France and Germany.* London: Centre for Advanced Land Use Studies, College of Estate Management, 1973.
Délégation à l'Aménagement du Territoire et à l'Action Régionale. *La Politique d'aménagement du territoire.* Paris: Documentation Française, 1970.
Direction Départmentale de l'Agriculture des Bouches-du-Rhône. "Charte des zones d'activités agricoles des Bouches-du-Rhône." Mimeographed. 1973.
———. "Habiter à la campagne." Mimeographed. 1972.
Etablissement Public Régional de Provence–Alpes–Côte d'Azur. "Politique foncier: Etapes de l'instruction d'une demande d'acquisition." Mimeographed. Marseilles, 7 November 1975.
Falque, Max. "Plus value, moins value: Essai d'étude comparative dans quelques pays européens." Mimeographed. Le Tholonet, June 1974.
——— "Recherches sur la maîtrise foncière des espaces ouverts." Paper presented to the Land Commission of the Provence–Alpes–Côte d'Azur Regional Council, 29 December 1974.

————. "Servitudes contractuelles et protection des espaces ouverts." Mimeographed. Le Tholonet, 1974.

Fédération Nationale des Sociétés d'Aménagement Foncier et d'Etablissement Rurale. *S.A.F.E.R.: Organisation, fonctionnement.* Paris: Fédération Nationale des Sociétés d'Aménagement Foncier et d'Etablissement Rurale, 1970.

Jacquignon, Louis. *Le Droit de l'urbanisme.* 5th ed. Paris: Editions Eyrolles, 1975.

Jamois, Jean. *Les Zones à Urbaniser par Priorité.* Paris: Berger-Levrault, 1968.

Lacassin, Christian. "L'Aménagement touristique du Littoral Languedoc-Roussillon." Thesis, University of Aix-en-Provence, 1969–70.

*Les Lois d'orientation à l'épreuve des faits. Economie Rurale* 108. (July–August 1975).

Levy, Michel. "Problème foncier et politique foncière." Mimeographed. Marseilles, 21 March 1968.

Mascart, Alain. "Les Zones d'Aménagement Concertées: La Zone du Jas de Bouffan d'Aix-en-Provence." Thesis, University of Aix-en-Provence, 1970–71.

Ministère de l'Agriculture and Ministère de l'Equipement. *Aménager l'espace rurale.* Paris: Ministère de l'Agriculture and Ministère de l'Equipement, 1976.

Ministère de l'Aménagement du Territoire, de l'Equipement, du Logement, et du Tourisme. "La Redevance départmentale d'espaces verts." Mimeographed. Groupe d'Etudes Régionales, Service Regional de Provence–Côte d'Azur, 1973.

Mission d'Aménagement de l'Etang de Berre, "Des logements oui, mais aussi des villes." Report. Vitrolles: Mission d'Aménagement de l'Etang de Berre, 1972.

————. "L'Aménagement de l'Etang de Berre." Report. Vitrolles: Mission d'Aménagement de l'Etang de Berre, no date.

Omnium Technique de l'Habitat. "Problèmes fonciers: Etat de la recherche et orientation d'étude." Internal office memo. November 1971.

Organisation pour les Etudes d'Aménagement de l'Aire Métropolitaine Marseillaise. *Fos-Information.* Marseilles, 1972.

————. *Perspectives d'aménagement de l'aire métropolitaine marseillaise.* Région Provence–Côte d'Azur–Corse, Ministère de l'Equipement et du Logement. Marseilles, January 1969.

————. *Schéma d'aménagement de l'aire métropolitaine marseillaise.* Marseilles, June 1970.

————. *Tableau de bord de la zone de Fos.* Marseilles, 1 September 1972.

Organisation pour les Etudes d'Aménagement de l'Aire Métropolitaine Lorraine. *Maîtrise foncière dans la métropole Lorraine.* Pont-à-Mousson, November 1971.

Organization for Economic Cooperation and Development. "Structural Reform Measures in Agriculture." Mimeographed. Paris, 1972.

Parfait, François, and la Commission Urbanisme de l'AGHTM. *La Planification urbaine: Alibi ou espoir.* Paris: Editions Eyrolles, 1973.

Pisani, Edgard. *Utopie foncière.* Paris: Gallimard, 1977.

Service de Presse. Conseil Régional de Provence–Alpes–Côte d'Azur. *La Région: D'où vient l'argent?* Marseilles, 2 November 1976.

Service Promotion Industrielle, Port Autonome de Marseille. *Doing Business at Fos.* Marseilles: Service Promotion Industrielle, 1972.

Société Centrale pour l'Equipement du Territoire, Département d'Aménagement, Groupe des Conseillers Techniques. *Répertoire des opérations d'équipement urbain et touristique.* Paris, 1972.

Société d'Aménagement Foncier et d'Etablissement Rural. *Pour mieux connaître votre S.A.F.E.R.* Paris: Société d'Aménagement et d'Etablissement Rural, 1972.

————. "S.A.F.E.R.," *Dictionnaire Permanent Entreprise Agricole* 29 (1 May 1976).

————. *SAFER.* Paris: Société d'Aménagement Foncier et d'Etablissement Rural, 1970.

Strong, Ann Louise. *Planned Urban Environments: Sweden, Finland, Israel, the Netherlands, France.* Baltimore: The Johns Hopkins Press, 1971.

Swan, Hedley Maurice. *Land Market Control Strategy in France: The Case of the ZAD.* Discussion paper B.75.4. Ottawa Ministry of State for Urban Affairs, 1975.

————. "Land Market Control in France: An Evaluation of the ZAD." Mimeographed. Ottawa, 1975.

Thompson, Ian B. *The Lower Rhône and Marseilles.* Oxford: Oxford University Press, 1975.

Vedrenne, R. "Les Principaux Aspects de la réforme des finances des collectivités locales en France." *Local Finance* 2, no. 6 (November 1973).

Vergnet, Sylvie. "La Z.U.P. de Nîmes." Thesis, University of Aix-en-Provence, 1972–73.

# 5

# The Potential
# for Land Banking
# in the United States

Land banking has been a reality in many countries of Western Europe for much of the twentieth century. It is widely accepted as a desirable means of implementing land use plans. The major problems being encountered with current programs are not intrinsic to land banking. In the Stockholm region and in the large Dutch metropolitan areas except for Rotterdam the problems arise from the shift of political power and wealth from the central cities to the suburban municipalities, while in France the problems arise from inadequate acquisition funds and irresolution concerning public retention of the unearned increment in land values.

In order to evaluate the short-term prospects for land banking in the United States, one needs to consider the contemporary American setting, including the actualities of public land ownership and public control of land use and the apparent climate of opinion concerning land speculation and the role of the public sector. It also is important to consider the specific forms that land banking might take here and the issues that these various forms raise.

## Lessons from Europe

The Swedish land banking system, and in particular that of Stockholm, has received considerable attention and widespread praise. The Dutch system, which has strong parallels to the Swedish, is much less well known,[1] while French endeavors in land banking—to my knowledge—have not previously been looked at as a composite. Before considering what each of these systems may offer Americans as a useful precedent, it may be helpful to step back from the detail of the three preceding chapters and restate the principal features of each system.

Sweden and the Netherlands exemplify those countries that stress the provision of opportunity to all people to enjoy a high quality of life. One policy that supports this goal is that society as a whole should share the increment in land values resulting from planning decisions. Land banking is a tool that is entirely compatible with this policy.

France, like the United States, has stressed individual opportunity over equality of opportunity. Both countries have a 200-year tradition of free enterprise in land. Protection of a landowner's right to make decisions affecting his land has taken precedence over protection of those affected by these decisions. Recently, both countries have been moving toward greater restriction on private land use to promote the public interest. Because France has been subject to a more extreme set of development pressures than the United States, it has moved faster. Various forms of land banking have been adopted as part of the expanded public role in the control of land use.

A comparison between land banking as it has functioned under near optimal conditions in Sweden and the Netherlands and under numerous limitations in France suggests that, even when constrained by societal attitudes and by inadequate funds, land banking still can be an effective means of realizing land use policies. Its continually expanding use in France over the past twenty years is particular testimony to that. The role of land banking in each country in holding down land prices and inhibiting speculation unfortunately remains an open question due to lack of information. In Sweden and the Netherlands, the entire land use control system inhibits speculation; the particular role of land banking cannot be determined. In France, the ZADs are alleged to have proven a potent force against speculation, yet widespread speculation persists. To what extent it has been checked by the ZADs and the other land bank programs is unknown.

## Characteristics of the Swedish and Dutch Systems

Sweden and the Netherlands have been and remain opposites in terms of densities and growth pressures; today the Netherlands has a density twenty times that of Sweden and is growing almost twice as fast. These countries initially engaged in land banking for very different reasons. Early in this century, the large cities of Sweden decided to provide moderately priced land and housing to try to stem the exodus of Swedes to free land in the United States. Land banking was part of the response to the exodus of one-third of the population. On the other hand, the Netherlands has long been overcrowded. To add to its settlement problems, the Randstad, its dominant urban region, is below sea level, and construction there is both difficult and expensive. For the Dutch, land banking was one of the two principal ways of maximizing their country's land potential; the other way was to create new land.

Although the motivations that led them to initiate land banking were dissimilar, both countries shared and still share common values about land. They view land as a private good, which properly is subject to extensive public control in order to achieve the use that best promotes the common welfare. Both countries believe that landowners are not entitled to unearned increments in land values. Given these common values, their land bank programs have evolved through various stages and today are roughly comparable.

The large Swedish and Dutch cities, on whose peripheries most development is occurring, formerly had purchased so much land so far in advance of need that they had a vast stock of land available for development. It was the custom for the central cities to annex land, install infrastructure, extend transportation services, prepare sites, determine what uses were desirable, and offer the sites for sale or lease in accord with their plans. It has been common practice to subsidize some land uses at the expense of others, and some cities have subsidized all land prices from their general treasuries.

Today these practices of many decades have altered, because of a new combination of forces. The central cities either are declining slowly in population and income or are just holding their own. They are receiving revenues from their leased land but are buying little new land. Some still hold enormous amounts of undeveloped land outside their boundaries—Stockholm owns land outside the city totaling twice the city's area—but the annexation of that land has ceased to be politically acceptable to the suburban municipalities. This unbuilt extraterritorial land will be developed in cooperation with the municipalities in which it is located. Other central cities have developed their stocks of land and have ceded their former role of land banker to suburban municipalities.

The suburban municipalities are not rich, as the central cities used to be, and must depend on national government aid and on borrowing to finance their purchases. However, there is no longer any reason to buy twenty or thirty years in advance of need, carrying the cost of land over that period, since current laws specify that the existing use value, not development value, is to be paid for land. Swedish and Dutch municipalities have the right of eminent domain, so the property owner has little alternative but to sell when land is sought for a land bank. All landowners, whether or not their land is purchased for a land bank, are treated equitably under both systems. Dense development occurs on land bank land, acquired at its rural use value. Other land is subject to municipal land use regulations, which can prohibit any use denser than that currently existing.

Municipal acquisition of land in advance of development is customary in both countries. In the Stockholm metropolitan area, approximately 70 percent of all residential deveolpment occurs on municipally owned land. Sixteen of the twenty-three municipalities in the metropolitan area lease rather than sell their lands for development. In the Netherlands, municipal land banks are the source of over 80 percent of all land being developed, about one-third of which is offered on lease terms only. In both countries, virtually all dense development is on municipal land.

Even though each country can control development by means of regulation, land banking continues to be desirable on the grounds of efficiency and equity. Public ownership enables municipalities to time development with the provision of public services and to exercise control over the mix of land uses. It also assures that owners of development sites will not benefit from land sales and thus work an injustice on those landowners restricted to farming or other low-density uses.

There are several current, unresolved problems affecting land banking in both Sweden and the Netherlands. Leases in the past were for terms of many decades with no provision for rent revision; this is still current practice in some cities, while others have introduced rent revision provisions in new leases. Often, however, lease income falls far short either of the market rental value or of the sum needed to pay off land acquisition costs. This practice subsidizes many, unevenly, without a rational basis. Particularly now that the land banks are financed predominantly by the national governments, it is time for a reevaluation of leasing policies.

Another set of problems is that of the disparity between the objectives of the national government and suburban land banks. Suburban municipalities tend to be small, inadequately staffed, parochial in outlook, and short of funds. They are likely to compete for financially attractive development, and these pressures at times conflict with regional and national planning objectives. The state can and sometimes does influence local land bank activities by granting or withholding financial assistance. In the future, however, a more direct means of programming the purchase and disposition of land to implement regional and national objectives is likely to be needed. Whether this may be a metropolitan government, such as the Stockholm County Council, a regional agency, such as the Rijnmond Public Corporation, or some other form of organization remains to be decided.

## The Varied Land Bank Programs of France

France did not initiate land banking until 1958, and then it was the national government, not the municipalities, that took the initiative. The government was committed to a high rate of housing construction (to compensate for wartime losses) and to growth pole development. These objectives took more specific form in the national economic and physical development plans and consequent national investment. Land banking became one tool for plan implementation. Its initial use was in Priority Urbanization Zones (ZUPs), designed as one means to counteract massive concentration in Paris. While municipalities designated these zones and acquired land in them, the state exercised ultimate control over their approval and granted the funds essential for acquisition, improvements, and housing. The ZUPs were later followed by other Zs, by the SAFER farm program, and by the regional council land banks. Today's mix of land bank programs has been shaped by a number of factors; among them are the emergence of local land use planning, pressure for greater decentralization of power, increasing concern over the loss of farmland and environmentally sensitive areas to development, and repugnance toward much of the new development. These new forces coexist with continued wholesale speculation. The six land bank programs have as a common starting point the conviction that it is proper for the public sector to avert gross inequities of planning decisions by intervention in the market. Thus, excessive windfalls may be avoided by public purchase of sites intended for intensive development. Conversely, the loss of all development value may be avoided by public purchase of developable land planned for continued open space use. Some land bank acquisitions are at current market value, some at the land's value one year prior to designation of a ZUP or Deferred Development Zone (ZAD). The various land bank programs authorize different public or private groups and/or units of government to acquire land, they may or may not create a right of preemption in the acquiring agency, and they provide different financing mechanisms. With this considerable diversity of actors and purposes, it is very difficult to assess accurately the impact of the French programs. Two illustrations give some sense of their scope.

As of 1974, 1 percent of France had been placed in ZADs. These zones include most land planned for intensive development and its related open space. In comparison to this, 1 percent designated for potential development, 6 percent of the country already is urbanized. All land in the ZADs is subject to preemption and, while most will not be acquired, the leverage obtained by the preemption power provides extensive control over the land market. Creating Planned Development Zones (ZACs) within the ZADs then makes it possible to develop intensively in accord with plans.

In recent years the SAFERs, private corporations operating with the power to preempt and with the aid of national subsidies, have bought 12 percent of all farmland offered for sale and have resold the land subject to restrictions that assure continued farm use for fifteen years. The impact of this program on the preservation of farmland varies widely by location; the greatest need for it is in those areas where farmland is under strong pressure for development. Overall, its role is significant.

All of the French land bank programs have been well conceived in legal and administrative terms. The programs are in extensive use and, for the most part, are regarded as worthwhile and important. One can say that they are successful in the sense that they have made possible the acquisition of significant amounts of land and the control of future use of that land. The programs that purchase land planned for development have captured for the public sector some portion of the value added to land as a result of government actions. The programs that purchase land planned for farming or other open space use have succeeded in barring development from those lands.

Having said this, it is necessary to say as well that neither the land bank programs nor any other government actions have brought France close either to control of land speculation or to widespread realization of land use planning objectives. The fault is not in the design of the programs but in the lack of sufficient political or financial commitment to them. As Edgard Pisani said, comparing Stockholm's land bank program with the French programs:

I return from Stockholm full of admiration and richer by at least two lessons: public acquisition of land and long-term leasing of it constitute the only system that responds simultaneously to the needs of urbanization and to the exigencies of a certain public morality while permitting development of a dynamic economic system. But also—but especially—the land problem is an easy problem to solve since it is viewed from a rigorous economic and financial perspective. For us, one must add to this an entire aggregate of legal, political, sentimental, and sociological givens that obscure rationality.[2]

France, like the United States, has not resolved the issue of how much of a landowner's value it is equitable to remove through planning decisions or, on the other hand, how much a landowner is entitled to be rewarded for speculative efforts. One result of this indecision is that political pressure often leads to the granting of permission to develop sites not in development zones for private market housing. In addition to the usual consequences of scattered development, this increases the proposition of subsidized housing in the development zones, makes it more difficult to attract private market housing to them, and fosters socioeconomic segregation there.

A different problem is that none of the land bank programs enjoys enough financial support to enable the acquiring agencies to operate at an adequate level. These problems and the underlying issues that they reflect are recognized by many French planners and politicians. Whether they will be resolved is uncertain.


### The Current Setting in the United States

For approximately a decade, land banking has been touted as a necessary and/or desirable tool for the management of future development in the United States. In the words of Anthony Downs:

Any attempt to exert significant public influence over the nature, location, magnitude or physical form of urban growth requires public ownership or other direct control of a significant part of the land in a major metropolitan area, especially on the growth periphery.[3]

This conviction is widely shared. A series of commissions[4] and prominent individuals[5] have advanced a range of land bank proposals. The setting for these proposals, and for the land bank experimentation that has occurred so far, is the peculiarly American pattern of dispersed urbanization. Private ownership of urban land, public infrastructure investments, and land use controls all have fostered this pattern. A brief review of the current distribution of land ownership between the public and private sectors and of trends in the exercise of land use controls precedes a description of some recent American land bank programs and proposals. The Puerto Rico Land Administration Act, the principal ongoing land bank program, and the land banking provisions of the American Law Institute's *Model Land Development Code* receive emphasis as the outstanding examples to date.


### *Land Ownership*

Today the public-private ratio of land ownership in the United States is 42 percent to 58 percent.[6] The components of the public share are 34 percent federal, 6 percent state and local, and 2 percent Indian. There is little prospect of significant, imminent change in this distribution. While public ownership is very substantial, most public lands are remote from urban areas and, therefore, offer the public sector little direct control over urbanization.

Federal lands constitute approximately one-third of the area of the country, or 761 million acres. This is less than half the total once held in the public domain. The Bureau of Land Management (BLM)[7] of the Department of the Interior administers 62 percent of the federal lands; these lands are the residual public domain, managed by the bureau "pend-

TABLE 5.1. Agency Jurisdiction over Federal Lands, 1974

| Agency | Acres (in Millions) | Percentage |
|---|---|---|
| Dept. of the Interior | | |
|     Fish and Wildlife Service | 31 | 4 |
|     Bureau of Indian Affairs | 5 | 1 |
|     Bureau of Land Management | 470 | 62 |
|     National Park Service | 25 | 3 |
|     Bureau of Reclamation | 8 | 1 |
|       Subtotal | 539 | 71 |
| Dept. of Agriculture | | |
|     Forest Service | 187 | 25 |
| Dept. of Defense | 31 | 4 |
| Other | 4 | |
|     Total | 761 | 100 |

SOURCE: U.S., Department of the Interior, *Public Land Statistics, 1975* (Washington, D.C.: Government Printing Office, 1976).

ing final disposition." With the exception of the parts of the Alaskan public domain, the probability is that the final disposition of the public domain will be either retention by BLM or transfer to other public agencies for specific uses. Table 5.1 shows the distribution of management responsibility for the federal lands as of 1974.

The shift in federal policy away from disposition of the public domain occurred at the start of the twentieth century. At that time the government decided to retain ownership of much of the remaining public domain and to offer land for lease on terms designed to earn a profit.

Timber rights were among the earliest to be leased. In 1905, the Forestry Service was established in the Department of Agriculture and the forest reserve, which had been created in 1891, was transferred to it from the Interior Department. The more productive timber lands were offered for lease, a practice that has continued over the years. As of 1975, 23 million acres were under lease for commercial timber harvesting.

The leasing of mineral rights also dates back to the turn of the century.[8] As of 1975, there were 104,000 mineral leases covering 82 million acres; income to the federal government from these leases totaled $2.8 billion in fiscal 1975.

Whether the federal government has obtained a fair value for its leases and whether the resources subject to lease are being wisely managed are not at issue here. What warrants emphasis is that the policy of retaining the fee to lands with resource development potential and offering the lands for private lease has been widely supported throughout the twentieth century. Public acceptance of this policy can be a precedent for a policy of public ownership and lease of development lands.

There have been substantial additions to the federal public lands during the century. Here, too, there may be a precedent to aid acceptance of land banking. Despite enormous federal holdings, Congress repeatedly has responded to specific needs for further acquisition.

An early example is the Weeks Act of 1911. This law authorized the federal government to buy additional lands for the forest reserve when a vast public domain already existed. The acquisitions were justified on the ground that forest cover, by absorption and slow release of precipitation, contributes to the maintenance of stream flow, which, in turn, promotes navigability. Since enhancement of navigability as an aid to commerce was acknowledged to be a federal governmental function, by this line of reasoning forest purchases were appropriate federal expenditures.

A series of large, unintended acquisitions occurred during the 1930s. During the opening of the west, most settlers had bought, preempted, or been granted title to the more productive of the public domain lands. Many, however, had acquired marginal land. The settlers' failure to understand the limitations of the arid lands for cultivation contributed to the Dust Bowl conditions of the 1930s, to widespread bankruptcy for the settlers, and, in the heart of the Depression, to federal reacquisition by purchase of millions of acres of this land. Some of the land later was resold, while some was retained as part of the public domain.

Recent federal land purchases have consisted of comparatively small scale acquisitions for parks, recreation areas, wildlife management areas, and federal facilities, particularly Department of Defense installations. While small, the acquisitions are notable because many have been in or near densely settled urban areas. Despite high land acquisition costs, Congress has authorized purchases to retain open space and to make recreation opportunities readily available to urban residents. This reflects a shift in priorities toward the needs of urban areas and a recognition that smaller holdings near an urban population may serve these needs better than vast tracts hundreds or thousands of miles away.

Map 1.1 of the federal lands shows vividly the extreme imbalance in distribution of the federal lands between the eastern and western United States. This imbalance resulted, first, from the absence of federal lands in the original thirteen states and, second, from the east to west progression of the sale and grant programs for the public domain. When the policy shifted to one of public domain retention, most of the remaining public domain was in the far west. Today, less than 1 percent of the land in Connecticut, Iowa, Maine, and New York is in federal ownership, while over 60 percent of the land in Alaska, Idaho, Nevada, and Utah is federal. Although recent population shifts to the Pacific Coast and to the Southwest are bringing urban settlement into closer proximity with the federal lands, it remains true that the federal lands are located predominantly in the less settled areas of the country. While the holdings are vast, they therefore are of limited potential as reserves for future development.

The extent and distribution of state-owned land varies widely among the states. The states created from the public domain received federal land grants, some of which were inalienable, with the income earmarked for specified public purposes. These holdings create patterns of state land ownership comparable to that of the state of Washington, shown in chapter 1. Some states lacking substantial federal holdings, such as New York and Pennsylvania, own extensive state forests managed in part for timber income and in part for recreation. In Pennsylvania, for instance, only 2.3 percent of the land is federally owned but 11 percent is state owned. State forest land acquisitions have increased substantially over the past decade, particularly in the more heavily urbanized states. State and local government acquisitions for parks and public facilities also have increased recently. Total state land holdings rose over 12 percent from 1959 to 1974.[9] Still, as with most of the federal lands, the state forest and recreation lands tend to be remote from major urban concentrations; therefore, they have only a limited potential as a reserve for future development. (See map 5.1.)

### Land Use Determinants

Since the current stock of federal and state lands is far from most of the pressures for land use change and, therefore, of limited suitability for incorporation into a land bank system, institution of land banking will be dependent upon legislative authorization and appropriation of funds for new land acquisition.

Until this occurs, urban development will continue to be shaped by public investment in specific programs such as sewers and housing and by public land use controls. The long prevalent division of influence between federal public investment and local regulatory controls is changing. Investment and tax expenditures affecting urban development are still predominantly federal, but now both the federal and state governments have joined local governments as regulators of land use. Greater recognition of the scarcity of some resources and of the impacts of development on other resources is leading to increasing regulation at a level of government high enough to affect an entire system, such as a watershed or airshed. Since this regulation is designed to protect resources, its impact on development tends to be to shift it elsewhere. Where the development will go remains a private market decision, but it is a decision influenced by direct and indirect actions of all levels of government. These actions are uncoordinated and often at cross purposes with one another.

The federal influences are powerful but disparate and diffused, for they were not adopted with relation to any common set of national objectives.

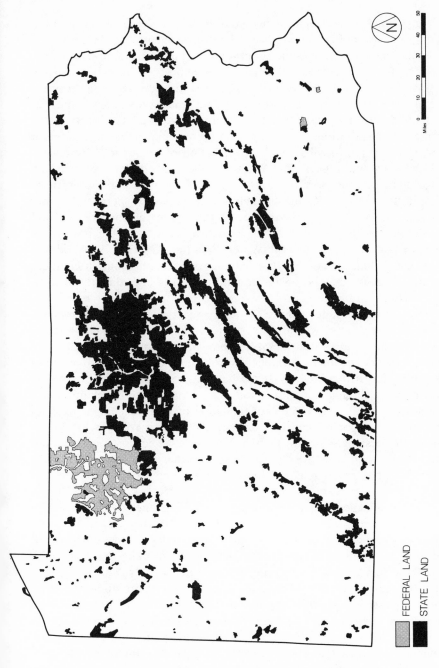

MAP 5.1. Federal and state lands in Pennsylvania

SOURCE: Adapted from Commonwealth of Pennsylvania, Department of Environmental Resources (untitled map) (Harris-burg, 1974)

FEDERAL LAND

STATE LAND

To date, Congress has rejected a commitment to the development of a national land use policy. Therefore, federal investments, tax expenditures, and regulations advance specific program aims that are often inconsistent. Until recently, the federal influences were almost exclusively financial, taking the form of grants or subsidies. Highway and sewerage grants, home mortgage interest deductions, and energy and water subsidies are illustrative of the federal programs that have major impacts on the location and character of urbanization. Shifts in allocation formulas under federal grant programs can result in substantial redistribution of grant funds by region. The Urban Institute reports that "in 1970, the Sunbelt states received an average of 12 percent more per person in federal grants than the northern industrial states; by 1976, the Sunbelt states received 9 percent less per capita than their counterparts in the North. The divergence of regional funds accelerated in 1977."[10] In the past few years, with the passage of the Clean Air Act, the Federal Water Pollution Control Act, and the Coastal Zone Management Act, the federal government, acting in conjunction with the states, has begun to regulate resources and, directly or indirectly, to affect land use.

The influence of state actions on land use is increasing but remains modest when compared with that of the federal government. The level of intervention also varies considerably from state to state, depending on growth pressures and local attitudes toward them. Only Hawaii has state-level zoning for all land. Many states have taken the initiative to protect critical areas, including wetlands, flood plains, and prime farmland, and a few states are attempting to control the siting of development of regional significance.[11] Oregon's Land Use Control Act, which requires local governments to designate urban growth boundaries and to zone all land beyond those boundaries for farm, forest, or other open space uses, is a measure that has great potential for influencing the location of development.

The local influence on land use is powerful, sometimes as a deterrent to development, sometimes as a stimulus. It also is highly fragmented, because of the different aims of the multiplicity of local governments that enact land use controls. Central cities, with their shrinking tax base, high demand for services, and aging infrastructure, regularly lose out in the competition to attract or hold desirable ratables. The surrounding municipalities respond in various ways to the prospect of development. Some actively seek intensive development consisting of lucrative ratables. Some actively seek to avoid development. Some do little planning but fight when threatened with undesired development. Others, both unprepared and passive, receive the residual development. Thus, some local governments are far more successful than others in controlling the use of their land. All are influenced in their actions by their dependence on the real property tax as a principal source of income. This creates a pressure to screen out residential development that does not pay its own way. Large lot zoning has been the usual local land use control adopted to limit residential development to more expensive housing. In the 1970s, many courts have struck down large lot zoning on the ground that it is exclusionary and acts as an unreasonable constraint on people's choice of a place to live.[12] Nonetheless, large lot zoning remains a major influence on urban development, contributing both to the scattering of development and to low densities. A few local governments—some of them acting in response to court pressure—have developed land use control systems intended to encourage a planned mix of development over a period of years.

Even given the recent increase in sensitivity to people's needs for a better living environment and the response to this by regulatory innovation at all levels of government, there still remains a need for land banking. First, public plans often are not implemented and regulations are subject to change. There is a considerable disparity between the development decisions of the private market, constrained by a variety of uncoordinated public-sector regulations, and the development decisions called for by plans. Second, plan implementation through land banking advances the public interest because there is a redistribution toward the public sector of the profits arising from development.

The major effort that will be required to introduce a new approach to land use control is warranted because there will be substantial, continued urban growth. There is no question but that population growth will continue and that most of the impact of this growth will be on urban areas. The Census Bureau's most conservative projection, based upon an average reproduction rate of 1.8 children per family, shows a population of 265 million in 2020, up from 205 million in 1970. As of 1970, 149 million people were classified as urban, while another 40 million were nonfarmer residents of rural areas, usually located within commuting distance of urban areas. Only 5 percent of the population were classified as rural farm residents.[13] (See map 5.2.)

Which land will be converted from rural to urban use to meet the demands of the increasing population will be determined by a number of forces, including the amount of growth, locational preferences, and density of development, as well as the previously discussed public investment and regulatory controls. If recent migration trends continue, much of the growth will occur in the sunbelt and along the West Coast. The Northeast and North Central regions of the country will show little growth, and some parts of these regions are likely to decline.

The densities at which people wish to live are of great significance to land conversion, as well as to the future character of urban areas. Even in nongrowth areas, land conversion will be significant in amount if central

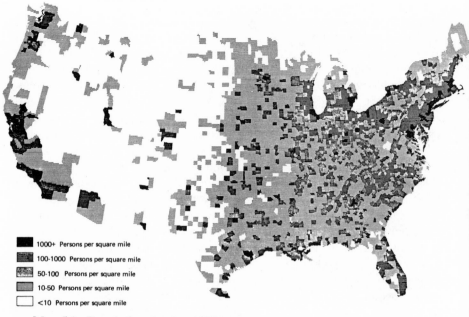

■ 1000+ Persons per square mile

▤ 100-1000 Persons per square mile

▦ 50-100 Persons per square mile

▤ 10-50 Persons per square mile

☐ <10 Persons per square mile

MAP 5.2. Population density, 1970

SOURCE: Adapted from Regional Plan Association, *Growth and Settlement in the U.S.* (New York, 1975), p. 36

city residents continue to move out to settle fringe areas at low densities. In 1970, the urban population occupied only 1.5 percent of the nation's land; another 1.5 percent was developed for public uses, especially roads. While the amount of developed land in the nation is small, recent settlement patterns show a high level of land consumption. Between 1960 and 1970, each new urban resident used 0.4 acres. The New York Regional Plan Association calculates that, by the year 2020, 8 percent of the nation's land, or an additional 90 million acres, will be urbanized.[14] This estimate is based on what the Census Bureau terms its currently probable population projection, based on an average rate of reproduction of 2.1 children per family, and it assumes a continuation of recent low-density development patterns. Many factors may change: for instance, rising energy costs may stimulate denser development, Congress may vote more aid to the declining central cities and stem the outflow, and the increasing number of elderly in the population may choose to live in high-density concentrations. Nevertheless, it is certain that an enormous amount of what is now rural land will be developed in the coming decades.

This short summary of the varied impacts of government actions on urban development may be persuasive that confusion among objectives is unlikely to lead to patterns of land use that best advance the public interest. There are many who argue that land banking can do better.

### Land Bank Programs and Proposals

Some American proponents of land banking have moved beyond conceptual advocacy to the development of detailed proposals and the enactment of programs. The most fully articulated proposal and program, respectively, are the land banking article of the American Law Institute's *Model Land Development Code (hereafter cited as Code)*[15] and the land bank operated by the Puerto Rico Land Administration.[16] Because the Puerto Rican land bank antedates the American Law Institute's *Code* by eleven years, it will be discussed first. A number of other programs and proposals will be mentioned briefly to illustrate the range of concerns already being addressed by land banking.

Puerto Rico has long been faced with the problem of inadequate housing for the waves of rural poor who have migrated to the urban areas. Land speculation was endemic, placing private housing beyond the reach of even moderate income people and causing subsidized housing to be inordinately expensive for the public sector. In 1962, the Puerto Rican legislature adopted a far-reaching, comprehensive bill[17] that created a public agency designed to fight urban speculation and to implement development plans through the creation of a land bank.

The act's statement of findings expresses fully the concerns of the legislature:

Urban lands, or lands adapted to urban development, are monopolized and kept unused by their owners, which creates an artificial shortage of land and raise in price of other properties and staple commodities; that the speedy raise in the price of land makes it impossible for persons of moderate or low resources to purchase land in appropriate areas; . . . that the raise in the price of land makes for undesirable urban expansions, which, in turn, creates serious financial problems to the Commonwealth and municipal governments.[18]

Monopoly control of urban land leading to high land prices, exclusion of low- and moderate-income people from the land market, pressure for development in unsuitable locations, and high infrastructure costs attributable to a lack of control over the timing and location of development are the problems that faced Puerto Rico; these problems are different from those facing many American urban areas only in their severity. The Puerto Rican legislature, in choosing to respond to the problems by initiating land banking, acknowledged explicitly the inadequacy of existing land use controls:

This ever-increasing price of land cannot be controlled, nor the problems thereby created can be solved, by any of the tools available to the Commonwealth and municipal governments; that the levy of taxes and the regulations of physical planning are insufficient; that the regulation on subdivision and zoning operates prospectively for undeveloped and underdeveloped areas and cannot prevent the undesirable, but legal, use of the land; . . . that it is in the public interest to avoid, as soon as possible, the excessive and disproportionate increase in the market price of land.[19]

The intent of the act is a broad, encompassing protection of natural areas as well as the location of new development:

It is the intent of the Legislative Assembly that the activities of the Administration hereby created promote, in a planned and efficient manner, the welfare, the economic freedom and the social justice of the present and future inhabitants of Puerto Rico through the efficient utilization of the land and the fitting out of new areas anywhere in Puerto Rico, to insure a better balance between the needs of future communities and the economic and geographic media; preserve historical values and the natural values of the land, the beaches, the forests, and landscapes; . . . avoid the concentration of landholdings for speculative purposes by any one person; and develop programs for the acquisition of the necessary land for the carrying out of any type of project.[20]

To carry out the purposes of the act, the legislature created the Puerto Rico Land Administration, a public corporation governed by a board whose members are: the governor, as chairman; the chairman of the Puerto Rico Planning Board, as vice chairman; the secretaries of the Treasury, Public Works, and Agriculture; the director of the Urban Renewal and Housing Corporation; the administrator of economic development; and two gubernatorial appointees.

The act authorizes the Land Administration to acquire land, by purchase, eminent domain, barter, or otherwise. When the Land Administration acquires land by eminent domain, the statute directs that just compensation shall be calculated as follows: just compensation is the market value exclusive of any increase in value occasioned by expectations that the land or nearby land would be publicly acquired by the Land Administration or the Commonwealth and exclusive of any increase in value attributable to public improvements in the vicinity made by the Land Administration or the Commonwealth to advance the purposes of the act.

Land acquisition may be financed by the borrowing or issuance of bonds whose payment is secured by the Land Administration's revenues and holdings. Debts of the Land Administration are not secured by the full faith and credit of the Commonwealth. Although the act appropriated $20 million to the Land Administration, it was not anticipated that this alone would suffice as a revolving fund for land acquisition.

Land may be acquired anywhere in the Commonwealth and held in reserve for a variety of future uses, including housing, industrial development, public works, new community development, and the maintenance of natural areas. The future use need not be known at the time of acquisition. The only general constraint on future use is that the purpose should insure "the utilization of lands on the basis of the most reasonable costs in behalf of the welfare of the community."[21]

The Land Administration may improve land in its reserve by drainage, filling, or irrigation. It may act as the developer of its land or it may contract with government agencies or private developers for use of the land in accord with the purposes of the act. Land may be sold or leased for development. While the Land Administration is prohibited from giving away land, other than to the Commonwealth, it is authorized to dispose of it for less than either the purchase price or the land's market value in order to further the purposes of the act. All sales or leases of property for housing development must include provisions limiting the profits to be made by the purchaser.

The Land Administration Act was attacked on the ground that it unconstitutionally authorized the taking of land for future uses unknown and unspecified at the time of taking. The act was upheld in 1967, by the Supreme Court of Puerto Rico, which held that the acquisition of land, even though its future use was unspecified, was for a social benefit and that this was a valid public use justifying the use of eminent domain.[22]

To implement the act, the Land Administration prepares plans showing how much land, in what locations, it *may* acquire for the land reserve. These plans are submitted to the Puerto Rico Planning Board for review for conformity with the board's master plan for Puerto Rico and its more detailed plans for the various municipalities. Once the planning board approves the Land Administration plans, the Land Administration publishes notice that it may buy the land. By 1973, Land Administration acquisition plans were under way or completed for three metropolitan areas and forty-one smaller municipalities.[23]

As of 1977, the Land Administration had acquired almost 55,000 acres and had disposed of 18,000 acres, either by lease or sale. The legislature has appropriated a total of $95,876,062 to the Land Administration. The Land Administration also has borrowed to finance its operations but has not issued bonds. On 30 June 1977, outstanding loans from the Government Development Bank for Puerto Rico, carrying interest at 9 percent, and from the Commonwealth of Puerto Rico, interest free, totaled $40 million. Also as of that date, the Land Administration held 36,600 acres distributed in 510 parcels in seventy-two municipalities, acquired at a cost of $148 million.[24] Ninety-five percent of the land disposed of has been leased. Lease terms are for from five to twenty-five years, and options to

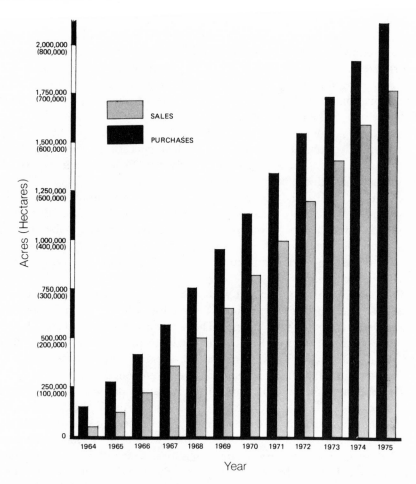

FIGURE 5.1. Puerto Rico Land Administration: Acquisition and disposition of land, 1964–1975

SOURCE: Adapted from Administracion de Terrenos de Puerto Rico, *Informe Anual* (1964–75) (Santurce, Puerto Rico)

renew may carry the total term to as long as ninety-five years. Land is sold at market value or leased at a percentage of the market value except to governments; for governments the land may be offered at either the market or the book value or, rarely, it may be offered as a gift. Some leases provide for rent increases at the time of each renewal, while others do not.[25] (See fig. 5.1.)

Land has been acquired at the request of public agencies, either for specific projects or to hold down speculation in land around those projects

FIGURE 5.2. La Marina project, Puerto Rico (photo courtesy of Puerto Rico Land Administration)

so that the public sector would realize any increments in value attributable to the projects.[26] Land from the reserve has been used for two new communities, for the construction of thousands of units of low- and moderate-income housing, for industrial development, and for the management of natural resources. Marinas have been built, habitat preserved, and historic areas protected (see fig. 5.2). Land still held in the reserve often is leased pending future disposal. Although some advocates of the land bank program would like to have seen a higher level of activity, the act is working effectively and the Land Administration has had considerable success.

New York's Urban Development Corporation (UDC) has many of the same land assembly powers as the Puerto Rico Land Administration.[27] As of 1973, UDC held $20 million worth of land, mostly as a reserve for its planned new communities of Radisson and Audubon. Funds for land acquisition and for the construction of infrastructure came from a state non-interest-bearing loan. Radisson, a 2,700-acre site twelve miles from Syracuse, was acquired by purchase. The federal government sold UDC 2,000 acres at less than $1,000 per acre, and the remainder was purchased from a private owner at approximately $3,500 per acre. Land at Radisson is being sold for residential and industrial development. Audubon is a

FIGURE 5.3. Roosevelt Island, U.S.A. (photo by Jack Brennan, courtesy of Urban Development Corporation)

2,400-acre site near Buffalo. Land costs there were high, averaging $6,500 per acre; to hold down acquisition costs somewhat, UDC did not reveal its plans for the site and bought through agents who did not name their principal. Audubon was planned to be a new community serving the already acquired site for the new Buffalo campus of the State University of New York.[28] Roosevelt Island, a 152-acre tract in New York City's East River, was acquired under a ninety-nine-year lease. Accompanying the lease was UDC's development plan, which provided for five thousand units of mixed-income housing, community facilities, and parks. The first two thousand housing units have been built by housing companies organized by UDC and holding the land as sublessees. Construction of another one thousand units is expected to begin in 1978. (See fig. 5.3.)

There are several land bank programs whose purpose is limited to the provision of sites for low- and moderate-income housing. Fairfax County,

Virginia, decided, in 1973, to create a $500,000 revolving fund for land acquisition. The original intent of the county board of supervisors was to buy critical sites, such as those adjacent to Metro stops, so that the county could profit from publicly caused increases in land values and so that the desired mix of development could be assured upon sale of the sites. By 1974, the county had modified its objectives to the acquisition of land for future use for low- and moderate-income housing.[29] There now are over 100 units of subsidized housing under construction on land purchased and resold by the county.

The Fairfax County land bank initially was funded by an allocation by the county board of supervisors of $2 million of federal revenue sharing funds to the land bank account. On further consideration, the county decided that it should appropriate its own funds for land banking, since, if revenue sharing funds were used for land acquisition, the cost of land could not be counted as a matching contribution for other federal funds for housing development.

In fiscal 1978, the county has nearly $800,000 available for land bank acquisitions and projects a fund in excess of $1.2 million for fiscal 1979. The Department of Housing and Community Development administers the fund, lending money to the Redevelopment and Housing Authority for the acquisition of housing sites in accord with the county plan. Once permanent financing is obtained for a housing project, the land acquisition loan is repaid. In fiscal 1978, over $200,000 of the money in the revolving fund came from repaid loans for land acquisition for two housing projects. It is county policy not to draw down the fund in order to subsidize land costs. With land accounting for only 5 percent of the cost of housing, the county has decided that it is more important to build up the revolving fund so that more sites can be acquired than to subsidize the cost of the acquisitions.[30]

In High Point, Winston-Salem, and Greensboro, North Carolina, each town has a private, nonprofit housing development corporation that buys land to hold for future development for low and moderate income housing. These corporations differ in structure, but all have local business and political backing. They are dependent on the voluntary purchase of land, since they have no eminent domain power.[31]

Davenport, Iowa, agreed in the settlement of a suit to allocate funds from its community development grants to acquire land to be used in the future for multifamily housing. Its 1977 allocation for this purpose was $225,000.[32] Congress, in the Community Development Act of 1974, specifically authorized use of community development grants to local governments for

the acquisition of real property . . . which is (a) blighted, deteriorated, deteriorating, *undeveloped* or inappropriately developed from the standpoint of sound community development and growth; (b) appropriate for rehabilitation or conservation activities; (c) appropriate for the preservation or restoration of historic sites, the beautification of urban land, the conservation of open spaces, natural resources, and scenic areas, the provision of recreational opportunities, *or the guidance of urban development*; (d) to be used for the provision of public works, facilities, and improvements eligible for assistance under this title; or (e) to be used for other public purposes. (emphasis added)[33]

Numerous communities have created industrial development corporations that acquire land for subsequent resale, often at a write-down, as a means of attracting new industry or retaining existing industry in search of a different or larger site.[34]

The various land bank proposals address different critical aspects of a land bank program, such as who should acquire land, how much land must be acquired, and what means of financing should be used.

A proposal for the state of Maine suggests the creation of a public agency that would be "a permanent repository of land that is held for ever as a public trust for the people of Maine, their welfare, and enjoyment" as well as an agency active in leasing other land for intensive development.[35]

Charles Haar, having concluded that "a feasible way to eliminate sprawl and leapfrogging, and the consequent distortions in land values and in the taxpayers' costs of producing public services, is through some mechanism of land reserve,"[36] goes on to propose the creation of metropolitan authorities with the power to acquire, manage, and dispose of land in accord with a metropolitan plan. These authorities would have the power of eminent domain and would receive federal financial assistance.

Marion Clawson has concluded that

measures to make the present suburban land conversion process work better, to improve the functioning of the urban land market, and to reorganize local government might well have considerable importance. But, could they be sufficient without public acquisition of land, even under the best of circumstances? In the judgment of this writer, they could not. If we wish really to cure the major deficiency in the suburban land conversion process, public land purchase must be instituted and carried out on an adequate scale.[37]

For Clawson, an adequate scale is approximately 60 percent of the land to be converted to urban use, with the land acquired from five to twenty years in advance of need.

The Douglas Commission concurred with Haar and Clawson that public acquisition is vital to the control of urban land development. It also emphasized that it is proper for the government to capture and retain land value increases resulting from development decisions.

A study carried out for the Urban Land Institute[38] proposed that special-purpose corporations be created with the power to acquire land, by eminent domain or otherwise. These would be similar to the Puerto Rico

Land Administration. They would be able to borrow money or to issue bonds secured by the holdings and revenues of the corporation and would be eligible for federal and state aid.

The most complete proposal for land banking is article 6 of the American Law Institute's *Model Land Development Code*. Drafted by Allison Dunham and Fred Bosselman, the reporter and associate reporter for the *Code*, respectively, the land banking article is also the product of considerable debate among members of the institute. As presented in the *Code*, it is, therefore, the distillation of the opinions of a number of leading professionals in the land use field. The provisions of article 6 proceed in a logical sequence—creation of the implementing agency, general powers and obligations of the agency, acquisition of land, disposition of land, and the role of local government—with the reporters' commentary accompanying each section. A summary of the provisions and commentary follows.

The opening section is a statement of purpose that sets forth the scope of land banking:

The acquisition of interests in land for the purpose of facilitating future planning to maintain a public land reserve, and the holding and disposition thereof in accordance with the purposes of this Code, are hereby declared to be for the public purpose of achieving the land policy and land planning objectives of this State whether or not at the time of acquisition or expenditure of funds for acquisition or maintenance any particular future use, public or private, is contemplated for the land. Appropriations for, issuance of bonds for, and taxation for a land reserve system; acquisition of land for a land reserve by gift, purchase or condemnation; management of land so acquired; and disposition of land so acquired; are hereby declared to be for a valid public purpose.[39]

Responding to the key issue in *Puerto Rico* v. *Rosso*,[40] the *Code* asserts that it is a valid public purpose to acquire land for a then undetermined future use. The commentary notes that the constitutionality of this provision is not a certainty but concludes that, in light of *Puerto Rico* v. *Rosso*, other recent opinions, and the general broadening in judicial interpretations of public purpose, it is probable that the provision would withstand challenge.

The *Code* posits that the state will be the level of government to create a land bank, and there is no discussion of alternative possibilities. It provides for the creation of a State Land Reserve Agency, which, depending upon the preference of a particular state, may be placed within an existing department or established as a separate agency. The *Code* states that this agency may create regional divisions, provided that they have the same boundaries as regions of the state's land planning agency.[41] There is no provision for the delegation of any of the agency's powers to regional divisions if these are created.

The State Land Reserve Agency is required to adopt a land reserve policy. The proposed policy must be submitted to the state's land planning agency for review and comment prior to adoption. The *Code* offers alternative provisions for rejection: the policy cannot be adopted either if the land planning agency disapproves of it or if the land planning agency finds it inconsistent with a state land development plan then in effect.[42] Adoption must be preceded by public notice and the opportunity for citizen participation.

The portion of article 6 that sets forth the general powers and obligations of the State Land Reserve Agency offers a number of alternative provisions. The agency may be established as a conventional government agency or as a public corporation analogous in its tort liability to a private corporation. In either case, the agency is empowered to apply for grants, enter into contracts, receive lands or funds, borrow money, and buy, improve, and manage land. The agency is authorized specifically to lease land while it is in the reserve.[43] It is the intention of the *Code* that the agency should not act as a land developer.

Whether or not lands held by the agency are to be subject to real property, capital gain, income, excise, transfer, special improvement, or other taxes is left open as an option for the adopting state. The reporters' commentary acknowledges the inherent conflict between the needs of local government for revenue from the real property tax and the need of the agency to hold land until a propitious time for sale. The alternatives raised for consideration concerning the real property tax are that the agency shall be exempt, that it shall be fully taxable, or that it shall pay the largest of the following:

(a) [15] percent of the gross rental income from the parcel; (b) at the current levy of the taxing district on the assessed value of the land of the Agency in the last full tax year preceding the year of acquisition by the Agency; (c) at the current levy of the district on a value representing [40] percent of the price paid by the Agency to acquire the land.[44]

The State Land Reserve Agency is authorized to acquire any land or interest in land that could be used to carry out its policy. It may condemn land in accord with the state's eminent domain law. It is also authorized to contract with local governments to acquire and hold land for them. The agency may acquire land without disclosing to the seller that it is the purchaser.[45]

Disposition of land is governed by the same *Code* provisions as are proposed for other sales of land by government agencies.[46] The only differences proposed for the agency are that it not be permitted to dispose of land by lottery or at less than the use value, except for sales of land acquired for local governments.[47] The agency must publish notice of any proposed land disposition, including a description of the land, the proposed purchaser, and the proposed use. A copy of the notice must be sent to the state land planning agency, which can bar the disposition by notifying the agency that such action will not advance the state's planning goals. Once the agency has disposed of land, it must so notify the state land planning agency, which in turn must publish notice of the disposition. Third-party challenges to the disposition would be limited in time; the *Code* suggests a limit of three months from the publication of the notice of disposition.[48]

Finally, the land banking article also establishes a procedure for local governments to follow when they wish the State Land Reserve Agency to dispose of its lands located in their jurisdiction. First, the local government may request the agency to sell the land to it or to others for a proposed use. If the agency denies or fails to respond to the request, the local government may submit the request to the state land planning agency, which is required to give notice and to hold a legislative-type hearing. Following the hearing, the land planning agency may order the State Land Reserve Agency to dispose of the land either if this is appropriate to advance the goals of a state land development plan or if the latter agency has held the land for over twenty years and it "is no longer needed to accomplish the land reserve policy."[49]

Article 6 is positive in tone. While the reporters acknowledge that certain problems will arise, including the question of the constitutionality of an acquisition for an unknown future use and the conflict between long-term land holding and short-term fiscal needs, they urge that land banking be tried:

As is true with any untried technique of controlling development, land banking will undoubtedly have different consequences than either its proponents or opponents originally forecast. But only experimentation with actual land banking programs will enable a valid evaluation of their real effects. This Article is designed to serve as a basic framework for those states that wish to work in this challenging area.[50]

I concur fully that experimentation is necessary and desirable. There are major policy and procedural issues that need resolution; a review of them follows, illuminated where possible by experiences from Europe.

### Critical Land Bank Issues

The preceding section described some current land bank programs and proposals. With the exception of excerpts from the commentary to the *Code*, the presentation was factual, with little discussion of underlying issues. This is in keeping with the tenor of the programs and proposals.

Most of the commissions and individuals who have endorsed land banking have done so in very positive terms; first they have described the short-comings of present approaches to the control of urban development, then they have advanced land banking as the promising alternative. Many undoubtedly adopted this nonanalytic approach to land banking because they felt that a certain measure of advocacy was required to promote a new approach so divergent from current practice. Despite my own substantial enthusiasm for land banking, it would be misleading to conclude this account by creating the impression that a land bank program modeled on the experience in Europe is the panacea for American urban development problems. It may well be the best hope, but that does not mean that it waits on our horizon, trouble free. There are critical issues of both policy and organization to be considered and resolved.

### Compatibility of Land Banking with American Values

The major policy issue that must be faced is whether land banking is compatible with current American attitudes toward public land ownership and public capture of unearned increments in land value. Related issues are whether we are ready to shift from a speculative land investment system toward a system that offers substantial equity among landowners and whether, if we are, the only option is to embrace a land bank program that includes all land planned for intensive development.

One could separate the question of ownership from that of gain and posit a public land bank that acquired land at its development value. Although many would attack even this as socialistic, our acceptance of continued federal ownership of the public domain, of extensive state land ownership, and of widespread public acquisition for redevelopment suggests that public land banks also are likely to be acceptable, given acquisition at development value. However, in considering the question of public acceptability of land banking, I do not believe it proper or practical to separate ownership from the realization of gain. I concur with other proponents of land banking that it is legitimate and necessary for the land bank to realize the gains resulting from public investment and development. As the American Institute of Architects said, "We favor public acquisition and preparation of land in advance of development. We believe that the appreciating value of urbanizing land should be recycled into the cost of developing, serving, and maintaining it."[51] The Douglas Commission took a similar stand: "Where actual purchase will result in the government's recapturing increases in land values for the public, government should deem this a legitimate function and an added incentive for direct action."[52]

The Puerto Rico Land Administration Act is designed to achieve public capture of gain by the application of its definition of just compensation. By specifically excluding land value attributable to expectations of public purchase and investment, acquisition is to occur at a price reflecting private investment only. This legislation adopts the same logic as the holding of the New York Court of Appeals in the Grand Central Terminal case.[53]

Other land bank programs have other rules governing acquisition price; their common trait is that gains attributable to public decisions accrue to the public sector. In Sweden and the Netherlands, municipalities generally pay the rural use value for land. Negotiated agreement on this price is usual in Sweden; landowners know that, if they do not agree to the price offered, the municipalities always have recourse to eminent domain. If a landowner insists on eminent domain, the law specifies that the price to be paid shall be the lesser of the market value or the market value ten years previously (corrected for any change in the value of the kronor). In most instances this results in the payment of the rural use value. Dutch law provides for the payment of the rural land value plus the value of structures, moving expenses, and other expenses directly related to the acquisition. The Swedish and Dutch systems treat landowners equitably. Virtually all intensive development occurs on public land. Almost all development in both of these countries is intensive, and so there is little market for land for single-family, unsewered housing development. Therefore, landowners whose land is not acquired for a land bank have little opportunity to sell for more than the rural use value. French law, both for condemnation and preemption, states that the price to be paid for land is to be its existing use value one year prior to the initiation of specified condemnation or preemption proceedings and, further, that this value is to exclude expectations of increases due to public investments or to the probable relaxation of land use controls. The price is corrected to reflect any change in the value of the franc up to the date of establishing the amount of compensation.

Another possibility, but one that results in heavy carrying costs, is acquisition many years ahead of development, before development value has settled on the land. This was the Swedish system throughout much of this century.

Whatever the rules governing the determination of an acquisition price, if the underlying principle is that the private landowner shall not benefit from the increment in value attributable to the public decision to buy, the same question remains. Is this acceptable public policy in the United States? Is Puerto Rico's land bank a bellwether or an aberration?

As the discussion of taking and just compensation in chapter 1 pointed out, many courts have considerably expanded their definitions of public use. Some have reconsidered the degree of loss of value necessary to constitute a taking. In a number of states, the combined effect of this judicial reinterpretation has been to uphold a broader range of regulations that cause a substantial drop in property value. As it becomes more common for landowners to be subject to regulations, such as flood plain, wetland, or agricultural zoning, which provide no compensation for limiting land use to low-intensity activities, the concept of paying the rural use value for land bank acquisitions should become more acceptable.

There are qualifications to this statement, and they raise the issue of equity. First, if there is a general expectation that zoning will change to permit development when timely, then rural use zoning will be viewed as temporary and will not hold the market value of the land down to its rural use value. Consequently, the zoning will be less severe in its impact on the landowner than acquisition for a land bank at rural use value. Second, if a substantial share of development continues to occur on private land, and if the owners of this land continue to profit handsomely from its development, the disparity between the gains realized by these landowners and the price paid for land bank acquisitions can be expected to wither support for land banking. The French have had precisely this problem with their development districts. Although the government intended that all major development—defined as a development of 100 or more units—would take place in the development districts, lack of enough money for land acquisition combined with political pressure for development permission elsewhere has led to much private development outside the development districts. This, in turn, has led to high profits for some landowners and strong opposition from other landowners to public acquisition of their land for the development districts.

Americans have welcomed inequity, an essential element of speculative land investment, so long as they have received a measure of protection from loss caused by government action. It is probable that they would respond just as the French have to a program of public acquisition in which there was a substantial gap between the price paid for land by the public sector and the price paid by the private market. However, if publicly caused inequity is unacceptable, this does not imply that legislated equity will be endorsed. A powerful tradition of speculation in land will not be easily cast aside.

Is there some possible modification of the European policies that would permit limited private return and yet achieve substantial equity? This question is linked to the question of whether all land planned for development must be acquired. Sweden, the Netherlands, and France agree that a land bank should control all land to be developed intensively. They believe that there should be enough of a stock of land in public hands to meet several years' development demand, offering some flexibility as to which land will be developed first. They also agree that other land must be under some form of public control that is effective in preventing intensive development.

This control might take the form of regulations and/or a right of preemption. Acquisition costs are prohibitive at this scale of land banking unless the acquisition is at a rural use value or at a market value unaffected by public investment expectations. Even with eventual public realization of the gain from development, there is a gap of at least several years between the acquisition and the recovery of the acquisition costs. The French failure to provide enough acquisition funds for the purchase of land needed for all intensive development might well be paralleled in the United States. The scale of land acquisition necessary here may be beyond any commitment that we would be prepared to make. Our approach to new towns financing is not an encouraging precedent.

It is unfortunate that the systems of accounts in the three European countries have not made it possible here to determine what the returns to the public from land banking have been or when the returns have been realized. Such information would be extremely useful to U.S. policy makers evaluating the desirability of undertaking a large-scale land bank program. In Sweden and the Netherlands, land policy is so closely tied to housing and development policies that separate accounting for land investments has not been thought appropriate. In France one could obtain the necessary data from SEMs or from regional agencies such as EPAREB, but such an undertaking would be difficult and time consuming. One would need a means of selecting a representative sample from the many completed projects. Then extensive cooperation from the staffs of the organizations selected would be vital to obtain access to the data and an interpretation of the very complex financing arrangements used by the French.

Even if a study of the return from public land investments in France yielded very positive results, Americans might conclude that the priorities of the two countries were sufficiently different so that we would not choose to finance land bank acquisitions on a scale comparable to that of France, let alone that of Sweden and the Netherlands.

There is an alternative. The land bank can operate at a modest scale in relation to the totality of land that will be urbanized. Acquisition can be limited to the sites where the more intensive development is planned, such as sites for what the *Code* describes as development with regional impact. An essential component of this approach, however, is that there be a rough equity of the returns from land between people whose land is acquired by the public and people who are allowed to develop privately. If the land bank pays the market value less the value attributable to actual public investment or expectation of public investment, the landowner will receive that gain that is attributable to private activity. Of course, stating this as policy is substantially easier than defining a method for application of the policy. To achieve equity, those landowners who are allowed to develop privately would be taxed on their gain from development at a rate that would afford them approximately the same return from the sale of land as that obtained by the person who sells to a land bank. To make this tax proposal more attractive and easier to administer, development might be defined as in France—by a minimum number of units, or by the need for sewerage. Other construction, such as of a limited number of low-density, single-family houses, would not be subject to the special capital gain tax.

In proposing a limited-scale land bank coupled with a tax on private land development, I qualify the proposal with the skeptical observation of Sylvan Kamm, an astute critic of land banking:

Far more optimum strategies could be devised if land banking were coupled with effective administration of existing police power controls on land use, effective use of taxing powers to control development, or effective use of public facilities construction to guide development. But to couple a land bank proposal to such hypothetical action raises a number of questions. Such tools have been available for many years and experience in attempting to use them in a coordinated fashion gives little basis to believe that they can ever be coordinated. However, if they were so used, most of the beneficial effects might well result from their use rather than from land banking.[54]

Despite these concerns, Kamm does endorse land banking on a limited scale: "Most of the problems involved in land banking arise from scale. Lesser scale uses of public acquisition could serve valid public purposes without the problems involved in large scale land banking.[55]

Both the systems used in the three European countries and a system of limited-scale public acquisition combined with a tax on gains from private development assure that the public sector will benefit from the gain arising from its development decisions and, at the same time, that the landowners will be treated equitably. All of the systems substitute the value of equity for the prevailing American value of speculative opportunity. The European systems present particular difficulties because of the scale of initial funding required and the necessity for the acceptance of public ownership of all land to be intensively developed, which might be defined as all areas to be sewered. The alternative, a smaller scale land bank for all major developments coupled with a tax on other private development, presents a lesser difficulty, namely, the problem raised by Sylvan Kamm: will it be possible to gain the adoption of an adequate tax and of effective controls on land not planned for development and to coordinate the use of the tax and the controls with the operation of the land bank?

In my opinion, a land bank limited, at least initially, to acquisitions of sites for major developments stands both a real possibility of creation and a better chance than a land bank designed to acquire all land intended for intensive development. I think that Americans are ready to accept a pro-

gram that stops huge speculative gains, often tied to inside political knowledge, for a very few and that leaves some gain, albeit a modest one, for the
many who have investments in land. There probably are some communities so committed to comprehensive growth management that they are
ready to embark on a program for a land bank designed to accommodate
all intensive development. Because I view this as a more efficient approach, if one that is less attractive for general adoption now, I would
grant those communities top priority for financial assistance so that their
experience could serve as a prototype for others.

### Land Bank Powers

The *Code* offers explicit recommendations on the powers and organization of a land bank agency; in some instances it suggests alternatives,
but more often it does not. It raises a number of issues that need resolution
before any legislative body adopts enabling legislation creating land banks.
Among these are: who may create a land bank, what methods of acquisition will be authorized, how compensation shall be determined, what planning requirements shall exist, how acquisition may be financed, how land
banks shall be taxed, who may develop the land, how long the land may be
held, and what principles shall govern land disposition. European and
Puerto Rican experiences and American proposals provide some insight on
alternative approaches to these questions.

Any level of government, or a nongovernmental organization such as
France's SAFERs, might be authorized to create and manage a land bank.
There is considerable diversity of opinion among land bank proponents as
to what is preferable. Some favor one model for all states, while some
suggest that the choice of agency or agencies should turn upon the circumstances in a given state. Some advocate the creation of a hierarchy of
agencies, while some prefer limiting the authorization to a single agency.

Few proposals envision a direct role for the federal government as a
land bank agency. The Advisory Commission on Intergovernmental Relations did suggest two alternative possibilities, one similar to the French
SEMs:

Direct Federal involvement in large-scale urban development could be achieved
in a number of ways. One would be to create a mixed, public-private land
development corporation chartered by Congress with capitalization in the form
of capital stock carrying voting rights and eligibility for dividends. Substantial
private stock participation with accompanying voting rights could be provided,
but with majority control remaining with the Federal Government. . . .

Another approach would involve creation by Congress of a national urban
development agency or authorizing the Department of Housing and Urban

Development to acquire, hold, improve, and dispose of land for urban development. Such an agency or HUD could also be authorized to undertake large-scale urban and new community projects in conformance with a national urbanization policy.[56]

The Kaiser Committee recommended that the federal government buy land, but only for the development of subsidized housing and appropriate community facilities. Their report proposed that the federal government be authorized to use eminent domain where necessary, override local land use controls where they were inconsistent with federal plans, and lease the land for development.[57] Had these recommendations managed to win Congressional support, a program implementing them would have resulted in large developments segregated by income. The unhappy American experience with concentrations of public housing might well have been duplicated, even though a broader range of incomes would have been served.

The *Code* limits authorization for land banking to the state. Similarly, the Puerto Rico Land Administration Act authorized only the Commonwealth to operate a land bank. There are several reasons given for preferring the state as the land bank administrator. First, other choices may be less desirable. Assuming that much of a land bank's activity would be in metropolitan areas, it is evident that few units of general purpose government have jurisdiction over all or most of a metropolitan area. Regional planning agencies have the jurisdiction but, for the most part, have no power to regulate or acquire land. Central cities in much of the country do not have extraterritorial land acquisition powers. Further, central cities in the United States do not have a historic commitment comparable to that of the Swedish and Dutch cities to provide a place to live for newcomers to the region. Suburban municipalities located where growth will occur may not have the will and capacity to engage in land banking. Political power in these municipalities is likely to rest with large landowners; if their primary interest is in return from their land, this is antithetical to the interests of a land bank. There are other positive reasons for preferring the state as land bank administrator. The state should have a more comprehensive picture of land use needs and, therefore, should act less parochially than any lower level unit of government. It can acquire land for major developments to occur outside as well as within metropolitan areas. And it is more able than lower level units of government to fund land acquisition.

Opponents of state land banking argue that the state government is too remote to understand the development needs of each of its urban areas. Admitting that the state has greater financial resources than the lower levels of government, they say that, just as with the federal government, funding can be separated from land acquisition and management.

There are counterproposals to state authorization that advocate placing land bank powers with particular categories of government. Three such proposals are: (1) Central cities should act if they have powers of annexation. Recent experience in Stockholm and several of the large Dutch cities suggests that, where annexation is politically infeasible, central cities are unlikely to undertake extraterritorial land bank programs. (2) Where counties or regional governments cover entire urban areas, they should be the land bank agencies. (3) Where there are special-purpose regional agencies, such as the Port of New York Authority or the Delaware River Basin Commission, and no regional governments, these agencies should be authorized to be metropolitan land bank agencies.

There is little support for placing land banking power exclusively at the municipal level. This would place responsibility for action primarily with the suburban municipalities where most growth is expected to occur. In addition to the argument that land banking often is counter to the interests of those in power in the suburban municipalities, there is the argument that limiting authorization to multiple local governments destroys a major advantage of land banking. If a land bank agency has jurisdiction over a large area, it can pool costs and revenues from its land program. This makes it possible to allocate land to its most appropriate use, rather than to a use constrained by the need for a return to balance the investment in a given site.

France offers interesting precedents in the design of land bank agencies. Acquisition and land management can be by a corporation with mixed public and private participation. The SEMs that operate the ZUPs and ZADs are the primary example of this form of organization. There also are private nonprofit corporations, such as the SAFERs, and profit-making corporations, such as are common in ZACs. The SEM is the most widely used structure for land banking in France. Since one or more local governments must subscribe between 50 and 65 percent of the stock of an SEM, this assures local government a dominant role vis-à-vis other participating organizations such as banks and chambers of commerce. While the state holds only a few shares, its power is considerable because it is the primary source of acquisition funds. This local-state-private structure is responsive to many of the complaints about either a state or a local land bank agency and warrants consideration.

The report of the Advisory Commission on Intergovernmental Relations, in addition to describing two possible models for federal action, suggested the possibility of authorizing a state land bank agency, which in turn could charter regional or local land bank agencies.[58]

The Douglas Commission recommendation for legislation enabling a state to authorize land banking suggested that several alternatives be provided:

The Commission recommends that State Governments enact legislation enabling State and/or local development authorities or agencies of general purpose governments to acquire land in advance of development for the following purposes: (a) assuring the continuing availability of sites needed for development; (b) controlling the timing, location, type, and scale of development; (c) preventing urban sprawl; and (d) reserving to the public gains in land values resulting from the action of government in promoting and servicing development.[59]

In my opinion, no fixed choice of agency or level of government will be appropriate for all states. Each state should frame its legislation after considering factors such as the size of the state, the urban/rural split of its population, the expectations of urban growth, the existing structure and powers of local government and of special purpose agencies, and the willingness to innovate.

All of the proposals and programs authorize acquisition by purchase, gift, or eminent domain and acquisition of the fee or lesser interests. There is a general agreement that the power of eminent domain is essential. The power of barter included in the Puerto Rico Land Administration Act and in the French SAFER law offers desirable flexibility. The *Code*'s authorization for a state to acquire land on behalf of a local government makes sense, assuming that only the state is empowered to engage in land banking.

The power to preempt private market sales, which is not now authorized in the United States, would be the most useful additional acquisition tool. In Sweden and France, the land bank agency must receive notice of all proposed sales and can preempt to restrain speculation. The existence of the power to preempt has an effect on land transactions similar to the existence of the power of eminent domain. Once the affected public is aware of its existence it can be used sparingly, as a backup to negotiated purchase. Also, if proposed private sales are compatible with land use plans, there is no need for public purchase. The preemption power affords the land bank agency the opportunity to make this judgment. Preemption is effective only if the land bank agency has adequate means at its disposal to act when it deems necessary. Some of the French SAFERs have been handicapped by insufficient funding and therefore have not been a powerful force to counteract land speculation.

Preemption is a land use control compatible with the American legal system and with American values. There is ample precedent for it in the private market's use of the right of first refusal.

The legislation allowing land banks should specify how land to be acquired will be valued. I think it essential that acquisition be at a price unaffected by public investment decisions. There are several methods of achieving this.

THE UNITED STATES 273

The Dutch acquisition at the rural use value plus any improvements and costs of moving is the simplest to administer of the various methods of valuation. It is not well suited to the United States urban fringe, where land values reflect private as well as public actions. The Puerto Rican Land Administration Act offers another approach. Its inclusion of anticipated as well as actual public actions as elements of the market value is paralleled in the French condemnation and preemption law. The French law adds another element—increments in the market value due to expectations of change in land use controls to permit more intensive development. The Puerto Rican and French laws require that these specified elements be excluded from the acquisition price. The Swedish law, requiring the use of the lesser of the current market value or the market value ten years previously (corrected for any change in the value of the kronor), is relatively simple to administer and has the same general objective. Unlike the Puerto Rican and French laws, it does not present the treacherous task of differentiating increments in value attributable to public actions from those attributable to private actions. Whereas the Puerto Rican and French laws are logically appealing but difficult to implement, the Swedish system is somewhat arbitrary but workable. It would be more arbitrary in its impact in the United States than in Sweden. In Sweden there is little variation in the value of land a decade or more away from development, other than variation due to the natural characteristics of the land. In the United States, fragmentation in planning, public facility construction, and development decision making lead to much scattering in suburban land values. The market value of some land ten years prior to public acquisition might approach the development value while that of other land might be close to the rural use value. Therefore, owners of land with similar value at the time of acquisition might receive very different payments under the Swedish method of valuation. Variants on the Puerto Rican, French, and Swedish methods can be developed. The ideal would be a system that is both evenhanded and simple to implement. Such a system for American conditions has yet to be devised.

Assuming that, whatever method of valuation is chosen, the price paid will exclude the value attributable to public actions, it is undesirable to authorize covert acquisitions to keep the price down. The French government bought much land at Languedoc-Roussillon through straw parties and paid low prices because the public remained unaware of the development plans. This was before the use of preemption in ZADs had been tested, and the government feared relying on a new technique for such a vast project. However, the outcome of secrecy, in addition to inexpensive land acquisition, was widespread and lasting public resentment. In any event, secrecy is incompatible with the planning requirements that are recommended here.

The European and Puerto Rican programs and the *Code* all include the requirement that land bank acquisitions be in accord with adopted plans and/or be approved by the relevant planning agency. These requirements are vital. They assure public accessibility to information about which land might be acquired and curb possibilities of the abuse of acquisition powers by the land bank agency. Because the plans to which the acquisitions must conform are of a general nature, they do not bind the land bank agency to use specific parcels for specific uses.

There is one issue to be resolved concerning planning requirements: to which level of government's plans must the land bank acquisition proposals conform? If the land banking is carried out by a state, the Puerto Rican and *Code* provisions concerning the approval of acquisition proposals by the Puerto Rico Planning Board or the state planning board are appropriate. However, if the land banking power rests with another level of government or with some other agency, such as an SEM or SAFER, there may be a problem of multiple, inconsistent plans. The degree of consistency between local, regional, and state plans varies widely, and in many locations there are no land use plans at one or more of these levels of government. Even if there are both local and regional plans, it is rare for states to review them for consistency with their plans, if such exist. Therefore, the European practice of provincial or national review and approval of lower level plans so that there is a consistency among the tiers of plans is not a model readily adaptable to the present relationship of the state to regions and local governments in this country.

If land banking is limited to major development, such as that described in the *Code* as the development of regional impact, then it is probable that there would be state plans for the siting of such development and it is reasonable to provide that a land bank agency, however constituted, should obtain state planning board approval of its acquisition proposals.

If land banking is authorized for all development sites, the issue is harder to resolve. It would be logically consistent to require that whatever level of government is authorized to engage in land banking should conform to its own plans. If some agency that is not a unit of a general purpose government, such as a regional planning commission or an SEM, is authorized to be a land bank agency, it could be required to act consistently with the plans either of all governments having planning jurisdiction over the area proposed for acquisition or only of the highest level of government. The choice here will be shaped within a state by the relative strengths of state and local governments.

If a nonstate land bank agency is dependent on state funds, should the state have a planning veto power? For example, if a county land bank agency proposed to acquire land in conformity with the county plan, should the state have the right to refuse to fund an acquisition that would not be in accord with the state land use plan? If we were to follow the European practice, there would be no grant unless the proposal was in accord with the state plan. Similarly, if a state land bank agency applies for federal funds, should the federal government have a planning veto power? Many American grant programs, particularly those of the federal government, have avoided this issue by omitting substantive planning requirements or by stating federal policy in very general terms. In this way local autonomy has been preserved. If one favors a policy role for the grantor of acquisition funds, it is necessary to recognize that creating a planning veto at the state level, and especially at the federal level, is counter to prevailing American practice.

Land banks can be expected to be profitable undertakings over time. In the short run they face two difficult financial problems—assembling large sums for land acquisition and operating with little or no revenue. The larger the scope of the land bank's activity and the farther in advance of development it acquires land, the longer delayed will be its shift to a profitable operation. Funds in the early years are needed for land acquisition, land improvement, administration, taxes, and payment of the carrying costs of borrowings.

Federal, state, and local government and the private sector are the potential sources of funds. There are a number of means by which the funds can be made available. The Advisory Commission on Intergovernmental Relations lists them as follows:

The agencies' operations could be financed, as appropriate, through direct appropriations, charges and rents, grants, sales of land, and borrowing, if authorized. Borrowing authority could be granted on a revenue basis in anticipation of land sales and rents. Revenue from land sales and rent could provide a major source of income and a significant part of the operations of State land development agencies could be on a revolving fund basis after an initial appropriation of working capital, supplemented only as needed by subsequent direct appropriations or borrowing.[60]

Virtually all land bank advocates believe that federal financial participation is essential to place land bank agencies in a position to acquire land at requisite speed and scale. The proposals differ as to what form the federal assistance might take and include grants, loans, earmarked trust funds, and guarantees. The Douglas Commission recommended the creation of a federal revolving fund to make loans to local land bank agencies.[61] The Advisory Commission on Intergovernmental Relations recommended federal grants, loans, and loan guarantees:

Section 704 of the Housing and Urban Development Act of 1965 (the Federal program for advance acquisition) could be amended to include capital grants for the acquisition of land for public facilities and large-scale urban and new community development. In addition, Title X of the National Housing Act (the land purchase and development loan guarantee program) could be expanded to include low interest loans to State land development agencies for land purchase and site development. . . .

The large initial investment and extended holding period necessary in a successful and on-going program of advance acquisition has proven to be a major deterrent for States and localities already hard pressed to support current operating and construction programs.

. . . it seems clear that for State land development agencies to accomplish their objective of carefully planned acquisition of land for future urban use, they must be in a position to acquire land considerably in advance of development. The ready availability of Federal loans, at the time when they are needed, and at low interest rates would help provide States with the resources to enter actively into a land acquisition program.[62]

Although the advance acquisition program no longer exists, community development grants under the Community Development Act of 1974 may be, and are being, used for land bank acquisitions.

If federal financial support is critical, there is also the expectation that state assistance will be needed. Appropriations for grants and/or loans are the most direct form of aid. Land bank agency bonds could be backed by the full faith and credit of the state. Taxes, including some portion of real estate transfer taxes and/or a capital gains tax on development, could be placed in a special trust fund to provide a source of grants or loans to land bank agencies.

Most local governments have a very limited capacity for funding land acquisition. Most must rely on bond issues and borrowing and need state or federal backing either to obtain favorable bond ratings or to borrow at low interest. If local governments were authorized to form mixed public-private corporations akin to the French SEMs, they could seek participation from local interests concerned with development.

The three European countries are sources of some alternative approaches to funding land acquisition. The Swedish government offers much more favorable loan terms for land to be leased rather than sold—a loan of 95 percent of site value is repayable over forty years at market interest with repayment of the principal deferred for ten years if the land is to be leased, while the terms are ten years with principal deferred two years if land is to be sold. Deferring principal payments on loans long enough for revenues from the land to cover loan repayments is of significant assistance to a land bank agency.

The Bank of Netherland Municipalities, capitalized in equal shares by the state and the member municipalities, is the principal source of land bank loans in the Netherlands. The bank is able to attract private investment, particularly from institutional investors, offering a source of funds that would not be available to many of the municipalities acting individually.

French acquisitions are funded by state loans whose terms vary from program to program depending on government priorities. Whatever the terms, they are very favorable when compared to private borrowing costs. Government loans are not available unless projects accord with budget priorities in the national economic plan. SAFERs receive subsidized loans plus direct state grants equal to 2 percent of the cost of all acquisitions and the revenue from all sales. There are other sources of funds. The departments tax subdivision in Picturesque Zones and earmark the revenue for open space acquisition in those zones. The tax is a fixed charge per lot with additional increments as the lot size increases. The regional councils levy a tax and earmark part of the revenue for grants to municipalities for land bank acquisition. The grants vary as to percentage of land acquisition cost in accord with regional council priorities.

Stockholm's long-term practice of granting sixty-year leases with no provision for rent revision and Amsterdam's fifty-year leases, revised only for inflation or deflation, are startling illustrations of how to prevent a land bank from becoming self-supporting. The objective of subsidizing housing costs could have been met in many other ways without fixing land use and creating large inequities between tenants of old and new housing.

State legislation must be explicit as to which taxes will be applicable to land bank agency holdings. A number of taxes, including special assessments, transfer tax, capital gains tax, and real property tax, could be imposed. The Puerto Rican legislation exempts the Land Administration from all except the real property tax, the tax most likely to pose a serious conflict between the interests of the land bank agency and the jurisdictions that levy the tax. As the *Code* commentary notes, local governments and school districts are highly dependent on the real property tax for their revenues. If large tracts of land within jurisdictions providing a number of public services become exempt, either the tax burden must be shifted to other property owners or services must be reduced. These jurisdictions would be likely to oppose state law exempting land bank holdings from the real property tax. In more rural areas with few school children and no public sewers, public water, police force, library, or other public services, large-scale land bank acquisition could forestall development and the accompanying need to raise taxes to provide new services. Therefore, these jurisdictions would be less affected by real property tax exemption for land bank property.

From the perspective of the land bank agency, the obligation to pay real property taxes creates one further need for revenue; for land acquired early in the life of the agency the taxes will be a burden at a time when the land is generating little or no income. This may cause pressure on the agency to dispose of land sooner than it otherwise might choose. The Advisory Commission on Intergovernmental Relations recommends that the state make payments in lieu of taxes to local tax jurisdictions, equal in amount to lost revenues, for all lands held in reserve by land bank agencies. If the assessment is at the market value, this merely shifts the burden from the agency to the state and may not alleviate the pressure to sell prematurely.

The *Code* offers several real property tax alternatives other than full market value assessment or exemption and proposes that the agency pay whichever would be the highest tax. Instead, a state might adopt one of the alternatives, the proposal to set the tax at a percentage of the gross rental income. The tax would fluctuate with the rental value of the land, which is fair to the agency. Further, the tax would be likely to provide the taxing jurisdictions with revenue compatible with the cost of the services provided to the agency lands.

Reducing local government reliance on the real property tax is highly desirable but is a reform beyond the scope of this study.

The Puerto Rican law authorizes the Land Administration to act as developer of its land but, so far, it has not done so. The *Code* contains no such enabling provision, thereby committing a land bank agency to dispose of its holdings when it is timely for them to be developed. In the American setting it probably is preferable for the land bank agency not to be the developer. Instead, land planned for public use, such as for parks, schools, and roads, would be transferred to the appropriate public agencies. Land planned for private open space use, such as farming or forestry, would be leased or sold subject to easements barring development. The remaining land would be sold or leased to the private sector for development in accord with detailed public plans.

The French innovation of the mixed public-private company is one alternative that merits consideration as a developer of land bank sites. With state, local, and private participation, each partner to the enterprise contributes to acquisition, site preparation, and development in accord with its abilities and resources. The SEMs have the further advantage of access to the government- and bank-backed SCET, which, for a contract fee, provides legal and financial advice and assists them in obtaining acquisition and development funds. A comparable structure here could provide financial security and strong links between all parties involved in the development process. Particularly where the development is of large, high-density sites, there will be a major role for the public sector. Better coordination of development may be achieved by creating an agency in which public agencies participate jointly with private entrepreneurs.

There is a difference of opinion as to whether enabling legislation should fix a limit on the time during which land can be held in reserve. Those who favor a limit are concerned that agencies will be insufficiently responsive to changing needs for land. Others say that carrying costs will be a sufficient pressure on the agencies to dispose of land at an early date. In the United States, there is likely to be a greater problem with disposition too early than with extended retention. The Douglas Commission recommended setting a maximum holding period but did not suggest how long it should be.[63]

The *Code* reflects the reporters' concern that ossification may overtake a land bank agency, yet does not require disposal within a given time. It recommends that, if an agency fails to dispose of land within twenty years of its acquisition, the state planning agency and the municipality in which the land is located may act to require the agency to dispose of the land. This provision places the power of decision with the state planning agency, which also has the option of allowing the land bank agency to continue holding the land.

France's SAFER law requires that land be disposed of within five years of acquisition or, under special circumstances, within ten years. Since the intent of the SAFER program is to acquire farm land, improve and/or replat it, and resell it for farming, a short holding period is desirable. However, the statutory limitation may be an occasional impediment, since the SAFERs may need longer to assemble several parcels and create a more efficient farm unit. French law limits the duration of the right of preemption in development districts but does not require land, once acquired, to be sold within any stated period.

The traditional practice in Sweden was to acquire land whenever it came on the market, often several decades ahead of need. Now, with strong land use controls, explicit statutory language on the price to be paid for expropriated land, and tighter municipal budgets, it is likely that most land will be acquired only a few years in advance of development. In the Netherlands, a turnover time of several years already is customary.

With the exception of the SAFERs, none of the European programs calls for the disposition of land within a given period, and there is no indication that land bank agencies are thought to hold on to land too long.

There are two issues here: what interest in land should be conveyed, and how should the price be set? Land can be conveyed by lease, sale, sale subject to conditions, or gift. The price can be set with reference to market value, acquisition price, intended use, agency costs during the holding period, and/or agency policy on return from land.

Land bank authorization statutes usually permit disposition by lease or sale and may permit gifts to public agencies, particularly for subsidized housing. The prevailing preference among operating agencies is for the use of a long-term lease, because this permits the land bank agency to benefit from appreciation in land value, either through increased rents or through a new lease for more intensive use. Swedish and Dutch cities vary in their methods of land disposition; a fair generalization may be that they would prefer to lease all land but that many must sell some land in order to obtain immediate cash to pay off debts incurred by acquisition. Swedish leases are for an indefinite number of years but, at stated intervals, municipalities may terminate them on showing that the land is needed for another use. When this occurs, the municipality must pay the lessee what is then the value of structures on the site.

French disposal terms vary with the land bank program and the intended use of the land. At Fos, the public has retained control by leasing port and industrial sites so that terms can be adjusted to increase the competitive attraction of the port. Land in development zones usually is sold. SAFERs sell land subject to the condition that the buyer's family must farm the land for fifteen years. This is a very short restriction period; while the land is placed in more productive agricultural use than previously, the government subsidies to the SAFERs pay for a public benefit sharply limited in time.

The Puerto Rico Land Administration is relying primarily on leasing, and most American commentators agree that leasing is preferable to sale. As the Douglas Commission said, "Wherever feasible, long-term leases should be the preferred method of disposing of any public land, and lease terms should be set so as to permit reassembly of properties for future replanning and development."[64]

A major advantage of a land bank is that it can set land prices so as to attract the desired use to a particular site. Unless the government allows a deficit operation, as has been the practice for Dutch cities, this flexibility in pricing is constrained by the need for the land bank agency to be solvent. The usual practice in Europe is for industrial and commercial site prices to be set high enough to provide a subsidy for housing sites. Stockholm leases office and residential land at a fixed unit price regardless of the acquisition and improvement costs at any given site. The totality of lease prices is calculated to cover the interest on loans, acquisition and improvement costs, and administration costs. In the Netherlands, the state sets regional maximum prices for land. In France, sites for subsidized housing are sold at a lower price than sites for private housing. SAFERs sell farmland to whomever they consider the "best" purchaser from the perspective of farm use rather than to the highest bidder.

The practice of Stockholm and a number of Dutch cities of granting long lease terms with little or no provision for rent revision is not recommended. This practice has led to irrational variations in rents, to the consequent unwillingness of tenants in low rent sites to move, and to inadequate income for the land bank agencies.

The *Code* recommends that sales below the market price be authorized only to local governments. The Puerto Rico Land Administration Act permits such sales if the developer accepts a limited return. This is enforced by a provision for the reversion of the title to the Land Administration should the developer violate the provisions.

This concludes the review of the principal issues that must be resolved as part of the process of land bank authorization. The arguments for land banking have been made, and the experiences with it in other countries have been analyzed. Now it is for the reader to decide whether the new land use control capabilities that would result from the use of land banking are significant enough to justify the very considerable effort required to bring about its adoption.

From my perspective, the effort seems warranted and the prospect of success sufficient. We are facing a long period of continued urban growth. Development under our present system of land use controls is widely agreed to be inefficient, unattractive, and unsatisfying. Respect for the natural environment and recognition of human needs are increasing. New Jersey's fair share housing decisions, Wisconsin's wetlands protection under the public trust doctrine, and New York's architectural preservation decision rejecting a private right to the increment in value contributed by the public sector all exemplify shifts in attitude. With these shifts comes increased support for public intervention in private land use decisions. I do not believe that we will accept a system of public intervention that is avowedly inequitable to landowners, such as a system that restricts some urban fringe land to farming and to sale at the farm use value while permitting other comparable land to be developed intensively and to be sold at the value for that development. Nor do I believe that we will accept a system that is altogether equitable but that, like the Swedish and Dutch systems, limits landowners to the rural use value of their land. I believe that we would accept a system that assures substantial equity, that offers a return for privately created value, and that calls for public purchase only for the larger, more intensive developments.

For those prepared to work for land banking in the United States, the most important lessons to learn from Sweden, the Netherlands, and France are that the agencies authorized to act must have constituencies supportive of their goals, that these agencies must have enough money available to buy land when the need or opportunity arises, and that the national government (and, in the United States, the state governments) must be prepared to provide most of the financial backing for the agencies. These observations may be obvious, yet, where the European programs have foundered, one or more of these elements has been lacking.

The Puerto Rico Land Administration and the New York Urban Development Corporation are forerunners of American land banking. Community Development grants arc funding other land bank acquisitions. At last there is a combination of concern about the quality of urban growth and recognition of the inadequacy of past efforts at growth management that make the time propitious for the widespread inauguration of land bank programs.


## APPENDIX A

Land Administration Act of Puerto Rico

An Act*

To create the Puerto Rico Land Administration; to fix its powers and duties; and to appropriate funds for the carrying out of the purposes of this act.

Statement of Motives

It is hereby declared:

(a) That the Commonwealth of Puerto Rico is one of the most densely populated areas in the world; that urban lands, or lands adapted to urban development, are monopolized and kept unused by their owners, which creates an artificial shortage of land and raise in price of other properties and staple commodities; that the speedy raise in the price of land makes it impossible for persons of moderate or low resources to purchase land in appropriate areas, and forces such persons to build homes outside of close-to-town areas and far from their places of work and other activities; that the raise in the price of land makes for undesirable urban expansions, which, in turn, creates serious financial problems to the Commonwealth and municipal governments, as the costs of providing public services such as roads, water removal, public parks, public health, fire prevention and fire fighting, police vigilance, and others such as are necessary for the protection of life and property, so essential for the development of a community, increase several times; that the raise in the price of land increases the overhead cost of industrial and commercial enterprises and, therefore, sets their products at a disadvantage in commercial competition locally as well as abroad; that the relatively speedy raise in the price of land increases differences in income, inasmuch as unused land in Puerto Rico, both urban and rural, is controlled, to a large extent, by a small number of persons;

(b) that this ever-increasing price of land cannot be controlled, nor the problems thereby created can be solved, by any of the tools available to the

* Puerto Rico, Laws, Statutes, *Laws of Puerto Rico Annotated*, Act 13, 16 May 1962.

Commonwealth and municipal governments; that the levy of taxes and the regulations of physical planning are insufficient; that the regulation on subdivision and zoning operates prospectively for undeveloped and underdeveloped areas and cannot prevent the undesirable, but legal, use of the land; and that the regulation on land subdivision is insufficient to control either the expansion of city limits or the disconnected and inadequate expansion of the cities;

(c) that the raise in the price of land also affects or prevents the implementing of the master plans and is a cause of worry for the public conglomerate and constitutes a serious problem, to control which available public funds may be put to maximum use, by authorizing the acquisition of private property whenever necessary;

(d) that it is in the public interest to avoid, as soon as possible, the excessive and disproportionate increase in the market price of land.

It is hereby declared, as a matter of legislative determination, the desirability of the approval of the provisions of this act, as a necessary public policy; and, likewise, it is hereby declared that the land reserve authorized in this act constitutes in itself a public end.

It is the intent of the Legislative Assembly that the activities of the Administration hereby created promote, in a planned and efficient manner, the welfare, the economic freedom and the social justice of the present and future inhabitants of Puerto Rico through the efficient utilization of the land and the fitting out of new areas anywhere in Puerto Rico, to insure a better balance between the needs of future communities and the economic and geographic media; preserve historical values and the natural values of the land, the beaches, the forests, and landscapes; insure the best conditions of health, safety, and social life; larger recreational facilities and greater and better essential services; avoid the concentration of landholdings for speculative purposes by any one person; and develop programs for the acquisition of the necessary land for the carrying out of any type of project, by itself, or through or jointly with agencies of the Commonwealth of Puerto Rico or of the Government of the United States, or with private entities; promote action leading to a better utilization of and profiting from the land on the basis of more reasonable costs in behalf of the welfare of the community, especially in the towns and areas adapted to urban development, creating adequate land reserves in order thus to assist the Commonwealth of Puerto Rico in the carrying out of its public policy of industrial, commercial and housing development, and of providing public services so that there may be an orderly development in keeping with the master plans, and of more effectively meeting its governmental responsibility of preserving the health, safety and welfare of the inhabitants of Puerto Rico at the highest level compatible with community resources. Likewise, it is the intent of the Legislative Assembly that the Administration hereby created exercise all necessary powers and rights, in order to carry out all its activities; to acquire any right, interest or easement in any property which favors the development, utilization and conservation of open areas in their natural state, protect water bodies, preserve soils and forest, and the beauty of places devoted to public use, protect the public from the effects of floods, and facilitate the utilization and development of areas which are reserved for projects of public interest, especially those related to the health, safety and welfare of the inhabitants; to make use of such portion of its real property as may be necessary, establishing, in so doing, such conditions or limitations as it may deem necessary or proper regarding its use and utilization; to insure compliance with the provisions of this act and prevent that the use given to such property may facilitate or tend to create or maintain undesirable or adverse conditions to the public interest; to impose such restrictions, when selling or otherwise disposing of its property, as will limit the profits which, in the price to be paid by the public, is to be made by the acquirer regarding the land; and to evolve land rehabilitation projects through drying, filling, irrigating, or any other proper means for increasing land utilization.

Be It Enacted by the Legislature of Puerto Rico:

Section 1. This act may be cited as the "Puerto Rico Land Administration Act."

Section 2. The following terms, whenever used in this act, shall have the following meanings, except where the context otherwise clearly indicates:

(a) "Administration" means the Puerto Rico Land Administration.

(b) "Board" means the Governing Board of the Administration.

(c) "Bonds" means bonds, notes, or other obligations or evidences of indebtedness.

(d) "Agency" means branch, department, bureau, commission, board, office, dependency, instrumentality, public corporation, political subdivision, or any other government body.

(e) "United States" includes the Federal Government and its agencies, territories, possessions and political subdivisions, and the states of the Union and agencies thereof.

Section 3. (a) There is hereby created a body corporate and politic which shall constitute a public corporation or government instrumentality having a juridical personality separate and apart from that of the Commonwealth of Puerto Rico, and shall be known as the Puerto Rico Land Administration.

(b) The powers of the Administration shall be exercised, and its general policy determined, by a Governing Board composed of the Governor of Puerto Rico, who shall be chairman, the Chairman of the Puerto Rico Planning Board, who shall be vice-chairman, the Secretaries of the Treasury, Public Works and Agriculture, the Director of the Urban Renewal and Housing Corporation, the Economic Development Administrator, and two additional members to be appointed by the Governor, with the advice and consent of the Senate, for a term of four years and until their successors are appointed and qualify.

The members of the Board shall receive no compensation for their services as such.

Section 4. The Executive Director of the Administration shall be appointed by the Board, shall hold office at the will of the appointing authority and until his successor is appointed and qualifies, and shall discharge such duties and bear such responsibilities as may be assigned to him by the appointing authority, pursuant to the bylaws of the Administration. The bylaws of the Administration may provide for the delegation to the Executive Director of such powers and duties of the Administration as the Board may deem proper.

Section 5. The Administration shall have a secretary, who shall hold office at the will of the appointing authority and until his successor is appointed and qualifies.

Section 6. The debts, obligations, contracts, bonds, notes, debentures, receipts, expenditures, accounts, funds, printed matter, and property of the Administration shall be deemed to be those of the said Administration and not those of the Commonwealth of Puerto Rico or of any agency, official or employee thereof.

Section 7. Duties and Powers. The Administration shall have a juridical personality of its own and may exercise such rights and powers as may be necessary or proper for the carrying out of the purposes hereof, including, but not limited to, the following:

(a) To have perpetual succession;

(b) To approve, amend or repeal bylaws;

(c) To appoint all its officials, agents and employees, and to grant and impose on them such powers, faculties, responsibilities, and authority as it may deem proper; to determine their duties; to fix, change and pay such compensation as it may determine, subject to the policy, bylaws, regulations and procedures approved by the Board. All personnel matters of the Administration shall be regulated without subjection to the laws governing the Office of Personnel of the Government of Puerto Rico or to the rules and regulations promulgated by said Office;

(d) To adopt, alter, and use a seal which shall be judicially noticed;

(e) To draft, adopt, amend, and repeal rules and regulations governing the policies of its activities in general, and to exercise and discharge the powers and duties granted to and imposed on it by law. Upon the approval and promulgation of said rules and regulations by the Board, the same shall have the force of law as soon as filed in Spanish and English in the offices of the Secretary of State. Such rules and regulations shall be published in the Bulletin of the Commonwealth of Puerto Rico and shall, not later than ten days after filed in the offices of the Secretary of State, be published in a newspaper of general circulation;

(f) To sue and be sued;

(g) To establish the accounting system required for an adequate control of all expenditures and revenues pertaining to or administered by it, in consultation with the Secretary of the Treasury;

(h) To have full powers for the carrying out of the public policy of the Commonwealth of Puerto Rico as herein established;

(i) To make contracts and to execute all instruments necessary or expedient in the exercise of any or all of its powers;

(j) To acquire property in any lawful manner, including, but without limitation, the following: by purchase, option of purchase, purchase by installments, at public auction, by lease, legacy, devise, assignment, exchange, gift, or by the exercise of the right of eminent domain in the manner provided by this act and the laws of Puerto Rico; and to hold, maintain, use and avail itself of, or utilize any real or personal property, including, but not limited to, securities and other movables or any interest therein, deemed by it necessary or desirable to carry out its purposes;

(k) To sell, grant options of sale, sell by installments, convey, exchange, lease or otherwise dispose of its property in the course of its normal operations, except by gift, which may only be made for the benefit of the Commonwealth of Puerto Rico and its agencies. There shall not be considered as a gift any disposal of property, or of any right or interest therein, which, in fulfillment of the purposes hereof may be effected by the Administration at a lower price than it paid for same, or lower than the value of such property, or right or interest therein, in the market;

(l) To sell or otherwise dispose of any real or personal property which in the judgment of the Administration is no longer necessary to carry out the purposes of this act subject to the same limitation imposed thereupon by the preceding paragraph;

(m) To borrow money, give security and issue bonds for any of its corporate purposes or for the purposes of funding, refunding, paying, or discharging any of its outstanding or assumed bonds or obligations, and to secure payment of its bonds and of any and all other obligations by pledging, mortgaging, or otherwise encumbering all or any of its contracts, revenues, income or property;

(n) To accept in its own behalf, or in behalf of the Commonwealth of Puerto Rico, financial aid of any nature, including subsidies, gifts, advances and suchlike, from the Commonwealth of Puerto Rico or its agencies, from the United States Government or its agencies, and from private persons; to enter into contracts, leases, agreements, or other transactions with both or any of such governments or their agencies, and to expend the proceeds of the funds so received for the purposes of this act;

(o) To have complete control and supervision of any and all of its property and activities, including the power to determine the character of and necessity for all its expenditures and the manner in which they shall be allowed, incurred, and paid, without regard to the provisions of any laws governing the expenditure of public funds and such determination shall be final and conclusive upon all officers and employees of the Commonwealth of Puerto Rico, without prejudice to the provisions of section 10 of this act;

(p) To prescribe by regulation the policies governing all matters with relation to the personnel of the Administration. Such policies shall, insofar as compatible with the efficient effectuation of the purposes of the Administration, be similar to those governing the personnel of the commonwealth government;

(q) To acquire, in the manner provided in this act, private property and keep it in reserve, for the benefit of the people of Puerto Rico, for the use of the Commonwealth of Puerto Rico or its agencies. Whenever properties or property rights are condemned for specific purposes of public-work development and social welfare, such purposes shall be carried out within a period of year which shall never exceed fifteen, from the date of acquisition. The property so acquired may be assigned or conveyed to the Commonwealth of Puerto Rico or its agencies, under reasonable terms and conditions;

(r) To enter, after obtaining permission to do so from the owner or holder, or his representative, any land or premises, for the purpose of making surveys, taking measurements, or conducting investigation with regard to the nature, conditions and price of such lands or premises, for the purposes of this act. Should the owner or holder, or his representative, refuse to grant permission to enter the property for the above mentioned purposes, any judge of the Court of First Instance shall, upon presentation to him of an affidavit setting forth the intention of the Administration to enter such lands or premises for the stated purposes, issue an order authorizing any official or officials, or employee or employees of the Administration to enter the property described in the affidavit, for the purposes mentioned in this provision;

(s) To acquire real property, urban or rural, which may be kept in reserve towards facilitating the continuation of the development of public work and social and economic welfare programs which may be under way or which may be undertaken by the Administration itself, by the Commonwealth of Puerto Rico or its agencies, and by private persons for the benefit of the above-mentioned public entities or of the community, including, but not limited to, housing and industrial development programs, in order to prevent the inflation brought about by speculative practices in the purchase-sale of real estate and to allow for populational growth in an organized and planned manner;

(t) To promote and share in the fitting out of new areas anywhere in Puerto Rico, within the frame of the policies which will insure a better balance with regard to the needs of future communities, aiming, among other things, to preserve the natural values of the lands, beaches, forests, and landscapes; to insure the best conditions of health, safety, comfort, recreational facilities, essential services, and aesthetic activities; to preserve historical values; to insure the utilization of lands on the basis of the most reasonable costs in behalf of the welfare of the community; to this end, but not to be construed as a limitation, to develop programs for the acquisition of the necessary lands, and for encouraging all kinds of projects, such as will favor such development, either on its own or through or jointly with agencies of the Commonwealth of Puerto Rico or of the Government of the United States, or with private entities;

(u) To barter for the purpose of improving the utilization of the lands;

(v) To exercise all necessary powers and rights for developing land rehabilitation projects through drying, draining, filling, irrigating, or any other proper means for increasing land utilizations;

(w) To carry out by itself, or through or jointly with agencies of the Commonwealth of Puerto Rico or of the Government of the United States, or by means of covenants with private persons or entities, programs and work, including housing projects, to insure the most effective development and the fullest utilization, in keeping with the purposes of this act, of lands owned by the Administration, or by the Commonwealth or any of its agencies;

(x) To acquire any right or interest or easement in any property in order to: promote the development, utilization and maintenance of open areas in their natural state so as to protect bodies of water; to protect the public from the effects of floods; to preserve soils and forests; to preserve the beauty of places devoted to public use, including green areas and public parks; and to facilitate the use and development of areas which are in reserve for projects of public interest, especially those related to the health, safety and welfare of the inhabitants;

(y) To enter into agreements with the Commonwealth of Puerto Rico and its agencies so as to acquire real property for them, to sell real property owned by them, or intervene in or carry out the development of programs in connection with such property, subject to the laws that fix the official activities of said agencies. To such ends, the parties to these covenants are hereby authorized to make such transfers of funds as may be necessary;

(z) To establish, in disposing of any real property, all such conditions and limitations regarding its use or utilization as it may deem necessary and desirable to insure the fulfillment of the purposes of this act, so that the use made of said property will not facilitate or tend to create undesirable conditions, or conditions adverse to the public interest, which this act aims to protect. Whenever the Administration sells or otherwise disposes of property for the acquirer to erect thereon housing developments or any other type of project involving a subsequent sale to private persons, it may fix such restrictions as it may deem necessary for the effectuation of the purposes of this act. In any event, it shall include one limiting, through a proper formula, the profits to be had by the acquirer with respect to the land and all other costs of the project;

(a-1) To transmit, in perpetuity or for a limited time, to urbanizers, for housing developments, and to other persons for the undertaking of any work having social interest, any right, real or personal, or any interest in the lands that it may hold; and

(b-1) To sell, whenever it may deem it necessary and desirable, lands or any interest therein, at such price as it may consider reasonable in order to lower the cost of the houses or to fulfill any of the purposes of this act.

Section 8. The Administration may, subject to the applicable regulations of the Planning Board, subdivide the lands acquired by any of the means authorized, by law, according to the topography of the land, its fertility, the local conditions, and the desirable policies to achieve the best development or utilization of such lands for the benefit of the Puerto Rican community, and thus to fulfill the purposes of this act. The size and value of such lands shall be determined by the Administration on the basis of the existing needs in the zone, urban or rural, where a program of public work or activity is to be undertaken for the better utilization of such lands. The Administration shall promulgate the necessary regulations to fulfill the purposes of this section.

Section 9. All funds of the Administration, including the proceeds from the sale of its bonds, shall be deposited with recognized depositories for funds of the Commonwealth of Puerto Rico, but such funds shall be kept in a separate account or accounts registered in the name of the Administration. Disbursements shall be made by the Administration according to its own regulations and budgets.

Section 10. The Controller of the Commonwealth of Puerto Rico shall, whenever he may deem it necessary, but at least once a year, examine all accounts and books of the Administration, and shall report thereon to the Legislative Assembly, the Governor, and any other public officer, as he may see fit. No provision of this act shall be construed as a limitation to the power of the Controller of Puerto Rico.

Section 11. The public corporations of the Commonwealth are hereby authorized to assign and convey to the Administration, at the latter's request and under such reasonable terms and conditions as they may agree upon without the need for auction or other legal formalities additional to the execution of the proper instrument, any property or interest therein, including property already devoted to public use, such as the Administration may deem it necessary or desirable to possess for the effectuation of its own purposes.

The Secretary of Public Works may, free of any cost whatsoever, convey to the Administration, with the approval of the Governor, such lands of the Commonwealth of Puerto Rico as said Administration may need for the effectuation of its purposes. This provision shall not be construed in the sense of authorizing the assignment or conveyance of property specifically devoted to other purpose by legislative provision.

Section 12. On request of the Administration, the Commonwealth of Puerto Rico may acquire, by purchase, condemnation, or by any other lawful means, for the use and benefit of the Administration, in the manner provided for by this act and by the Commonwealth laws on condemnation, the title to any real property and the interests therein that may be necessary or convenient for its purposes. The Administration shall advance the necessary funds estimated as the value of the property or rights to be acquired. Any difference in value which may be decreed by the competent court may be paid from the public treasury, but the Administration shall be under obligation to reimburse said difference. After reimbursement in full is made, the title to said property shall be transferred to the Administration, upon order of the court to that effect. In those cases where the Governor of the Commonwealth of Puerto Rico should deem it necessary and convenient that the title to the property and rights so acquired be directly recorded in behalf of the Administration so as to speed up the fulfillment of the ends and purposes for which the same was created, he may so request from the court at any time within the condemnation proceedings, and the court shall so order. The power hereby conferred on the Governor shall not limit or restrain the authority of the Administration to institute itself the condemnation proceedings when it may deem it convenient.

Section 13. All real and personal property or interests therein necessary to carry out the purposes of this act, are declared of public utility, also every work or project carried out by the Administration, and said real and personal property or any less estate or interest therein, may be condemned without the previous declaration of public utility provided in the General Law of Eminent Domain, either by condemnation proceedings instituted by the Commonwealth of Puerto Rico, or directly by the Administration.

Section 14. (a) In any proceeding which has been or may be instituted by and in the name of the Administration for the acquisition of land for the purposes specified in this act, the Administration may file in the same cause, at the time the petition is filed or at any time before judgment is rendered, a declaration of taking for the acquisition and material delivery of the property the object of condemnation, signed by the person or entity empowered by law to seek the condemnation in question, declaring that said property is sought for the use of the Administration. Said declaration of taking and material delivery shall contain and be accompanied by: (1) a statement of the authority under which, and the public use for which, the acquisition of said property is sought; (2) a description of the property sufficient for the identification thereof; (3) a statement of the estate or interest in said property the acquisition of which is sought for the utilization purposes specified in this act; (4) a plan, in the case of property which can be so represented; (5) the fixing of the sum of money estimated by the Administration to be just compensation for the property the acquisition of which is sought;

(b) As soon as said declaration of taking and delivery is filed and the deposit is made in the court, for the benefit and use of the natural or artificial person or persons entitled thereto, of the amount estimated as compensation and specified in said declaration, title to the said property in fee simple absolute, or such less estate or interest therein as is specified in said declaration, shall vest in the Administration or in the Commonwealth of Puerto Rico, as the case may be, and such property shall be deemed to be condemned and acquired for the use of the Administration or of the Commonwealth of Puerto Rico. The right to just compensation for the property shall vest in the person or persons entitled thereto; and said compensation shall be ascertained and awarded in said proceeding and established by judgment therein; and the said judgment shall include, as part of the just compensation awarded, interest at the rate of six per centum (6%) per annum on the amount finally awarded as the value of the property as of the date of taking, from said date to the date of payment; interest shall not be allowed on so much thereof as shall have been deposited and paid into the court. No sum so deposited and paid into the court shall be subject to any charge for any reason whatsoever;

(c) Upon application of the parties in interest, the court may order that the money deposited in the court, or any part thereof, be paid forthwith for or on account of the just compensation to be awarded in said proceeding. If the compensation finally awarded in respect to said property, or any part thereof, shall exceed the amount of the money so received by any entitled person, the court shall enter judgment against the Administration or the Commonwealth of Puerto Rico, as the case may be, for the amount of the difference;

(d) Upon the filing of the declaration of taking, the court shall have power to fix the time within which, and the terms upon which, the natural or artificial persons in possession of the property the object in the proceeding shall surrender material possession to the expropriating party. The court shall have power to make such orders in respect to encumbrances, rentals, taxes, insurance and other charges, if any, burdening the property, as shall be just and equitable. No appeal in any such cause, nor any bond or undertaking given therein, shall operate to prevent or delay the acquisition by, or the vesting of the title to such property in, the Administration or the Commonwealth of Puerto Rico, as the case may be, and its material delivery thereto.

(e) In any case in which the Administration shall have acquired title in fee simple to and the possession of any land and the structures located thereon, during the course of a comdemnation proceeding, before final judgment is rendered, and in which the Administration is obliged to pay the amount finally awarded as compensation, the Administration shall have power to destroy such structures erected on said land.

(f) In case of condemnation of property for the purposes of this act, the just compensation shall be based on the value in the market of such property, without taking into consideration any increase in such value due to the condemnation project having been announced and publicized.

The valuation to be made shall not include any increase due to well-founded and reasonable expectation that the property to be acquired by the Administration or by the Commonwealth, or other property similar thereto, or other situated within the locality where the former is situated, may now or later be required for public use or social benefit, or be necessary for some use to which it can be applied only by the Administration or the Commonwealth or any agency or instrumentality thereof with power for the condemnation of private property.

In case of condemnation, the just compensation shall likewise not include any new increase by reason of the public improvement or expenditures made in the locality by the Administration or the Commonwealth or any agency thereof, nor shall it include any increase by reason of any other work done by or at the initiative thereof, to effectuate the purposes if this act, when the increase be the result of plans or resolutions, officially adopted, for the acquisition of land for public works or for the purposes of this act.

(g) The provisions of Act No. 182, approved May 5, 1949, and of Act. No. 441, approved May 14, 1947, as amended, shall not apply in respect to the properties acquired by the Administration. In case of sale of real property acquired by condemnation and no longer useful for the purposes of this act or for the public purposes of the Commonwealth or any of its agencies, preference shall be given to the former owners of the condemned property, or in default thereof, to their forced heirs, subject to the conditions which the Administration may establish for the sale of said property. In no case, however, shall the Administration be obliged to sell to the former owner or to his heirs at a price lower than the market value of the property in question at the time it is sold by the Administration.

When the Administration shall determine that the acquired property or any part thereof is no longer useful for the purposes of this act or for the public purposes of the Commonwealth or its agencies, it shall notify the person or persons from whom said property was expropriated, or the forced heirs thereof, of their preferent right to require such property. The notification, showing the price and conditions of the sale offer, shall be sent by registered mail, if the addresses of the interested parties are known: if unknown, the notification shall be by edicts, published in a newspaper of general circulation once a week for two consecutive weeks. If the edict is published, it shall be presumed, subject to evidence to the contrary, that the address was unknown.

Upon expiration of the term of thirty (30) days from the notification by mail, or of forty (40) days from the publication of the last edict, which terms shall be unextendable, the Administration shall be at liberty to dispose of the property as best befits the public interest.    •

When the person or persons entitled to such preference accept, within the term prescribed by this section, the price and conditions of the sale, said person or persons shall be obliged to send to the Administration the amount of the value of the property, by certified check or in legal tender. If the aforesaid requisites are not complied with, acceptance of the preference shall have no validity whatsoever, and the Administration shall be entitled to dispose of the property as expressed in the preceding paragraph.

Section 15. The properties belonging to the Administration, and any interest in any property held by it, shall be exempt from the payment of all kinds of fees, taxes (except property taxes), commonwealth or municipal tariff fees or imposts, heretofore or hereafter required by law. This exemption covers the execution of all kinds of instruments, the prosecution of proceedings of any nature, or the issuance of certifications, and recording in the registries of property.

Section 16. (a) By authority of the Government of Puerto Rico, hereby granted, the Administration may issue and sell its own bonds from time to time, and have them outstanding;

(b) The Administration, through resolution or resolutions to that effect, shall determine everything related with the date; time of maturity; rate or rates of interest; denomination or denominations; series; form; registration or conversion privileges; medium of payment; place or places of payments; terms of redemption, with or without premium; date they may be declared due, even before their maturity; replacement of mutilated, destroyed, stolen or lost bonds, and all the other conditions and stipulations which it may consider convenient;

(c) The bonds may be sold at public or private sale for such price or prices not lower than ninety-five (95) per cent of the par value thereof as the Board shall determine; refunding bonds may be exchanged for outstanding bonds of the Administration on such terms as the Board may deem to be in the best interest of the Administration. All bonds of the Administration shall be negotiable instruments;

(d) The bonds of the Administration bearing the signature of the officers of the Administration in office on the date of the signing thereof, shall be valid and binding obligations, notwithstanding that before the delivery thereof and payment therefor any or all of the officers of the Administration whose signatures or facsimile signatures appear thereon have ceased to be such officers of the Administration;

(e) Temporary or interim bonds, receipts or certificates may be issued in such form and with such provisions as may be provided in such resolution or resolutions;

(f) Any resolution or resolutions authorizing bonds may contain provisions which shall be part of the contract with the bondholders: (1) as to the disposition of the entire gross or net revenue and present or future income of the Administration, including the pledging of all or any part thereof to secure payment of the bonds; (2) as to the covenant of pledging all or any part of the revenues, income of property of the Administration; (3) as to the setting aside of reserves for amortization funds, and the regulation and disposition thereof; (4) as to limitations on the purposes to which may be applied the proceeds of the sale of any issue of bonds made; (5) as to limitations on the issuance of additional bonds; (6) as to the procedure by which the terms of any resolution authorizing bonds, or any other contract with the bondholders may be amended or abrogated; (7) as to the amount of the bonds whose holders must consent thereto, and the manner in which such consent may be given; (8) as to the events, default, and terms and conditions upon which any or all of the bonds should become or may be declared due before maturity, and as to the terms and conditions upon which such declaration and its consequences may be waived; and (9) as to any other acts or conditions which may be necessary or convenient for the security of the bonds, or that may tend to make the bonds more marketable;

(g) No officer or employee of the Administration executing bonds shall be liable personally on the bonds;

(h) The Administration is authorized to purchase any outstanding bonds issued or assumed thereby, with any funds available thereof, at a price not exceeding the principal amount or the redemption price thereof plus the accrued interest;

(i) The bonds issued by the Administration shall be lawful investment and may be accepted as securities for all trust funds, special or public, whose investment or deposit is under the authority and jurisdiction of the Commonwealth Government or of any officer or employee thereof;

(j) The bonds and other obligations issued by the Administration shall not be a debt of the Commonwealth of Puerto Rico or of any of its agencies; nor shall such bonds or other obligations be payable out of any funds other than those of the Administration;

(k) The bonds issued by the Administration and the income deriving therefrom shall be exempt from taxes and imposts from the Commonwealth of Puerto Rico and its agencies;

(l) The Commonwealth of Puerto Rico does hereby pledge to, and agree with, any of its agencies, or with any agency of the Government of the United States or of any state of the Union, or with any person subscribing to or acquiring bonds or other obligations of the Administration, that it will not encumber, limit nor restrict the properties, incomes, revenues, rights or powers hereby vested in the Administration until all such bonds or other obligations at any time issued, together with the interest thereon, are fully met and discharged; and

(m) In addition to the rights which they may have, subject only to the restrictions arising from the contract, the bondholders shall be entitled to compel the Administration, its officers, agents or employees, by mandamus, action or proceeding at law or in equity, to fulfill any and all the terms, agreements or provisions contained in the contract of the Administration with or for the benefit of said bondholders, and to require that there be carried out or performed any of the resolutions and covenants of the Administration or of the duties required by this act. They may likewise, by action or proceeding at law, challenge any illegal act in violation of their rights on the part of the Administration.

Section 17. The provisions of Act No. 272, approved May 15, 1945, as heretofore or hereafter amended, shall be applicable to the Administration.

Section 18. Where the provisions of this act are in conflict with the provisions of any other act of the Legislature of Puerto Rico, the provisions of this act shall be controlling and no law hereafter passed shall be construed to apply to the Administration unless so specifically provided.

Section 19. No injunction shall be issued to prevent the application of this act or any part thereof.

Section 20. If any provision of this act is declared unconstitutional by any court, said judgment shall not affect the rest of the statute.

Section 21. There is hereby appropriated to the Administration, from unencumbered funds in the Commonwealth Treasury, up to the sum of twenty million (20,000,000) dollars to carry out the purposes of this act. From this sum there is hereby appropriated and placed at the disposal of the Administration, effective July 1, 1962, the sum of seven million (7,000,000) dollars, and the remaining thirteen million (13,000,000) dollars shall be appropriated and placed at the disposal of the Administration on July 1, 1963. For the initial expenses of organization and operation of the Administration there is hereby appropriated, from unencumbered funds in the Commonwealth Treasury, the additional sum of two hundred thousand (200,000) dollars.

Section 22. The Secretary of the Treasury is hereby authorized to advance to the Administration, from any available funds in the Commonwealth Treasury, the sums necessary to carry out the purposes of this act; provided, that the Secretary of the Treasury shall recover the sums advanced, on and after July 1, 1962, chargeable to the appropriation of seven million (7,000,000) dollars provided in Section 21 of this act.

Section 23. The Administration shall submit to the Legislative Assembly at the close of each fiscal year:

(1) A financial statement;
(2) A report on the transactions made by the Administration during the preceding fiscal year;
(3) A report on the status and progress of all the activities of the Administration since its creation, or since the date of the last of these reports.

Section 24. This act shall take effect immediately after its approval.

## APPENDIX B

A Model Land Development Code*

Article 6. Land Banking

PART 1

*State Land Reserve Agency*

Section 6–101.    *Land Reserve as a Public Purpose*

The acquisition of interests in land for the purpose of facilitating future

* Endorsed by the American Law Institute, 21 May 1975.

planning to maintain a public land reserve, and the holding and disposition thereof in accordance with the purposes of this Code, are hereby declared to be for the public purpose of achieving the land policy and land planning objectives of this State whether or not at the time of acquisition or expenditure of funds for acquisition or maintenance any particular future use, public or private, is contemplated for the land. Appropriations for, issuance of bonds for, and taxation for a land reserve system; acquisition of land for a land reserve by gift, purchase or condemnation; management of land so acquired; and disposition of land so acquired; are hereby declared to be for a valid public purpose.

Section 6–102.    *Organization of State Land Reserve Agency*

(1) There is hereby created a State Land Reserve Agency authorized to exercise the powers granted to it by this Article.

(2) The State Land Reserve Agency shall be an office within the [designate appropriate department of state government or create a new agency].

(3) The State Land Reserve Agency may employ a director and subordinate personnel necessary to carry out the powers conferred upon the Agency within the limits of available funds. The Agency may determine the conditions and terms of employment as if it were the board of directors of a private corporation under the laws of this State.

(4) The State Land Reserve Agency may by rule create one or more regional divisions having the same boundaries as a Regional Planning Division after consultation with the State Land Planning Agency and after complying with the procedures for designating regional divisions under Section 8–102(1).

(5) The Governor may designate a state advisory committee consisting of no more than [11] members to be appointed by him and to serve at his pleasure. For any region created under subsection (4) the Governor may designate a regional advisory committee.

Section 6–103.    *Land Reserve Policy*

(1) The State Land Reserve Agency shall adopt by rule and may amend from time to time a land reserve policy describing the general purposes for which it intends to acquire, hold and dispose of land under this Article.

(2) Before adopting any land reserve policy the Agency shall submit the proposed policy for review and comment to the State Land Planning Agency and any appropriate advisory committee created under Section 6–102.

(3) The State Land Reserve Agency shall not adopt any land reserve policy which the State Land Planning Agency has by order [disapproved] [determined to be inconsistent with a currently effective State Land Development Plan].

PART 2

*General Powers and Obligations of State Land Reserve Agency*

Section 6–201.    *Corporate Capacity and Financial Provisions*

(1) The State Land Reserve Agency shall [be regarded as if it were a private corporation and] have capacity to contract, to sue and be sued in its

name. It shall be liable in tort for its acts and omissions and those of its agents [to the same extent as the State is liable for acts and omissions concerning property belonging to the sovereign] [to the same extent as a private corporation is liable for acts and omissions concerning property owned by it].

(2) The Agency may apply for grants from state and federal government as [if it were] an Agency for this State and it may do everything necessary and proper to comply with the terms of a grant.

(3) The Agency may enter into contracts with local governments as provided in Section 6–501, receive funds from them, and acquire, manage and dispose of land pursuant to the agreement as if it were an agent of the government with whom the agreement has been signed.

(4) The Agency may receive funds appropriated to it by the State Legislature, and furnished to it by local governments pursuant to contracts under § 6–501, both for the purpose of carrying out its day-to-day operations and for the purpose of acquiring, managing and disposing of land.

(5) The Agency may receive funds appropriated to it [from funds raised for it by the issuance of general obligation bonds of this State in accordance with applicable law for the issuance of this type of bonds].

(6) The Agency may borrow money to make improvements to land held by it necessary for the management and retention of the land and give as security an interest in the land so improved.

(7) Any contract to improve land executed by the Agency is subject to the mechanics lien law of this State as if the Agency were a private corporation.

(8) The Agency may purchase land and subject it to a security interest to secure payment of the price.

(9) The Agency may receive land or funds by way of a life time or testamentary gift and hold or dispose of the land or funds subject to any conditions attached to the gift.

Section 6–202.    *Management of the Holdings of the Agency*

The State Land Reserve Agency may construct, demolish or repair existing or new improvements and otherwise manage any interest in land it may own. The Agency may enter into a lease for the purpose of maintaining the property and making appropriate use of the land while it is in the reserve. Any action taken under this Section shall be consistent with the land reserve policy adopted under § 6–103 and any other applicable regulations under this Code or other requirements of law.

Section 6–203.    *Taxation of the Agency and Its Property*

(1) The real estate owned by the State Land Reserve Agency [shall] [shall not] be subject to real property tax. A leasehold in land of the Agency [shall] [shall not] be subject to a real property tax. [The Agency shall pay in each tax year prorata to the real property taxing districts in which the land is situated a sum of money that is the largest of the sums calculated in the following manner:

(a) [15] percent of the gross rental income from the parcel;

(b) at the current levy of the taxing district on the assessed value of the land of the Agency in the last full tax year preceding the year of acquisition by the Agency;

(c) at the current levy of the district on a value representing [40] percent of the price paid by the Agency to acquire the land.]

(2) Notwithstanding any other provision in this or any other law of this State, gains arising to the Agency from disposition of a parcel of land by it [shall] [shall not] be subject to taxation. [If the realized gain exceeds [25] percent of the cost of the land sold, the gain in excess of [25] percent shall be distributed to the taxing districts in which the land is located in the same proportion as payments made during the previous tax year by the Agency in lieu of real property taxation under the preceding subsection. The [Department of Revenue] shall adopt rules to carry out the provisions of this Section.]

(3) The income of the Agency [shall] [shall not] be subject to the income or corporate franchise tax laws of this State [as if it were a private corporation].

(4) The Agency [shall] [shall not] be subject to excise, transfer taxes and other taxes not provided for in the preceding paragraphs arising from its activities as if it were a private corporation.

(5) Any special assessment or improvement tax imposed in accordance with the law applicable to the particular improvement on other land in the district [may] [may not] be imposed on the real estate of the Agency as if it were privately held land.

PART 3

*Acquisition of Land*

Section 6–301.    *Purposes of Acquisition*

(1) The State Land Reserve Agency may acquire any land that is used or is capable of being used to carry out the Agency's land reserve policy, and that the Agency by resolution finds necessary and proper in carrying out the policy. The land may be acquired from private owners and from governmental agencies of this State and of the United States.

(2) The State Land Reserve Agency may also acquire land for any lawful purposes of a local government pursuant to a contract authorized by § 6–501. Such acquisition must be consistent with the Agency's land reserve policy unless the acquisition is made solely with funds supplied by the local government.

(3) The power granted by this Article to acquire land includes the power to acquire any interest in land as defined in § 5–101.

(4) Land acquired under this Article shall be treated, for purposes of future disposition, as land acquired for planning purposes under § 5–401.

Section 6–302.    *Method of Acquisition*

(1) In acquiring land, the State Land Reserve Agency may acquire the land by purchase, gift, exchange, interagency transfer, devise or other means. It may use its own agents or licensed real estate brokers with or without disclosure to the seller of the fact that the Agency is the intended purchaser.

(2) The Agency may advertise for offers of sale and buy the parcels offered at the lowest price among the offers for comparable land. The Agency shall advertise its offer to buy for at least one day in each of three successive weeks and the advertisement shall state that sealed bids are requested and the time and place at which the offers will be opened. The advertisement shall describe in detail the characteristics of the land sought and shall state the time before which offers must be received. No offeror may change his offer after it is submitted. Nothing in this Section requires the Agency to accept any offer to sell, or prevents the Agency and a rejected offeror from negotiating subsequently for a sale to the Agency at a price comparable to or below that accepted on the opening date.

Section 6–303.    *Method of Payment for Acquired Land*

(1) The State Land Reserve Agency shall pay the price for a parcel of land to be acquired in cash at the time of delivery of the deed of transfer, or in any of the following ways which are acceptable to the seller:

(a) in cash periodic payments of not more than 300 monthly payments;

(b) in bonds issued by the appropriate state agency to finance land purchases by the State Land Reserve Agency, at the market value of the bonds at the close of the business day before delivery of the deed of the land; or

(c) by purchase of an annuity contract from an organization qualified to write annuity contracts in this State.

(2) Notwithstanding any statute or rule applicable to claims against the State and notwithstanding any clause in the contract between the Agency and the seller, the right to receive payment is assignable by the seller. Until the State Land Reserve Agency has received notice of the assignment in a form acceptable to it, the Agency may continue to pay the person to whom payment was due according to the contract and it is discharged of its obligation to the extent of the payment so made.

Section 6–304.    *Condemnation Power*

(1) The State Land Reserve Agency shall have the power to condemn land, subject to the conditions of this Section and the [general eminent domain statute].

(2) The condemnation shall comply with the provisions of § 5–303 governing assumptions regarding development permission made in valuing the land, with the provisions of § 5–304 governing the valuation of temporary interests, and with the provisions of § 5–301 regarding compliance with local regulations if the condemnation is for the purpose of undertaking specific development.

PART 4

*Disposition of Land by State Land Reserve Agency*

Section 6–401.    *General Provisions*

Land which the State Land Reserve Agency is authorized to dispose of under this Part shall be disposed of as provided in Part 4 of Article 5 on disposition of land held for planning purposes. Whenever Part 4 of Article 5 gives a choice of the method of disposition, the transferee or the price to be obtained, the State Land Reserve Agency may make the same selection as any other governmental agency holding land for planning purposes, except that it may not dispose by lot under Section 5–409 or at less than use value under Section 5–407.

Section 6–402.   *Notice of Proposed Disposition*

( 1 ) At least [4] weeks prior to disposing of any land, other than by short term lease under § 5–410, the State Land Reserve Agency shall publish in a newspaper of general circulation a notice describing the land, naming the proposed purchaser, and stating in general terms the proposed use. The Agency shall send a copy of the notice to the State Land Planning Agency.

( 2 ) If the State Land Planning Agency notifies the State Land Reserve Agency prior to the date of disposition that the proposed use of the land will not further proper planning of the area, the State Land Reserve Agency shall not dispose of the land except for a use that has been approved by the State Land Planning Agency.

Section 6–403.   *Notice of Completed Disposition of Land; Limitation of Actions*

( 1 ) The State Land Reserve Agency shall file with the State Land Planning Agency a notice of completed disposition each time it disposes of land, other than by short term lease under § 5–410, within [four weeks] after such disposition has been completed.

( 2 ) The State Land Planning Agency shall publish each notice received by it under this Section in the next available weekly land development notice published pursuant to § 8–208.

( 3 ) No person other than the State Land Reserve Agency or the purchaser may bring any action to contest the validity of any disposition of land by the State Land Reserve Agency under the terms of this Article more than [3 months] after the publication of notice regarding the disposition in the weekly land development notice.

PART 5

*Participation of Local Governments in Land Reserve System*

Section 6–501.   *Powers of Local Governments*

( 1 ) A local government may appropriate money for or issue bonds in accordance with [applicable law governing borrowing procedures] to finance in whole or in part acquisition of land by the State Land Reserve Agency on behalf of the local government.

( 2 ) The contract between the local government and the State Land Reserve Agency may direct the Agency to acquire land with funds supplied by the local government and to hold and maintain the land so acquired.

( 3 ) Regardless of the terms of the contract, the State Land Reserve Agency may hold and dispose of the land so acquired in accordance with the land reserve policy except as the contract may limit the Agency's power in the following respects:

(a) the contract may provide that the distributable gain provided for in Section 6–203(2) shall be paid to the contracting local government.

(b) the contract may specify conditions under which the property may be disposed of at less than market price with the loss, if any, deducted from funds held by the Agency for the benefit of the local government.

(c) the contract may provide that no security interest or lien attaching to holdings of the Agency can attach to land acquired under this Part without the consent of the local government.

(d) the contract may require the approval of the local government for any disposition of the land.

(4) No existing power of any local government to acquire land is limited or modified by this Section.

Section 6–502.    *Request by Local Government for Disposal of Land*

(1) Any local government may from time to time request that the State Land Reserve Agency dispose of land within the local government's jurisdiction by transmitting to the Agency a notice identifying specific land and stating the use proposed therefor. The notice may request that the land be sold to the local government or that it be offered to specified other purchasers or the public generally.

(2) If the local government's request has been denied or has not been acted upon within [three months] after it was transmitted, the local government may transmit a copy of the notice to the State Land Planning Agency which shall publish it in the weekly land development notice under § 8–208 and hold a legislative-type hearing on the request under the procedures of § 2–305.

(3) After the hearing the State Land Planning Agency may by rule direct that the land be disposed if it finds

(a) that disposition of the land is appropriate to achieve the purposes of a State Land Development Plan; or

(b) that the land has been held by the State Land Reserve Agency for more than 20 years and is no longer needed to accomplish the land reserve policy.

NOTES

1. See, however, Neutze, "Land and Land Use Planning."
2. Pisani, *Utopie foncière*, pp. 5, 6.
3. Anthony Downs, "Alternative Forms of Future Urban Growth in the United States," *Journal of the American Institute of Planners* 36, no. 1 (January 1970).
4. See, for example, National Commission on Urban Problems (also known as the Douglas Commission, because it was chaired by Senator Paul Douglas), "Building the American City," report (Washington, D.C.: Government Printing Office, 1968); Advisory Commission on Inter-Governmental Relations, "Policy Statement on New

Communities," report (Washington: Advisory Commission on Inter-Governmental Relations, 1968); National Committee on Urban Policy, "The New City," report (Washington, D.C., 1969); American Institute of Architects, "A Plan for Urban Growth: Report of the National Policy Task Force," report (Washington, D.C.: American Institute of Architects, 1972); and American Law Institute, *Model Land Development Code*.

5. John Reps, "The Future of American Planning: Requiem or Renascence?," *Planning* (1967); Downs, "Future Urban Growth"; Haar, "Two Federal Levers"; Marion Clawson, *Suburban Land Conversion in the United States: An Economic and Governmental Process* (Baltimore: The Johns Hopkins Press, 1971); Parsons, *Public Land Acquisition*; and Flechner, *Land Banking*.

6. Data supplied by U.S. Department of Agriculture, 1978.

7. BLM was created in 1946, through a merger of the General Land Office and the Grazing Service.

8. The following are among the pertinent acts: Mining Law of 1872, Act of 10 May 1872, 17 Stat 91 as amended; Mineral Leasing Law of 1920, Act of 25 February 1920, 41 Stat 437, 30 USCA section 181 et seq. as amended; Act of 7 August 1947, 61 Stat 913, 39 USCA 351–359; and, on geothermal leasing, Act of 24 December 1970, 84 Stat 1566, 30 USCA 1001 et seq.

9. *U.S. News and World Report*, 20 February 1978.

10. Peterson and Muller, cited in *Search*.

11. Bosselman and Callies, *Land Use Control*, is an excellent source of information about direct state efforts to affect the use of land.

12. See *In re Appeal of Kit-Mar Builders, Inc.*, 439 Pa. 466, 268 A.2d 765 (1970), which held two- and three-acre residential lot zoning unconstitutional, for a statement of this view.

13. Regional Plan Association, *Growth and Settlement in the U.S.*

14. Ibid.

15. See appendix B for the full text of article 6.

16. See appendix A for the Puerto Rico Land Administration Act.

17. The Puerto Rico Land Administration Act, Act 13, 16 May 1962.

18. Ibid., Statement of Findings.

19. Ibid.

20. Ibid.

21. Ibid., section 7(t).

22. *Puerto Rico* v. *Rosso*, 95 P.R.R. 488 (1967), appeal dismissed 399 U.S. 14 (1968). In 1946, Act 282 had amended the Civil Code of 1902 to add social benefit as one of the public purposes for which eminent domain might be used.

23. Parsons, *Public Land Acquisition*.

24. Commonwealth of Puerto Rico, Puerto Rico Land Administration, "Financial Statements As of June 30, 1977 and 1976 Together with Auditors' Report."

25. Letter from José A. Santiago Padró, Executive Director, Puerto Rico Land Administration, 8 February 1978.

26. Flechner, *Land Banking*.

27. N.Y. unconsolidated laws, sections 6251–85 (McKinney, 1973).

28. Letters dated 28 February 1978 and 28 March 1978 from Edward J. Logue, President of Logue Development Co., Inc., and former Chief Executive Officer of New York Urban Development Corp. from 1969 to 1975.

29. *Washington Post*, 8 April 1974.

30. Virginia, Fairfax County, Office of Research and Statistics, "Proposed Land Banking Program."

31. Van Alstyne, *Land Bank Handbook*.

32. *New York Times*, 15 February 1977.

33. 42 U.S.C. 5305(a)(1), 1974.

34. For example, the Rhode Island Industrial Land Development Corporation Act, chapter 276, Public Law of 1970, authorizes the creation of semipublic corporations empowered to use eminent domain to acquire land for industrial land banks.

35. Barringer, Richard, "A Maine Manifest," p. 66.

36. Hong, "Two Federal Levels," p. 372.
37. Clawson, *Suburban Land Conversion*, p. 355.
38. Einsweiler, "Selected Municipal Guidance Systems."
39. Section 6–101.
40. See note 22.
41. Section 6–102.
42. Section 6–103.
43. Sections 6–201, 6–202.
44. Section 6–203 (1).
45. Sections 6–301, 6–302, 6–304.
46. Article 6, pt. 4.
47. Section 6–501.
48. Sections 6–401 to 6–403.
49. Section 6–502.
50. American Law Institute, *Model Land Development Code*, p. 229.
51. American Institute of Architects, "Plan for Urban Growth."
52. National Commission on Urban Problems, "Building the American City," p. 250.
53. *Penn Central Transportation Co.* v. *City of New York*, 42 N.Y.2d 324 (1977); 438 U.S. 104, 98 S.Ct. 2646, 57 L.Ed.2d 631 (1978).
54. Kamm, "Land Banking," p. 14.
55. Ibid., p. iii.
56. Advisory Commission on Inter-Governmental Relations, "New Communities," p. 161.
57. The President's Committee on Urban Housing, *A Decent Home*, p. 146.
58. Advisory Commission on Inter-Governmental Relations, "New Communities," p. 161.
59. National Commission on Urban Problems, "Building the American City," p. 251, recommendation 7(b).
60. Advisory Commission on Inter-Governmental Relations, "New Communities," p. 162.
61. National Commission on Urban Problems, "Building the American City," p. 252, recommendation 7(c).
62. Advisory Commission on Inter-Governmental Relations, "New Communities," pp. 151, 152.
63. National Commission on Urban Problems, "Building the American City," p. 251, recommendation 7(b).
64. Ibid.

## REFERENCES

Administracion de Terrenos de Puerto Rico. *Informe Anual, 1976–77*; *Informe Anual, 1973–74 y 1974–75*; *Informe Anual, 1972–73*; *Informe Anual, 1971–72*; *Informe Anual, 1970–71*; *Informe Anual, 1970*; *Informe Anual, 1968–69*; *Informe Anual, 1967–68*; *Informe Anual, 1966–67*; *Informe Anual, 1965–66*; *Informe Anual, 1964–65*; *Informe Anual, 1962–63*. Santurce, Puerto Rico.

The American Law Institute. *A Model Land Development Code*. Philadelphia: The American Law Institute, 1976.

Barringer, Richard. "A Maine Manifest." Report. Bath, Me.: The Allagash Group, 1972.

Bosselman, Fred, and Callies, David. *The Quiet Revolution in Land Use Con-*

*trol*. Council on Environmental Quality. Washington, D.C.: Government Printing Office, 1971.

Clawson, Marion, and Held, R. Burnell. *The Federal Lands: Their Use and Management*. Baltimore: The Johns Hopkins University Press, 1957.

Commonwealth of Puerto Rico. Puerto Rico Land Administration. "Financial Statements As of June 30, 1977 and 1976 Together with Auditors' Report." Mimeographed. San Juan, 26 August 1977.

Einsweiler, Robert C., et al. "Comparative Descriptions of Selected Municipal Guidance Systems." In *Management and Control of Urban Growth*. Washington, D.C.: Urban Land Institute, 1974.

Flechner, Harvey L. *Land Banking in the Control of Urban Development*. New York: Praeger Publishers, 1974.

Haar, Charles. "Wanted: Two Federal Levers for Urban Land Use—Land Banks and Urbank." Excerpted in *Land Use Controls: Present Problems and Future Reform*, edited by David Listokin. Center for Urban Policy Research. New Brunswick, N.J.: Rutgers University, 1974.

Hawaii Senate. Ways and Means Committee. *A Bill for an Act Establishing a State Development Corporation and Land Bank*. 1973, S 1350.

Kamm, Sylvan. *Land Banking: Public Policy, Alternatives and Dilemmas*. The Urban Institute Papers 112–28. Washington, D.C. The Urban Institute, 1970.

"Land Banking Can Ease Some Growing Pains." *Conservation Foundation Letter* (December 1975).

Neutze, G. Max. "The Price of Land and Land Use Planning: Policy Instruments in the Urban Land Market." Report for the Organization for Economic Cooperation and Development. Paris, 1973.

Parsons, Kermit C., et al. *Public Land Acquisition for New Communities and the Control of Urban Growth*. Center for Urban Development Research. Ithaca, N.Y.: Cornell University, 1973.

Peterson, George, and Muller, Thomas. Cited in *Search*. Washington, D.C.: The Urban Institute, 1977.

Pisani, Edgard. *Utopie foncière*. Paris: Gallimard, 1977.

The President's Committee on Urban Housing (chaired by Edgar Kaiser). *A Decent Home*. Washington, D.C.: Government Printing Office, 1969.

Regional Plan Association. *Growth and Settlement in the U.S.: Past Trends and Future Issues*. New York: Regional Plan Association, 1975.

U.S. Department of the Interior. *Public Land Statistics, 1975*. Washington, D.C.: Government Printing Office, 1976.

Urban Land Research Analysts Corporation. *Investment Policy for Land Banks*. Lexington, Mass.: Urban Land Research Analysts Corp., 1967.

Van Alstyne, Carol, ed. *Land Bank Handbook: Advance Acquisition of Sites for Low and Moderate Income Housing*. Greensboro, N.C.: Piedmont Triad Council of Governments, 1972.

Virginia. Fairfax County. Office of Research and Statistics. "Proposed Land Banking Program for Fairfax County." July 1974.

Wisconsin. Milwaukee Department of City Development. "The Land Bank: Eight Years of Industrial Development Progress, '64–'71." Report to the Common Councils Committee on Economic Development, March 1972.

# Index

305

**Library of Congress Cataloging in Publication Data**

Strong, Ann Louise.
 Land banking.

 (Johns Hopkins studies in urban affairs)
 Includes bibliographies.
  1. Land use, Urban—Case studies.  2. City
planning—Case studies.  3. Public lands—Case
studies.  I. Title.  II. Series.
HD111.S76      333.1'094      78–11804
ISBN 0–8018–2169–X

Ann L. Strong is chairman of the Department of City and Regional Planning at the University of Pennsylvania. She also currently serves as trustee and chairman of the Litigation Review Committee of the Environmental Defense Fund and as a member of the Pennsylvania State Planning Board. Her earlier books include *Planned Urban Environments: Sweden, Finland, Israel, the Netherlands, France; Private Property and the Public Interest: The Brandywine Experience* (both described on the back of this jacket); and *Open Space for Urban America.*

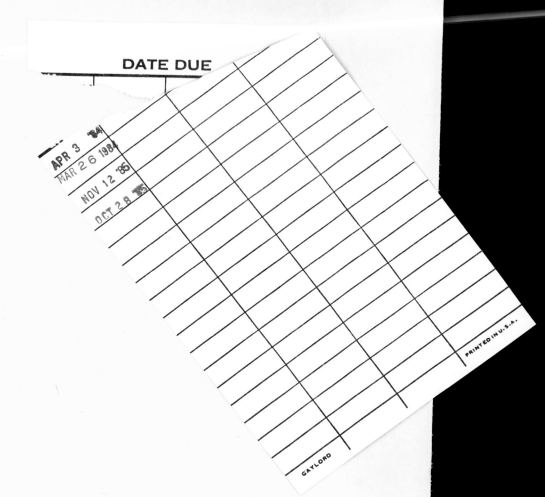

**DATE DUE**

APR 3 '84
MAR 2 6 1984
MAR 12 '85
NOV 12 '85
OCT 2 8

PRINTED IN U.S.A.

GAYLORD